Options
Explained

N. Brewer.

Options
Explained

Robert Tompkins

M
stockton
press

Published in the United States and Canada by
STOCKTON PRESS, 1991
257 Park Avenue South,
New York, N.Y. 10010, USA

ISBN 1-56159-043-6

First published in the United Kingdom by
MACMILLAN PUBLISHERS LTD, 1991
Distributed by Globe Book Services Ltd
Brunel Road, Houndmills
Basingstoke, Hants RG21 2XS, England

ISBN 0-333-56911-3

A catalogue record for this book
is available from The British Library.

Typeset by Hodgson Associates, Tunbridge Wells, Kent TN2 5DD
Printed in Great Britain by
Antony Rowe Ltd, Chippenham, Wiltshire

Contents

Dedication

This book is dedicated to Stuart David Katz, who not only taught me everything I needed to know about options but also taught me the true meaning of friendship.

Preface

In almost every human generation, a revolution occurs. Some generations are blessed by innovations that forever change the world in which they live. Some of us are fortunate enough to witness these events and explain their significance. This is the task I have undertaken with this book. In my generation, the financial world experienced such a revolution. Many brilliant minds were able for the first time to discern the basic building blocks which form our financial markets and then turn these insights into products which touch the lives of us all. My career has been intertwined with the development of one of these most basic building blocks of financial markets: that of options.

The mecca of option markets was Chicago during the 1970s where, in April 1973, the Chicago Board Options Exchange opened. For the first time, standardised option contracts were listed on a regulated market open to all. In addition, two professors at the University of Chicago — Fischer Black and Myron Scholes — were able to uncover the puzzle of options pricing with a brilliant insight. Fate led me to the University of Chicago in 1976 and quickly I was caught up in the electricity of that time. After earning three degrees from the University, my career path led me to the research department of the Chicago Mercantile Exchange, where Fred Arditti was leading a team of economists investigating the introduction of option contracts on a wide variety of financial products and commodities. The opportunity to work with two brilliant financial economists, Michael Asay and Rick Kilcollin, allowed me to immerse myself in the option area and help develop products (on currency options, stock index products and interest rate securities) which would forever change world financial markets.

I was also fortunate to have the opportunity to apply these concepts in the marketplace at Harris trust and Savings Bank and at Continental Illinois National Bank. At Harris, I helped set up one of the first currency option desks in Chicago and later, at Continental Illinois, I traded and managed options on interest rate products. At both institutions, I was again fortunate to come into contact with extremely clever colleagues who helped me understand the limitations of options theory.

Although my education was solid, I found that the concepts underlying options contracts eluded me. The seminal papers were buried in exotic mathematics which were removed from my daily experience. Slowly, the commonsense of these concepts became uncovered as I read and reread the seminal papers and combined these concepts with daily trading activity. Then, with extraordinary luck, I was asked to prepare seminars on these markets for banks in America and Europe. My first seminar in Finland for Postipankki in January 1985 literally changed my life as I could no longer veil option concepts in mathematical terms but had to find a common sense explanation for these products. With the assistance of the educational departments from many of the major futures and options exchanges, a series of seminars was developed that distilled the consistencies among the markets. As this occurred, certain patterns became obvious and the mystery of options was solved for me. Since that first course, I have delivered over 200 courses on options in 28 countries worldwide. As these courses were refined and extended to a wide variety of different underlying instruments, it became even more apparent to me that option contracts were fundamental securities that applied equally well to all markets.

As I will show in the appendix this hypothesis seems to be borne out. Currently, 18 countries have established exchanges to trade options on a range of contracts from energy, metals, commodities, stocks, indices, fixed income securities, interest rates, and currencies. As will be demonstrated in this book, the concepts which spurred the development of options imply that any risky instrument can have an option market associated with it. Given the growth of exchange traded option markets and other related markets, there is little doubt that many more countries will include options in their capital markets in the near future.

Yet as I devoured each new option book that came to press, I found that most books were either too technical, hiding behind mathematics, too basic or too specialised. Many books would only concentrate on one kind of underlying instrument (like stocks, commodities or financial products) and seemed to suggest that the concept framework of options depends on the asset that underlies the option. These books failed to recognise that all options are based upon the same fundamental concepts. I felt that a book needed to be written that showed the similarities among options instead of the dissimilarities. In addition, I could find no book that could explain the logic behind these products without delving into mathematics. It became apparent that others shared my view. Many well informed people found the literature on options markets unsatisfying. Books could not answer basic questions such as why options exist, what gives them value and how these products can be used for trading and hedging needs; furthermore, since these products are so fundamental to an economy, why has their introduction been delayed until this generation only to then grow faster than any other financial product in history? In this book, I will examine all these issues and provide solutions to questions which have generally gone unanswered in other books on the subject.

To examine these critical issues, I have broken the book into four broad subject areas. In the first three chapters, I examine option basics and pricing. Each chapter (throughout this book) will feature a different option market, with the goal both of explaining the concepts and leading the reader to recognise the overlap that exists among all options markets. Chapter 1 presents basic definitions but differs from other texts by showing how options are created from any underlying market by separating that market into 'good' and 'bad' parts. In Chapter 2, the basics of option pricing are presented, featuring a different explanation of the Black and Scholes pricing formula; examining how the problem was solved. For the first time, the link between the Black and Scholes model and the world of physics is explained without the need for differential equations. In Chapter 3, the reader is shown what option pricing models are used for by option traders, and a variety of alternative pricing formulae are also presented. However, rather than emphasising the trivial differences between these formulae and the Black and Scholes model, I explain the similarities shared by all these option formulae. Finally, I finish Chapter 3 with the most fundamental relationship between options and their underlying markets (put-call parity), reaffirming my contention in Chapter 1 that options are nothing more than an underlying asset split into two parts. To show this, both formulae and 'magic graphing' rules are presented to help the mathematically and visually-inclined to understand this critical concept.

The second major area covered in this book includes trading strategies with options. Unfortunately, too many texts overemphasise this area and lead the reader to conclude that options are simply a more sophisticated way to gamble. In Chapter 4, I explain how to use options to benefit from a viewpoint on the movement of the underlying market. However, I present not only the possible returns from various strategies but also discuss how options allow the investor to limit his risk exposure. In Chapter 5, the most fundamental use for options — the trading of risk — is examined. I present the range of possible strategies and also indicate when these are most appropriate. Finally, in Chapter 6, the trading strategies which assure that an equilibrium occurs in these markets is reviewed. These arbitrage trades are probably outside most users' options experience, but must be understood to appreciate the mechanisms within which option pricing works.

The third area I cover is how the investor can use options to manage the risk of his investments. Chapter 7 examines how to protect fixed income securities using options, and compares options and futures contracts for managing risk. Next, in Chapter 8, applications of options to the portfolio manager are reviewed: how can options be used to revise a portfolio manager's risk/return objectives. Here I concentrate on stock index products and demonstrate how to achieve guaranteed investment funds, discuss how portfolio insurance works, why 'delta neutral' hedging techniques should be avoided, and how to create option hedging strategies with no cost. Finally, in Chapter 9, I show (for the first time in any book) how to measure and hedge the risk of an option portfolio. With the use of a popular options risk management computer program, the reader will see how all the theoretical concepts presented in Chapter 3 apply in the daily world of the risk manager.

The final area I examine can roughly be categorised as the structure of options markets and the regulatory environment for these products. Chapter 10 is a survey of over-the-counter (OTC) option markets for managing interest rate risk, and shows how many exotic option products are simply an extension of those option concepts already discussed. Chapter 11 reviews how exchange traded options markets work. Specifically, I describe the role of the clearing house in option markets, how margin works, and how the structures of four popular option markets around the world differ. Finally, Chapter 12 provides a current review of the regulatory, accounting and taxes environments for those countries where options contracts are currently trading. The aim of this book is to show that the concepts which underlie options are consistent across all markets. I hope that for most readers *Options Explained* will be the only book they require in order to understand these products and apply them to their investment needs.

Since I first put pen to paper in November 1989, many of my staff have been involved in the evolution of the final draft. I would like to thank Michael Addor, Adrienne McConnell, Christine Schloder, and Andrew Loose for their assistance in 1989 and 1990. The final and successful completion of the book, though, was due to the superhuman efforts of my current employees: Juan Villen and especially Stephanie Garcia-y-Costa. Without their help, this book would never have made the deadline we promised to our patient editor, Andrea Hartill. I would also like to thank Arthur Andersen & Company for their contributions to the final chapter of this book (which examines the accounting issues worldwide), especially Victor Levy and Philip Broadley in the London office. Finally, I would like to express particular thanks to my brother Timothy, who helped turn my illegible first draft into correct English. Any mistakes or errors remaining are solely my responsibility.

Robert G. Tompkins
August 1991

1: The Basics of Options

INTRODUCTION

Obviously, the best way to become familiar with traded options is to trade. As happens in many fields, a book can serve as a useful guide to new concepts and later provide a perspective once experience has been gained; but there can be no substitute for the experience itself. I have therefore written this as a guidebook and not as a textbook; to assist and accompany the reader as he learns, applies and trades the financial products described hereafter. Additionally, the book is meant to help develop an understanding of the mechanics of how option trading works and thereby also help potential market traders anticipate and benefit from the experiences encountered in the actual market.

The material for this book has been derived from over 200 workshops on options that I have delivered since 1985. These courses have allowed me at one time or another to explain options on stocks, stock indices, fixed income securities, interest rates, currencies, commodities and a whole range of exotic options such as options on interest rate swaps, Cap agreements and options on options. Fortunately, the concepts that underlie almost all options markets are the same. Once one understands the theoretical underpinnings for one of these securities, one can apply the same rationale to almost any other option or option-like security. To illustrate the degree of overlap that option securities have, each chapter of this book will feature a different kind of option contract in its examples. The reader can be confident that when they understand the basics of stock or currency options pricing, the same principles will apply to other options. In addition, the trading and hedging examples covered can apply equally well to all markets. As in the courses, I have arranged the text here into a progression of topics with the ultimate objective of giving the reader a sufficient understanding of these products and their markets to be able to trade competently in them and understand the foundations of all option markets.

I begin the book by describing what options are and what they can do, and defining the terminology commonly used in the industry. Then, theoretical topics such as option pricing and arbitrage are examined, followed by a practical explanation of how to use options, including trading approaches, hedging strategies and portfolio applications. After this, I discuss how to manage the risk of an options portfolio. Next, I examine the development of over-the-counter option products. The book ends with a review of exchange traded option markets in four representative exchanges and finally reviews the regulatory environment for option trading throughout the world.

WHY OPTIONS EXIST

Options serve several purposes. On a purely speculative level they offer investors a sort of limited risk wager. Buying options is analogous in some ways to playing the casino game of roulette. In roulette, what one risks on each spin of the wheel is simply the cost of the chips placed on the table. But at the same time, depending on where the chips happen to be placed and where the ball comes to rest in the wheel, there is an opportunity for significant gain. Similarly to a roulette player, someone who purchases an option is buying the right to wager for profit, but in this case by buying or selling an asset of some kind. The option to buy or sell, like the face value of a roulette chip, costs a fixed and known amount. In option trading, the face value of this 'roulette chip' is called the 'option premium'. Once an option is purchased, it is immediately placed on the table (so to speak) and the market begins to spin.

Again, viewing option trading as a speculative product, an investor can wager for amounts significantly greater than the value of his option premium, since the cost of the premium is nearly always a very small percentage of the potential value of the asset it represents. This is called leverage and in simple terms is defined as the opportunity to gain an equivalent profit at the risk of a capital sum considerably smaller than the actual purchase and sale of the asset itself would involve. Again, the likeness of the roulette chip to the option premium may be applied — very large potential gain in relation to the size of the risk.

We will leave the roulette table here, though, since options have an important feature not shared by simple games of chance. In addition to loss or gain, options are defined in terms of time. An option contract to buy or sell an asset has a specific buy-by or sell-by date and in most markets exercising that option may occur at any time within that period. This allows the myriad forces of the market to act upon the option and thereby permits those traders skilled in the market to create effective trading strategies both in the long and the short term. Market volatility, interest rates, and time to option expiration — indeed all the things which affect our economic markets generally — come to bear in option trading and, if properly allowed for, may be beneficially used. With so many possible variables, the permutations of creating option trading strategies are endless but I have endeavoured to provide a number of examples later in the book by way of illustrating how such strategies work.

If we put the purely speculative uses to one side, the primary purpose of option trading — and in fact the main reason options came to exist in the first place — is one especially suited to industry. Options function as insurance, and in this area the needs of the world of commerce and the services provided by the world of finance dovetail perfectly. As insurance, traded options are bought or sold against actual requirements. A typical example is the need of an export manufacturer to protect the exchange rate on a particular contract. Having taken an order on a price calculated at a given exchange rate in a foreign currency, the manufacturer wishes to protect the price against adverse changes in the exchange market for the period between accepting the order and being paid for it. To do so, he purchases an option on the foreign currency covering the period of manufacture, delivery and payment. Another typical case would be a processing company wishing to protect the cost of imported raw materials on long deliveries. This would be done by purchasing an option in local currency against anticipated future delivery requirements of the material. In both cases, however, the option offers a significant flexibility over either simple insurance or plain speculation, since it offers the benefit of both at no additional cost. The insurance is obtained by buying the option at a known exchange or commodity rate and at a known option premium. However, should the exchange or commodity rate have changed to the advantage of the option holder by the time the option is to be exercised then the speculative choice becomes available as well. If it is more profitable for the option holder to purchase the required asset on the open market than to exercise the option, the option is simply allowed to lapse. Option trading is one of the rare financial instruments which really does let traders have it both ways.

THE TWO KINDS OF OPTIONS

A *call* option gives the holder the right to *buy* the underlying asset at a fixed price. This is also known as the strike price. A *put* option provides the holder with the right to *sell* the underlying position at the strike price. When buying either type of option, whether a call or a put, the buyer must pay the option seller a premium either immediately or at some later point (as is the case at some marketplaces where the premium payment is deferred until the expiration date).

A call option is the right to acquire an asset, hold an asset, or own the underlying asset at a fixed price. A put option is the right to sell an asset at a fixed price. A call option gives the holder the ability to assume a buying (also known as a long) position in the underlying market. A put option gives the holder the right to a selling (also known as short) position in the underlying market.

I must explain here a point which confuses many people. The principal difference between options and futures contracts relates to rights and obligations. Futures contracts are obligations to perform. Option contracts, conversely, provide the choice to perform.

To understand the beneficial aspects of the rights provided by options, think about more ordinary rights that you have. One right is to cross the street as you please, excluding jay walking. Now picture yourself deciding whether to use that right. You approach the curb at the street corner, and what do you do? If you follow your mother's advice, you will look both ways to see if the street is clear and free from traffic. If it is, and you want to cross the street, you will choose to use your right. What happens if the street is not clear, but instead heavily congested with speeding traffic? You will choose not to use your right at that moment and instead wait until it is safe.

When you purchase an option, you have the right, but not the obligation, to buy or sell the underlying market. Your criterion for crossing the street is the traffic. For options, the criterion is called the strike price, or exercise price. Given that you have the right to buy or not to buy, you will decide which to do depending on whether exercising your right would be profitable to you.

Suppose the market is trading below the strike price of your option contract. If you had the right to buy (a call option) and you did so, you would have a cash outflow, so you would choose not to buy. If, however, the prevailing market price exceeds the strike price, you may choose to buy since this would result in a cash inflow. With options, therefore, the strike price is the benchmark by which a decision to buy or sell will be made, just as the curb is the 'threshold' to evaluate the traffic.

For example, assume a situation where a Gold futures contract is trading at $367 per ounce, and a call and put option on the Gold futures both have strike prices of $360. Someone holding a $360 call option will have a cash inflow if he uses his right. He can buy at $360 and immediately sell the underlying futures at $367 for an inflow of $7 per ounce. Someone holding a put option under similar circumstances would not choose to use his right. He would have an outflow of $7 if he exercised into a selling position at $360 and then had to buy the position back at $367. However, he could also wait and hope that the market price would fall below his strike price of $360 at some point prior to the expiration of his option.

In contrast to an option, a Gold futures contract is an obligation which one must accept regardless of the outcome. It is as if one were forced to cross the street regardless of the traffic conditions. Options obviously provide a tremendous benefit because of the rights they confer. Maybe all the best things in life are free but, understandably, the benefits provided by options have a cost: the premium.

DEFINITIONS

While we are here, what does the term 'underlying' mean? This is the asset you will deal in if you exercise the option, and the range of financial instruments that can be used with options is quite diverse. Theoretically, options can be offered on *any* kind of asset. Option contracts exist on stocks, currencies, interest rates, gold, commodities and many other markets. The appendix at the end of the book lists the worldwide exchanges where options contracts are traded. Fortunately, all the basic principles of options hold regardless of the characteristics of the underlying asset. Thus, the reader can be assured that all the concepts in this book can be applied to any option he might trade. To prove it, I will examine a different underlying asset in every chapter:

Chapter 1: Gold futures at the COMEX
Chapter 2: IBM shares at the CBOE
Chapter 3: US $/£ at the PHLX, the IMM and in the Interbank market
Chapter 4: Crude Oil futures at the NYMEX
Chapter 5: Soyabean futures at the CBOT
Chapter 6: Eurodollar futures at the IMM
Chapter 7: T-Bond futures at the CBOT
Chapter 8: The S&P Stock Index at the CBOE and S&P 500 futures at the IOM
Chapter 9: Live Cattle futures at the CME
Chapter 10: Over-the-counter Interest Rate Products.

UNIT OF TRADING	**1 GOLD FUTURES CONTRACT**
DELIVERY MONTHS	**FEBRUARY, APRIL, JUNE, AUGUST, OCTOBER AND DECEMBER**
EXERCISE TIME	**15:00 PRIOR TO EXPIRATION 16:00 ON LAST TRADING DAY**
DELIVERY DAY	**FIRST BUSINESS DAY AFTER EXER-CISE DAY**
LAST TRADING DAY (= EXPIRY DAY)	**SECOND FRIDAY OF THE MONTH PRIOR TO THE DELIVERY MONTH**
QUOTATION	**MULTIPLES OF $0.10**
MINIMUM PRICE MOVEMENT (TICK SIZE & VALUE)	**$0.10 PER TROY OUNCE**
EXERCISE PRICE INTERVALS	**$10 (<500), $20 (500-1000), $50 (>1000) PER OUNCE**
TRADING HOURS	**08:20 - 14:30 NEW YORK TIME**

Table 1.1 Options on Gold Futures (COMEX)

Now consider the option on Gold futures traded at the Commodity Exchange (COMEX) in New York (which I will use in this chapter). The prices will be in dollars per ounce. Table 1.1 outlines the contract specification for this underlying. The asset underlying the option is a COMEX Gold futures contract which is the obligation either to buy or sell gold in the month following the expiration of the option.

Before proceeding, let us define some terms. There are *holders* and *writers* in the options market. A holder is a buyer of an option in an opening transaction. Writers are sellers of an option in an opening transaction.

All options which trade on the same financial instrument belong to a particular option class. Options of a particular class which have the same strike price (exercise price) and the same expiration date are classified as an option series. With options, the underlying instrument is defined in the contract specifications (see Table 1.1). However, there is a difference between August Gold futures and December Gold futures because they represent different points of time in the future; therefore, options on these different underlying instruments belong in different option classes.

DISPOSITION OF OPTIONS CONTRACTS

Assume you have acquired an option position. What can you do with it? You have four alternatives to dispose of that option. You can offset the option in the market, let the option expire worthless, exercise the option, or allow the exchange to exercise the option automatically for you. Let us look at each of these in turn.

5

Offsetting an option means cashing it in by doing an opposite trade. Exchanges provide a marketplace where people can find an opportunity to offset positions acquired earlier. In the best markets, one can offset a position at any time until the position matures. Therefore, if the rationale for the transaction has changed, you can cash in the option, get some money back and — who knows? — you might even make a profit!

The second alternative is to let the option expire worthless. If a potential loss would occur were you to exercise the option, you have the ability to walk away from the option and let it expire worthless. Your only loss for not using the option is the premium you paid to acquire it.

The third alternative is to transform the option into a position in the underlying market by exercising it. Once the option is transformed, it cannot be changed back into an option. A transformed option is analogous to a caterpillar which has metamorphosed into a butterfly. It cannot decide after it has emerged from the cocoon as a butterfly that it liked it better as a caterpillar, munching leaves all day long. Once it climbs out of that cocoon there is no going back.

Once an option is exercised into the underlying it is likewise transformed. The trader now holding the new position in the underlying asset cannot return to the features of the option. When the holder transforms an option it remains a full position in the underlying asset as either long (if a call) or short (if a put). As with all options, exercise is the right of the holder. An important question is: who actually provides the position to the holder who exercises?

The individual who must assume the opposite side to the holder is the one who has written that option. If only one holder and one writer exist, then it is obvious who exercises and who honours the option contract. In reality, many option writers exist, and the one assigned to honour a contract when a holder exercises is determined by the clearing house associated with an exchange market. This is done by random assignment on the COMEX, which will be discussed extensively later. In practice, because options can be offset easily, very few people choose to exercise their options, and most people generally offset the option contracts before their expiration. (The reason why people generally prefer to offset an option rather than by exercising it will be discussed in Chapter 2.)

The fourth alternative for options at a number of option markets (and at the COMEX) is an automatic exercise. Sometimes the situation occurs in which a profitable option has been forgotten, and the profit can be lost when the option expires. To avoid this oversight, the market provides procedures for automatically exercising the option. At the COMEX, if the underlying Gold futures price is $1 or more above the strike price of a call option (or $1 or less the strike price of a put), then the option will be automatically exercised.

For example, let us suppose that you had a call option on Gold with a $360 strike price, and the futures market ended up at $365 on the expiration day of your option. You are on holiday on this day and cannot be reached regarding whether or not to exercise the option. The COMEX would assume that you would want to exercise the option at $360 and receive the inflow of $5. This is an instance where automatic exercise would come in handy.

One might think that automatic exercise makes automatic sense. This is not always true. Risks may be introduced by automatic exercise which the holder might not want. Imagine that the price of an underlying physical security was barely above the strike price of a call option. If automatic exercise occurred, to realise that profit the option holder would have to deal in the underlying market. It could be that significant transactions costs in doing this would wipe out any small positive cashflow for the option. If instead the option was cash settled at the moment of exercise, the holder simply has cash deposited into his account and no position in the underlying asset. So, for cash settled options (especially on stock indices) automatic exercise makes sense. However, given that many options are exercised into an underlying asset which may require physical delivery, an irrevocable automatic exercise feature might be detrimental.

Imagine that on a particular date the underlying Gold market settles at $350.50 and a $350 call option expires on the same day. Since you have the right to buy at $350, you might want to exercise the call and have a 50¢ inflow. However, the 50¢ profit is not immediately paid in cash but instead one is assigned a futures position. To realise immediately the cash inflow one would have to place an offsetting trade in the futures market. Now suppose that the last traded price on the Gold futures is $350.50, but the market makers on the floor of the COMEX will only buy the futures at a price of $349.50 (known as the bid price). If you were to exercise the option, you would receive a buying position in the Gold futures at $350 but you could only sell it at $349.50 for a loss of 50¢ . In this case, since the bid price for the futures is lower than the strike price, you would lose if an automatic exercise forced you to buy the underlying futures. If you decided not to close the futures position immediately, you could hold the futures position uncovered and wait until the final settlement occurred for the futures (in the next calendar month); but by then the futures market could have dropped below $350 and you would have a loss on the exercised option. So, in this example, the automatic exercise would not be beneficial to the option holder.

An even more stark example is for options on stocks or other actual securities, where one might have to come up with substantial capital to perform on the contract only to be stuck with the proverbial truckload of soyabeans dumped on the front lawn. To add to your misery, you might be unable to unload the position you have just been automatically exercised into at a profit. So for most options on physical securities, exercise of these contracts is left to the discretion of the trader.

EXERCISE AND ASSIGNMENT OF OPTIONS

Now that your brain is brimming with new terms, let us squeeze in a few more. Two styles of exercise features exist for most options: American and European. (Sometimes, options that allow one to exercise at the average price for a period, are referred to as having an 'Asian' exercise feature. These will be discussed in Chapter 10.)

An American-style option allows you to exercise the option into the underlying asset at any time until expiration. For example, if one buys a December 1991 expiration option on Gold futures, it can be converted to a Gold future at any time from the date of purchase until 8 November, which is the final trading day for the December options.

The European-style options can only be exercised on a single day, usually the expiration day of the option. In our example, if the option on COMEX Gold were European-style, then only on 8 November could it be transformed into the underlying Gold futures market. The COMEX options instead have an American-style exercise feature which gives confidence to holders since at any time they can 'force' the options to follow movements in the underlying asset through the mechanism of exercise and liquidation of the futures thus obtained. If at any time American option prices become unreasonable, holders can exercise them to receive the appropriate cash inflow rather than having to accept unfair offsetting option prices which would be below the 'intrinsic' amount. (In the next chapter I will discuss what this amount is.)

As mentioned earlier, when an option is exercised there has to be someone on the other side who is assigned to honour that particular contract. Note that assignment means the obligation of the writer to fulfil the contract terms. As discussed, the clearing house must assign these positions to writers in a fair and equitable way. The random solution process used at the COMEX is similar to a box full of bingo balls. If a holder decides he wants his position immediately and he exercises his option before expiration, the clearing house pulls a numbered ball at random from the box. Each number is associated with a particular selling option position held by a particular option writer, and this random process determines who takes the opposite position to the holder. In reality, no bingo balls exist, but a random number generator on the clearing house computer performs a similar task.

The number of exercises that has occurred is entered into the clearing system. The computer matches exercised options with writers each night, and assigns futures positions to holders and writers of options which appear on their statements the next morning. When the holder of a call option exercises, the option writer who is selected by the (clearing house of) COMEX will be assigned a selling position in Gold futures at the strike price of the option. Furthermore, the short option position the writer previously had then disappears. Suppose someone sold ten call options and that night the (clearing house of) COMEX assigned three contracts to this writer. Next morning, on the writer's books, he would have seven short call options and three short futures.

However, people generally do not exercise options prior to expiration unless there is illiquidity, silly prices, or if they have made a mistake. If they made a mistake, they essentially have given the writer 'free' money. (This will be discussed in some detail in Chapter 2, when we examine the relationship between the pricing of American and European options.) Most options are only exercised if they are deep 'in-the-money' (which I will define in the next chapter) and at that point the writers already expect them to be exercised. However, the existence of the exercise feature is generally sufficient to assure that option prices behave efficiently. If it were the case that option positions did not mirror a position in the underlying market, the mechanism of early exercise would allow the holder immediately to cash in the option.

WHY OPTIONS ARE TIED TO THE UNDERLYING MARKET

Because of the threat of exercise, option positions must behave like positions in the underlying market. Call option premiums have to increase as the underlying market prices increase because if they do not, people who hold call options can exercise them into the underlying market and realise this gain. If your put option price does not increase as the market price falls, you can exercise it to realise the gain associated with the downward movement in the underlying market. The call option becomes an underlying long position when you transform it by exercise, and exercising the put option yields a short position in the underlying market. Thus, holding a call option must act like a long underlying position, and holding a put option must act like a short underlying position (see Figure 1.1). What about those who sell the options to the holders? Option writers must have positions which have payoffs exactly opposite to the payoffs of option holders. Let us return to our insurance analogy. People who sell options act like insurance agents. If I sold someone 'buying' insurance, or a call option, then he or she has the right to buy the underlying asset in consideration for the payment of a premium. When the holder exercises the 'buying' insurance he assumes a long position in the underlying asset. The call option writer must assume the opposite side to this transaction; therefore, I have the obligation to sell the underlying asset to the holder. When the holder transforms his option, my position as the writer is also transformed into a selling position in the underlying market. Thus, writers of call options have positions that behave like short positions in the underlying market (see Figure 1.1); that is, they will make money when the market goes down and lose money when the market goes up, exactly the opposite payoff structure to the call option holder.

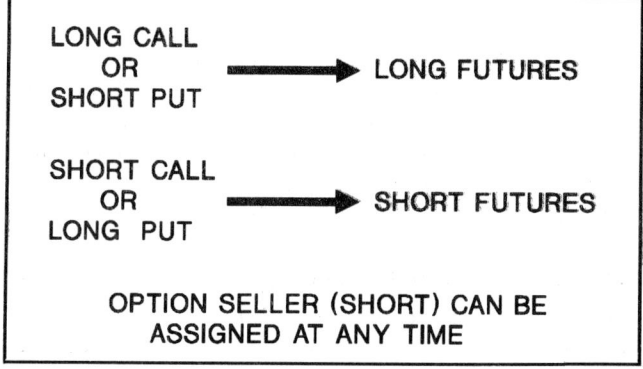

Figure 1.1 Exercise Results

Let us now consider the writer of the put option. If the put holder decides to exercise his right to sell, the writer of the put must assume a buying position. Therefore, the writer must assume a long position when the put holder decides to exercise. Holding a put provides the buyer with the right to have a short position. Those who write puts, however, have an obligation to buy from the holder whenever exercise occurs (see Figure 1.1).

Now wait a minute! Can you think of any other market where when you *buy* something you become a seller, or when you *sell* something you become a buyer? Options are unique: buying or selling options may not act in the same way as buying or selling the underlying market.

Buying or selling calls behave in a similar way to buying or selling the underlying market. If you buy calls when (underlying) prices go up, you expect to make money; and when market prices fall you expect to lose. Writers of call options have similar profit and loss biases to selling the underlying market. When prices fall they expect to profit and when prices rise they expect to lose.

Puts act conversely. Buyers of puts expect to lose money when prices rise, and expect to make money when prices fall. Writers of puts expect to profit when prices rise and lose money when prices fall. The key point to remember is that holders of options, either calls or puts, have a limited loss potential equal to their premium expenditure with potentially unlimited profits. The maximum amount writers of options can make is the premium that has been paid to them. For this assured initial cash inflow, they accept an unlimited risk potential.

Options are currently traded on underlying assets as diverse as currencies, interest rates, raw materials, stocks, and a wide variety of other markets. Theoretically, any asset you can buy or sell can be the basis for an options market. Before I can demonstrate this, I must clearly define what a profit/loss profile is. A profit/loss profile is the profit and the loss associated with a range of underlying market prices for a particular transaction.

PROFIT/LOSS PROFILES

Assume that you buy a Gold futures contract at a price of $360. (This is the obligation to buy at $360 a certain date in the future.) As the futures price increases to $363, your profit will be $3. If you buy the futures contract at $360 and the market remains constant, then the profit or loss is zero. Had it dropped to $358 you would have a loss of $2. So, now we put a point at the intersection of these profit/loss numbers and the associated prices and connect the points with a line. This has been done for you in Figure 1.2.

This figure illustrates the relationship between profit/loss and prices for buying the underlying asset (in our case, futures) described above. The line going to the northeast on the table continues infinitely in that direction, and the line towards the southwest until the Gold futures price is zero. For didactic purposes, I consider this to be an infinite loss. The logic is that if Gold futures prices are at zero, this probably means

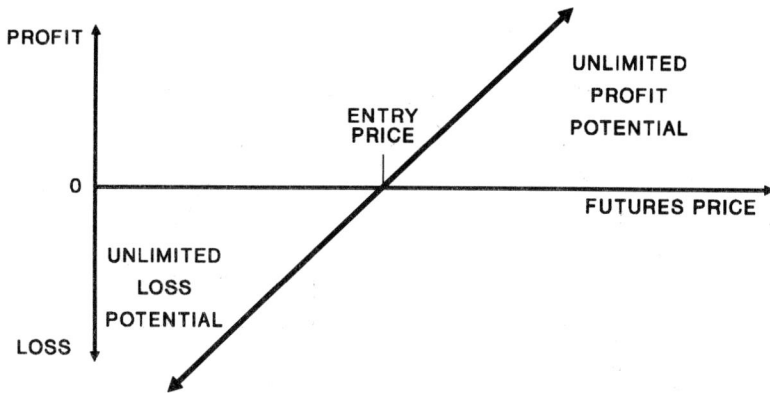

Figure 1.2 Long Futures

the end of the world. What I really mean is not an infinite loss but a linear loss which has a constant slope equal to the profit slope until the Gold futures is worthless. So, I do grant the point that the individual who purchases a Gold futures knows his maximum loss potential. However, given that these contracts are margined, the actual dollar loss potential could be much greater than the initial investment the holder of the futures initially placed as margin. (Margin is a deposit placed with futures or options exchanges which is sufficient to guarantee that the holder or writer of the position will be able to perform at the levels agreed to when the position was established. This is generally a small percentage of the value of the contract.)

OPTIONS AS THE 'GOOD' AND 'BAD' FEATURES OF THE UNDERLYING

Where do options come in? Option contracts simply take this position which is buying the underlying asset and split it into a good part and a bad part. The good part is the profit line which rises to the northeast, and the bad part is the loss potential portion of the diagram which falls to the southwest.

First, consider the good part. If we cleanly divided the good and bad parts as in Figure 1.3, then the good part is terrific: no losses and only gains. This is analogous to going to the casino and the croupier giving you an unlimited supply of free chips. In this case, what would you do? Play roulette all the time, of course. However, the casino does not do this; it prevents you from playing the roulette wheel indefinitely by charging for the chips. Likewise, to keep you from playing the option market perpetually with no risk, you are charged a premium, and that premium is what you stand to lose.

People only vaguely familiar with options cannot fathom why it is necessary to pay for options. By paying the premium, you pay for an unlimited upside potential and you have the ability to walk away from it with a fixed loss (the premium). Would these

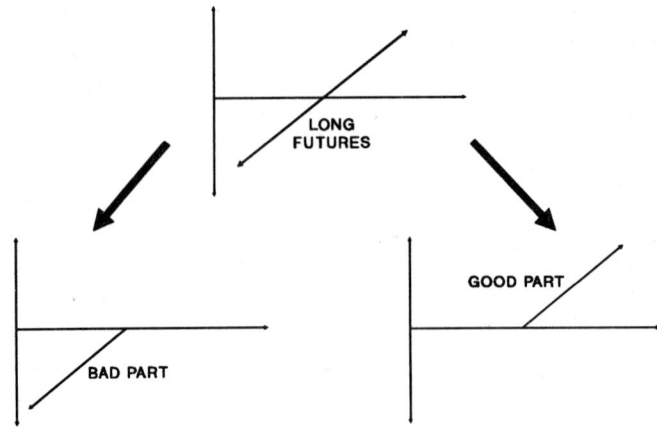

Figure 1.3 Long Futures

same people expect to play roulette at no expense or receive their fire insurance policies for free? Of course, they would not. Nor should they expect option contracts to be free.

Therefore, when you purchase a call option, you have to pay a premium to gain the right to buy the underlying asset and get the good parts of buying the market. The most you can lose is your premium when the market is at or below your strike price, and you have an unlimited profit potential when the market rises. The profit/loss diagram for buying the call can be seen in Figure 1.4.

What about the 'bad' part of going long in the market? This is the unlimited loss potential which in Figure 1.3 goes towards the southwest. If you made this kind of transaction (where you only got the 'bad' things and never any gains), you would be most unhappy. This trade is not the way to get ahead in any business. Therefore, if you decided to accept this terrible trade, you would only be induced to do so if someone made it worth your while.

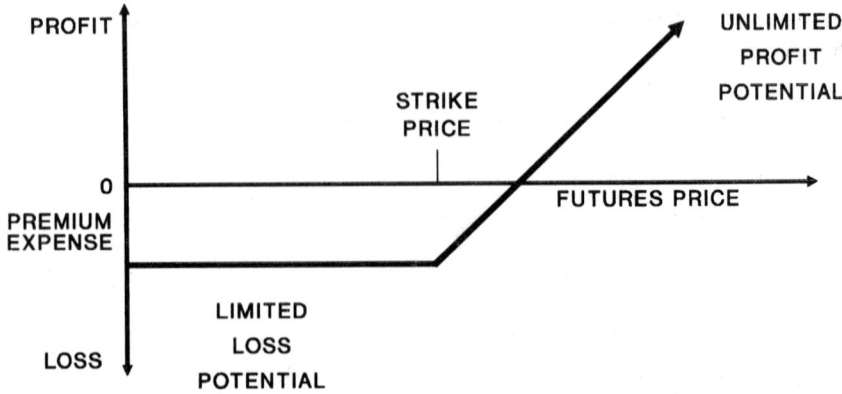

Figure 1.4 Holding a Call

Again, this situation can be compared to insurance. Insurance companies assume the potentially unlimited losses of their policy holders. What do they get from the insurance buyer in exchange for taking this risk? They receive a premium. An insurance company assumes all the risks in return for the receipt of a premium. Furthermore, the maximum gain it can hope for is the amount received for assuming that risk. Therefore, writers of options, like insurance writers, face an unlimited loss potential in exchange for a limited gain. Thus, the trade which is the unlimited loss potential in Figure 1.3 is the obligation to buy, which is writing a put option. The most you can make is the premium received when the market is stable or rises, and you have an unlimited loss potential when the market price falls. The profit/loss diagram for writing a put can be seen in Figure 1.5.

Hence, we take the original long underlying position and simply split it into the right to buy (holding a call option) and the obligation to buy (writing a put option). (See Table 1.2.) Consider a put writer. He sold a Gold option to someone who is now holding the right to sell at a strike price of $360. The put writer sold the option and received $5 in premium. If the market goes up to $370, the put holder who has the right to sell at $360 will choose instead to sell at the market price which is higher than this strike price (if he decides to sell at all). At any price equal to or above the strike, the put writer walks away with the entire premium of $5. At $360, the put holder is indifferent to exercising the put option or selling the underlying asset directly since he will achieve the same selling price of $360. When the market price is at $360, the put writer is still happy because he retains the entire premium paid to him.

If the market collapses to $350, the put holder has the right to sell at $360. He could conceivably cover it by buying the underlying market at $350, and the put holder would have a tidy sum less the premium he paid. The put writer must take the loss by buying the underlying asset at $360 from the put holder, and the best price he can sell at is the prevailing price of $350. Hence, by writing put options, the writer loses money when the market goes down, and makes money when the market goes up. This is comparable to the loss potential from holding the underlying asset.

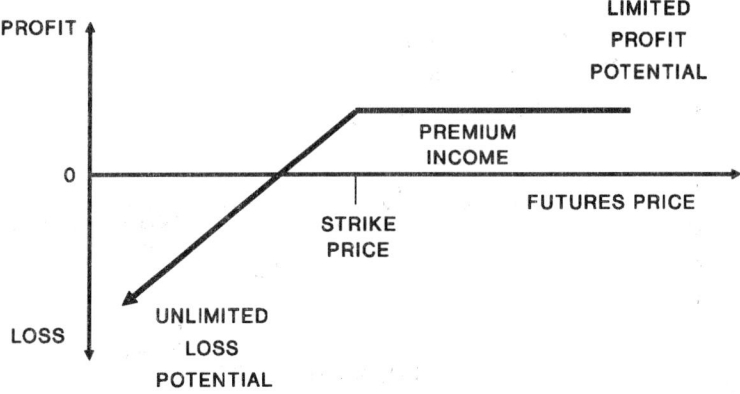

Figure 1.5 Writing a Put

UNDERLYING MARKET

	BUYING	SELLING
HOLDING	**HOLDING A CALL** RIGHT TO BUY	**HOLDING A PUT** RIGHT TO SELL
WRITING	**WRITING A PUT** OBLIGATION TO BUY	**WRITING A CALL** OBLIGATION TO SELL

OPTIONS

Table 1.2 Alternative Strategies

SPLITTING A SHORT UNDERLYING POSITION INTO 'GOOD' AND 'BAD' PARTS

Now I will examine the selling side of the underlying market. Short selling is selling something without owning it, with an implicit agreement to buy it back later. Futures contracts are ideal for this kind of transaction because they can be established with only a margin payment.

In futures markets, buying and selling positions are equally easy to do and are no different in terms of transaction costs. If you sell a Gold futures contract at $360 and the market decreases to $358, then there is a profit of $2. If you sell at $360 and it remains at $360, you have no profit or loss. If you sell at $360 and the market increases to $363, there is a loss of $3. Therefore, you have an unlimited profit potential as market prices fall and an unlimited loss potential as market prices rise (see Figure 1.6). Again, the option market simply splits this position into two parts: a good part and a bad part.

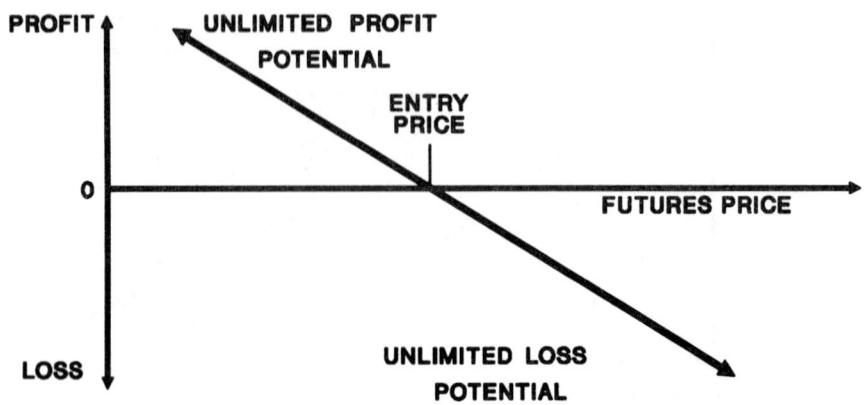

Figure 1.6 Short Futures

14

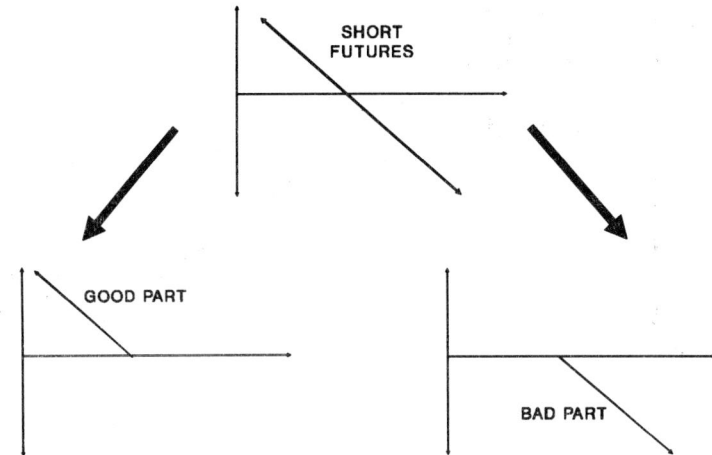

Figure 1.7 Short Futures

Figure 1.7 shows the short position split into its good and bad parts. The put option, the right to sell, has an unlimited profit potential heading towards the northwest. Once you have paid the premium for the put, you acquire an unlimited profit potential and a limited loss potential (see Figure 1.8). The bad part (the unlimited loss) goes to the writer of the call option. He has a limited gain as prices fall but can lose a bundle as prices rise (see Figure 1.9).

The writer of the call option has the obligation to sell the market at the strike price no matter how high the price goes. The writer receives a premium and assumes for that premium an unlimited loss potential as the market rises. People who purchase options pay for the right to unlimited gain potentials. Those who sell options (the writers) accept the unlimited loss potential in exchange for the premium paid to them by the option holders.

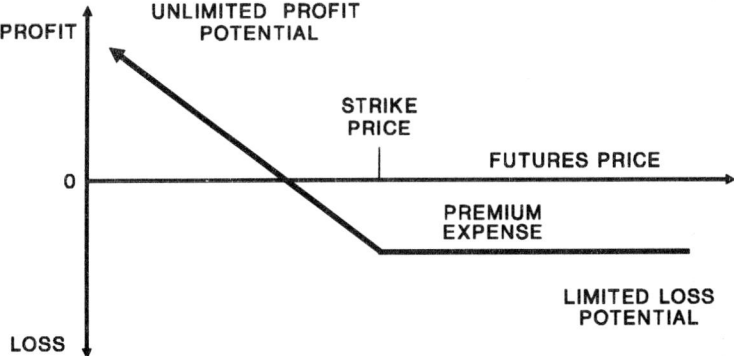

Figure 1.8 Holding a put

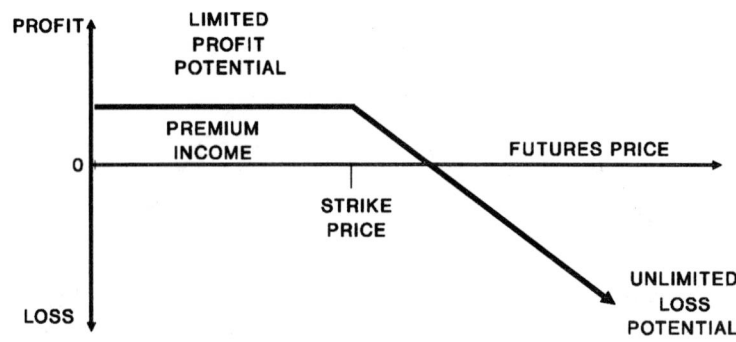

Figure 1.9 Writing a Call

SUMMARY

Summing up, option markets split buying or selling positions in the underlying market into purely 'good' and 'bad' parts. If we wish to establish a buying position, meaning trades which benefit as prices rise, we now have three alternatives (if we use both the option and underlying markets). First of all, we can purchase a futures contract with unlimited profit and loss potential. Second, we can purchase a call option with unlimited profit potential and a limited loss. Finally, if we write a put option, we achieve a limited gain potential with an unlimited loss.

If we wish to establish selling positions, meaning trades which profit as prices fall, we also have three possible transactions. First, the most straightforward way to benefit from drops in market prices is to sell a futures contract. Second, we can purchase put options (the right to sell) without a potentially unlimited loss by paying a premium. Finally, we can sell a call option which yields a limited premium if the market moves down and an unlimited loss if the market moves up.

As can be discerned, a key difference between trading options and trading underlying assets is the option premium paid or received. Therefore, it is crucial to understand how this is determined and what the critical factors are in that determination. This will be discussed in the next chapter.

2: Basic Concepts in Options Pricing

In this chapter, I will examine option concepts by using options on IBM stock as our sample underlying. Table 2.1 displays the contract specifications for this option contract traded at the Chicago Board Options Exchange (CBOE). This allows one either to buy or sell 100 shares of IBM stock at or before a variety of expiration dates.

TRADING UNIT	100 SHARES OF IBM
DELIVERY MONTHS	JANUARY, APRIL, JULY, OCTOBER
EXERCISE TIME	16:30 (CHICAGO TIME)
EXPIRATION DAY	THE THIRD SATURDAY OF THE EXPIRATION MONTH
LAST TRADING DAY	THIRD FRIDAY OF THE DELIVERY MONTH
QUOTATION	DOLLARS PER SHARE
EXERCISE PRICE INTERVALS	$5 WHEN THE STOCK PRICE IS MORE THAN $25. $40 WHEN THE STOCK PRICE IS MORE THAN $200
TRADING HOURS	10:00 - 16:00 (CHICAGO TIME)

Table 2.1 Options on IBM Shares (CBOE)

Before option pricing can be properly examined, a few important terms must be introduced. Three key concepts to understand are: in-the-money, at-the-money, and out-of-the-money.

IN-THE-MONEY

If, as a holder of an option, you transact at the strike price of the option and relative to the underlying market, you have a cash inflow. That option is called in-the-money. For example, if the current price of IBM stock is $105 and you could buy it at $100 using a call option, you would have money coming in. Thus, a $100 option would be known as an in-the-money call (see Figure 2.1).

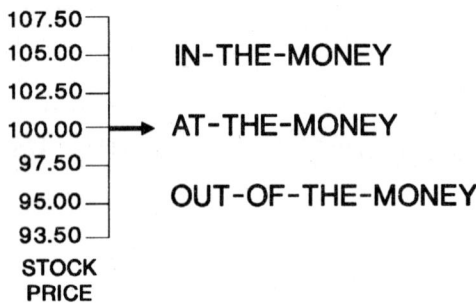

Figure 2.1 100.00 IBM Stock Call Option

AT-THE-MONEY

An option is at-the-money when the market price is trading at the same level as the strike price. If you have an $105 call option on IBM and the current market price of IBM is $105, the option is an at-the-money call option.

OUT-OF-THE-MONEY

If you transact at the strike price of the option and relative to the underlying, you have a cash outflow. That option is called out-of-the-money. Consider a put option on IBM with a strike price of $100. If you exercised the put option, selling the stock at $100, and then bought the stock back at $105, you would have an outflow of $5 per share. The $100 put option would then be called out-of-the-money (see Figure 2.2).

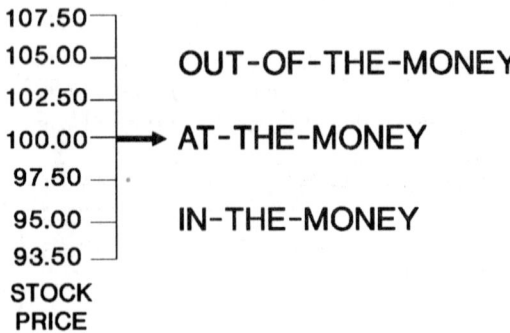

Figure 2.2 100.00 IBM Stock Put Option

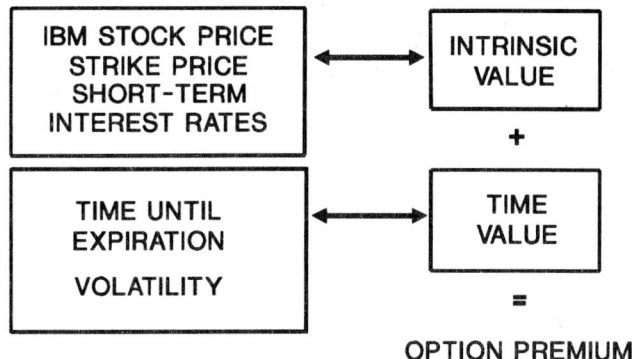

Figure 2.3 Variables Used in Pricing

THE FUNDAMENTAL COMPONENTS OF AN OPTIONS PRICE

In this section, I will examine the basis of option pricing. The fundamental idea in option pricing is that an option price can be split into two components, intrinsic value and time value (see Figure 2.3).

Intrinsic Value

The intrinsic value is simply the in-the-money amount. In-the-money is a cash inflow from exercising the option. What happens if you hold a call option on IBM with the right to buy at $105, and the IBM stock price is currently at $105½? If the option were exercised, the inflow of $½ per share would result, making it an in-the-money option. Since the intrinsic value is the in-the-money amount, it is also $½. If the price of IBM decreased to $105, the in-the-money amount and the intrinsic value would dwindle to zero (see Table 2.2).

What would occur if the price of IBM shares decreased further to $104? You would not exercise this call option at $105 because it is out-of-the-money. Because the option is out-of-the-money, the in-the-money amount is zero. The intrinsic value must then also be zero. It follows that the intrinsic value of an option will always be either greater than or equal to zero. It can never be negative.

The put option is the mirror image of the call option. A positive inflow will not result if you can sell at $105 when everyone else can also sell at that price (i.e., the put is at-the-money).

If the underlying market price fell to $102, you could exercise the put and establish a short position at $105. Then, you could buy the underlying market back at $102, resulting in a $3 inflow per share. The put option is in-the-money by an amount of $3 when the price of IBM is $102.

IBM STOCK PRICE	INTRINSIC VALUE 105.00 CALL	INTRINSIC VALUE 105.00 PUT
102.00	0	3.00
104.50	0	0.50
105.00	0	0
105.50	0.50	0
108.00	3.00	0

Table 2.2 Intrinsic Value Calculation

Determining the Time Value

Calculating the intrinsic value is very straightforward; but how do we determine the time value? It is easy. Just take the actual option's price and subtract the intrinsic value. This gives you the time value.

For example, suppose that IBM is trading at $105 and you can buy a $100 call and a $100 put. The price of the $100 call is $5¾, and the price of the $100 put is $¾ (see Table 2.3). The in-the-money amount for the call option is $5, thus the intrinsic value is also $5. As the call option is trading at $5¾, the remaining $¾ is the time value for the call. What about the $100 put? Since the market price is higher than the put strike price, the put is out-of-the-money and its intrinsic value is zero. Since the put has a price of ¾ of a dollar (75¢), the entire value of the option is composed of time value.

IBM STOCK PRICE	100.00 CALL	100.00 PUT
105.00	5 3/4	3/4

CALL: INTRINSIC VALUE	= 105.00 - 100.00	= 5.00		
TIME VALUE	= 5 3/4 -	5.00	= 3/4	
OPTION PREMIUM	= 5.00 +	3/4	= 5 3/4	

PUT: INTRINSIC VALUE	= 100.00 - 105.00 OR 0			
TIME VALUE	= 3/4 -	0	= 3/4	
OPTION PREMIUM	= 0 +	3/4	= 3/4	

Table 2.3 Intrinsic Value versus Time Value

The Black and Scholes Model

As anyone can see, the intrinsic value component of an option price is trivial to estimate. The problem with option pricing, by process of elimination, must lie with the time value. Fischer Black and Myron Scholes — two professors then at the University of Chicago — made a breakthrough in options pricing in 1972-73 when they 'cracked the nut' of time value.[1] To understand the steps they took to solve the problem, we need to examine the stochastic dominance arguments which they used to define the boundary limits for option prices.

Stochastic Dominance Arguments
A stochastic dominance condition is a statement about the relative benefit of different alternative investments. For instance, suppose we are comparing two alternative investments in a market that can go up, down, or remain the same. If investment 1 provides the same payoff as investment 2 when the market goes up or down, but provides a superior payoff when the market is stable, then we say that investment 1 is stochastically dominant over investment 2. Furthermore, we can say that the value of investment 1 must be greater than or equal to the value of investment 2.

The first stochastic dominance condition compares the option's price to its intrinsic value. Consider that an option is American-style, meaning it can be exercised at any time. The option's price must be greater than or equal to its intrinsic value (see Figure 2.4).

If the option price were less than the intrinsic value, the option buyer could earn immediate and risk-free profits by purchasing the option, exercising it and covering the exercised position in the underlying market. For example, suppose a $100 call option on IBM was trading at $2 when the underlying IBM stock was trading at $105. In this situation the option buyer could buy the call for $2, immediately exercise it and simultaneously sell the IBM stock at $105. The result of this series of transactions would be an inflow of $5 from the stock trades (long IBM stock through the call

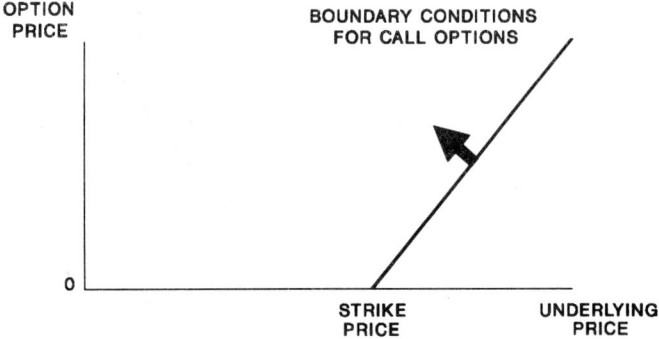

Figure 2.4 Boundary Conditions

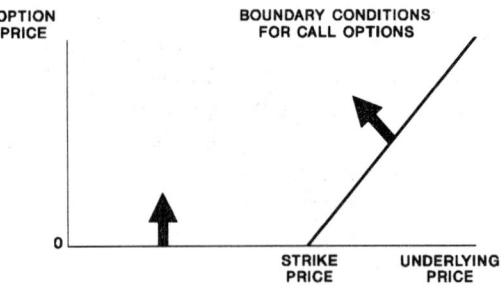

Figure 2.5 Boundary Conditions

exercise at $100 and selling the stock obtained at $105) and an outflow of $2 on the options purchase. The net effect would be a risk-free inflow of $3.

The second stochastic dominance condition is that an option must be worth at least zero (see Figure 2.5). As discussed before, options can be compared to insurance policies. Imagine an insurance broker providing you with insurance and not only giving you the insurance for free, but throwing in a cash rebate as well. This is a negative insurance price and, of course, impossible. While an insurance agent may give you a free calendar, he will not give you free insurance and then pay money to you to take on your risk. Likewise with an option; the option price might conceivably be zero if there were no risk, but it can never be negative. An option price must be greater than or equal to zero.

The third stochastic dominance condition is that an option price must be less than or equal to the value of the underlying asset price (see Figure 2.6). For example, consider the relationship between the value of a six-month option on gold with the actual price of gold. The option will only last six months while the gold may well last forever. So, how can the option on gold be worth more than the gold itself? It cannot.

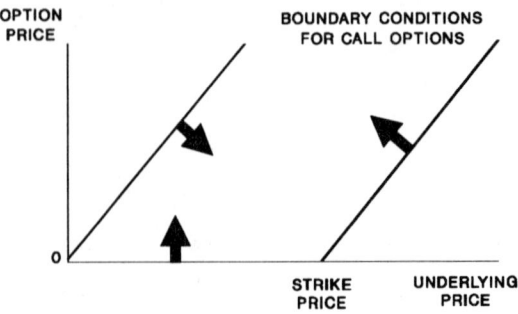

Figure 2.6 Boundary Conditions

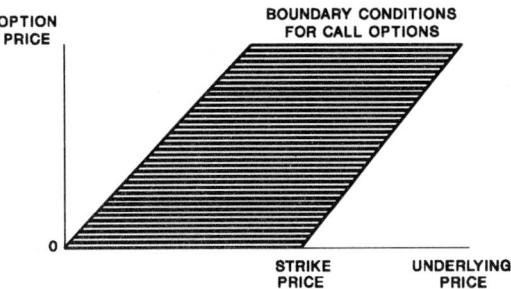

Figure 2.7 Boundary Conditions

The value of the option will be less than or equal to the value of the underlying asset. The option price must be some positive non-zero value between the intrinsic value and the value of the underlying asset. This is shown in Figure 2.7.

Assumptions of the Black and Scholes Model
With these stochastic dominance arguments defining the boundaries for call option prices, Black and Scholes set about determining where in that range the call option price would be. To make things simpler, they assumed that the call option had a European-style exercise feature, the underlying market price was distributed lognormally, interest rates and volatility of the underlying asset were constant, and that the asset paid no dividends or coupons before the expiration of the option.

What does a log normal process for prices imply? Assume that yields are presently at 9 per cent and the market can fluctuate up or down. Over the short term, there is a higher probability that yields will be at 8.90 per cent or 9.10 per cent than at 15 per cent. If I had to guess what tomorrow's yields would be, my best guess would be that they would remain at 9 per cent. This is the fundamental assumption of the normal curve, also called the Gaussian curve, displayed in Figure 2.8.

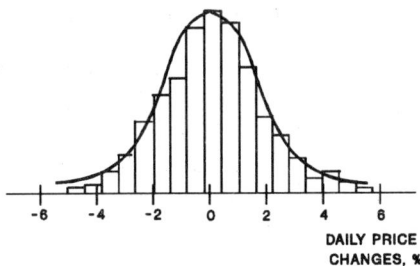

Figure 2.8 Normal Distribution

However, since interest rates cannot fall below zero, but can go up to infinity, we must adjust the normal distribution to take this into account. To do this, we simply multiply the normal distribution by a natural logarithm to enable the rates to be non-zero but retain the ability to reach positive infinity. Black and Scholes assumed that the price for assets also moved in this pattern of distribution; that is, prices too cannot fall below zero.

With these few assumptions regarding how underlying markets behave (which turns out to be the same as geometric Brownian motion in physics), Professors Black and Scholes were able to identify and solve a partial differential equation for the option's value. Curiously, their assumptions about how markets tend to behave are similar to the random movement of particles in physics. Therefore, it is not surprising that an important breakthrough in solving the Black and Scholes formula for option pricing was the adaptation of a heat transfer equation from physics.

To illustrate the comparative logic between the heat transfer equation and option pricing, assume you have a block of metal in a room which is at 20 degrees Celsius. If the block were heated until its temperature reached 200 degrees Celsius and then allowed to cool, the centre of the block would remain hot for quite some time, but at some point would begin cooling down rapidly. If you plotted the decay of heat over time, you would see a curve similar to that in Figure 2.9.

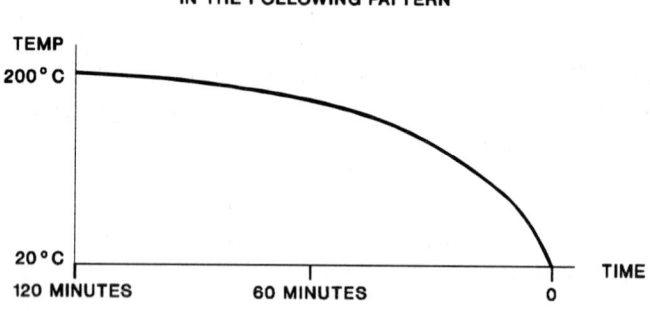

**THE BLOCK COOLS DOWN OVERTIME
IN THE FOLLOWING PATTERN**

**THIS CURVE ALSO DESCRIBES
THE TIME DECAY OF OPTION PRICES**

Figure 2.9 Black and Scholes Model 'Heat Transfer Equation'

This pattern of decay is identical to the time decay predicted for options by the Black and Scholes option pricing model. This breakthrough allowed, for the first time, a closed form solution for the pricing of European call options. The theory behind adapting the heat transfer equation to options was that if one could simply determine the market volatility (the 'heat') that exists and the time left until expiration, the time value of an option could be estimated. Once this is added to the intrinsic value, one has determined the 'fair' option price.

CALL OPTION

$$\text{CALL} = S \times N(d_1) - [E \times N(d_2) \times e^{-rt}]$$

WHERE:

$$d_1 = \frac{[\ln(S/E) + (R + \sigma^2/2\sqrt{t}\,]}{\sigma\sqrt{t}}$$

$$d_2 = d_1 - [\sigma\sqrt{t}\,]$$

t = TIME TO EXPIRATION % OF A YEAR
E = EXERCISE PRICE OF OPTION
R = RISK FREE INTEREST RATE OF PERIOD T
N = CUMULATIVE NORMAL DENSITY FUNCTION
ln = NATURAL LOGARITHM FUNCTION
σ^2 = VARIANCE OF THE RATE OF RETURN
S = SHARE PRICE
e = EXPONENTIAL FUNCTION
σ = SQUARE ROOT OF VARIANCE, ie. VOLATILITY

Figure 2.10 The Black and Scholes Option Pricing Model

Figure 2.10 displays the Black and Scholes formula. The formula is really quite easy to understand when one remembers that the price of an option is simply made up of intrinsic value and time value. For a call option, the intrinsic value is determined by the difference in the underlying stock price and the exercise price. In the equation, the reader can see that S is the price of a stock and $E \times e^{-rt}$ is the present value of the exercise price of the option. If the price of an option is only made up of the intrinsic value (as is the case at the expiration of the options) then the Black and Scholes formula simply subtracts the difference between the stock price and today's equivalent exercise price $(S - E \times e^{-rt})$ to yield the intrinsic value of the call. The intrinsic value for this can be seen later in this chapter in Figure 2.11b, and the reader will notice that the exercise price has been discounted to present value.[2] Obviously, at expiration the 'future is now' and the intrinsic value is simply $S - E$.

By process of elimination, the time value for the Black and Scholes model must be determined by the other factors in the formula which are $N(d_1)$ and $N(d_2)$. The N factors are the cumulative normal distribution of the stock price centred at the current price S and at the discounted exercise price $E \times e^{-rt}$. The factors d_1 and d_2 simply apply the logarithmic function outlined above and determine how big these distributions are. Again, the formula says that we must take the difference between these distributions. Figure 2.11a displays these two bell-shaped distributions subtracted from one another. As the reader can see, the intersection of these two bell-shaped distributions is the 'pointy' peaked area that lies between them, and is differentiated by vertical lines. The very top of this intersected area is the time value of the option.

What will happen to time value as the stock price increases or decreases? Since the exercise price is fixed, only the distribution of the stock price can move around. If S rises, then the peak of the distribution rises as well. In the mind's eye, the reader can see that as the stock price goes to the right, the amount that the two distributions will intersect increases as will the peak of the crossover. When the stock price is equal to the discounted exercise price, the distributions are exactly on top of each other and their overlap is at the highest degree with the highest peak. If the stock price continues

THE INTERSECTION OF THE DISTRIBUTIONS
AT VARIOUS STOCK PRICE LEVELS

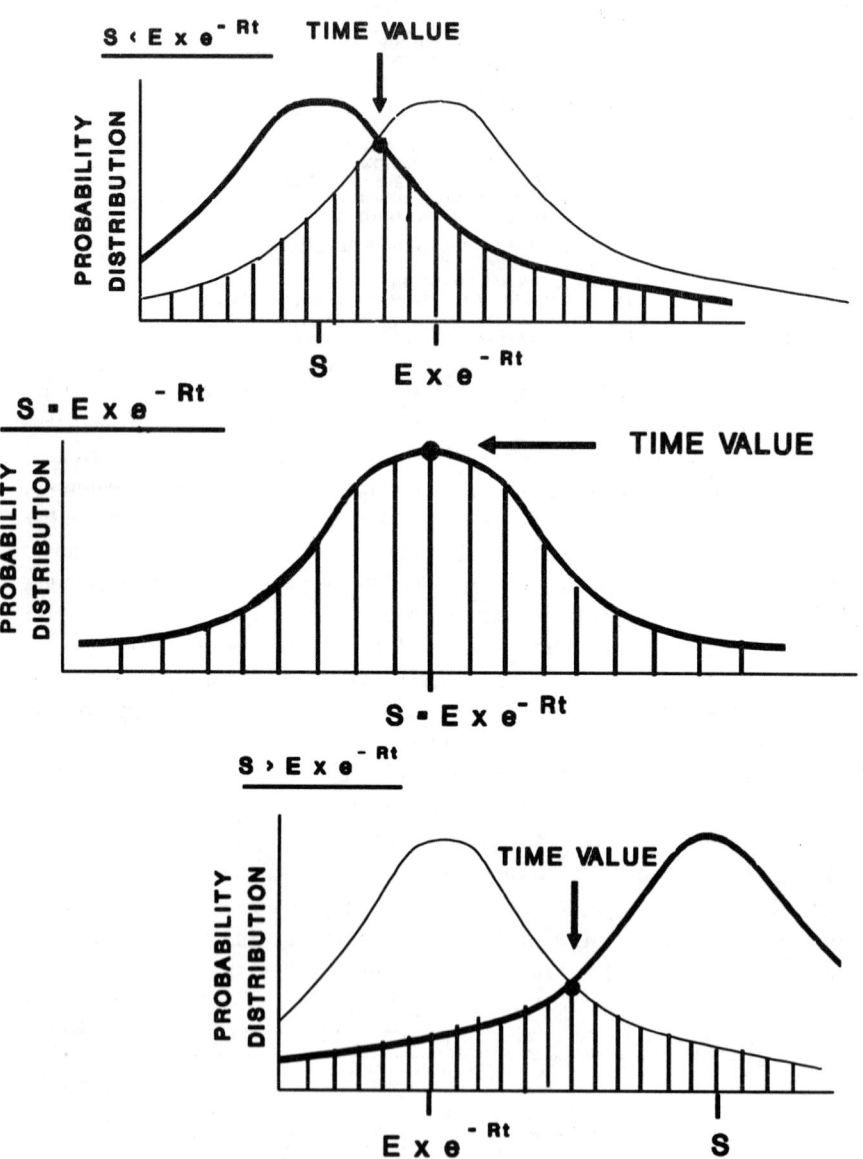

Figure 2.11a

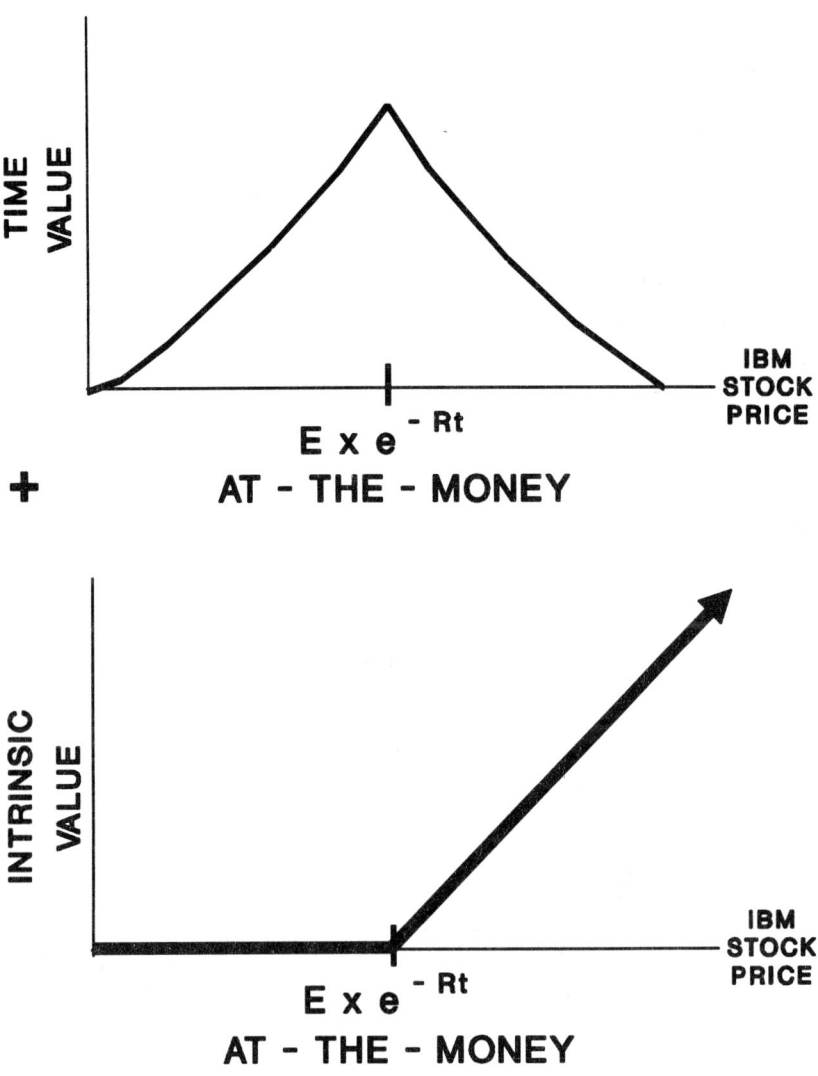

Figure 2.11b The Time Value and Intrinsic Value of an IBM Call Option

to rise above the discounted exercise price, then the crossover peak will begin to fall. This can be seen in Figure 2.11a. So, in conclusion, all the Black and Scholes formula is saying is that the intrinsic value is equal to the difference in the *prices* of the stock and strike, and that the time value is equal to the difference in the *distributions* of the stock price at current levels and at the level of the exercise price.

Figure 2.11b is an extension of Figure 2.11a and shows the time value function of an option as I examine the entire continuous range of possible stock prices. The reader can see the same 'pointy' shape displayed before, and that the maximum time value is when the option is at-the-money ($S = E \times e^{-rt}$).

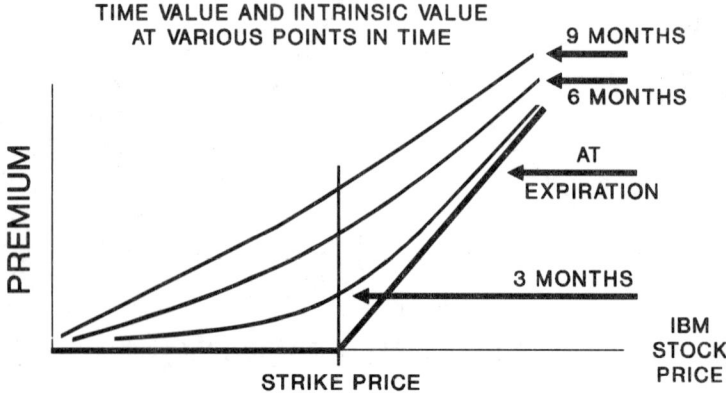

Figure 2.12 3-6-9 Month Call Options

Again, the intrinsic value of an option is determined by using the market price and the discounted strike price, and this is presented in the lower portion of Figure 2.11b. Volatility, time to expiration, and our normal distribution function allow us to determine the time value component. Figure 2.12 displays prices generated by the Black and Scholes model for call options. In this table, the intrinsic value and the time value are combined. So, if the reader combines the two graphs in Figure 2.11b, he will achieve the same result as Figure 2.12. After the addition of the time value, the relationship between the options' premium and the underlying price is represented by a smooth curve. Prior to expiration, a call option's relationship to the underlying market is defined by this curve instead of the angular 'hockey stick' shape of the (intrinsic value) profit/loss profiles I have presented until this point. What the reader will notice is that the longer the period until expiration, the greater the price for an option and the straighter the shape of the curve. Only at expiration — when there is no time remaining — does the call option's profit/loss profile resemble a 'hockey stick' shape, and the price of the option is only determined by the *prices* of the underlying asset and the strike.

In a similar vein, the put option's price is also made up of two components: the intrinsic value and the time value.[3] The intrinsic value for a put option is its in-the-money amount. That is, the strike price minus the current underlying price if that amount is positive, or else zero. Again, the time value is equal to the intersection of the distributions centred at the underlying price and at the discounted exercise price of the option.

To solve the equation, Black and Scholes had to make some pretty onerous assumptions. Since most options have an American exercise feature (including the stock options on IBM), and the Black and Scholes model is only for European-style options, isn't this a problem? The answer is 'not necessarily', and I can illustrate this best by an example. How many people do you know who will reach into their pocket, take out a $100 note, drop it on the ground and then walk away? I would venture to say not very many. Now consider the theoretical difference between an American option and a European option. The American should be more valuable because you can do something with it that you cannot do with the European option — you have the choice to exercise early. However, consider what one actually receives when one exercises the option. They will assume a position in the underlying market at the strike price of the option. Thus, only when the option is in-the-money will the holder decide to exercise it. When they exercise the option, it 'disappears' and a position in the underlying market replaces it. The amount of money they will receive is equal to the difference between the strike price and the prevailing underlying price, and the reader will recognise that this is simply equal to the intrinsic value of the option. However, prior to expiration, an option's price will also contain time value. Upon exercise before the final expiration date, this time value is lost. It is comparable to taking the $100 note out of your pocket and throwing it away. If one wanted to offset the option rather than exercising it, one could sell it back and always receive at least as much and in almost all cases considerably more. So, for almost all assets, the American exercise feature does not add value to the value of a call option since there is no value in being able to exercise early if you can instead sell the option back.[4] This also explains why most people choose to offset options rather than exercise them (with this I fulfil my promise to explain the statement made in Chapter 1).

Perhaps the other assumptions of the Black and Scholes model seem more severe: that volatility and interest rates are constant and no cashflows (like dividends) are associated with the underlying asset over the life of the option. Consider options on interest-sensitive securities. If interest rates are constant, so will be the prices of these assets. What would be the point of having options if the underlying asset and the risk of that market were fixed? There would be no point. Furthermore, almost all stocks pay dividends (and bonds pay coupons), and when these dividends are paid the stock price will fall. These are indeed serious drawbacks to the formula. However, I will examine these problems later in the book and show the reader how adjustments can be made to address these problems. Nevertheless, the Black and Scholes model is remarkably good as an estimation tool for the 'fair' price of an option. Essentially, Black and Scholes required these assumptions to take a 'snapshot' of what the options price would be at a single point in time. At the moment of estimation, the Black and Scholes formula is as accurate as a Nikon camera. It will give you a 'fair' picture of the situation. If, however, the scene changes, the photograph you have taken is no longer an accurate representation of current reality. As with the Black and Scholes model, one must retake the picture when the scene changes and do so every time a change occurs. Does this imply that a Nikon camera is not good simply because the scenes it records change? Of course not. Equally, it does not mean that the Black and Scholes formula is invalid because it assumes the 'scene' will remain unchanged. Remember, that is why the Black and Scholes formula is referred to as a 'model' and not as a 'reality'.

Rather than dwell upon the assumptions of the model now, I will examine in detail the variables required to determine the Black and Scholes option prices. In subsequent chapters, I will discuss the practical application of theoretical options pricing models and how these assumptions are factored in. In review, the two components that determine intrinsic value are the strike price and the underlying price (discounted by the interest rate for the life of the option). The elements used to assess the time value include the time until expiration and the expected volatility.

Effects of Time on the Price of an Option

How does time affect the time value of an option? Once again, we can apply an insurance example to infer an answer. If we compare a one-year insurance policy with a two-year insurance policy, both beginning tomorrow, we would expect them to have different prices. The longer the term of the policy, the more expensive the insurance will be. Since we now know options are similar to insurance, the greater the time to expiration, the higher the time value of the option. However, because time value is not a linear function of time, there are optimal times to consider purchasing options, and times when it is optimal to sell them, purely from the aspect of time decay.

For example, assume you have two choices for purchasing 125 days of option protection. Figure 2.13a and 2.13b describe the time decay of an option. The first choice would be to buy an IBM call option with 125 days left until expiration for $6, and hold it until it expires. Upon expiration there is no time left, and the time value is zero. Since the 125 days of protection costs $6, the total cost is $6 per share and since each IBM option contract is for 100 shares that represents a loss of $600. This can be seen in Figure 2.13a. The second alternative would be to buy an option with 250 days until expiration. The cost is $8½. After 125 days, when it is no longer needed, you offset the option by selling it back. If you sell it back for $6, then your total cost is only $2½. This can be seen in Figure 2.13b.

A significant problem for commercial users of options is that they consider them too expensive for their needs. They are only too expensive if you buy them at $6 and hold them until expiration when they become worthless. However, if you buy the option at $8½ and sell it back at $6, then the expected cost is only $2½.[5] The time to consider buying options from a time decay standpoint is when the option has a long term until expiration. The time to consider selling options is when the option has a short term until expiration. If one recognises this fact, then why would anyone buy options close to the expiration date? This is especially puzzling when one considers that the most concentrated trading activity in exchange-traded options seems to occur in those options close to expiration. Obviously, that means a lot of people are buying

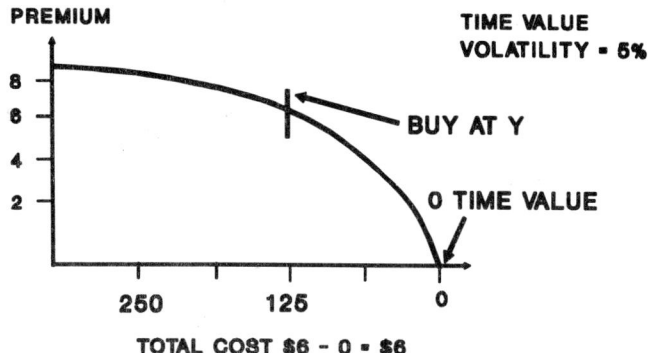

IF YOU BUY THE 125 DAY OPTION AT EXPIRATION,
IT WILL HAVE LOST ALL TIME VALUE

TOTAL COST $6 - 0 = $6

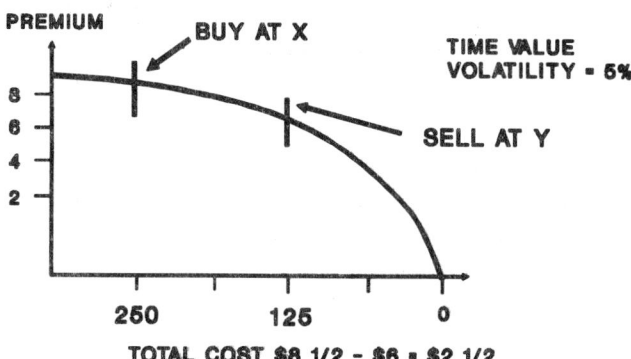

IF YOU SELL BACK THE 250 DAY OPTION WITH
125 DAYS LEFT, WHAT IS EXPECTED COST?

TOTAL COST $8 1/2 - $6 = $2 1/2

Figures 2.13a & 2.13b

options at a time where the heaviest rate of time decay occurs. To understand why people choose to buy options close to expiration, one must consider another factor I previously introduced: that of leverage. By examining when during the life of an option the heaviest trading activity occurs, we can draw some interesting conclusions about who is buying these option contracts and why.

Suppose there are three kinds of players in the market: hedgers, market makers, and speculators. A hedger is interested in reducing his risks and — when buying options — reducing his expected net cost of hedging. Therefore, hedgers are more likely to buy long-dated options and sell them back prior to expiration to reduce the expected cost. Most economists would categorise hedgers as 'risk adverse'. Market makers should be indifferent about when they buy or sell options because they generally hold the positions only long enough to find someone else to pass the contracts onto. Therefore, market makers might be called 'risk neutral' regarding the

31

time decay of options. On the other hand, the speculator wants to make a quick profit; therefore, he is interested in leverage (percentage returns) and would be a 'risk seeker'. Since these individuals have an appetite for risk, they will want to maximise the amount of leverage. As Figure 2.14 shows, leverage is maximised as options approach expiration.

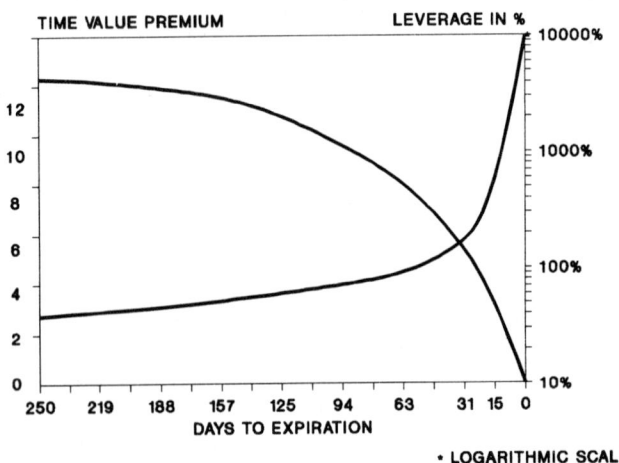

Figure 2.14 Time Value versus Leverage

What I mean by leverage is the percentage profit for an at-the-money option for a certain movement in the underlying market. In Figure 2.14, I assumed an at-the-money call option on IBM and determined the percentage profit for an increase in the stock price of $5 at various points prior to expiration. To contrast the leverage with the time value of the option, I plotted the percentage returns on a logarithmic scale on the right-hand side of Figure 2.14, and the time value of the option on the left-hand side of the graph. As the reader can see, the further back in time one goes, the greater the option's cost and the lower the leverage. However, if one does purchase a long-dated option, the time decay impact is significantly less. Hedgers — who often have more capital to work with — want to minimise the net cost of their option premium. They can achieve this by paying more for the options initially and then offsetting them before the heavy time decay begins to occur (as was demonstrated in Figure 2.13b).

Why would a speculator prefer inexpensive options near the expiration date? Suppose the speculator considers buying an option with 200 days until expiration costing $8, or an option with approximately a week of life left (that costs only $¼). If the underlying stock price increases by $5, then the long-dated option's value will increase to $10½ from $8 for the $5 increase in the price of the underlying share. This is only a 31 per cent return on the investment of premium. Now, consider the short-dated option, bought at $¼. When the market moves by $5, then the option's value will increase to $5. The percentage return is then 2000 per cent. As a result, the leverage is inversely related to the time remaining, and the shape of the leverage curve is the mirror image of the time decay curve.

Of course, this kind of leverage could lead the unscrupulous to contemplate manipulation. For this reason, many exchanges have very strict regulations on trading near expiration. Unscrupulous speculators can make a huge percentage return by buying options with strike prices which are close to the prevailing market price. If the market happens to move dramatically, the returns can often exceed 100 per cent. For example, with one day to expiration, someone buys an IBM $105 call for $¼ when the underlying share is trading at $104¾. If IBM's price just happened to move to $105½ the next day, the holder would exercise the option, sell the stock and make a profit of $¼. This would be a return of 100 per cent in one day on the capital invested. Therefore, there exists an incentive to manipulate the underlying market near expiration to drive the market price through an option strike price. Because of the highly levered, limited loss gamble that exists during the last week before expiration, many option professionals have termed this period 'lottery time'.

The Implications of the Lognormal Distribution

The reader will recall that the Black and Scholes model assumes that markets are distributed in a lognormal distribution. To understand the implications of this, the game of roulette is a good way to explain the probabilistic features of time value.

There are 38 numbers on (an American) roulette wheel. These numbers run from 1 to 36, which pay off the gambler who has placed a bet on one of these numbers, and 0 and 00 which pay off nothing. The object is to win by betting on a particular number and having the ball land in the slot represented by that number. If the ball lands on the number, you win. By placing a one-dollar bet on a single number, the probability of winning is one in 38, with a payoff of $35. The payoff is very high, but the probability is very low that your number will be a winner.

To guarantee you get some payoff in roulette, you could place a bet on each of the 36 available numbers. In this strategy, the amount of cash winnings is high and the probability of winning is also high (94.74 per cent). However, the net payoff is negative because the cost of this betting tactic exceeds the potential payoff, and you will always lose. However, if over time a particular bias can be discerned on the wheel, then the player can devise a strategy to earn superior profits. Basically, the highest expected return strategy would be to place selected bets on those numbers observed to occur most often.

Since Black and Scholes assume that markets are distributed log normally (instead of a uniform distribution on a fair roulette wheel), the highest probability event is at the current market price, and this is the best guess for the outcome of the next market price. Thus, at-the-money 'bets' have the highest probability and, as a result, the highest time value. When the option's strike price is deeply out-of-the-money, the option is a long shot and not very expensive. If the option is deeply in-the- money, it will be very expensive. This is similar to the strategy of putting a chip on every available number in roulette. One reduces the leverage and potential profits of the option because of the high premium expenditure. So, from a net profit standpoint, the lowest expected profits are for deeply out-of-the-money and deeply in-the-money options. The greatest profit potential is for the at-the-money options. Thus, again, the expected payoffs (probability times payoff minus the cost of the bet) will resembling the bell-shaped curve in Figure 2.8.

The Impact of Volatility on the Price of an Option

The other major component in determining time value is volatility. Volatility is far and away the most important variable in the determination of the time value of an option premium. Assume you want to buy health insurance. If you are in perfect health, the policy will be less expensive than if you had a terminal disease.

The policy is more expensive if you become gravely ill because the perceived risk (the probability of pay out) is much higher.

However, if you had purchased the insurance when healthy and then were told that you had a terminal disease, you could probably sell the policy back to the insurance agent. You could receive more than you had paid for it initially if the insurance agent were anxious enough to get out of his obligation. If you did this, you would be able to recognise a monetary gain owing to the fact that the perception of risk had changed.[6] If you did sell back the insurance and then learned your terminal disease was simply a misdiagnosis, you could go to another agent and buy insurance again at a lower premium. Hence, you were able to buy low risk, sell high risk, buy low risk again, and make money in the process. Your underlying health did not change, but the perception of the risk of your health did change.

The key to understanding volatility is that the greater the risk, the higher the option premium. Hence in option markets, risk is measured by a concept known as volatility. The more volatile the underlying market, the riskier it is. The riskier the market, the greater the time value of the option.

How Volatility is Measured

Volatility is measured in three primary ways: historical volatility, implied volatility, and forecasted volatility.

Historical Volatility
Historical volatility is measured by the actual deviations in the underlying market over some recent past period. As an example, assume that IBM shares are currently trading at $104¾. Suppose the price of the market yesterday was $105 and the day before yesterday the price of the market was $104½. The difference between these numbers shows a profit of $½ on the underlying markets yesterday and a loss of $¼ today. To standardise things, I will convert this number into a percentage change since it is easier to compare. Some days it will increase by 0.10 per cent and other days it will decrease by 0.10 per cent. However, in a world with random fluctuations over time, percentage

returns average to around zero and are distributed in a bell-shaped curve as in Figure 2.8.

Suppose we took the distribution of the movements up and down which have occurred in the market over the last 30 days. In most markets, we would get a normal curve as I discussed previously. The nice thing about normal curves is that they can be completely described and understood by two numbers: the average (or mean) and the standard deviation. Since the average change in random walk markets is zero, the only thing we must concentrate on is the standard deviation. The concept of random walk in financial markets is the assumption that there should not be any systematic pattern in the time series of security returns. One way to think of random walk is to consider a drunkard. After he leaves his favourite watering hole — and assuming that he has satiated his thirst — his ambulatory process will be random. That is, each step he takes has no relation to the direction of the steps he took previously. He wanders around and hence the term 'random walk'. A useful feature with the standard deviation is that it defines the probability of the price being certain levels. For example, when the normal curve deviates up or down by one standard deviation, there is a three-to-one chance that tomorrow the market price will be plus or minus this number multiplied by today's price.

Suppose the yearly standard deviation for IBM shares is 25 per cent. Now we must estimate what the price of IBM shares should be in one year. If a futures market existed for IBM shares, then it would be a simple matter to use the futures price as our estimate. Unfortunately, no futures market yet exists for IBM shares. To determine the forward price for IBM shares, we must apply the same methods used to determine the price of futures contracts. This formula is simply the current stock price multiplied by 1 plus the interest rate for the period, and then one subtracts the expected dividends from this result.[7] The expected level for IBM stock in one year is equal to $106½. This is determined by multiplying the current price of $104¾ by 1 + 6.5 per cent (the rate for interbank borrowing in London for one year US dollars) and subtracting $5, which is the expected dividend IBM will pay over this period. Therefore, our best guess for what the IBM price will be in one year is this level of $106½ with a 50/50 probability that it could turn out to be higher or lower. What would be the probability that the price turns out to be $135? If we looked up one standard deviation or an increase of the expected price of $106½ by 25 per cent, that would say that the one upward standard deviation would give us a price of $133⅛. Given the present dispersion of possible prices in one year, there would be a low probability that a $135 price would occur (less than, roughly, 1 in 6). The lower boundary could also have a price level 25 per cent *below* the projected futures price, and 75 per cent of $106½ is $79⅞. So, I can say with confidence that in one year I am sure that the price of IBM stock will be between $79⅞ and $133⅛, with three-to-one odds.[8]

Suppose you purchased a one-year IBM call option with a $135 strike price which benefits you if prices rise above $135. Given that $133⅛ is the one standard deviation limit, this option is not worth very much because it has a low probability of being used. At the very best, only in 1 year out of 6 would you expect prices to be above $135. If you can determine what volatility is, then you can make some probabilistic predictions of what could happen in the future at various levels. For example, the call option with a strike price of $135 is worth very little because the probability is low that prices will be that high (and that the options will subsequently be profitable).

Now, consider a call option with a strike price of $75. That option is deep in-the-money and is very expensive. Similar to the chip on every number strategy, this option has a high probability of payoff but a low net cash inflow because of the high premium expense. So the leverage is low.

However, since the expected future price has the highest probability of occurrence, options (both calls and puts) with strike prices equal to that level have the optimum tradeoff between probability and leverage. These options, therefore, have the greatest time value.

To determine historical volatility, one simply examines the percentage differences between the day-to-day prices for a period in the past. To eliminate the offsetting positive and negative changes, we square each observation, add them up, divide them by the number of days monitored[9] and then take the square root. Now we have determined a daily standard deviation. Then, we will convert that figure to an annualised basis and assume that the past can be used to predict the future. The problem is that when you rely on past events to predict the future, you must assume that the future will be like the past. While this can be valid for some markets, it might make more sense to take into account what is happening now rather than what has happened in the past. This is done by determining the volatility implied today in the options prices and obtaining an estimate for today's price of risk.

The time value of option premiums is simply a method to securitise risk or volatility. When the volatility in any market changes, option prices on that market can also change. Options prices not only reflect market moves but also reflect on fluctuations in volatility. Figure 2.15 displays the historical volatility of IBM shares from 1990 to

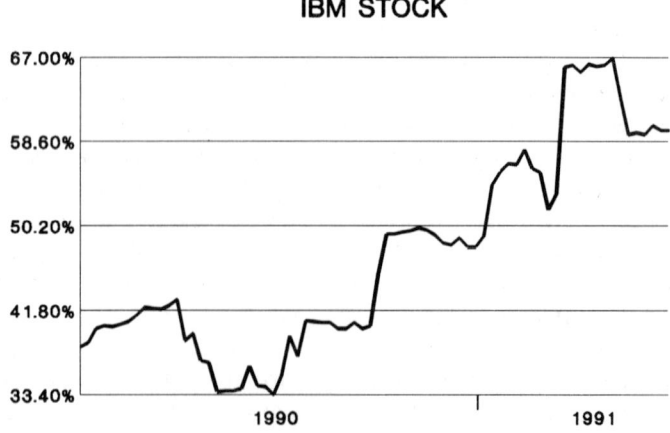

Figure 2.15 Historical Volatility (Source: Bridge Information Systems)

1991. Because significant changes in risk occurred over this period, substantial opportunities existed for volatility traders. These opportunities can be realised into profits simply by buying low volatility and selling high volatility. Just like our health insurance example, if one can predict changes in the perceptions of risk, one can make money trading risk.

Implied Volatility

Implied volatility is the risk perceived by the market today and built into the time value of the premium. It can change as quickly as any market-generated factor. To determine implied volatility, all that one requires is an actual option price and a theoretical option pricing model.

You simply input the strike price of the option, the underlying asset price, the expiration date, a short term interest rate, the expected dividends that will be paid and finally the actual option price into a theoretical option pricing model. The price of the underlying market, the option premium, the term, the short-term interest rates, the dividends and the time to maturity are all known factors. The only unknown variable is the volatility. One determines the implied volatility by running the option pricing formula backwards with the actual price as an input. The model will inform the trader what volatility input had to be entered into that model to yield the actual option's market price. The trader can then assume that the market's price for volatility should be consistent for other option strike prices on the same underlying and maturity. If a 25 per cent volatility is implied by the price of a $105 call option, you would expect the volatility of a $110 option to be equal, given that both options share the same underlying. Therefore, one could use the implied volatility of the $105 call to predict the price of the $110 option. Essentially, implied volatility is determined by supply and demand for risk in the market just like any price series. Later, when I discuss volatility trading, I will display a plot of implied volatility (see Figure 5.1b).

Forecasted Volatility

Another way to determine volatility is to forecast it using statistical techniques. Heteroscedasticity is a statistical term for nonconstant variance. Since volatility perceptions in the market are based on people's perceptions, there must be a link between volatility and real events which affect risk. In a particular country the government might change its policies due to the release of macroeconomic statistics. If the economy is doing well, the perception of risk might be low for certain markets. If the economy is expected to fall into a recession, there is a higher risk for these same markets. One might hypothesise that when the economy is weak, the risk of the market is high, or vice versa.

I wrote a paper in 1983 which examined this very hypothesis in relation to the US stock market.[10] The theory propounded was that during expansionary periods in the economy, the risk of stock markets is low, and during recessions the risk becomes higher (see Figure 2.16). If you have a forecast on the health of the economy, you can forecast volatility. In a stock market recession, if volatility increases then you have an entire category of trading strategies you can use which do not have to be directionally

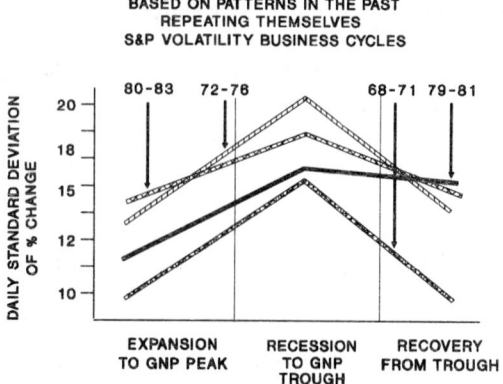

Figure 2.16 Forecasted Volatility

biased. There are ways of trading with options when you do not have a view on the movement of the underlying market. The most important element in the option price is the volatility you predict; since it is the only unknown element, it is the only factor you can trade.

Consider the situation where you buy a $105 call option when IBM shares are trading at $105 and the volatility is 35 per cent. The price paid for the option is $7⅛. If the price of IBM falls to $100, the value of the call should decrease. However, if the volatility increases to 50 per cent concurrently with the market's fall, the value of the option will increase to $7¾. Thus, the increase in time value caused by a rise in volatility can sometimes overwhelm the impact from underlying market moves (see Figure 2.17).

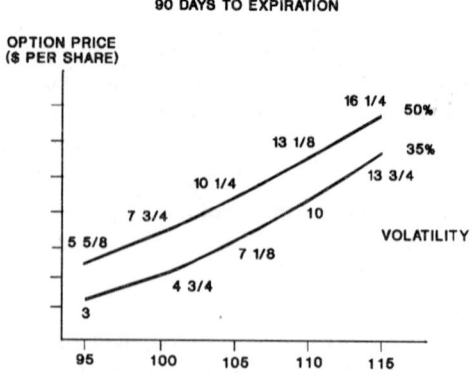

Figure 2.17 Volatility Impacts

When I traded treasury bond options in the United States, I once bought put options while the market was rising. Theoretically, the puts should have lost their value. However, exactly the opposite occurred because the volatility increased. I made money because the increase in the perception of risk overwhelmed the loss potential from the move in the market. Remember, volatility is easily the most critical element in the time value of an option.

Interest Rates and Dividend Impacts for Options

The final variable in the Black and Scholes options pricing formula is the interest rate factor. When they developed their model, they wanted to cover all the angles and to do so they needed to consider what alternative investments an option investor might consider. What made sense to Black and Scholes was an investment in risk-free deposits for the term of the options life, especially if the investor could combine the option purchased (or sold) with a position in the underlying asset to create a risk- free position. Then the combined position should have a return equal to the interest rate offered on the comparable deposit. This final variable made sure that the option holder (or writer) would not be able to make money for nothing. (This condition is also known as a 'no arbitrage' constraint). For many option markets, this interest rate factor is trivial. For options on futures contracts — which I will discuss later — the impact can be completely eliminated. However, to show this to be the case, I need to cover a little more theoretical ground and this will be done in the next chapter.

The effects of dividends and other cash inflows like coupons are fairly straightforward. One can treat these payments as 'negative' borrowing and a reduction in the net borrowing cost required to purchase equity or bonds. Later I will discuss both continuous dividend payments and what happens when dividends are paid in a lump sum.

[1] This is the 'big one': F. Black and M. Scholes, 'The Pricing of Options and Corporate Liabilities', *Journal of Political Economy*, May-June 1973, pp.637-59. While Black and Scholes got all the glory, Robert C. Merton of MIT was hot on the trail of solving the problem and barely missed out. See R. Merton, 'Theory of Rational Option Pricing', *Bell Journal of Economics and Management Science*, Spring 1973, pp.141-83 for what may be the best of the early articles on options pricing.

[2] The reason why the Exercise Price is discounted is that the Black and Scholes formula is for European-style options only.

For the American-style option, the fact that immediate exercise could occur means that the intrinsic value must be equal to the difference between the underlying price and the strike. For the European option, the only time exercise could occur to realise the intrinsic value is at the expiration in the future.

To determine today's equivalent exercise price, we must discount the future exercise price back to present value and e^{-rt} is the continuous interest rate factor that achieves this.

3
Black and Scholes did not actually come up with a model for pricing put options. However, through some very simple arbitrage techniques that will be explained in the next chapter, one can determine put prices from the Black and Scholes call option prices.

4
This may not be the case for a call option on an asset which pays coupons or dividends. Furthermore, there can exist circumstances where the early exercise of a put option may make sense; an elegant argument is presented in the Robert C. Merton article previously referenced.

5
This only works if the other variables which determine an options price are constant. This argument is known as *Ceteris Paribus*. However, given that one cannot predict the future, decisions must be based upon expected outcomes. One expects that buying longer dated options and selling them back prior to expiration will be a cheaper alternative to buying shorter dated options and letting them expire.

6
The comparable situation in the options market is to sell the option previously purchased back into the market. If the volatility has risen, the option will be worth more and result in a profit to the option holder.

7
This formula for forward or futures prices assumes an equivalent portfolio in shares and borrowing that mimics the cashflows of a futures contract. Since a futures or forward contract costs nothing today with settlement of the contract in the future, the equivalent portfolio in stock requires one to buy the stock and borrow money to pay for the shares, repaying the borrowing at the future date. Over the time period of the holding, the profit of the portfolio of shares and borrowing will be determined by the change in the share price, the cost of borrowing and any dividends paid to the share holder. The formula for the forward price of a share is $F = S \times e^{rt} - D$ where F is the forward price, S is the current price, r is the borrowing interest rate for the period t, and D the dividends paid over the period t.

8
In a normal distribution, the plus and minus one standard deviation range covers roughly $\frac{2}{3}$ of the distribution.

9
To be truly accurate, one would divide by the number of days monitored minus one. In Figure 2.15, the number of days monitored was covering the previous three months. The formula for the standard deviation is

$$\sigma = \sqrt{\sum (x_i - x^*)^2 / n - 1} ,$$

where x_i is the individual observations in the period, x^* is the average of these observations for the period, n is the number of observations, $\sum$ is the summation notation indicating that the difference between each observation and the average must be summed up and $\sqrt{}$ is the square root function.

10
R. Tompkins, 'S&P 500 Stock Index Volatilities: Business Cycle Patterns', *Market Perspectives*, Vol.1, No.3, June/July 1983.

3: Advanced Concepts in Options Pricing

Now that I have identified the key factors in option pricing (the underlying instrument market price, the strike price, the underlying instrument volatility, the time to expiration, and the interest rate), I will examine how these factors are synthesised into an option pricing model.

In this chapter, the underlying asset which will serve for our examples will be the US Dollar/Pound Sterling exchange rate. Options on foreign exchange are traded in the interbank market on an over-the-counter basis (OTC), and are also traded at a number of exchanges worldwide. Of these exchange traded currency options, the Philadelphia Stock Exchange (PHLX) and the International Monetary Market (IMM) in Chicago are the most popular. I will examine both the OTC currency option market and the $/£ options traded at both the PHLX and IMM markets. The contract specifications for both the PHLX $/£ option on physical currency and the IMM $/£ option on currency futures are presented in Tables 3.1 and 3.2.

THE ROLE OPTION PRICING MODELS PLAY IN OPTION EVALUATION

A common misconception about option pricing models is that they indicate the 'right' price for an option. Option pricing models do not necessarily give the 'right' price of an option. The 'right' price of an option is what someone is willing to pay you for a particular option. The best pricing method found up to now is the market; an efficient market will give the best and truest prices for options. The true benefits of an option pricing model are that they provide an accurate 'snapshot' of current market conditions (remember the Nikon camera example in Chapter 2) and, more importantly, the option pricing models break the option's market price into each of the factors that comprise it. Thus, you can examine each factor separately and assess their individual contribution to the determination of the option's price. Furthermore, by forecasting each of the individual factors, one can forecast an option's price over a wide variety of different scenarios.

For example, once you have an actual market price for an option, you can determine the implied volatility associated with that market price by setting the theoretical price generated by your model of choice equal to the actual price. Furthermore, an option pricing model can predict how the market price of the option should change given that

UNDERLYING CURRENCY UNITS	£ 31,250
EXPIRATION MONTHS	MARCH, JUNE, SEPTEMBER AND DECEMBER. IN ADDITION THE 2 NEAREST-TERM MONTHS.
EXPIRATION DATE	SATURDAY BEFORE THIRD WEDNESDAY OF THE MONTH
MINIMUM PREMIUM CHANGE	0.01
MINIMUM PRICE MOVEMENT	$3.125
EXERCISE PRICE INTERVALS	2 1/2 CENTS PER UNIT
EXERCISE METHOD	AMERICAN OPT.: ANYTIME UNTIL EXPIRATION EUROPEAN OPT.: EXERCISE ON LAST TRADING DAY
DELIVERY METHOD	FOREIGN CURRENCY PURCH.: DELIVERS $ TO OCC ACCOUNT IN THE U.S. FOREIGN CURRENCY SELLER: DELIVERS CURRENCY TO OCC ACCOUNT IN THE COUNTRY OF CURRENCY

Table 3.1 Options on $/£ (PHLX)

the volatility changes, or given that any of the other factors that determine the value of an option change. Therefore, option pricing models should be used to inform you how option prices can change in the market and not necessarily what the correct option price is. This might seem to undermine the usefulness of option pricing models, but this is far from being the case.

TRADING UNIT	ONE BRITISH POUND FUTURES CONTRACT (£62,500)
EXPIRATION MONTHS	ALL CONTRACT MONTHS DELIVERABLE INTO MARCH, JUNE, SEPTEMBER AND DECEMBER FUTURES
EXPIRATION DATE	19:00 ON THE LAST TRADING DAY
PREMIUM QUOTATIONS	U.S. $ PER BRITISH POUND
MINIMUM PRICE MOVEMENT (TICK SIZE)	0.02 CENTS, EQUAL TO $12.50 PER CONTRACT
EXERCISE PRICE INTERVALS	2 1/2 CENTS ($1.625, $1.650...)
TRADING HOURS	7:20 - 14:00 (CHICAGO TIME)
LAST TRADING DAY	TWO FRIDAYS BEFORE THE THIRD WEDNESDAY OF THE CONTRACT MONTH

Table 3.2 Options on British Pounds (IMM)

OPTION DERIVATIVES COMPARED TO AEROPLANE GAUGES

For an analogy of the option pricing model, let us look at another model that has the sole purpose of measuring the present state of the world and indicating the impact on that state from changes in several factors. Consider the instruments in an aeroplane. When you fly an aeroplane you will probably rely mostly on the visual feedback you receive from looking out of the window. However, you also have gauges to confirm and quantify your visual feedback, and also to guide you when your view out of the window is unreliable, such as when you are flying through a storm.

Suppose you were designing an aeroplane instrument board. If you could select only one instrument, which one would you choose? Would you measure the altitude, pitch, speed, fuel or the outside temperature? As you contemplate which gauge is most important, you will begin to realise that since many factors are necessary to keep the aeroplane airborne, you will require gauges on all these factors. If you had altitude but not speed, you might stall the plane and crash. If you had altitude and speed but not fuel, you could also plummet to earth as your aeroplane ran out of fuel and the engine stopped. However, regardless of the gauges you choose, only a very foolish pilot would rely solely on his instruments and never look out of the window. With options markets, relying on the market price is like looking out of the window when flying an aeroplane. The option pricing model acts as a surrogate for reality by providing gauges to inform you how the options price could change as the factors determining options prices change. But no matter how good your option pricing model, you cannot neglect to 'look out of the window' as you trade options. Remember that at some point, however, your gauges can be the difference between success and 'crashing' when the actual market conditions may become too foggy to fathom.

The factors we need to measure — and, therefore, create 'gauges' for — include: the underlying instrument market price, the underlying instrument volatility, the time to expiration, and the interest rates.

THE DELTA CONCEPT

The first and perhaps most important gauge we will use in options markets is commonly called the delta. The delta tells us how sensitive the option's price is to changes in the value of the underlying asset. There are at least four ways to think about delta.

Delta as the Measure of Relative Change to the Underlying

The first way to define delta is as the relative change that an option price will experience for a given change in the underlying market. Suppose that the exchange rate for Dollars and the Pound Sterling is \$1.675, and the price of a call option on the exchange rate is trading at 2.5¢ . Suppose the underlying market moves from \$1.675

to $1.685, a change of 1¢ , and at the same time, the option on Pound Sterling changes from 2.4¢ to 2.9¢ . The option has experienced a change of .5¢ simultaneously with the underlying's change of 1¢ (see Table 3.3).

DELTA: THE AMOUNT THE OPTION PRICE CHANGES FOR A SMALL CHANGE IN THE UNDERLYING PRICE

EXAMPLE:

	T	T+1	Δ
$/£ PRICE	1.675	1.685	0.010
OPTION PRICE	0.024	0.029	0.005

Table 3.3 Definition

The delta is the actual change in the option's price divided by the actual change in the underlying price. Therefore, the relative change (or delta) for the option would be 0.5 of a cent divided by the underlying market change of 1¢ , or 0.5. This suggests that for every point of the underlying asset movement, the option price will move by 50 per cent. For this reason, the delta is also known as a hedge ratio. This allows one to determine the proper hedged position for an options contract using a position in the underlying Pound Sterling. If the size of the underlying foreign exchange transaction were £1,000,000, then in this example, two options would be required to offset 100 per cent of the movement in £1,000,000. Conversely, you could also create a neutralised position with one option and £500,000 (half) of the underlying amount of the Pound Sterling.

Delta as the Sloped Relationship between the Option Price and the Price of the Underlying Asset

The second way to understand delta is to define it as the ratio between the change in the options's price for a change in the underlying price. This ratio is equal to the slope of the curved relationship between the option's price and the price of the underlying market. This relationship is shown in Figure 3.1. At expiration, the value of the option is zero or it is the in-the-money amount (intrinsic value). If the option is out-of-the-money, it has a value of zero everywhere from $1.675 to the left. Since a slope of zero implies a horizontal line, the option's price is flat from $1.675 to the left. If the option is in-the-money it will be exercised into a long futures position. This will occur everywhere to the right of $1.675. So, the value of the option at that point will

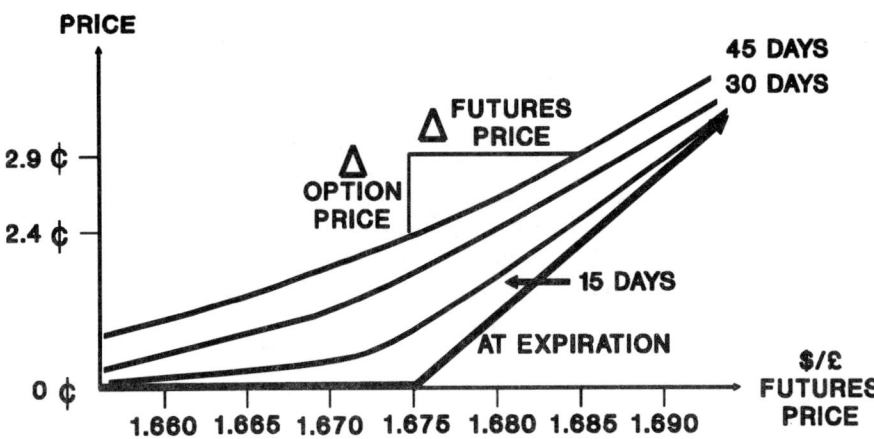

Figure 3.1 Fair Value Premiums

be solely determined by the level of the underlying asset. The value of the option will then increase one point for every one point increase in the futures. Therefore, the slope for the option in this region is 1.0 or a 45-degree angle. Hence, at expiration the option will have either a slope of zero (if out-of-the-money) or one (if in-the-money).

Only at the expiration of the option will we know for certain whether the option is exercised or not. Prior to this date, it is unknown whether the underlying market price will finish above or below the option's strike price. Therefore, before the expiration, the slope of the relationship of the option's price to the underlying market lies somewhere between zero and one. The higher the probability the option will finish at a value of zero, the closer the slope will be to zero. The higher the probability the option will be exercised into a full underlying position, the closer the slope will be to one. Intuition should tell us that at some point the slope should be halfway between 0 and 1 and that value would be 0.5. Suppose a slope of zero is associated with an out-of-the-money option and a slope of one with an in-the-money option. We could speculate that the at-the-money option (which lies in the middle between these extremes) might have a slope of 0.5. Hence, anytime before expiration, an out-of-the-money option will have a delta between 0 and 0.5, and an in-the-money option will have a delta between 0.5 and 1.0.

Delta as the Measure of Relative Risk of the Option to a Buying Position in the Underlying Market

The third way one might evaluate the delta is to examine the relative risk of the option to an underlying position as the underlying price changes. For example, if one held £1,000,000 in nominal value of Pound Sterling at a price of $1.675, that means the contract value is $1,675,000. If the price changes from $1.675 to $1.665 the new contract value is $1,665,000 or a loss of $10,000. To eliminate completely the risk of holding this position, we must sell an equivalent amount of Pound Sterling which in this example would be £1,000,000.

An option's risk relative to the exchange rate of the $/£ is thus dependent on two factors: the amount held in the underlying asset, suppose £1,000,000, and the delta factor which might be 0.50 if the option's strike price is $1.675 (at-the-money). Suppose a call option with a strike price of $1.675 has a price of 5¢ at a market price of $1.675. If the market price fell to $1.665, then the new option price would be 4.5¢. Thus, the contract value was originally worth $50,000 ($0.05 × £1,000,000) and the new value is $45,000 ($0.045 × £1,000,000) for a loss of $5000. What would be the equivalent position in Pound Sterling which would generate the same loss for the same price change from $1.675 to $1.665? Recalling that £1,000,000 in Pound Sterling lost $10,000, then it is clear that £500,000 in Pound Sterling would generate a loss of $5000 for the same price change. Therefore, the call option with a strike price of $1.675 would have the same equivalent risk as holding 50 per cent of a £1,000,000 position. Again, to eliminate the price risk of holding the option, one would be required to establish an equivalent short position in Pound Sterling with the same relative exposure and this would be £500,000.

Since the delta indicates the relative risk of an option to a full long position in the underlying market, deltas allow easy consolidation of complicated options and underlying positions. This is because the netting of all 'positive' and 'negative' deltas provides the trader with his total risk relative to holding a long position in the underlying market. Remember that a long position in the market corresponds to a delta of 1, and a short position corresponds to a delta of −1.

Delta as the Probability that the Option will Finish at Expiration In-the-Money

The fourth way to define delta is as the probability that the option will finish in-the-money. Suppose the current spot exchange rate for $/£ is $1.70 and the forward price of Pound Sterling at expiration date of the option is $1.675. Since we are interested in the expected future rate of the currency exchange, the forward price is the appropriate rate to compare. What is the probability that the next price of the forward $/£ could be either $1.68 or $1.67 when the current forward rate is $1.675? In a random market, the probability is 50/50. Therefore, if I have an option with the right to buy (or sell) at $1.675, the probability is 50/50 that it will be in-the-money after the next trade. What would be your guess that an option would be in-the-money in five minutes given the prevailing market price and the strike price are both at $1.675? Again the probability is 50/50. What about in an hour, a day, a week or a month? It is always the same, 50/50. Therefore, the delta of an option which is at-the-money is always approximately 0.5.

Now, consider options which are out-of-the-money. These options have less than a 50 per cent chance of finishing in-the-money (i.e. the delta is below 0.5). The reason is that if the prevailing price remains where it is, when the options expire they will finish out-of-the-money. Therefore, the probability that the market will be 5¢ lower in 45 days is less than 50/50; it might be only 33 per cent. On the other hand, there is an approximately 67 per cent probability that the market will be higher than that level in 45 days. Hence, the delta states the probability that the option will be above or below the strike price at the maturity depending on whether it is a call or a put option.[1] For calls, the delta is the probability that the market price will be above that level, and for puts it is the probability that the market will be below that level.

Uses of Delta

Deltas are very valuable because they show both the probabilities of exercise and the risk relative to the underlying market. Also, deltas show you how many options or futures are required to hedge the underlying market price risk. Finally, the delta indicates what the profit or loss will be for a particular option contract when the underlying futures price changes. When the option is at-the-money, the delta is always 0.5. When an option is deeply in-the-money, the delta approaches 1.0 for a call and —1.0 for a put. If the option is out-of-the-money, then you will not exercise the contract, and the delta of these options approaches zero.

As you approach expiration, people who hold in-the-money call options have a position which mimics a full long position in the underlying asset. As a result, their exposure relative to the underlying asset (definition 3) is 100 per cent of a position, or a delta of one. The person who holds an in-the-money put has a position that acts like a full short position in the underlying asset which, compared with an underlying long position, would be minus one. Similarly, if you have agreed to buy £1,000,000 for dollars in the future and you want to be flat or risk-free, you can close out the position by selling 1,000,000 Pound Sterling for that same date. If you are long the equivalent of one delta and want the position to be flat or zero, you must simply combine with it some strategy that yields a minus one delta position. Since one minus one equals zero, you would then have a flat position relative to the underlying exchange rate.

Therefore, deltas allow you to evaluate the risk of any options position (or combination of options) as if it (they) were a position in the underlying foreign exchange market. Then, it is a simple step to establish offsetting delta exposures (with either spot or forward currency contracts, or with other options) until the net delta exposure is zero; achieving a position with no exposure to the underlying market. Alternatively, one can become delta positive or negative to benefit from a bullish or bearish sentiment. Since a positive delta offsets a negative delta and we have identified those option positions that are long (positive delta) or short (negative delta) relative to the underlying market, the relative risk can easily be determined. They cancel out if they are balanced correctly, yielding a hedged position. Determining the overall delta position is crucial to assessing the overall risk of a combination of options. The ability to determine the net delta is an important feature in risk management.

Delta Exposures of the Basic Strategies

Generally, if you buy any underlying market, your exposure will always be one or 100 per cent of that market. If you buy a put option (the right to sell), the relative exposure to a long underlying position is negative. That is, if the price of the underlying asset rises and the other factors do not change, the value of the put option will fall and the holder of the put will lose money. Therefore, relative to the underlying asset, holding put options are negative positions and provide negative deltas. When the market rises, put options should lose money; conversely, if the market falls, put options should make money. Therefore, put prices have an inverse relationship to movement in the price of the market. If an option is out-of-the-money, it will have a relatively small exposure relative to the underlying market; that is, if the market price changes the price of the option will remain almost unchanged. If it is deeply in-the-money, it acts almost like a full long or short position in the underlying market. When it is eventually transformed into the underlying market by exercise, it assumes the risk of the underlying market and then has a delta of either plus or minus one.

In the currency markets, if you have a position with a delta of positive 0.95, then you have a position which is as risky (in nominal term) as 95 per cent of one million Pounds Sterling (or £950,000). The buyer of a put option finds that his risk will range from no exposure to a full short position (minus one delta) depending on whether the market price lies above or below the strike price. Similarly, this inverse exposure also exists for those who sell call options. As I discussed in the previous chapter, both writing calls and holding put positions are equivalent short positions relative to the underlying market and, thereby, have delta exposures which are negative. All deltas are relative to one standard, which is a position buying one million Pounds Sterling for dollars in our examples.

The Concept of Delta Neutral

Because of the wide variety of strike prices for calls and puts that are available for $/£ both on exchange markets and on an over-the-counter (OTC) basis, the ways to achieve a flat position are almost infinite. When the net delta for a combination of options (and spot or forward contracts) is equal to zero, it is commonly referred to as a 'Delta Neutral' position. Consider hedging a single $/£ option series with an offsetting position in the $/£ forward market. To determine a 'risk-free' hedge ratio, one simply takes the inverse of the option's delta to determine the number of options required for each $/£ forward contract. Alternatively, one would simply multiply the delta by one $/£ forward position to determine the quantity of the currency that must be sold forward to hedge each option position. Unfortunately, because option deltas are by definition less than or equal to 1.0, the amount of currency required to hedge a single option may easily be less than the £1,000,000 which is generally the minimum dealing size for most forward contracts. In the exchange traded Pound Sterling futures market (and in almost all exchange markets), it is not possible to buy or sell less than one futures contract. So, if we adjust the quantity of the forward currency position to hedge the option, we will have either to deal in a size smaller than is generally traded (and have to pay a wider spread), or use standardised futures contracts in 'round lots' (i.e. integer amounts). Let us consider instead using the inverse of the delta to determine the number of options for a one million $/£ forward contract. For example, assume the $/£ forward price is at $1.675 and there is a call option which is trading with a strike price of $1.70. This option has a delta of 0.33 because it is out-of-the-money. If one purchased this call option it would be equivalent to being long 33 per cent of a single million Sterling forward contract. If you bought a $/£ forward contract to create an equivalent position, how many would you have to buy? To create an equivalent position you would have to buy 33 per cent of one million Sterling in the forward market which would be equal to £330,000 for each call option you bought. What happens if we decide that we want to deal only forward contracts at a minimum size of £1,000,000? We must find out how many options are required to establish a position exactly equal to buying the £1,000,000 forward contract. In delta terms, this strategy would have to be equal to a positive one delta. Let us consider an example. Suppose you are short one million $/£ in the forward market and you wish to offset the risk of this transaction using these call options expiring on that forward date. Since the options are equivalent to one third of a long position in a $/£ forward contract, you would need to purchase three call options to offset the risk exposure and become delta neutral. So, the proper hedge ratio would be the inverse of 0.33 which is three option contacts.

The real beauty of deltas is that they not only allow comparisons between options and the underlying forward market, but also between call and put options with a wide variety of strike prices. Now, we will apply this technique to hedge a $/£ option's exposure with another $/£ option. When we purchase a call, we have an equivalent long position. If we sell a call, by symmetry, we have an equivalent short position. If these calls were on the same underlying asset, the same maturity and the same strike price, buying and selling these options would provide an exact offset. Suppose the options have different strike prices; then the options are also quite different. Suppose you purchased a Mercedes Benz automobile and then sold one. What would your risk position be, relative to the price of Mercedes Benzes? One might intuitively think the position is offsetting or flat. But what if the Mercedes purchased was a 500 SL model and the Mercedes sold was a 190 E model? The position may or may not be 'flat' relative to the overall price of Mercedes Benzes because you are holding two positions which do not exactly offset. Since the 500 SL costs more than the 190 E, we must adjust the number of cars held to be equivalent in value. What is important is that the relative exposure of each offsets the other. Since the 500 SL is more valuable than the 190 E, more 190 Es must be sold to provide a truly 'hedged' position.

Let us now return to the options on foreign exchange market. Suppose you have a $1.70 strike price call option and a $1.725 strike price call option. As indicated above, the $1.70 call has an equivalent risk of one third worth of one million $/£ forward contract because its delta is 0.33. Suppose the $1.725 call option has a delta of 0.17 (i.e. it is further out-of-the-money). If you sold the $1.725 call option it would create a position equivalent to selling one sixth of a million $/£ forward contract (0.17 is approximately ⅙). This occurs because when you sell a call, the delta position is negative (if you instead bought the call, the delta would be a positive 0.17). If your goal is to achieve an offsetting and risk-less position with these two options, then you must adjust the number of calls bought or sold to reflect their different relative risks. So, if buying the $1.70 call is equivalent to buying one third of a million Sterling forward, and selling the $1.725 call is equivalent to selling one sixth of a million Sterling forward, to have a position with no exposure to the forward $/£ exchange rate (that is a delta neutral position) you would have to sell two $1.725 calls for every $1.70 call you bought. The reader may be curious as to the reason why we did not sell one $1.725 call and then sell half of the $1.70 call. We could have done this, but it would have required the underlying $/£ amount for the $1.70 call option to equal only £500,000. Again, most options trade on a minimum underlying amount and it could be that the price for a 'micro' option might be less advantageous.

In exchange traded foreign exchange markets it would not be possible to sell half of the $1.70 call option because these trades are restricted to whole numbers. Nevertheless, even if we are restricted to a minimum purchase or sale of one option, the true risk of the option may not be equivalent to one lot in the underlying market.

The risk for an option is defined by both the number of lots bought or sold multiplied by the delta for that option.

The Problem with the Delta

The problem with deltas is that they only provide instantaneous information; they change as market conditions change. As with the aeroplane analogy, the altimeter will provide a valid measure of the altitude at that moment; however, as other factors such as speed, pitch or fuel change, so will the altitude. As the pilot must monitor how his altitude may change as the other factors which keep his aeroplane airborne change, so the options trader must also monitor how his deltas can change as the other variables that determine options prices change. To remain perfectly risk-free, a hedged position in options may have to be revised continuously.

For example, the Sterling forward market is at $1.675 and you buy three $1.70 calls with a delta of 0.33 (out-of-the-money call options). The relative risk of these options is therefore 1.0 delta (0.33 × 3) and this strategy is equivalent to buying a million Pounds Sterling on the expiration date of the option. Suppose that to hedge this risk, you sell a million pounds forward for that date. Since shorting the underlying forward contract provides a minus one delta, when you combine this trade with the three calls you have purchased, the net position is zero (a delta neutral position). If the market then increased to $1.70, the $1.70 call would now be at-the-money and the delta has increased to 0.50. This implies that the three call options each have an equivalency to 50 per cent of one million Pounds Sterling. In total, the equivalent delta position for all three together is a positive 1.50 or £1,500,000. The short position has remained at a −1.0 delta or short £1,000,000 because it is still a single short position in Sterling.

As the reader can see, the 'hedged' position is no longer neutral but has become an equivalent long position with the same risk as holding 50 per cent of one million pounds or a risk of £500,000.

As the market moves, the delta does not remain constant. Therefore, the option trader must measure the sensitivity of the deltas to changes in other factors, in this case to the movement in the underlying market. Again, the true value of option pricing models is that they allow you to determine this sensitivity. By using calculus and taking the derivatives of the option pricing formula relative to those factors of interest to us, we can easily generate additional gauges.

I can just imagine the words 'derivative' and 'calculus' hitting the reader right between the eyes and the attention starting to wane. Do not fear, as I will leave these concepts to other books where they are more appropriate. Our objective here is not to show you how to produce your own 'option gauges' but rather to show you how to read them and understand what they mean.

When I studied calculus, most examples seemed very abstract and sometimes even trivial to me. One of the most popular examples to explain derivatives used a graph with a vertical axis representing distance such as kilometers or miles and a horizontal axis representing time. A sloped line (looking very much like our call option) was drawn representing the change in distance for a given change in time. The intuition was quite straightforward, the relationship between the changes in distance and time is simply speed. Likewise, the relationship between an option's price and the underlying price is called the delta. So, the delta is like the speed of the option. However, speed is not the only thing that sells cars. Another important performance feature (besides the Dolby sound system) is the acceleration. This is the change in speed for a given change in time. While the speed (delta) is the first derivative of the distance per time at a particular point (simply the slope), the acceleration is the second derivative at that same point (the change in the slope). This derivative is determined by taking another derivative of the speed with respect to time. Since in options we are interested in determining how the delta changes when the underlying market changes, we simply take the derivative of the delta with respect to the underlying market and we get a new 'gauge' which is commonly referred to as the gamma.

THE CONCEPT OF GAMMA

The higher the gamma value, the more the delta will change when the underlying market price changes. Intuitively, gamma jointly measures how close the current market is to the strike price of your option and how close the option is to expiration. The closer the market price is to the strike price and the closer the maturity of the option is to the expiration date, the higher the gamma will be. For example, an at-the-money option with one minute remaining until expiration will have the highest possible gamma value. An option with more time remaining will have a lower gamma and the further away from expiration one goes, the lower still the gamma. Figure 3.2

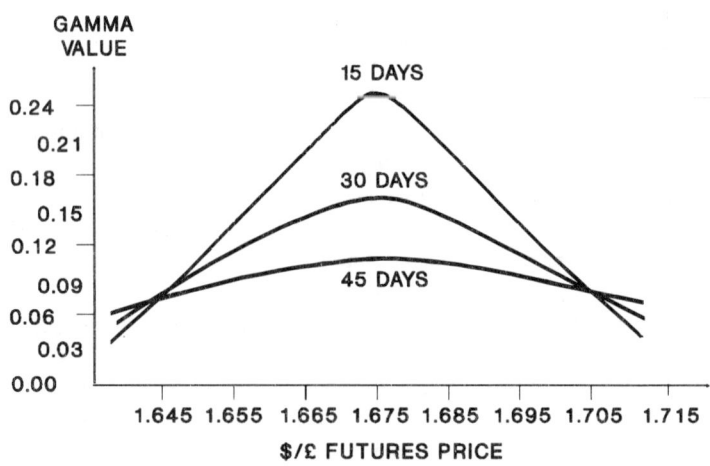

Figure 3.2 Gamma for a 1.675 Call Option

indicates gamma values for a particular $/£ call option with a variety of different maturities.

Consider a $1.70 call option with the underlying market trading at $1.6995 and one minute remaining until expiration. The delta is close to zero because it is out-of-the-money. If the market moves up .0010 (to $1.7005), the option is now in-the-money and the delta has become close to 1.0 due to the very small change in the underlying market. If the market oscillated above and below the strike price of $1.70, the delta would also swing between a 100 per cent exposure and a zero exposure. For those who purchase options, this impact represents an incredible leverage and many professional speculators purchase options at or near expiration with the goal of maximising this gamma impact. For sellers of options, the gamma has probably turned more hair white, caused more ulcers and broken more marriages than any other feature in options markets. People who buy options benefit from gamma and are often referred to as 'long gamma'. Those who sell options can be hurt when the gamma is high and the underlying market price moves. Therefore, they are often referred to as 'short gamma'.

Of course, if we are going to build gauges that measure the option's sensitivity to movement in the underlying market, we are also interested in all the other factors which determine an option's value. I have so far examined the speed (delta) and acceleration (gamma) features of options over the underlying market price. Now, I will look at the other factors, the most important of which is the volatility.

THE MEASURE OF VOLATILITY EXPOSURE — THE VEGA

The change in the option's price for a given change in volatility is called, among other things, vega. I prefer to call this measure the vega, but this is by no means a convention. In some markets, this derivative is called kappa, zeta, sigma, omega, epsilon and a

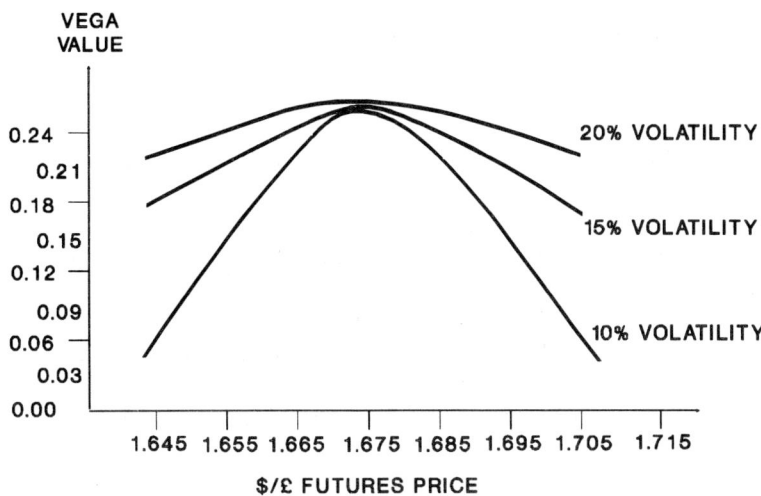

Figure 3.3 Vega for a 1.675 Call Option

variety of other Greek letters. Vega, as anyone who has pledged to a sorority or fraternity knows, is not a Greek letter but a now extinct sub-compact American car made by Chevrolet. I like vega because it has a 'V' for volatility and sounds rather Greek. Anyway, the vega measures the amount of money you make or lose from a given change in volatility. If the options market is trading at a 15 per cent volatility and your option position has a vega of +1.4, this indicates you will make (lose) $1400 for every 1 per cent increase (decrease) in volatility. Thus, if you had this vega position and volatility increased to 16 per cent, then if everything else remained constant you would expect to make this amount of money. Of course, if volatility drops to 14 per cent you would also expect to lose this amount (see Figure 3.3).

As was alluded to earlier, options are the most straightforward method to turn risk into a security.[2] As risk changes, so does the value of an options contract. Therefore, options dealing is nothing more than risk (or volatility) dealing. It is easy to understand why one must measure the vega to know what the volatility exposure of an option is. A key feature of most computer programmes based upon the Black and Scholes model is that they can quickly and accurately determine the exposure of the option to each factor that determines the option's value including this vega measure. Using our aeroplane analogy, one could consider the vega as the measure of an option's 'altitude'. Obviously, the altitude is one of the most critical elements in flying an aeroplane, and the volatility is one of the most critical elements in determining an option's time value.

What are the other variables which determine a currency option's value? These include the strike price of the option, the time until maturity and the interest rates for each country. Of these, there is no derivative relative to the strike price because the strike price is fixed. Since the strike price cannot change, it makes no sense to examine how the option's price will change for a change in the strike price. While this is true for most options, some option-like securities such as convertible bonds can have a variable 'strike' price and then such a derivative may be appropriate. However, for most options, including options on foreign exchange, such a derivative is not appropriate.

THE EXPOSURE OF THE OPTION TO TIME DECAY — THE THETA

Of these three remaining variables, the most important one to measure is the option price's time decay as the option approaches maturity. While time passing is not a probabilistic (sometimes known as stochastic) factor (since everyone knows that time is passing), the options price impact from the passage of time is not as easy to determine as one might think. If you recall from Chapter 2, options prices do not decay over time in a straight line but rather in the shape defined by the heat transfer equation. So, to determine the amount of time decay that would occur from today until tomorrow, one could simply plug in today's underlying price, volatility, interest rates and time to maturity (making sure that the theoretical price from the model equals the market price of an option). Then, one would reduce the amount of time to maturity by one day, keeping the other variables constant, and revalue the option. The difference between today's market price and tomorrow's theoretical price is the time decay. As one can imagine, this is tedious and time- consuming. To speed up the process, one can simply use calculus to determine the derivative of the option price with respect to time, which is commonly known as the theta. This derivative is simply the slope of the time decay curve at a particular point and it gives the change in the option's market price from one day to another. The theta decay (which is exactly the same as the time decay curve in Figures 2.13a and 2.13b) can be seen in Figure 3.4.

Using our aeroplane gauge analogy, the theta derivative can be thought of as the fuel gauge. It measures how long the option will live and when it starts running out of 'fuel'.

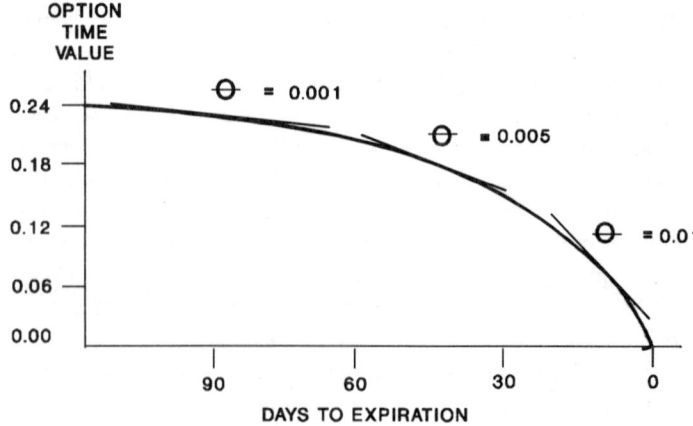

Figure 3.4 Theta for a 1.675 Call Option

THE SENSITIVITY OF OPTIONS TO INTEREST RATES — THE RHO

The final factor that we will measure is the sensitivity of the option's price to changes in short-term interest rates. The derivative of an option's prices relative to interest rates is commonly called rho. For currency options, two interest rates are important: the domestic currency interest rate and the foreign currency interest rate. Thus, one will have two rho derivatives. Again, using our aeroplane gauge analogy, the rho can be thought of as a thermometer measuring the outside temperature. For most flights in a small aeroplane, the outside temperature is fairly unimportant to its safe operation. However, if the altitude is very high, the temperature gauge can be quite important because ice can form. If ice forms on the wings, the aeroplane might become too heavy and plummet to earth. Figure 3.5 displays the domestic interest rate ($) rho for a call option on $/£.

To examine properly interest rate impact on options prices, we must wait until the end of this chapter after I have covered put-call parity. Until then, it is sufficient to say that the interest impact is generally of minor significance relative to the volatility, underlying market price movements and the passage of time. For options on forward foreign exchange, the interest rate impact is trivial and for certain kinds of options there is no effect from interest rates at all. However, for other kinds of options (especially long-dated OTC options) the interest rate impact can be important and must be closely monitored by dealers in these products.

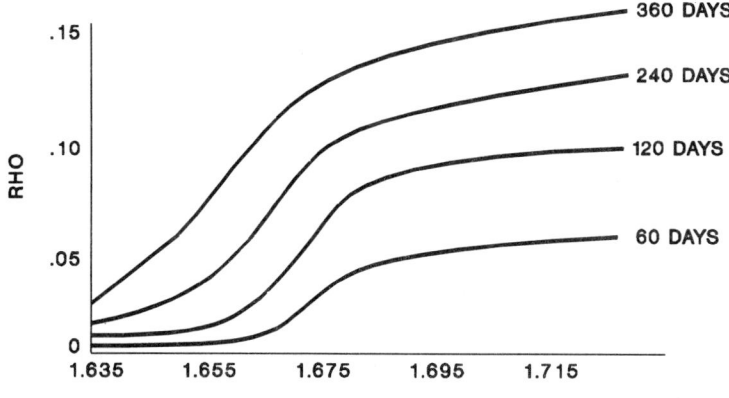

Figure 3.5 Rho for a 1.675 Call Option at Various Points Prior to Expiration.

THE APPROPRIATE PRICING MODELS FOR OPTIONS ON FOREIGN EXCHANGE

I feel that this is the point to present the reader with the appropriate pricing models for options on foreign exchange. I will also demonstrate how these same models are adapted for other kinds of underlying assets. The choice of the appropriate pricing model (for any kind of underlying) depends on whether the option is based upon the spot currency or upon the forward currency rate and whether the option can be exercised early.

European Options on Spot Currency

The formula for an option, which is based upon the current (or spot) foreign exchange rate and can only be exercised at expiration, may be seen in Figure 3.6. This formula was developed by Mark Garman and Steven Kohlhagen[3] and is remarkably similar to the Black and Scholes formula discussed in the previous chapter. In fact, the only difference between the two is that an additional interest rate factor is added to the

CALL OPTION

$$\text{CALL} = S \times N(d1) \times e^{-R_F t} - [E \times N(d2) \times e^{-R_D t}]$$

WHERE:

$$d(1) = \frac{\ln(S/E) + [R_D - R_F + (\sigma^2/2) \times t]}{\sigma \sqrt{t}}$$

$$d(2) = d(1) - \sigma \sqrt{t}$$

t = TIME TO EXPIRATION % OF A YEAR
E = EXERCISE PRICE OF OPTION
R_D = RISK FREE DOMESTIC INTEREST RATE
R_F = RISK FREE FOREIGN INTEREST RATE
N = CUMULATIVE NORMAL DENSITY FUNCTION
$\ln$ = NATURAL LOGARITHM FUNCTION

σ^2 = VARIANCE OF THE RATE OF RETURN

S = SPOT CURRENCY RATE
e = EXPONENTIAL FUNCTION

Figure 3.6 Garman/Kohlhagen FX Option Model.

Garman/Kohlhagen model for the 'foreign' country. It is one of the most comforting facets of option pricing theory that essentially all option pricing models are a refinement of the basic Black and Scholes methodology I have discussed so far.

One can view the evolution of option pricing theory as an adaptive progression from the initial innovative breakthrough. Consider, as an analogy, the evolution of internal combustion petrol engines. In the 1880s, Mr Daimler developed the first internal combustion petrol engine and fitted it into an automobile. This was a fundamental breakthrough that changed our world for ever. Since that time, many refinements have been made to the initial model, but every engine produced is still based upon the conceptual framework of its inventor.

One can think of the Black and Scholes model as being as great a breakthrough in the financial world as the first petrol motor was in the world of transport. As was the case with petrol motors, option pricing models since the initial invention have become more refined and sophisticated. Nevertheless, like the evolution of petrol engines, all option models are based upon the basic premises of Black and Scholes. From the extensive number of models that have been published in the financial literature, one might think that each new option pricing model is another breakthrough (for example the Binomial model which will be examined in the next few pages). However, this is not the case. The plethora of option pricing models do not reflect the invention of new 'engines' but rather present refinements to the original. It is as if when the first turbo-charger or fuel injection device was invented, the developer claimed that a new engine had been created. This is obviously not the case. The innovation would not be of any use had Mr Daimler not invented the basic engine for the refinements to fit onto.

So, it is not surprising that the Garman/Kohlhagen 'model' is really the Black and Scholes model with a 'currency interest rate' 'carburettor'. Furthermore, the most popular model for European options on dividend paying stock — the Merton 1973 model — is identical to the Garman/Kohlhagen model except that a continuous dividend payment is substituted for the foreign interest rate. So, the Merton model is really the Black and Scholes model with a Garman/Kohlhagen 'carburettor' painted a different colour.[4] Later in this book, I will present other models which have achieved fame in the pricing for a variety of underlying assets. But the reader can rest assured that all of these models are simply a refinement of the original Black and Scholes model presented in Chapter 2 and for the most part are only cosmetic changes.

European Options on Currency Forwards

The most appropriate model for European options on currency forwards is the Black (1976) model for options on forward contracts.[5] Figure 3.7 displays this model. Once again this 'model' is almost identical to the Black and Scholes model. The only differences are that a forward price F has replaced the stock price S and both the forward price and the strike price are discounted to present value. So, once again, a simple refinement to the original 'engine' has been introduced. However, this model has much broader applications than just for currency options. The Black (1976) model applies equally well to all futures contracts (for options with a European exercise feature) and many interest rate products I will discuss in Chapter 10. The reason why the Black (1976) model has such a broad appeal is because it assumes the underlying asset price that should be analysed is not the current price but what the asset price should be in the future (using basic arbitrage relationships). It has been convincingly argued by Mark Garman that the expected future price of the underlying asset on the expiration date of the option is more important than the current price of the asset.[6] In fact, what all option pricing models do is first estimate what the expected forward price of the underlying will be at the expiration date of the option and then estimate

$$\boxed{\text{CALL} = e^{-rt} \times [F \times N(d1) - E \times N(d2)]}$$

$$\boxed{\text{PUT} = \text{CALL} + e^{-rt} \times (E - F)}$$

WHERE:

$$d(1) = \frac{\ln(F/E) + (\sigma^2/2) \times t}{\sigma \sqrt{t}}$$

$$d(2) = d(1) - \sigma \sqrt{t}$$

t = TIME TO EXPIRATION % OF A YEAR
E = EXERCISE PRICE OF OPTION
r = RISK FREE INTEREST RATE OF PERIOD t
N = CUMULATIVE NORMAL DENSITY FUNCTION
ln = NATURAL LOGARITHM FUNCTION
σ^2 = VARIANCE OF THE RATE OF RETURN
F = FUTURES PRICE
e = EXPONENTIAL FUNCTION
σ = SQUARE ROOT OF VARIANCE, ie. VOLATILITY

Figure 3.7 The Black (1976) Option Pricing Model.

the option price. If, instead, the trader estimated the forward price himself, then for European options the Black (1976) model would provide the correct price for any kind of option contract.

American Options on Currency

Some have argued that the early exercise feature is so important that the Black and Scholes model cannot be correct. However, this argument is somewhat exaggerated in my opinion. If one remembers our discussion of the difference between European and American options in Chapter 2, one will recall that for securities which do not have discrete cashflows, the early exercise of call options is like throwing a $100 bill on the ground and walking away. The supposed problem is for those securities like stocks and bonds that do have cashflows periodically and would induce the option holder to exercise early to claim these cashflows. The most popular of the corrections to the Black and Scholes model for the possibility of American early exercise is the Binomial approach suggested by Cox, Ross and Rubinstein.[7]

Basically, the development of the Binomial model was spurred by an attempt by Professors Cox, Ross and Rubinstein to find an easier way to teach their students about how the Black and Scholes formula works. They used simple tree diagrams which can be seen in Figure 3.8 to explain how the price of the underlying security could change. These diagrams indicate that given you start out at a particular price for the underlying asset ($100 in Figure 3.8), the market price could either rise or fall by a discrete amount, say $1. After the initial up or down movement, the price could again move up or down by $1 and could be anywhere in the range $98 to $102. Then after this point, the process continues until the expiration date of the option.

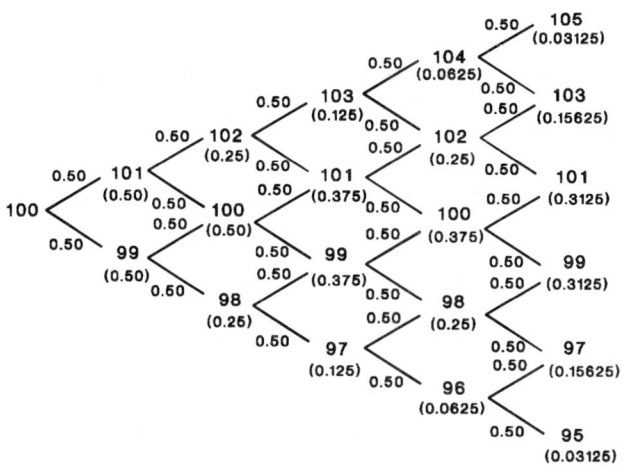

Figure 3.8 Binomial Model

The reader may recall that in the movement of markets, two factors are required to understand fully what is going on. One factor is the amount of the movement and the other is the probability of the movement. This was also the case when I discussed the expected return from playing roulette. How the Binomial approach incorporates probabilities is that it assigns to each branch of the tree the probability of an upward movement or a downward movement. Now consider that we are at $100 and the probability is 50/50 that the market could rise or fall.[8] So, this means a 50 per cent chance that in one unit of time, the price of the underlying market will be at $101 and a 50 per cent chance that the underlying market will be at $99. What about the probabilities for the next 'round'? Again, they will be 50/50. So if we are at either $101 or at $99, we face the same chances of upward or downward movement. However, if we are pricing the option at the beginning of the period, when the market price was at $100, we do not know whether the price will be at $101 or $99 after the first 'round'. To determine the probability that a given price would occur in 'round' two, given that we are starting at $100, we can simply multiply the probabilities along the branches to provide our estimate. These probabilities are also displayed on the tree diagram in Figure 3.8. For example, what is the probability now that in the second 'round' the price of the underlying will be $102 (or $98)? Well, it is a 50 per cent chance that the price will rise to $101 (or fall to $99) in the first 'round' and another 50 per cent chance that if it is at $101 (or $99) the next price will be $102 (or $98). So, we multiply 50 per cent by 50 per cent and that gives us a 25 per cent chance that in the second 'round' the price will be $102 (or $98). Furthermore, by the second 'round' the market price could either rise to $101 and then fall back to $100 or fall to $99 and then rise back to $100, each with a probability of 25 per cent. The combined probability that the market price will be at $100 in the second 'round' is 50 per cent (25 per cent + 25 per cent). This carries on over time and the reader can see that the further the market price branches up or down, the lower the probability of occurrence is; and that the highest probability remains at the current market price of $100. Does this sound familiar? The reader will recall that the lognormal distribution has exactly the same probability spread. The only difference between these distributions is that the Binomial distribution is plotted with discrete movements (like 100, 101 or 99) rather than continuous ones (like 100, 100.000001 or 99.999999).

$$\text{CALL} = S \times \phi\,[a;\ n,\ p'] - E \times e^{-rt}\,\phi\,[a;\ n,\ p]$$

WHERE:

S = PRICE OF THE UNDERLYING EXCHANGE RATE
E = EXERCISE PRICE OF THE OPTION
t = AMOUNT OF TIME UNTIL EXPIRATION
r = SHORT TERM INTEREST RATE UNTIL EXPIRATION
n = NUMBER OF DISCRETE PERIODS UNTIL EXPIRATION
r' = INTEREST RATE FOR A SINGLE PERIOD
u = POSSIBLE UPWARD MOVEMENT IN PRICES
d = POSSIBLE DOWNWARD MOVEMENT IN PRICES
p = (r' - d) / (u - d)
p' = (u/r) x p
a = SMALLEST NON-NEGATIVE INTEGER GREATER THAN
   $\ln(E/Bd^n)$ / $\ln(u/d)$
ϕ = BINOMIAL FUNCTION (WHICH CAN BE THOUGHT OF
   AS A DISTRIBUTION IN DISCRETE TIME)
ln = NATURAL LOGARITHM FUNCTION
e = EXPONENTIAL FUNCTION

Figure 3.9 The Cox, Ross, Rubenstein Options Pricing Model.

Instead of assuming a smooth lognormal distribution — like Black and Scholes — Cox, Ross and Rubinstein assume this jagged Binomial distribution in their model. Their equation, which can be seen in Figure 3.9, is often used for pricing American options on foreign exchange. While it initially looks different from the Black and Scholes formula presented in Chapter 2 (Figure 2.10), really it is based upon similar assumptions. Once again, the model has the underlying price S minus the strike price E which determines the intrinsic value just like the Black and Scholes model. The

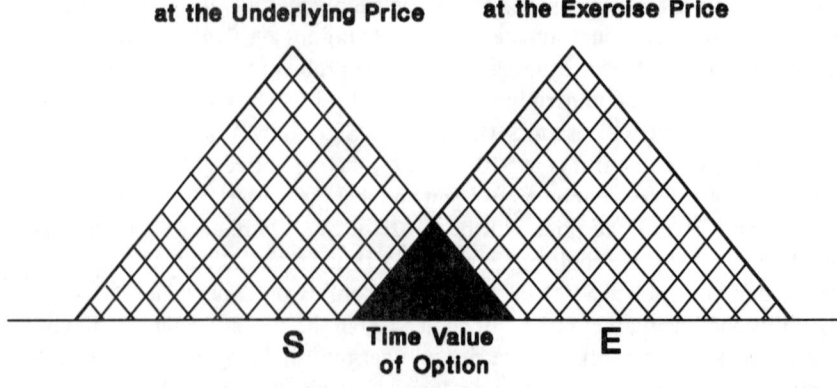

Figure 3.10a Binomial Pricing Options.

difference the Binomial and Black and Scholes models is the φ function in the Binomial formula. This is just like the lognormal distribution in the Black and Scholes model, but is instead the Binomial distribution with discrete time (assuming that the change in market prices is not continuous but can only vary by a minimum amount). Essentially, what one does is to take the Binomial tree diagram in Figure 3.8, turn it sideways and put in on the graph in Figure 3.10a centred at the projected forward underlying price and at the exercise price. Once again, the difference between the two distributions is taken to determine the time value of the options price. If the reader compares the result with the earlier Figure 2.11a for the Black and Scholes model, a remarkable resemblance will be seen. In fact, as the Binomial approach is extended to continuous time, the curve becomes identical to the lognormal distribution, and the Binomial result is equal to the Black and Scholes result.

This line of argument seems to suggest that the Binomial model is really no different from the Black and Scholes model. If this is so, what is the point of the Binomial approach? The answer is that when dividends or other cashflows occur at a single point in time, the Binomial model can take this into account and the Black and Scholes model cannot. For example, in Figure 3.10b we again have a tree diagram where, in this case, the underlying asset pays a dividend in the third period of 50¢ . When this occurs, the price in the branch at that point will drop by this amount. Then the branching process continues as before from these new prices which have been reduced by the dividend payment.

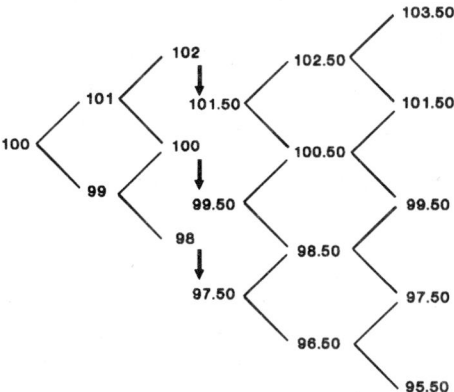

Figure 3.10b Binomial Model (Dividends Paid).

Also, the Binomial model is often used for American-style options where an early exercise feature exists. The Binomial model estimates the value of early exercise by assuming that, at a particular price for the underlying asset, the option will be exercised. Thus, all subsequent branches in the tree diagram have been 'pruned'. Because the option after that point no longer exists, it is no longer necessary to continue the branching process. When the option price is calculated (assuming that possibility of early exercise), once again all the possible prices for the underlying asset are multiplied by their probability of occurrence to give us our option price adjusted for the exercised event.

So, it appears that all options pricing models are based upon the same basic premises. But as was indicated at the beginning of this chapter, the purpose of an option pricing model is not necessarily to provide the correct price for an option but rather to indicate how an option price will change when the variables that determine that option price change. So I will return to the popular pricing models for currency options and examine the formulae for the derivatives of the important variables.

Formulae for the Derivatives of the Currency Option Pricing Models

The next figures list all the derivatives for the models I have spoken of and their formulae for calculation. As the reader can see, Figure 3.11 lists the derivatives for the Garman/Kohlhagen Model and is chock-a-block with exotic formulae. He should take comfort from the fact that, unless he is truly a 'quant' enthusiast (expert in

$$\text{CALL DELTA} = e^{-r_F t} N(d1)$$

$$\text{PUT DELTA} = - e^{-r_F t} N(-d1)$$

$$\text{CALL GAMMA} = \text{PUT GAMMA} = \frac{e^{-r_F t} N'(d1)}{S \sigma \sqrt{t}}$$

$$\text{CALL THETA} = r_F \times S \times e^{-r_F t} N(d1) - r_D \times E \times e^{-r_D t} N(d2)$$
$$- S \times e^{-r_F t} \sigma N'(d1) / (2 \sqrt{t})$$

$$\text{PUT THETA} = -r_F \times S \times e^{-r_F t} N(-d1) + r_D \times E \times e^{-r_D t} N(-d2)$$
$$- S \times e^{-r_F t} \sigma N'(d1) / (2 \sqrt{t})$$

$$\text{CALL VEGA} = \text{PUT VEGA} = e^{-r_F t} S \sqrt{t} N'(d1)$$

$$\text{CALL DOMESTIC RHO} = t \times e^{-r_D t} \times E \times N(d2)$$

$$\text{PUT DOMESTIC RHO} = - t \times e^{-r_D t} \times E \times N (-d2)$$

$$\text{CALL FOREIGN RHO} = - t \times e^{-r_F t} \times E \times N(d1)$$

$$\text{PUT FOREIGN RHO} = t \times e^{-r_F t} \times E \times N(-d1)$$

Figure 3.11 The Garman/Kohlhagen Model (Derivatives).

quantitative methods), the formulae may look like so much graffiti. Not to worry! Almost all popular computer programmes have these equations automatically coded in their routines. Therefore, the reader can leave the high-level mathematics to the 'rocket scientists' who solve these kinds of equations as a matter of course. The reader should instead try to understand the intuition I have presented in this text. Remember, you are not supposed to create the 'gauges', only to be able to read them. In addition, I have also included the Black and Scholes model and its derivatives for comparison's sake in Figure 3.12. Finally, in Figure 3.13, the derivatives of the Black (1976) model are also presented. These derivatives are the most important outputs for the option pricing models as they provide the critical 'gauges' necessary for hedging the risk of these securities.

CALL DELTA = N(d1)

PUT DELTA = - N(-d1)

CALL GAMMA = PUT GAMMA = $\dfrac{N'(d1)}{S\,\sigma\sqrt{t}}$

CALL THETA = $\dfrac{S\,\sigma\,N'(d1)}{2\sqrt{t}}$ + r x E x e^{-rt} N(d2)

PUT THETA = $\dfrac{S\,\sigma\,N'(d1)}{2\sqrt{t}}$ - r x E x e^{-rt} N(-d2)

CALL VEGA = PUT VEGA = S $\sqrt{t}$ N'(d1)

CALL RHO = t x E x e^{-rt} x N(d2)

PUT RHO = - t x E x e^{-rt} x N(-d2)

Figure 3.12 The Black/Scholes Pricing Model (Derivatives).

CALL DELTA = e^{-rt} N(d1)

PUT DELTA = - e^{-rt} N(-d1)

CALL GAMMA = PUT GAMMA = $\dfrac{e^{-rt}\,N'(d1)}{S\,\sigma\sqrt{t}}$

CALL THETA = - r x S x e^{-rt} N(d1) + r x E x e^{-rt} N(d2)
+ S x e^{-rt} σ N'(d1) / (2 $\sqrt{t}$)

PUT THETA = r x S x e^{-rt} N(-d1) - r x E x e^{-rt} N(-d2)
+ S x e^{-rt} σ N'(d1) / (2 $\sqrt{t}$)

CALL VEGA = PUT VEGA = e^{-rt} S $\sqrt{t}$ N'(d1)

CALL RHO = - t x CALL

PUT RHO = - t x PUT

Figure 3.13 The Black (1976)Pricing Model (Derivatives).

PUT-CALL PARITY: THE FUNDAMENTAL ARBITRAGE RELATIONSHIP

The final major theoretical topic which I will introduce in this chapter is put-call parity. When theoretical option pricing was in its nascent stage, many people began to discern that a relationship between the prices of call and put options seemed to exist. The only conundrum was that the payoff diagrams for these securities and their premiums seemed to be inversely related. As was discussed in the first chapter, all options can be created by simply splitting the underlying market positions into 'good' and 'bad' parts. Therefore, if we can break the underlying market into two parts, we can just as easily recombine them to recreate the underlying asset or try other combinations to see what we get. This can be done using a simple formula known as the put-call parity.

The formula for put-call parity is:

$$C - P = F - E$$

C is the value of a call, P the value of the put, F the value of the underlying forward foreign exchange market, and E the strike price for both the call and the put.[9] The put-call parity is the fundamental arbitrage relationship which forces call and put prices to be tied to their underlying market and to each other.

For example, let us examine the value of a call and the value of a put on the options contract's expiration day. Suppose the strike price for a $/£ put and call is $1.70. At expiration, relative to $1.70, the underlying price can be in one of three possible states of the world: the price could finish higher, lower, or exactly equal to $1.70. In the first case, when the market finishes higher than $1.70, consider the call option which is the right to buy at $1.70. With the market at $1.725, the value of the option would be equal to its intrinsic value of 2.5¢ . The $1.70 put option (the right to sell) would expire worthless. Hence, 2.5¢ (the value of a call) minus zero (the value of a put) must be equal to F minus E (1.725 – 1.70); which it is.

The second case is when the Pound Sterling exchange rate finishes below $1.70 at $1.685. If someone has the right to buy at $1.70 and the market is at $1.685, he will abandon the call because it is out-of-the-money. Thus, the value of the call is zero. Since the put option confers the right to sell at $1.70, with the market at $1.685, the put option will be worth its intrinsic value of 1.5¢ . So, on the left side of the equation, we find zero (C) minus 1.5¢ (P) must be equal to $1.685 minus $1.70 on the right side. Once again the arbitrage formula holds.

Finally, if the market finishes at $1.70, equal to the strike price, both the call and the put are at-the-money with no intrinsic value and worthless. The left side of the equation which reads zero minus zero must equal $1.70 minus $1.70. Hence, regardless of what happens to the market price at expiration, the put-call parity arbitrage formula will hold.

The reader can rest assured that put-call parity works not only at expiration but at all points prior to the expiration as well. For example, if the reader turns back to Chapter 2 and reviews Table 2.3, he will see put-call parity works for stock options in exactly the same way as it does for currency options. In that example, the price of IBM stock is $105 and the price for the $100 call is $5¾ and the $100 put is $¾. The put-call parity formula holds if $5¾ minus $¾ is equal to $105 minus $100. In this case, because $5 on the left side of the equation is equal to the $5 on the right side, the formula is not violated. This example not only demonstrates the arbitrage relationship between call and put prices, but also indicates the fact that the time value is identical ($¾) for calls and puts with the same strike price and time to maturity.[10]

Using put-call parity to Create Synthetic Securities

Apart from defining the most fundamental arbitrage relationship in the options markets, put-call parity also allows the trader a simple method to break strategies into their component parts and to recombine them. In essence, it helps the trader combine the basic building blocks of futures and options to create new 'synthetic' securities. To use put-call parity for this purpose, we first need to learn a few 'tricks'. The first trick in using put-call parity to develop synthetics is to put parentheses around the $F - E$ and treat this new variable as a buying position in the underlying market initiated at E.

Now the equation reads:

$$C - P = (F - E)$$

and we have three components: a call option, a put option, and the underlying market. The second trick is that if any of these three components has a positive or plus sign associated with it, it will be defined as a buying, holding or long position (this is also true for the case where there is nothing in front of it). If any of the variables has a minus sign in front of it, then it will be defined as a short, selling or writing position. Now, you can read the above equation aloud: if you buy a call (C) and sell a put ($- P$), that is equal to buying the underlying market at the price of E. Simple enough? I hope that the reader realises that we have just created our first synthetic security. When you buy a call and sell a put at the same strike price, that is the same payoff as buying a futures contract. Put-call parity allows us to determine many other synthetic positions as well.

In the first chapter, I defined three positions which are equivalent long positions relative to the underlying market: buying that market (or a forward contract on that market), buying a call option, and selling a put option. I also defined three positions which are equivalent short positions: selling that market short (or a short forward contract), buying a put option, and selling a call option. Since I have demonstrated how easy it is to create a synthetic long forward or futures position, I will give the reader in Table 3.4 the whole packet of actual and synthetic positions.

For example, what would you have if you had purchased £1,000,000 with dollars and expected to convert the Sterling back into dollars in the future? To protect against an adverse move in the exchange rate one would purchase a put option on Sterling. That series of trades would fit into our put-call parity equation as $+ (F - E)$ and $+ P$. To determine what the position would look like, all we need to do is to review our equation: $C - P = (F - E)$ and see if we can get $(F - E) + P$ on one side of the equation. If we can, we will then have on the other side of the equal sign what this combination is equivalent to. Those who excelled at algebra will see immediately that to get a $+ P$ over to the other side of the equation, along with the $(F - E)$, we simply have to add a $+ P$ to both sides. On the left side you will get $C - P + P$ and on the right side you get $(F - E) + P$. On the left side, the $- P$ and the $+ P$ cancel, leaving only C. So, the equation reduces to $C = (F - E) + P$. This means that buying a call is an equivalent

	ACTUAL POSITION	SYNTHETIC POSITION
BUYING THE UNDERLYING	+ (F - E)	C - P
BUYING A CALL OPTION	+ C	(F - E) + P
SELLING A PUT OPTION	- P	(F - E) - C
SELLING THE UNDERLYING	- (F - E)	- C + P
BUYING A PUT OPTION	+ P	- (F - E) + C
SELLING A CALL OPTION	- C	- (F - E) - P

Table 3.4 Actual versus Synthetic Positions

position to buying a futures contract and buying a put option. The left side of the equation is an 'actual' call and the right side is the synthetic call.

The 'Magic' Graphing Rules and Put-Call Parity

For those of us who like algebra, this process can make a lot of sense. But the rest of us are probably visually oriented, which means a picture is worth a thousand words. So not surprisingly, we can also tackle put-call parity with pictures. To do this I must first lay out what we call the 'magic' graphing rules.

And here they are: first, unlimited opportunities dominate limited opportunities; second, unlimited opportunities offset unlimited opportunities; and finally, limited opportunities offset limited opportunities. So, let us use these rules to prove the example I have just discussed: the composition of the synthetic call option.

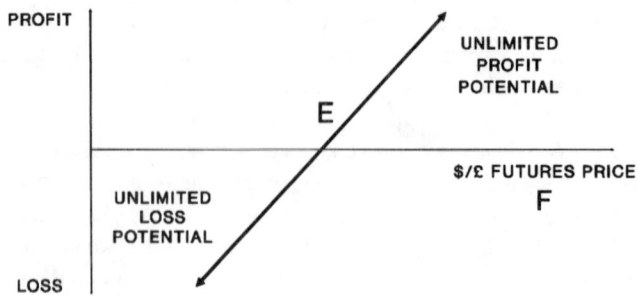

CONSTRUCTION OF A SYNTHETIC CALL:
SUPPOSE WE BUY THE UNDERLYING FUTURES
WHICH HAS THE FOLLOWING PROFIT/LOSS PROFILE?

Figure 3.14 Put-Call Parity: Applying Graphing Rules.

Figure 3.14 is a graphic example of a long underlying position $(F - E)$. If you buy a \$/£ forward contract at E and the market price F rises, the profit of that position will be equal to $F - E$. This implies the current price minus the price where you purchased it. Imagine you buy it at a price of \$1.70 (E) and the market price (F) falls below \$1.70 (E). The loss for the position E is equal once again to whatever the current price is minus \$1.70 $(F - E)$. There is an unlimited profit potential to the northeast and an unlimited loss potential to the southwest. Figure 3.15 displays a long put option which has an unlimited profit potential on the downside (to the northwest). The most you can lose when you buy the put option is the premium paid, which is a limited loss potential. This can be seen in the lower right quadrant. Now, let us consider the left of E in Figure 3.15. One line goes to the northwest (the profit potential for the put) and one

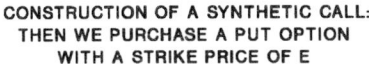

**CONSTRUCTION OF A SYNTHETIC CALL:
THEN WE PURCHASE A PUT OPTION
WITH A STRIKE PRICE OF E**

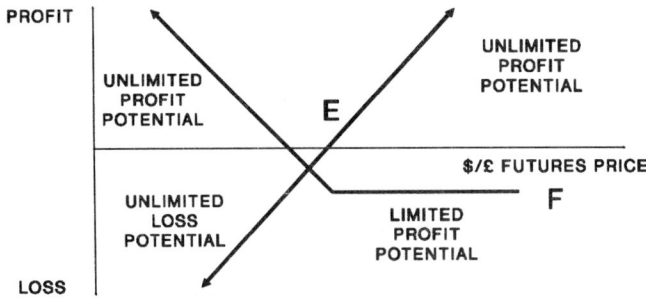

Figure 3.15 Put-Call Parity: Applying Graphing Rules.

line goes to the southwest (the loss potential for the futures). It is important to consider that these are equivalent and opposite unlimited exposures. The rule says unlimited and unlimited offset; so these two potentials cancel each other out.[11] Now, let us look at the right side of the graph. The underlying long position extends indefinitely to the northeast with a profit opportunity that is unlimited. What about the put option? It has a limited loss component to the right of E. Since the unlimited gain dominates the limited loss, the net effect is that the net position has an unlimited gain potential. To the left, the underlying market losses cancel the put's gains and to the right, the unlimited gains overwhelm the limited loss on the put. What does the net position end up looking like? This can be seen in Figure 3.16. It has a limited loss to the left (which looks like an option premium) and an unlimited gain as the market prices rises. Upon reflection, the reader will see that a synthetic call has been produced. This is hardly surprising. You will remember that when we combined buying the underlying asset with buying a put it produced a synthetic buying call: $C = (F - E) + P$. Hence, the put-call parity is a very easy way to separate each of the components in the forward (or futures) market and later recombine them.

CONSTRUCTION OF A SYNTHETIC CALL:
THE RESULTING SYNTHETIC CALL

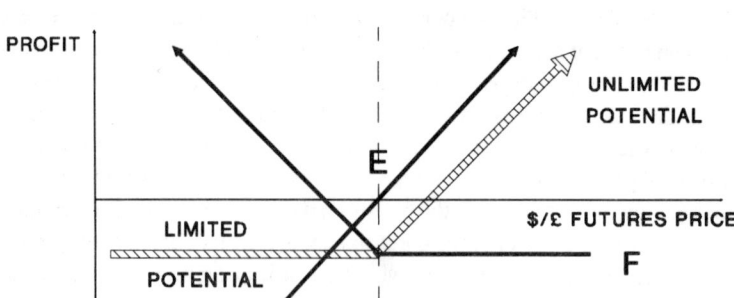

Figure 3.16 Put-Call Parity: Applying Graphing Rules.

It is probably not surprising that this simple technique is critical to ensure that fair and efficient pricing of each of the individual components occurs. For example, consider the value of a call option. As you will remember, it is made up of two components: time value and intrinsic value. Intrinsic value is simply $F - E$. So, a quick review of call and put prices in put-call parity would imply that the only difference between calls and put prices must be due to the intrinsic value. The time value for these must be exactly the same. If this turns out not to be the case, then an extremely low risk transaction can take place which will reap this profit through arbitrage. If the actual call option is 'over-valued' then it is a simple matter to sell this option and buy a fair valued synthetic call. Then the put-call formula would read:

$$0 = (F - E) + P - C$$

If this is valued at greater than zero: 'bingo'! An arbitrage profit exists. Of course, later in this book I will carefully examine these and other kinds of arbitrage strategies and will at that time use put-call parity extensively.

The Effects of Interest Rates on Option Prices

Now that I have introduced you to put-call parity, I can use this formula to gain further insight into the interest rate impacts on options. The interest rate impact for an option depends on the characteristics of the underlying asset. I will break these available underlying assets into three broad categories: costly assets, costless assets and neutral assets.

Costly assets require an immediate substantial cash outflow. For example, if you buy a 100 oz bar of gold when gold is trading at $400 per ounce, you will have to pay $40,000 to be 'long' Gold. A call option on gold might only cost $1200 and would still allow you the right to hold that asset if you bought the option instead of the gold. The remaining $38,800 could be placed on deposit to earn interest. Thus, the call option increases the leverage and frees up cash to place on deposit. As short-term interest rates rise, this leverage factor becomes more and more attractive. Therefore, buying gold call options and placing the balance in deposits will become increasingly attractive compared with buying the actual gold. To remain at equilibrium (also known as a 'no arbitrage' state), the call option's price must increase when the short-term interest rate rises to make the investor indifferent to either investing in the option/deposit trade or the outright gold purchase. Therefore, the higher the deposit rate, the higher the value for a call option. Conversely, the higher the short-term interest rate the lower the value of the put option. The actual formula for this put-call parity relationship can be seen in Figure 3.17.

$$C - P \bullet S - (E \bullet e^{-rt})$$

WHERE:

C - VALUE OF A CALL OPTION

P - VALUE OF A PUT OPTION

S - CASH SECURITY PRICE

E - EXERCISE PRICE FOR CALL & PUT

e - EXPONENTIAL FUNCTION

r - INTEREST RATE FOR OPTION'S LIFE

t - TIME (IN % OF A YEAR) UNTIL EXPIRY

Figure 3.17 Interest Rate Impacts for 'Costly' Assets.

The formula, $C - P = S - (E \times e^{-rt})$ requires a little more explanation. First, let us define the terms. I bet you can guess what C and P are. The S is the value of a spot security which is a costly asset, like gold or non-dividend paying shares. As before, E is the strike price for both the call and put; but now we have another factor, e^{-rt}. This is the interest rate factor. First, what is e? This is a continuous compounding factor. The letter 'e' is the mathematical exponential function also known as an anti-logarithm. This determines the present value of a pure continuously discounted instrument like a zero coupon bond or treasury bill. The letter 'r' is the deposit interest rate at which you could invest the money that buying options would free up (instead of buying the asset). Finally, 't' is the time period in the percentage of a 365-day year until the option expires and the deposit matures.

Say we want to find out what the continuous discount factor could be at 10 per cent for 182 days. It would be $e^{-(0.10)(0.50)}$ or 0.9512. Suppose we return to our put-call parity formula with an S equal to $100 and E equal to $90. Then $C - P = \$100 - (\$90 \times 0.9512) = \$14.39$. If the r rises to 11 per cent what happens? The new discount factor has become 0.9465. So back to the put-call parity formula: $C - P = \$100 -$

($90 × 0.9465) = $14.81. This increase from $14.39 to $14.81 reflects the increase in the value of the call relative to the put.

To prove this effect even more, I determined theoretical option prices with a maturity of 182 days and the strike and underlying prices consistent with the above example. Further, I assumed the underlying asset was a non-dividend paying stock with a volatility of 25 per cent. At an interest rate of 10 per cent, the $90 call option is worth $16.08. When the interest rises to 11 per cent the call is worth $16.41. So, the call gained in value by 0.33. The $90 put conversely was worth $1.69 at a 10 per cent interest rate and at the higher interest rate dropped to $1.60 for a loss of $0.09. The put-call relationship at 10 per cent interest was $16.08 minus $1.69 for a difference of $14.39. At the 11 per cent interest rate the new put-call relationship was $16.41 minus $1.60 and a difference of $14.81. The reader can see that this result is the same as that shown above.

In the currency option market, the formula is slightly different and reflects that both the currencies of the two countries involved in the contract pay an interest rate. This formula is seen in Figure 3.18 and is almost identical to the formula I have just presented. The only difference is that the S is also discounted back to present value by e^{-Rft}, where Rf is the foreign interest rate and Rd is the domestic interest rate. If the reader simply substitutes a dividend yield for Rf in the formula, he will have

$$C - P = (S \cdot e^{-r_f t}) - (E \cdot e^{-r_D t})$$

WHERE:

C - VALUE OF A CALL OPTION

P - VALUE OF A PUT OPTION

S - CASH SECURITY PRICE

E - EXERCISE PRICE FOR CALL & PUT

e - EXPONENTIAL FUNCTION

r_D - DOMESTIC INTEREST RATE

r_F - FOREIGN INTEREST RATE

t - TIME (IN % OF A YEAR) UNTIL EXPIRY

Figure 3.18 Interest Rate Impacts For 'Costly' Assets (for Currency Options).

defined the put-call parity relationship for stocks (or bonds) with continuous dividend (coupon) payments.

The second type of underlying assets I will consider are assets termed 'costless'. Examples of this kind of assets include options on forward foreign exchange and most options available on futures contracts.

If you decide to buy a forward contract in foreign exchange, you decide upon a price at which you will deal in the future. You pay nothing today because the agreement is to be settled at the forward date. If you buy an option instead of the forward contract, you have to pay a premium today. So, when comparing the value of an option to a forward contract, you must take into account that if you bought the option you give up a premium; and if you took the premium and deposited it, you could have earned interest. Thus, you give up interest by buying an option on a forward contract instead of simply dealing on the forward market; and in this case, options actually reduce the leverage. In many world exchanges (particularly in the United States), the premium for options on futures must be paid upon purchase while the underlying futures contract is margined. In these cases, non-margined options on futures have the same interest rate impact as options on forward foreign exchange. The reader can imagine that these kinds of options will have a completely different interest rate impact when compared to options on costly assets. What is interesting about costless asset options is that the interest rate impact for them is almost opposite to the impact of options on costly assets. That is, as interest rates rise, both the value of call options and put options fall. However, the impact tends to be small because the interest involved is on the option premium and not on the value of the underlying asset. In fact, for those futures options most likely to be traded (that is, options with maturities of three months or less), the effect on the option price from interest rate moves is generally minuscule. The put- call parity formula for these kinds of options can be seen in Figure 3.19. In that formula, the variables are identical to those in Figure 3.17. The only differences are that *F* is the futures or costless asset price and both the costless asset price and the strike price are discounted using the continuous discount factor.

$$C - P = (F - E) \cdot e^{-rt}$$

WHERE:

    C - VALUE OF A CALL OPTION

    P - VALUE OF A PUT OPTION

    S - CASH SECURITY PRICE

    E - EXERCISE PRICE FOR CALL & PUT

    e - EXPONENTIAL FUNCTION

    r - INTEREST RATE FOR OPTION'S LIFE

    t - TIME (IN % OF A YEAR) UNTIL EXPIRY

Figure 3.19 Interest Rate Impacts for 'Costless' Assets.

The Interest Rate Impact on Neutral Assets

The final interest rate impact is for options on assets which we will call 'neutral'. Neutral assets are in some ways similar to costless assets, except that both the underlying asset and the options are 'costless'. For example, options at London International Financial Futures Exchange (LIFFE) do not require payment when they are purchased, but are margined (like the underlying futures) and 'paid for' at the expiration date. Consider the interest rate implications of such an arrangement. Suppose you do not have to pay for an option up front, but are permitted to margin it just like a futures contract. Since you can margin both futures and options, they can be considered 'costless', especially if you are able to use interest-bearing securities as the basis for your margin. There is no opportunity cost lost from either the purchase of the underlying futures or the option on the futures. Therefore, there is no impact on the options prices from changes in the short-term interest rate because the investor comparing the two securities does not have to consider foregone interest. The value of the call minus the put will simply equal the difference between the strike price and the underlying futures contract (see Figure 3.20 for this final put-call parity formula). This is the purest form of the put-call parity formulae.

$$C - P = F - E$$

WHERE:

C - VALUE OF A CALL OPTION

P - VALUE OF A PUT OPTION

F - FUTURES PRICE

E - EXERCISE PRICE FOR CALL & PUT

Figure 3.20 Interest Rate Impacts for 'Neutral Assets'.

This concludes the theoretical portion of this book. From this point forward, *Options Explained* will shift the emphasis from the theoretical to the practical.

[1] This is actually a rule of thumb. In Figures 3.2 and 3.3, the reader will see that the delta is the $N(d_1)$ factor. The actual probability that the option will be exercised is $N(d_2)$ but in almost all cases this is very close to $N(d_1)$.

[2] The reader is referred to the health insurance example in Chapter 2 where the policy holder is 'trading' risk.

[3] Mark B. Garman and Steven W. Kohlhagen, 'Foreign Currency Option Values', *Journal of International Money and Finance*, 2, pp.231-37 (1983).

[4] Actually, since the Merton dividend adjustment came first in 1973, it is the original 'carburettor' and the Garman/Kohlhagen model is really the Merton 'carburettor' painted a different colour.

[5] Fischer Black, 'The Pricing of Commodity Contracts', *Journal of Financial Economics*, 3, pp.167-79 (January 1976).

[6] Mark B. Garman, 'Forward Prices, Option Prices and "Dividend Corrections"', *Working Paper, Department of Business Administration, University of California*, Berkeley (April 1983).

[7] John S. Cox, Steven Ross and Mark Rubinstein, 'Options Pricing: A Simplified Approach', *Journal of Financial Economics*, 7: pp.637-54 (September 1979).

[8] This assumes a random walk process, but is not critical to the Binomial methodology. For example, Cox, Ross and Rubinstein used a 60 per cent probability for upward movements and a 40 per cent probability for downward movements. However, we will assume a 50/50 probability and the reader is referred to the Cox, Ross & Rubinstein article to verify the result for a submartingale rather than a martingale process.

[9] In the original Black and Scholes formula, the strike price (E) in the put-call parity formula should be discounted at the risk-free interest rate for the appropriate time to maturity.

[10] Later in this chapter we will discuss the impacts of interest rates and dividends for the put-call parity equation for stock options. With dividends and interest rates, the stock price must be reduced by the dividend paid and the exercise price discounted by the interest rate. In this example, the interest rate impact was exactly offset by the payment of dividends so the put-call parity relationship was easily determined to be equal to the difference between the strike price and current stock price.

[11] The intuition is: if $F = 1.65$, the loss on the forward contract $= -5¢$, the profit on the put $= (+5¢ -$ premium$)$, therefore, the profit/loss of the net position $= -$ premium. This will occur whenever the \$/£ forward price is less than \$1.7000.

4: Directional Trading Strategies

In most markets, there are only two ways to profit: one can either buy or sell some underlying asset. To profit, you have to predict correctly which direction the market will take and when. With options, you can also profit from correctly predicting market direction, but in addition, you can gain from changes in the perceptions of risk, and from the passage of time. Furthermore, options allow you to arbitrage price discrepancies easily and completely. In this chapter, I will emphasise directional trading strategies that can be used with options on Crude Oil futures, covering volatility strategies and arbitrage for other underlying assets in later chapters.

As the reader learned in an earlier chapter, the value of an option is composed of the intrinsic value and the time value. Changes in intrinsic value are associated with movement in the underlying market, and time value is associated with changes in volatility and the passage of time. Therefore, when options are traded, a view must be taken on the movement of both the underlying and volatility. Very few people need to take a view on time because it is always passing. When I mention taking a view, I mean choosing a specific trading strategy which earns the maximum profit from particular market and volatility movements.

Now, consider the option on Crude Oil futures traded at the New York Mercantile Exchange (Nymex) which I will use for our examples in this chapter. The prices are in dollars per barrel. Table 4.1 outlines the contract specification for this underlying. The asset underlying the option is a Nymex Crude Oil futures contract, which is the obligation either to buy or sell 42,000 gallons of Crude Oil (1000 barrels) in the month following the expiration of the option.

TRADING UNIT	1 NYMEX CRUDE OIL FUT. CONTRACT
TRADING MONTHS	SIX CONSECUTIVE MONTHS
LAST TRADING DAY	FIRST FRIDAY OF THE MONTH PRIOR TO THE DELIVERY MONTH
MINIMUM PRICE MOVEMENT	$0.01 PER BARREL ($10 PER OPTION CONTRACT)
EXERCISE PRICE INTERVALS	$1 PER BARREL (7 DIFFERENT EXERCISE PRICES)
TRADING HOURS	9:45 - 15:10 (NEW YORK TIME)
EXERCISE	BY 16:30, ON ANY DAY UP TO AND INCLUDING THE OPTION'S EXPIRATION

Table 4.1 Options on Oil Crude Futures (NYMEX).

POSSIBLE VIEWPOINTS FOR THE UNDERLYING AND VOLATILITY

The three views that are possible with options are to buy, sell, or sit still. These three actions can be applied to both the underlying Crude Oil futures market and to volatility. For example, the trader may believe the Crude Oil market could increase, decrease, or remain the same. He could also form a similar view on volatility. With these two views, we can determine which trading strategy will be optimal under given conditions. Table 4.2 displays a trading strategy matrix that will be filled over the course of the next three chapters with all the option strategies I will present. In each cell, I will define the optimal strategy given one's view on the underlying market and volatility.

VIEWPOINT ON THE CRUDE OIL MARKET

	BUYER	SELLER	NEUTRAL
BUYER			
SELLER			
NEUTRAL			

VIEWPOINT ON VOLATILITY

Table 4.2 Option Trading Strategy Matrix.

What I will do in this chapter is to help the user combine his views on the underlying market and volatility to determine the most appropriate options strategy to employ. In later chapters, I will also show the reader how to take 'views' on time decay, intra market spreads (commonly defined as a spread between different futures contract months), and to consider the liquidity of the underlying and options markets when placing these trades. As a rule of thumb, if you have three out of these five elements in your favour and at least two of the three work in your favour, then the options strategy has a high probability of success. For example, if my view on volatility is bearish then I will sell options. When selling options, time decay works for me. Hence, even if the underlying price moves against my position, I might still profit more from time decay and a decrease in volatility. Thus, the unfavourable movement in the underlying market can be offset because two of the five factors produced a greater profit.

THREE WAYS TO BENEFIT FROM AN INCREASE IN THE UNDERLYING MARKET

Concerning market direction, there are three ways to assume an equivalent buying position in Crude Oil: one can buy a Crude Oil futures contract, buy a call option on Crude Oil futures, or sell a put option on Crude Oil futures. On the selling side, there are also three ways to assume a short position: one can sell a Crude Oil futures contract, buy a put option on Crude Oil futures, or sell a call option on Crude Oil futures. The choice of which trade to use depends on one's view on volatility.

When you buy an option, you buy the two components of its value: intrinsic value and time value. Intrinsic value is comprised of the in-the-money amount which is the maximum of the difference between the strike price and the current price of the underlying Crude Oil futures or zero. Volatility is the critical element in time value, comprising almost '97 per cent' of that value. If volatility increases, the time value increases as well, all other things remaining equal.

Buying an option implies buying volatility; consequently, when you sell an option, you sell volatility. If I buy or hold a call option, my position has a buying volatility bias. When volatility increases, I should make money. On the other hand, if I sell a put option I am selling volatility, and when volatility increases I lose money. However, when volatility decreases I should make money.

Finally, consider a long position in Crude Oil futures. Volatility does not impact the prices of these contracts. The price of Crude Oil futures is determined by supply and demand and is bound by the futures pricing relationship I discussed in Chapter 2 with the estimated forward price for IBM stock. The spreads for the futures price may widen when volatility increases, but the centre price (that is midway between the bid and ask prices) is based on cash prices and holding costs. Hence, the Crude Oil futures is not determined by volatility and therefore its exposure to volatility is neutral. If volatility increases or decreases, you will not make money from that fact. You only make money if the Crude Oil market moves up or down; in other words by directional moves in the underlying Crude Oil market.

Buying a Crude Oil Futures Contract

Buying a Crude Oil futures is the most aggressive position for benefiting from an increase in prices. If the Crude Oil market price increases, you profit instantly and significantly. But it must be emphasised that one also assumes an unlimited risk potential if the Crude Oil market price falls. The profit/loss potential of this strategy can be seen in Figure 4.1. This position can be thought of as 'long' the Crude Oil market and neutral to volatility. Therefore, if our view is to buy the underlying Crude Oil market and we have no view of volatility or expect it to be unchanged, one strategy we can employ is to buy the Crude Oil futures. In the trading strategy matrix, at the end of this chapter (Table 4.3), we would therefore place the long Crude Oil futures

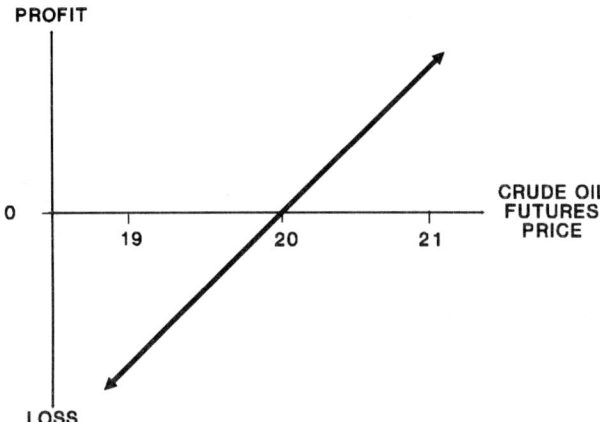

Figure 4.1 Profit/Loss Profile: Long Crude Oil Futures

strategy in the cell at the lower left, indicating a buying bias relative to the underlying Crude Oil market but neutral to volatility.

The problem with buying an underlying asset such as a Crude Oil futures contract is the unlimited loss potential. If, prior to the trading of options, you did not want an unlimited loss potential and had no view on volatility, there would not have been much you could have done. You would probably have abstained from involvement altogether. However, options on Crude Oil futures make loss-limited trading strategies possible. I will now examine the two other ways of going 'long' the Crude Oil market using these products. These positions include buying calls and selling puts. Let us first consider buying call options on Crude Oil futures.

Buying a Call Option on Crude Oil Futures

Suppose one buys a call option with a strike price of $20 per barrel. When the price of Crude Oil futures increases above that level, one has an unlimited profit potential. If the Crude Oil futures price decreases below $20, one abandons the call, and the most one loses is the premium paid for the option. Therefore, as indicated previously, holding calls allows one a limited loss potential. The profit/loss profile for buying a call option can be seen in Figure 4.2.

Suppose that instead of buying a call option, I tried to replicate the payoff diagram of a call option by buying Crude Oil futures when the futures price rose above $20 and selling the Crude Oil futures when the futures price fell below $20. In the mind's eye, this payoff should look like the intrinsic value of a call option. Unfortunately, as will be discussed in the section on portfolio insurance in Chapter 8, there is no guarantee that I will achieve the same result as a call.

The way this technique would work would involve buying a Crude Oil futures contract at $20 and, if the futures price rose, holding the position. If the futures price fell, then one would have to 'stop' the loss potential by selling the Crude Oil futures,

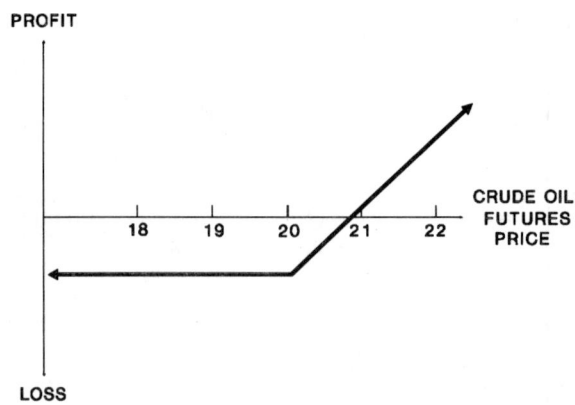

Figure 4.2 Profit/Loss Profile: Holding a Call Option.

hopefully at $20. To do this, one would place a 'stop loss' order after buying the Crude Oil futures. If the position was 'stopped out', the trader would then place another order — a limit buying order — again at $20. If the futures price then rose to this level, the trader would buy back in.

A stop loss order is an order which is triggered when a specific price is reached. When that particular price is reached, the broker has instructions to fill the trade at the best possible price. For example, if I bought the Crude Oil futures at $20 and then placed a stop loss order to sell at $19, when Crude Oil futures traded at $19, my broker would automatically sell my long futures position out at the best possible price. Unfortunately, the broker is not bound to sell at that price and the actual price of the transaction might be less than $19. A limit buying order instructs the broker to buy a Crude Oil futures contract if my target price is reached. Again, there is no assurance that my position will be filled at the price. If the market only trades at my target price, I am not assured a 'fill'. To assure I am filled, the market must trade higher than that target price.

The purpose of a stop loss order is to provide a limited loss feature to a trade previously filled in the Crude Oil futures. Therefore, a stop loss order attempts to provide the same limited loss potential of a call (or put) option. The problem with a stop loss order is that once it has been filled, the trader no longer has a position in the Crude Oil futures. If one was 'stopped out', and then if the Crude Oil futures price proceeded to rise, the trader would not be able to profit from this fact unless he bought another Crude Oil futures contract. A call option on Crude Oil futures, on the other hand, would allow the trader a limited loss and an unlimited profit potential, which trading the Crude Oil futures with stop loss orders and limit buying orders could not provide.

To create a synthetic call option by dynamically trading Crude Oil futures, one would have to sell every time the futures price fell to one's target price, and have to buy every time the futures rose above one's target price. Each time this occurred, the 'stop loss'/'limit buy' strategy would involve transaction costs and being on the wrong side of the bid/offer spread. This means that when a trader buys or sells from a market maker, the trader must buy at the market maker's offer price, and the trader can only sell at the market maker's bid price. This spread between bid and offer is typically 1¢ on the Crude Oil futures ($19.49 bid and $19.50 offer). An additional cost (which is variable) is associated with the fact that with a stop loss (sell) order (or a limit buy order) there is no guarantee that you will be able to sell (or buy) at the price you want. For example, if one had the stop loss sell order outlined above, the order would become 'active' when the Crude Oil futures market traded at $19. This 'active' order would mean the transaction was then completed at the best current price, even if the best current price were well below $19.

Most traders have been burnt by these kinds of orders. Inevitably, once a stop loss order (or limit buy order) is placed, the market will fluctuate sufficiently to trigger the order, resulting in a loss (or a new position). Then, as the fluctuation continues, the market will eventually rise (or fall) back to the previous level. Because of this, many traders refer to stop loss orders and limit orders as 'price magnets', which seem to the unlucky trader to draw the underlying price to the level of his order only to assure that it is filled. Thereafter, as if laughing at them, the market goes back to previous levels.

If you buy a call option, you establish a position at a known strike price which gives you 'automatic' sell stop and limit buying features. When you pay for a call option, you pay a premium. This premium can be thought of as (the present value of) the expected costs one would incur by replicating the payoffs of a call option using stop loss sell orders (and limit buying orders) in the underlying market. When volatility increases, time value increases because of the increased costs that would occur in a dynamic replication strategy using the underlying Crude Oil futures market. Thus, if the expected future volatility increases, it is favourable for those who have bought options because the prices of these securities rise.

When you hold a call on Crude Oil futures, since you are buying the right to buy a Crude Oil futures contract, you have an equivalent long position in Crude Oil futures in addition to buying volatility. In summary, the Crude Oil call option holder is both a buyer of the Crude Oil market and a buyer of volatility. If one expects both the Crude Oil market to increase and volatility to increase, the best strategy is to purchase a call option. Therefore in our strategy matrix at the end of this chapter (Table 4.3), the long call option fits into the cell in the upper left corner which indicates both a buying position in the underlying Crude Oil market and a buying position in volatility.

Selling a Put Option on Crude Oil Futures

The third way to achieve a long position in the Crude Oil market is to sell a put option on Crude Oil futures. Consider selling a $21 put, which is the obligation to buy the underlying Crude Oil futures at $21, the strike price. When I sell the put option, I receive a premium of say 90¢ , which is all that I will gain on the transaction. This position profits if the Crude Oil futures price is stable or rises above the strike price. If the futures price finishes at $21 or above, the holder will let the option expire and I will retain all the premium. If the market finishes below $21, the put holder will

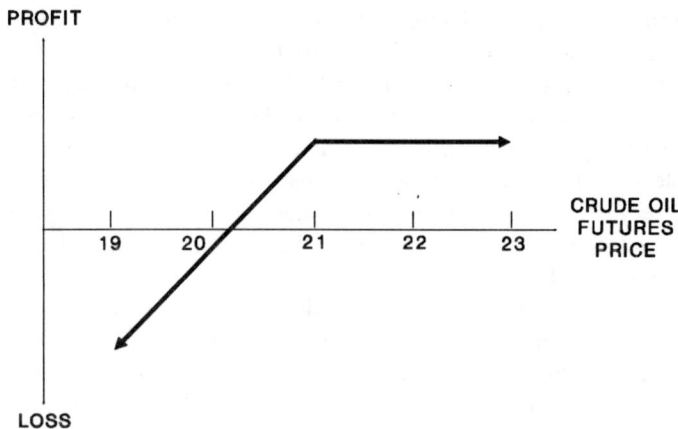

PROFIT

CRUDE OIL
FUTURES
PRICE

19   20   21   22   23

LOSS

Figure 4.3 Profit/Loss Profile: Writing a Put Option.

exercise the option. The profit or loss to the put seller depends on how far below the strike price the Crude Oil futures market finishes and how much premium he has received. If the market loss exceeds the premium inflow, the net impact will be a loss to the put writer. The profit/loss profile for selling a put on Crude Oil futures can be seen in Figure 4.3. Essentially, the put seller is betting on low volatility, stability, and slight bullish movement in the Crude Oil market.

When you sell a put option on Crude Oil futures, you assume the obligation to buy a Crude Oil futures contract. You have a long position not only because you profit as the futures price increase and lose when prices fall, but also because of this obligation to become a buyer of the Crude Oil futures. As you sold the two components of an option's value, intrinsic value and time value, you will benefit if the Crude Oil market increases and/or when volatility decreases. Thus, in our strategy matrix in Table 4.3, the short put option position will be placed in the middle left cell which is bullish on the Crude Oil market but bearish on volatility.

If you sell put options, you must realise that the most that can be gained is the time value. The intrinsic value must be returned at expiration if the option remains in-the-money. Therefore, if conditions are unchanged, the put writer has the intrinsic value on 'loan' that must eventually be paid back. Compared with buying the Crude Oil futures or buying a call on Crude Oil futures, selling the put option provides an inflow of premium. If the Crude Oil market stays at that particular level, you will earn a superior profit compared with buying the Crude Oil futures or buying the call. This is because 90¢ of time value will be credited to your account if the Crude Oil futures price finishes equal to or above your strike price. This can be a greater profit than buying the Crude Oil futures which will provide no profit if the eventual settlement price is equal to the present levels. The call option will actually experience a loss if the Crude Oil market is stable because the premium paid will be lost. Therefore, for stable to slightly rising Crude Oil markets, selling a put option is the ideal strategy.

Comparison of the Bullish Strategies

Figure 4.4 compares all these bullish positions. From the directional standpoint, the most aggressive position is to buy the Crude Oil futures. A less aggressive position is to buy a call option with the limited loss potential. The best strategy if one expects the Crude Oil market to move up minimally is to sell a put option. Which trade you choose will depend on how far you think the Crude Oil market will go, when it is going to move, and your viewpoint on volatility.

If you believe volatility will increase, the general rule is to buy options. Unfortunately, when you buy options you are subject to time decay. Unless volatility increases immediately, time decay can quickly waste the option's value. Therefore you should try to buy options with as long a maturity as possible.[1] While you will pay more for these long-dated options, you can sell them if volatility rises and should make a profit not offset by time decay. In this case, you are buying high to sell higher.

If you believe that volatility will fall, then you should sell options. But now you benefit from time decay, especially in the last 45 days of the options' life. Therefore, when selling short maturity options and volatility drops, the writer will benefit from both the volatility drop and the passage of time.

The consideration of loss potential, and whether it is limited or unlimited, is another consideration important to option traders. Selling options can be lucrative but requires the ability to apply 'damage control' quickly if the market starts to move against one's position. Thus, option writers must watch exposed short options positions very carefully indeed. Buyers of options must also watch their positions assiduously, even though they are assured of only a limited loss if things go wrong. Buying options is therefore a better strategy for those with a limited taste for risk.

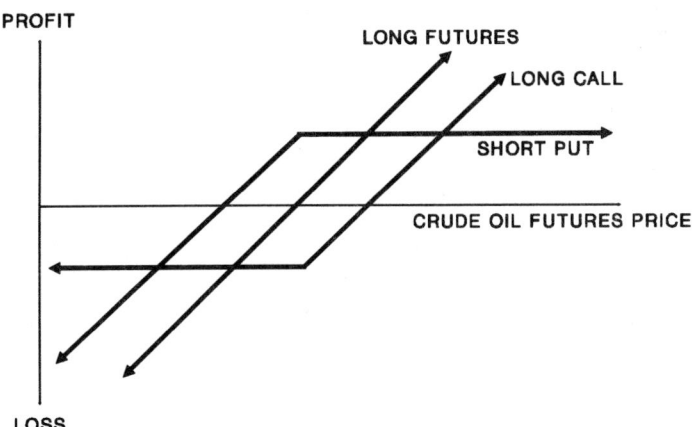

Figure 4.4 Option Strategies: Bullish Positions

THREE WAYS TO BENEFIT FROM A DECREASE IN THE UNDERLYING MARKET

On the selling side, there are three ways of going short in the Crude Oil market: selling the Crude Oil futures, buying a put on Crude Oil futures, or selling a call on Crude Oil futures. When selling the Crude Oil futures, you have an unlimited profit potential and an unlimited loss potential. When the Crude Oil market decreases, you make money because you can buy back the asset (futures) which you have sold at a higher level. Figure 4.5 displays the profit/loss profile of selling the Crude Oil futures.

When you purchase a put, you have the right to an unlimited profit potential as the Crude Oil market decreases. If the Crude Oil market rises instead, you will let the put expire with a maximum loss equal to the premium. Buying a put option, or any option for that matter, is similar to playing roulette in that the most you can lose is the chip you put down on the table. On the other hand, if you sell the call option, you are behaving like the casino. You assume an unlimited loss potential less the premium paid to you; the most you can gain is the 'chip' you have received.

Let us consider the volatility impacts of each of these short underlying positions. Consider a position where one sells a Crude Oil futures contract. This profits only when the price of Crude Oil falls and is not impacted by changes in volatility. When you buy a put option, you are buying both components of the option premium. The intrinsic value increases when the Crude Oil market price falls, and the time value — or 'insurance' — increases when volatility rises and decreases with the passage of time. Therefore, when Crude Oil market prices fall and volatility increases, the put option buyer gains a double benefit so long as not too much time decay has occurred.

When you sell a call option, you can benefit either from a drop in the time value or from a drop in the intrinsic value. Time value will decrease either when volatility drops or as the time passes. Intrinsic value for a call option will decrease to zero when the Crude Oil futures price falls equal to or below the strike price.

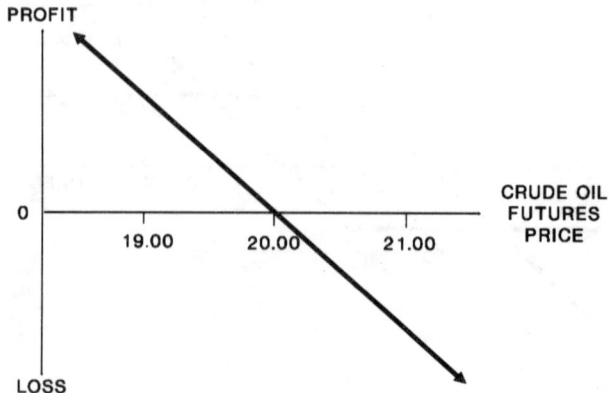

Figure 4.5 Profit/Loss Profile: Short Crude Oil Futures.

Selling a Crude Oil Futures Contract

I will now examine each of these short positions in turn, and identify each strategy's sensitivity to volatility. Suppose I sold the Crude Oil futures at $20, and the market price decreased to $19.50. By selling the Crude Oil futures, my position would be short relative to the underlying Crude Oil market, and neutral to volatility. As discussed earlier, the value of Crude Oil futures positions is independent of volatility. These positions only profit if the price falls. If my view were neutral to volatility but I wished to be a seller of the underlying Crude Oil market, then the trading strategy I might wish to consider would be to sell the Crude Oil futures. As with the long underlying position, I would face unlimited loss and profit potentials. Therefore, the selection of this strategy would depend on the ability to assume risk. Thus, in the trading strategy matrix Table 4.3 (p. 92), we will place the short Crude Oil futures strategy in the lower middle cell which indicates neutrality to volatility and a bias which is short the Crude Oil market.

Buying a Put Option on Crude Oil Futures

With a put option on Crude Oil futures, you pay a premium to establish the position. It is inconsequential when you pay, so long as you pay at some point. Therefore, when you buy this option, and hold it to expiration, the maximum loss will be equal to the premium value agreed upon when the option is initially transacted. If Crude Oil futures prices fall enough to cover the cost of the premium, the put holder will break even. If it falls further, he will then make a net profit. Anyone buying option positions has an unlimited profit potential and a limited loss potential. If you bought a put option at a strike price of $20 and paid $1 for it, and the Crude Oil futures prices dropped from $20 to $18.65 (a $1.35 move in the underlying futures), the net profit to the option holder would be 35¢ per barrel at expiration.

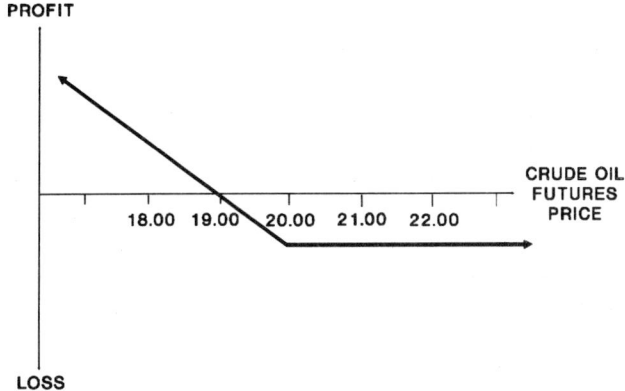

Figure 4.6 Profit/Loss Profile: Holding a Put Option.

In a situation where the put option is deeply in-the-money (a strike price of $22 when the Crude Oil futures price is at $20), its price will be made up of a substantial intrinsic value and a relatively small time value. In addition, since the delta of the put will approach -1.0, the change in the option price will move approximately one for one with the movement of one short Crude Oil futures position. At expiration, all in-the-money put options will be exercised into a short Crude Oil futures position and will at that point have a delta exactly equal to -1.0 for a put (and $+1.0$ for all in-the-money calls). Once the Crude Oil futures has moved sufficiently to cover the amount paid for the put option, you have broken even and only henceforth can make a profit. If the Crude Oil futures finishes equal to the strike price or higher, the put option premium is lost. The profit/loss profile of a put option at expiration is displayed in Figure 4.6.

A key point in options trading is profiting from changing volatility prior to expiration. Consider an at-the-money put option with a strike price of $20. Suppose the price of the option is 97.5¢ per barrel when the volatility is at 25 per cent. Then the OPEC makes an unclear announcement about a change in oil production policy. Everyone becomes nervous and boosts the expectation of Crude Oil volatility to 30 per cent. The put option premium will rise immediately to $1.17 per barrel. If I sold the put at this point, I would realise a profit of 19.5¢ per barrel even though the Crude Oil futures market had not yet moved. If the Crude Oil futures price happened to decrease as well, I would then achieve a double benefit from the increase in both intrinsic value and time value. Therefore, if my view is that volatility will increase as Crude Oil futures prices fall, purchasing a put option on Crude Oil futures will maximise my exposure to these two elements and provide the greatest profit if these events occur concurrently. If, instead, the Crude Oil futures price slowly rose as volatility fell, the put option would experience a double jeopardy and, in addition, lose from time decay. So, in our trading strategy matrix Table 4.3, the purchase of a put option fits into the middle upper cell of the strategy matrix, indicating biases of long volatility and short the Crude Oil market.

Selling a Call Option on Crude Oil Futures

The last trade that I will discuss on the short side is writing or selling a call option. For example, if we sell a $20 call, we receive a premium. For that premium, one assumes the obligation to sell. If the Crude Oil futures price decreases below $20 per barrel, the call option holder will not exercise his option and the option seller will retain all the premium received. Unfortunately, when the Crude Oil futures price increases, the option seller has to 'pay back' some of the option premium he has received (in the losses associated with selling the underlying position at what is now an unfavourable price). Consequently, if the Crude Oil futures price rises more than the premium the seller has received, the seller will have a net loss. However, this position is most advantageous when the Crude Oil futures price finishes at the strike

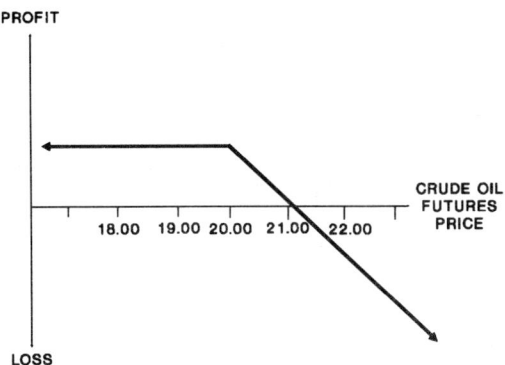

Figure 4.7 Profit/Loss Profile: Writing a Call Option.

price of the option or lower. Figure 4.7 displays the profit/loss profile from selling a call option.

Consider a stable market. This is the worst time for dealing since people attempt to make money out of sideways markets and often take large positions which they get stuck with and can only dispose of at a loss (or, at best, the bid/offer spread). Selling volatility via the options market is a better and more consistent way to make money when the market is stable compared with dealing in the futures.

If my view is that the underlying Crude Oil market is going to be stable, selling options allows me to profit from that opinion. This occurs because as Crude Oil market movements subside and risk decreases, option premiums fall. But which option should be sold: a call or a put? If I expect the drop in volatility to accompany a decrease in the Crude Oil market, the best position from that joint viewpoint is to sell the call option. In Table 4.3, since the call option seller is both a seller of the Crude Oil market and of volatility, this trade fits into our trading matrix in the centre cell.

Compared with buying a put option, the short call position has a limited gain if the Crude Oil futures market is steady or falls, while the put option has an unlimited profit potential. If the Crude Oil futures market rises, the call option seller has an unlimited loss potential less the premium he has received, while the put buyer has the limited loss of his premium. The worst strategy to use when the Crude Oil market increases is a short position in the Crude Oil futures, since it has an unlimited loss potential without any premium to cushion these losses.

Comparison of the Bearish Strategies

Figure 4.8 displays the three positions which are bearish relative to the underlying Crude Oil market. On the downside, the most aggressive position is to sell the Crude Oil futures because you make a profit immediately. If you expect the Crude Oil market to decrease 20 or 25 cents, then you will receive all this in gain. This is your best short-term trade. If you are concerned that the Crude Oil market might rise, you may

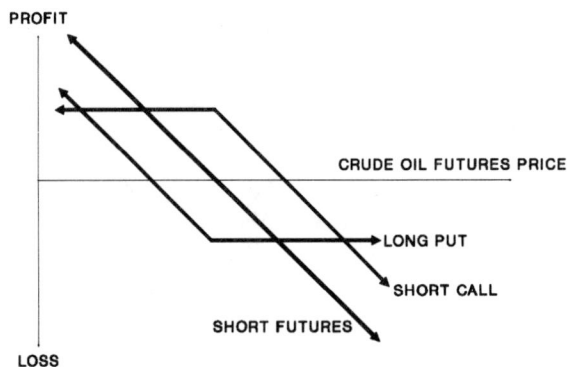

Figure 4.8 Option Strategies: Bearish Positions.

not wish to have the unlimited loss potential associated with a short Crude Oil futures contract.

Put option buyers have a short position because they benefit when the price of the Crude Oil futures goes down. They also achieve a great deal of leverage with a relatively small amount of capital invested. Unfortunately, when a put option is bought, the Crude Oil market must drop during the life of the option otherwise the option would expire worthless. Remember, options are wasting assets. The worst drawback when buying an option is waiting while the time value steadily depletes and the market fails to move. It is like driving a car up a hill and hoping you make it to the top before it runs out of petrol.

The benefit for all option sellers is that they do not have to pay a premium and therefore do not suffer time decay. It works for them. They receive a premium and, if the Crude Oil market is stable, they profit. As time passes, they earn their income and if they sell the options near expiration, they will benefit from a very rapid time decay and inflow of income. But never forget that the most they can make is the premium paid to them, and their risk potential is unlimited. Therefore, with options one must decide whether one wishes to buy an option with limited loss, or sell an option with a limited gain.

VERTICAL SPREADS

Fortunately, that is not the end of the story. With options one can use a wide variety of additional strategies by buying and selling options in combination. The strategist, by using both calls and puts of different strike prices, can create new 'instruments' with an infinite number of possible combinations. One of the most popular kinds of combination trades which provides a directional view is the vertical spread. In these trades, one buys a call and sells a call, or buys a put and sells a put. Both options will be on the same underlying position and with the same maturity. The twist is that one buys and sells options with different strike prices.

For example, suppose once again that you bought a Mercedes 190 E and sold a Mercedes 500 SL. What is your position versus Mercedes? You have a long position and a short position, but as I discussed in the previous chapter, the position may not be 'square' relative to Mercedes. You have the obligation to take delivery and make delivery on two different models. In the options market, if I buy a call I have a long position. If I sell a call, I have a short position. Since I have varied the strike prices, they are also not direct offsets. As in the Mercedes example, I am not directly offset because the 500 SL model is worth more than the 190 E. Nevertheless, even though they are not the same car, I will be able to reduce my exposure relative to the purchase of a single Mercedes Benz automobile.

The Bull Vertical Spread

If I expect the Crude Oil futures market to increase (that is, if I am bullish), then I might consider buying a bull spread. A bull spread is a vertical spread produced either by the purchase and sale of calls, or by the purchase and sale of puts. However, the rule for bull spreads is to buy the lower strike price option and sell the higher strike price option. For the Crude Oil futures, suppose I buy the $19/$21 bull spread, meaning I either buy the $19 call and sell the $21 call, or I buy the $19 put and sell the $21 put. This position profits when the Crude Oil futures increases. In this example, the Crude Oil futures is trading at $20.50 so the $19 call might cost me $1.90. To reduce my premium expense, I sell the $21 call option against it and receive 80¢ in premium. The net premium outflow is $1.10, which is the most I can lose.

Consider first the individual components in the bull spread. I have bought the $19 call which gives me the right to buy at $19. I have also sold the $21 call which is the obligation to sell at $21. If I bought at $19 and sold at $21, my inflow would be $2. But since I paid $1.10 for this strategy, the most I can make is the difference between these strike prices: $ 2, minus what I paid for the spread ($1.10) for a maximum profit potential of 90¢ .

Suppose the Crude Oil futures market can finish at either $19, $20, or $21. If the Crude Oil futures market finishes at $19, both the calls will expire worthless. My loss will be equal to the $1.10 in premium I paid for the spread. Furthermore, if the Crude Oil futures market finishes at any price below $19, both options will also expire worthless and again I will lose the premium I paid. If the Crude Oil futures market finishes at $20, the $19 call will be in-the-money by $1, and the $21 call we sold will expire worthless. So I have an inflow of $1 less my $1.10 outflow in the initial premium expense, which means I have a loss of 10¢ at that price. Finally, if the Crude Oil futures market finishes at $21, the $19 call will be worth $2 and the $21 call I sold will once again expire worthless; an overall inflow of $2 will result. Minus the $1.10 in my initial premium expenditure, this will once again yield a profit of 90¢ per barrel. So I achieve both a limited loss and limited gain with this strategy.

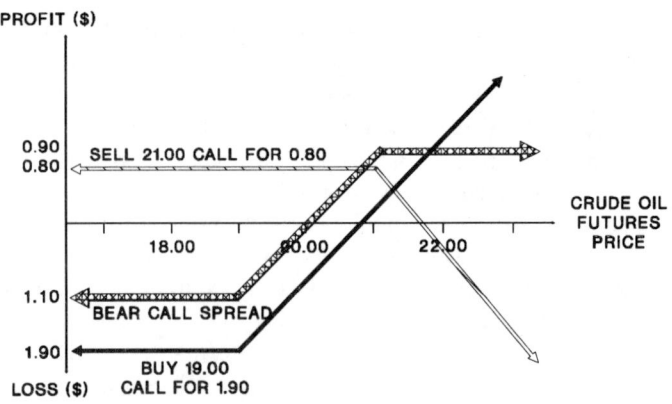

PROFIT ($)

0.90
0.80 — SELL 21.00 CALL FOR 0.80

CRUDE OIL
FUTURES
PRICE

18.00   20.00   22.00

1.10
BEAR CALL SPREAD

1.90
BUY 19.00
LOSS ($)   CALL FOR 1.90

Figure 4.9 Bull Call Spread: Crude Oil Futures at 20.00.

Figure 4.9 displays the profit and loss diagram for this trade. In this diagram, we have included all the component parts as well as the combined positions. To determine the combined position, we will use our graphing rules. We break up the profit and loss potentials into three sectors; the sector to the left of $19, the middle sector between $19 and $21, and the right sector to the right of $21. In the furthest left sector, the $19 call has a limited loss potential equal to the premium of $1.90, and the $21 call has a limited profit potential of 80¢ . The rule is: when you have two limited potentials, limited and limited cancel. Therefore, the bull spread to the left of $19 per barrel has a limited loss potential of $1.10.

In the middle sector, the $19 call has an 'unlimited' profit potential. That is, the profit rises one for one with the increase in the price of the Crude Oil futures. The $21 call has a limited profit potential over this range. The rule when we combine an unlimited and a limited is that the unlimited will dominate the limited. So, the combined strategy moves in the northeast direction, parallel to the profit/loss profile of the $19 call option.

Finally, in the right sector, the $19 call option still has an unlimited profit potential (above $21) and the $21 call option has an unlimited loss potential. The rule when we have two opposite unlimited potentials is that they cancel. So, to the right of $21, the bull spread has a limited gain potential of 90¢ per barrel.

Time Decay and Volatility Sensitivities of a Bull Spread
Why would one want to buy this? Two reasons may exist: time decay neutrality and volatility immunisation. If I buy an option outright (also known as a 'naked call') my exposure to time decay is extensive. If an option is sold, then time decay works in my favour. Therefore, if I am both buying and selling options, my exposure to volatility and time decay is reduced and can be neutral. Figure 4.10 displays the time decay characteristics of buying a $20 call compared with a $19/$21 and a $21/$22 bull spread. If I buy the $20 call, I pay a premium of $1.25 per barrel. The time decay for this option, as can be seen in the chart, is rapid and accelerating. The bull spreads, on the other hand, do not experience such time decay because the time value of the bought

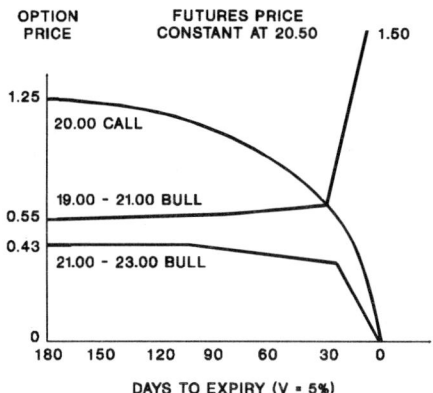

Figure 4.10 Time Decay Characteristics: Bull Spread.

option is decaying at a rate similar to the time decay of the option we have sold, and thus offsets. Therefore, an advantage for vertical spreads is that they can be held for a very long time without appreciable time decay, and also provide a limited loss feature. In the last 30 days, however, the reader can see that the time decay for the bull spreads is quite rapid. For example, the in-the-money bull spread ($19/$21) will rapidly decay to its intrinsic value of $1.50 (when the crude oil market is at $20.50), while the out-of-the-money bull spread ($21/$23) will rapidly decay to its intrinsic value of zero.

Assume for a moment your view is that over the next six months Crude Oil futures price will increase, but you do not know exactly when. Further, you feel that volatility may decrease over this period but you do not wish to be hurt if this occurs, and that you require a strategy with limited loss potential in case you are wrong. Finally, you want a strategy which will not be eroded by time decay. If you establish a bull spread, you will achieve all these objectives. Suppose Crude Oil futures take four months to rise. When that occurs, the bull spread increases in value owing to intrinsic value gain on the lower strike price call. Because the bull spread is neutral to time decay, you have not been hurt by patiently waiting for the Crude Oil market to move. In practice, if you hold the bull spread up to 30 days until expiration, and if the Crude Oil futures market still has not moved, then the spread should have approximately the same value it had when you purchased it and you should be able to sell it back at little or no loss. If you put on a bull spread and then have to unwind it, you may still believe the Crude Oil futures market may rise. So if your view is still bullish you can 'roll' the bull spread forward in time by doing exactly the same spread in the next expiration month. This spread will also have immunity to time decay and volatility. As long as you 'roll' out of bull spreads 30 days prior to expiration, you should not have any appreciable loss on the spread due to time decay. However, during the last 30 days, bull spreads can decay very rapidly which, incidentally, can be quite advantageous to sellers of these spreads. So, if you are a buyer of an out-of-the-money bull spread, make sure to roll out of it by that point.

The biases of bull spreads are directionally 'long' (buyers of the underlying Crude Oil market) and regarding volatility, neutral; since they are both buying and selling options. That is how you achieve a position with a limited loss and a negligible volatility exposure. So, if my view is that the Crude Oil market will increase and I wish to be neutral to volatility, then the bull spread is the ideal strategy to use. Thus, if we return to our strategy matrix in Table 4.3, the bull spread will be the cell in the lower left-hand side with a long underlying bias but neutral to volatility. It is important to note that also in this cell is the long Crude Oil futures position. The bull spread shares the same directional and volatility biases as a long Crude Oil futures contract. However, the bull spread's advantage is the limited loss feature which the Crude Oil futures position does not share.

The Bear Vertical Spread

While bull spreads benefit when the Crude Oil market increases, bear spreads benefit when the Crude Oil futures price decreases. Bear spreads are almost identical to bull spreads, except that the rule with bear spreads is that you buy the higher strike price option and sell the lower strike price option. Therefore, to create a bear spread one would buy the $21 put and sell the $19 put. However, if I buy the $21 call and sell the $19 call, this is also known as a bear spread but is termed a bear call spread. The bear call spread is referred to as a credit vertical spread because one's account will be credited with an inflow of premium. A bear put spread is known as a debt vertical spread because one must pay out premium for it. As with buying options, if I pay a premium to establish a vertical spread, this is the most I can lose (and if I receive a premium, this is the most I can make).

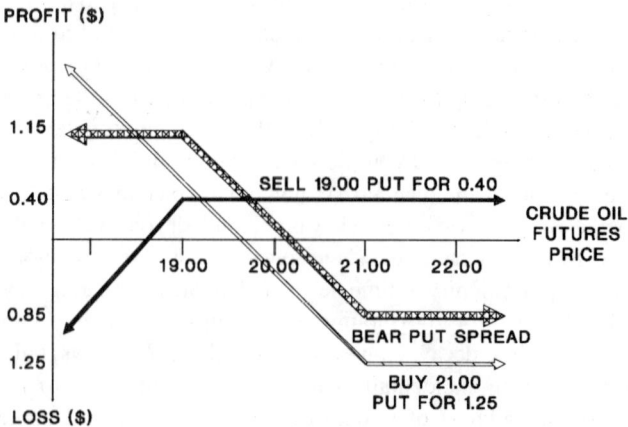

Figure 4.11 Bear Put Spread: Crude Oil Futures at 20.00.

Now, back to the bear put spread. If I buy a $21 put option, I might have to pay $1.25 for it: a limited loss and an unlimited profit potential, but at a dear price. To reduce this premium cost and protect myself against time decay, I also sell a $19 put option; receiving back 40¢ . The net cost of this combination is equal to an outflow of 85¢ ($1.25 minus 40¢). Again, this is the most I can lose and the profit potential for this spread is $1.15 (the $2 between $21 and $19 less the 85¢ I paid for the option spread). Figure 4.11 displays a buildup profit and loss diagram for this strategy.

Again using our graphing rules, we can break up the profit and loss potentials into three sectors. As with the bull spread, we will look at the left sector below $19, the middle sector between $19 and $21, and the right sector above $21. Below $19, the $19 put option I sold has an unlimited loss potential and the $21 put I purchased has an unlimited profit potential. Apply our graphing rules: since opposite unlimited potentials cancel, the bear spread has a limited profit over this range equal to the difference in the strike prices ($2), less the amount I paid for the spread (85¢) for a net profit of $1.15.

In the middle sector between $19 and $21, the $19 put I sold expires worthless and the $21 put I bought has an 'unlimited' profit potential. Because the unlimited dominates the limited, I achieve an unlimited profit potential sloping to the northwest.

Finally, in the right sector above $21, both put options expire worthless and therefore the combined position has both limited gain and loss profits. So I lose $1.25 on the $21 put I purchased, and gain 40¢ on the $19 put I sold, with a net loss of 85¢. Again, as with the bull call spread, I achieve a limited profit potential with the bear spread.

The advantages of bear spreads are that one is a seller of the underlying Crude Oil market, and the exposures to volatility and time decay are neutral since the trade involves both buying and selling options. Thus, the strategy offers a limited loss and a negligible volatility exposure, and is an equivalent short position relative to the underlying Crude Oil market. As with the bull spread, the time decay characteristics are neutral. So, if my view is that the Crude Oil market will decrease, and I wish to be neutral to volatility, then a bear spread is the ideal strategy to use. In our strategy matrix in Table 4.3, the bear spread will be the cell in the lower middle. This strategy is a seller of the underlying market but neutral to volatility. As was promised earlier in this chapter, we can use options to provide the same volatility neutrality as a Crude Oil futures position, but with a limited loss feature.

DIRECTIONAL TRADING STRATEGIES: PLACEMENT IN THE STRATEGY MATRIX

With the completion of our discussion of vertical spreads, I have filled Table 4.3 with eight possible strategies. What I will do in the next two chapters is to examine the category of option strategies that fit into the furthest right cells of the strategy matrix. These trades will be neutral to the underlying market but bullish, bearish or neutral on volatility. These trades include volatility strategies and options arbitrage.

VIEWPOINT ON THE CRUDE OIL MARKET

		BUYER	SELLER	NEUTRAL
VIEWPOINT ON VOLATILITY	**BUYER**	BUY CALL OPTION	BUY PUT OPTION	
	SELLER	SELL PUT OPTION	SELL CALL OPTION	
	NEUTRAL	LONG BUND FUTURES BULL SPREAD	SHORT BUND FUTURES BEAR SPREAD	

Table 4.3 Option Trading Strategy Matrix.

[1] In Chapter 2, the reader is referred to Figures 13a and 13b where we show that it is better to buy longer maturity options to minimise the time decay impact. Of course, if the option buyer is looking for the maximum leverage, then short-dated options are preferable (see Figure 2.14). However, the time decay for these options is also maximised.

5: Volatility Trading Strategies

In this section, I will discuss what may be the most creative of the options strategies: volatility trades. As previously explained, volatility is essentially the risk aspect of the market. It is the perception of risk that is 'securitised' in the time value component of an option premium. As I mentioned in Chapter 2, there are three ways to measure volatility. One method is the historical basis which measures what has happened in the past and is expressed as the annualised standard deviation of percentage changes in the underlying asset. The second method is the implied volatility, which is the current volatility associated with the option's price. Finally, there is the method of volatility estimation which forecasts future volatility by using econometric techniques which incorporate both the historical and implied techniques.

Traders buy or sell volatility as their perception of future risk in the future changes. When market makers get more 'edgy', they buy up volatility; and when they expect stability, volatility goes down. So, the current determination of volatility is simply the supply and demand for risk.

In this chapter, I will use the option on Soyabean futures traded at the Chicago Board of Trade (CBOT). The prices are in dollars per bushel. Table 5.1 outlines the contract specification for this underlying. The asset underlying the option is a CBOT Soyabean futures contract which is the obligation either to buy or sell 5000 bushels (a unit of measure of eight dry gallons) of Soyabeans in the month following the expiration of the option.

TRADING UNIT	1 CBOT SOYABEAN FUTURES CONTRACT OF 5,000 BUSHELS
TRADING MONTHS	JANUARY, MARCH, MAY, JULY, AUGUST, SEPTEMBER AND NOVEMBER
LAST TRADING DAY	LAST FRIDAY PRECEDING THE FIRST NOTICE DAY BY AT LEAST FIVE BUSINESS DAYS
EXERCISE PRICE	25 CENTS PER BUSHEL
MINIMUM PRICE MOVEMENT	1/8 CENT PER BUSHEL ($6.25 PER CONTRACT)
EXERCISE PRICE INTERVALS	$1 PER BUSHEL, (7 DIFFERENT EXERCISE PRICES)
TRADING HOURS	9:30 - 13:15 (CHICAGO TIME) LAST TRADING DAY: 9:30 - 12:00
EXERCISE	BY 18:00. AUTOMATIC EXERCISE FOR OPTIONS AT LEAST 30 CENTS IN-THE-MONEY ON THE LAST TRADING DAY

Table 5.1 Options on Soyabean Futures (CBOT).

HOW TO MAKE MONEY FROM A CHANGE IN VOLATILITY

How can someone make money from a change in risk? In an earlier chapter, I provided an example of risk trading with the story about the fellow who bought insurance and was later (incorrectly) diagnosed as having a terminal disease. Because the value of the health insurance increased dramatically, the policy holder sold it back to the insurance agent and made a profit. Then, when he was correctly diagnosed as not having a terminal disease, he was able to repurchase his health insurance at a low price once again. The insurance buyer had purchased low risk and then sold higher risk, to make money. The higher the perception of risk, the greater the value of the insurance. As risk recedes, insurance premiums and options prices both drop in value. So, if you expect risk to increase, you will buy risk and if you expect risk to fall, you sell risk. In this section, I will examine how to buy and sell risk using volatility trading strategies.

As was mentioned above, volatility is measured in percentage terms. How often does this perception of risk change? It can change as often as daily. Figure 5.1a displays the historical volatility of the July 1991 Soyabean futures from November 1990 until April 1991. To calculate the volatility each day, the previous 20 days of the percentage change in the Soyabean futures was used. As each day passed, the 20-day analysis period was moved forward one day to achieve a rolling 20-day historical volatility. Since the standard deviation is on daily returns, to turn it into an annualised number one simply multiplies the daily standard deviation by the square root of the number of trading days in a year (which is approximately 260 days). Each trading day the process was repeated (using the preceding 20 days) to provide the estimate of volatility for that period.

Over the period of time shown in Figure 5.1a, volatility increased initially and then fell, moving sideways until about 25 February 1991. Therefore, one would have benefited from 'selling' volatility over this period as the market began a period of slow activity. From the peak of 20 per cent, it would have been an ideal time to sell volatility and also benefit from time decay. As it was indicated, this is the historical Soyabean volatility. Would the actual implied volatility of traded options contracts also have dropped during this period? Figure 5.1b displays the implied volatility for the same period. As the reader can see, the implied volatility did indeed drop from about the beginning of December 1990 (when the historical volatility was at its peak of 20 per cent). However, in January the implied volatility increased more than the historical volatility. In most markets, historical volatility has a very close relationship to implied volatility. From a comparison of both plots, it can be seen that the trends are quite similar although the historical volatility seems to be less variable than the implied volatility.

When you trade volatility, the principles are the same as when you trade any price series. You buy when it is low and sell it at a higher level, or you sell it at a high level and buy it back at a lower level. For instance, over the time period represented in Figure 5.1b, one can see that after the initial surge in volatility there was a steady downtrend until the beginning of January when the activity of the Soyabean market

HISTORICAL VOLATILITY

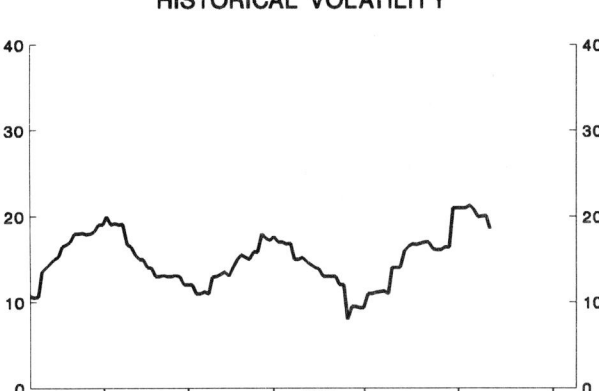

Figure 5.1a July 1991 Soyabean Futures Historical Volatility.

IMPLIED VOLATILITY

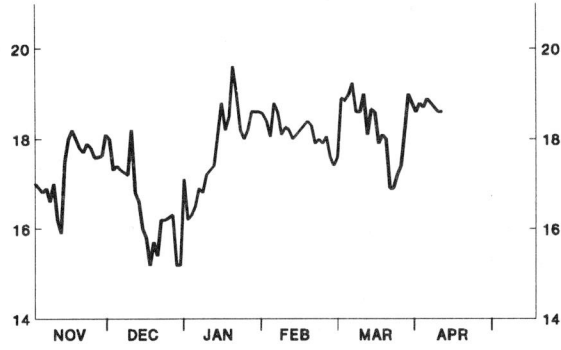

Figure 5.1b July 1991 Soyabean Options Implied Volatility

picked up. So, if you had sold volatility over the period from the middle of December 1990 until January 1991, and then reversed your view and bought volatility, you would have profited from these volatility changes.

Upon closer scrutiny of Figure 5.1a and 5.1b, the reader will observe that volatility seems to move like any other price series. It will rise and fall and then rise again. This can occur because the perception of risk changes over time. When new information comes into the market, people revise their opinions of risk and thereby change the prices at which they are willing to buy or sell options, which are after all insurance policies on that risk. *Ceteris Paribus* (that is, everything else remains the same), if volatility increases, option prices rise and if volatility decreases, option prices fall. Therefore, one buys options when the perception of risk rises and one sells options when risk is presumed to fall.

The ideal way to trade volatility is to maximise the exposure to volatility and minimise the exposure to the other factors which influence option prices, such as the movement in the underlying market. By doing so, the trader can focus his viewpoint on volatility alone. Then, one can trade volatility as though it were a simple price series. When one is completely neutral to the underlying market, and is just trading volatility, this is termed pure volatility trading. In addition to pure volatility trading, one can establish trading strategies that are initially neutral to the underlying market but can become an equivalent long or short position if the underlying market price moves to a particular level. These trades I will call 'leaning volatility trades'. In this chapter, I will examine in detail both pure and leaning volatility strategies.

Option prices (the time value component) are nothing more than risk channelled into a security. As risk increases it will increase the value of the security or the option derived from it. Sometimes, the increase in time value can be so extreme as to offset and even dominate changes in the intrinsic value. Figure 5.2 provides an example of how this can occur.

In this example, when the underlying market price is at \$5.75 per bushel, the \$5.75 call with 90 days to go has a price of 21½¢ if volatility is at 22 per cent. Suppose the market price goes down to \$5.60. If the volatility remains at 22 per cent, the call option price will fall from 21½¢ to 16¾¢ . But what happens if the market goes down because something dramatic – a catastrophic event such as the rumour of a bumper crop in Argentina, for example – has happened in the Soyabean market. If the fall in the market is concurrent with a volatility increase to 33 per cent, the option would then be worth 25¢ even though the underlying market price has fallen. Therefore, one would be able to make money buying the call option even though the underlying market price fell. In this case, the impact of volatility is more substantial than the other factors influencing the option price.

Let us assume my view is that both volatility and the market will increase, and therefore I buy the call option. Given that both events occur, I will make a substantial gain on this trade. Supposing the market increases to \$6 and volatility goes up to 33 per cent, I will more than double my investment of 21½ ¢ in the call. This is because

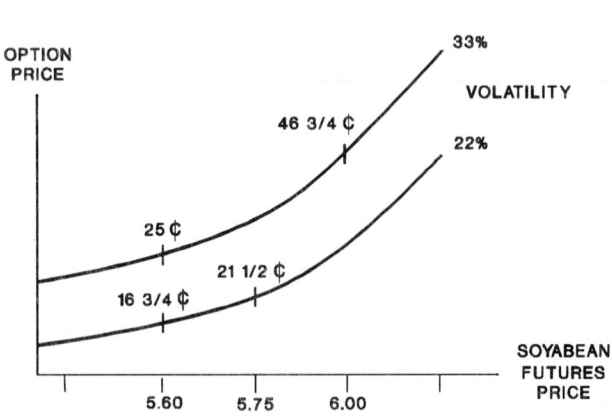

Figure 5.2 Volatility Impacts

I could then sell the call for 46¾ ¢ . As I demonstrated above, if volatility increases and the market is stable or falls, I can still make a profit from the purchase of the call.

Volatility is so important that in some circumstances one may wish to trade the volatility separately, owing to its critical impact on option premiums. To isolate for the volatility impacts, we must immunise the exposure to the underlying market. To do this, we will combine various options or underlying positions so that in combination, the strategy is immune to changes in the value of the underlying asset. Thus, the position will experience neither profits nor losses if the price of the underlying asset changes. The reader may recall that in Chapter 3 I mentioned that long equivalent positions offset short equivalent positions. So, in volatility trading, we will establish positions which have opposite and equivalent exposures to the underlying market to achieve this immunised position.

THE 'PURE' BUYING VOLATILITY STRATEGIES

Suppose a person purchases a call option which is an equivalent long position. As demonstrated above, if volatility increases he will profit. If he also buys a put option which is an equivalent short position, in combination with the long call what will he have? The put option has an opposite exposure to the underlying market (in other words, is short) but will also benefit if volatility increases. So, in combination, these two trades will be neutral to the underlying market but two options will still be held, both of which have a long volatility bias. That is how you go 'long' volatility; by buying options. If one buys both a call and a put, and adjusts carefully for the delta exposure of each, then the position can be neutralised to the underlying and will then be purely a volatility trade. Depending on which strike prices you choose, this combination trade is called either a straddle or a strangle.

Buying a Straddle

A long or buying straddle is achieved when you buy both a call option and a put option at the same strike price (generally both at-the-money). The call option you purchase is a long position relative to the underlying market, and the put option is a short position relative to the underlying. The total exposure of these two in combination will cancel out relative to the underlying position. Supposing we buy both options which are at-the-money; both options have deltas of 0.5. The call has a positive 0.5 delta and the put has a negative 0.5 delta. If we combine the +0.5 delta with the –0.5 delta, the net delta position is 0.0 or neutral to the underlying.

Even though you are neutral to the underlying asset, you are still holding two options having paid two premiums. Thus, for both options you are long volatility. One establishes this trade on the same underlying position, the same maturity and at the same strike price. Suppose when the underlying market is trading at $5.75 per bushel I bought a $5.75 call option on Soyabean futures, the most I can lose is the premium

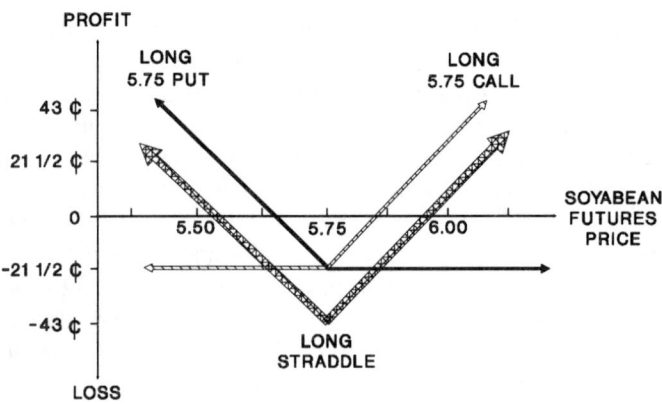

Figure 5.3 Buying a Straddle

paid but I have gained an unlimited upside potential. When I purchase the $5.75 put, I also have a limited loss potential and an unlimited profit potential to the downside. Figure 5.3 displays the two positions plotted together. To the left of $5.75, we have an unlimited profit potential for the put and a limited loss potential for the call. The graphing rule for the combination of an unlimited and a limited says that the unlimited profit potential will dominate the limited loss potential. Therefore, the combination has an unlimited profit potential to the left of the strike price. To the right of $5.75, we have an unlimited profit potential on the call and a limited loss potential on the put. Once again, the unlimited profit potential dominates the limited loss potential, and the combination will have an unlimited profit potential over this range. So, if you combine these two positions, the overall strategy looks like a big 'V'. You gain an unlimited profit potential to the left of $5.75 and an unlimited profit potential to the right of $5.75. Where this strategy fails is when the market stays level at $5.75 and both option premiums are lost.

If this position is initiated when the underlying Soyabean futures is at $5.75, it will be delta neutral. This is because the positions bought are at-the-money options with delta exposures that exactly offset. While you have no exposure to the underlying market, this trade will be extremely sensitive to volatility. By purchasing at-the-money options, they have the greatest time value and therefore the greatest volatility sensitivity. Unfortunately, these options are also extremely sensitive to time decay. Thus, very few traders can afford to maintain these strategies for long periods or until expiration; rather, most traders trade them for a short time period and take off the spread when and if the volatility increases. Often, these are effective strategies to establish prior to the release of government trade figures or other news events that tend to cause volatility or market uncertainty to increase.

Prior to expiration, both options will have substantial time value. As with the call option trade discussed previously, the value of each can increase dramatically from an increase in volatility. Straddles essentially double the exposure to volatility compared with the purchase of a single option. This means a doubling in the straddle profit for the same increase in the rate of volatility. Here is an example.

If the volatility is at 22 per cent, we may pay 43¢ per bushel for the at-the-money $5.75 straddle, each option valued at 21½¢ . Now, what happens if volatility goes up 1 per cent to 23 per cent? If the market price remains at $5.75, both the call and the put premiums will now be worth 22½¢ or a total of 45¢ for the straddle. If the straddle is sold at the now higher volatility, we have made 2¢ per bushel just from the 1 per cent increase in volatility. The market is still sitting there at $5.75; it has not moved. But because the volatility rose, you are able to make an immediate profit with the straddle. Unfortunately, if nothing occurs and both volatility and the market are stagnant, the trade will erode owing to the time decay. This is the reason most dealers rarely buy straddles for more than a few days. They use them as a short-term trade, expecting an immediate increase in volatility to occur. If this does occur, they will immediately close out the straddle, take their profits and run. These trades are often traded and quoted as spreads: buying the straddle at 43¢ and then selling it at 45¢ .

Buying a Strangle

A variation on this theme is buying the strangle, which costs less than the straddle to establish. With the strangle, you are buying a call and a put on the same Soyabean futures position for the same maturity, but at different strike prices. As before, the equivalent long position and the equivalent short position will offset each other relative to the underlying market. Generally, strangles are established with out-of-the-money options. If they are established with in-the-money options, they are often referred to as 'guts' positions. So, you are going to buy an out-of-the-money call and an out-of-the-money put. With the market trading at $5.75, you would buy the $6.00 call which is out-of-the-money. At the same time, you will buy an $5.50 put which is also out-of-the-money. In Figure 5.4, both of these trades are displayed and we will apply our graphing rules to see what the profit and loss profile of this combination will be.

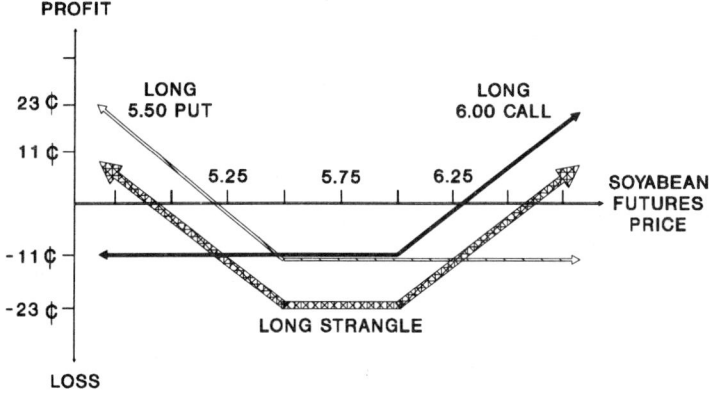

Figure 5.4 Buying a Strangle

To the left of $5.50, we have an unlimited profit potential on the long put option, and a limited loss potential on the call option. The graphing rule states that an unlimited profit potential will dominate the limited loss potential, so the strangle will have an unlimited profit potential below $5.50. Between $5.50 and $6.00, both the $5.50 put and the $6.00 call have a limited loss potential. In this case, they do not cancel but instead combine. Nevertheless, the loss potential is limited to the total premium cost. To the right of $6.00, the $6.00 call has an unlimited profit potential and the $5.50 put has a limited loss potential; so the rule is that the unlimited profit potential dominates the limited loss potential and the strangle will have an unlimited profit potential over this range.

Since with the strangle you are buying out-of-the-money options, you are paying a smaller premium compared with the straddle and – because you have purchased less time value – are not going to have the same amount of money exposed to time decay.[1] In this example, the $5.50 put price would be worth 11¢ and the $6.00 would be priced at 12¢ . Therefore, the strangle price would be 23¢ . With the strangle, you are no longer maximising your exposure to time value or to volatility. But you do have a position that costs less to establish and therefore has a smaller loss potential. These trades can perhaps be established for a longer time period than the straddle, but you still will want to take them off within seven to ten days if market volatility has failed to change.

While there are numerous other strategies one can establish to buy volatility, most traders will keep things simple and buy either the straddle or the strangle when trying to initiate a pure volatility strategy. This is because these strategies are the most sensitive to changes in volatility.

Where Long Straddles and Strangles Fit in the Strategy Matrix

With both straddles and strangles, the view is neutral to the market and long volatility. So, if we turn to our trading strategy matrix at the end of this chapter (Table 5.2), we will place the long straddle and long strangle into the upper right cell, which is neutral to the underlying market but with a buying bias to volatility. These trades work when one is uncertain where the underlying market is going but believes volatility will increase over the short term and before time decay erodes the position's value.

When establishing any of these trades, it is critical that the trader should remain disciplined, place and take off the trades as a spread. If one starts looking at each component separately and trades them not as a spread but one at a time, things can get very dangerous. Remember that the view with these trades is neutral to the underlying position: I do not care whether the market goes up or goes down, I will buy it and sell it as a spread because my initial view was to make my money on the increase in volatility. The disciplined trader remembers that he has 'bought' volatility at a low level expecting to sell it at a higher level, ideally in two or three days before the spread starts experiencing heavy time decay. What may occur is that the Soyabean market jolts one way or the other, and he will be very tempted to take off only one side of the spread. For example, if we bought a straddle and the market collapsed, one might want to take off the call and let the put 'ride'. What usually happens next is that the market rallies and you lose on both the call and the put. This kind of trading technique is called 'legging'.

To explain the risks of legging, I will use the analogy of a cowboy in the Old West facing the problem of crossing a barbed wire fence. The cowboy on his horse rides up to the barbed wire fence and plans to crawl over the fence and change onto another horse on the other side. He raises one leg at a time, keeping one leg astride his first horse and at the same time trying to place his free leg on the other horse on the other side. Now, as he is suspended over the barbed wire fence in the process of switching horses, what happens if one of the horses takes off? He is probably going to be badly hurt. Legging trades are essentially like this. If you decide not to trade these strategies as a spread but instead try to take off one leg at a time (hoping the other one will move in your favour), the results can be calamitous if the market fails to accommodate your technique. When one does this one is no longer purely trading volatility, but attempting a foolhardy trading technique. Whenever you trade, remember what your objectives are. More good trades go wrong when traders try to change position in midstream because they forget why they established the position in the first place. Whenever he considers legging a trade, the spread trader would be well advised to remember the old Wall Street adage: 'Bulls make money, bears make money, but pigs get slaughtered.' Remain disciplined; greed can cost you dearly!

Straddles and strangles are referred to as pure volatility trades because when you initially establish them, the positions are delta neutral and the trader profits equally if the market goes up or down. With both strategies, the unlimited profit opportunity is equal on both sides. What concerns the straddle and strangle buyer is that something happens quickly; either the market moves or volatility increases.

LEANING VOLATILITY BUYING STRATEGIES: RATIO BACK SPREADS

There are other ways to buy volatility which do not have the same balanced view on the underlying market, and these trades are called leaning volatility trades. These trades start out as delta neutral, but as the market moves they develop a bias on the movement of the underlying asset. The two most common of these trades are known as call back spreads and put back spreads.

Call Ratio Back Spreads: the Callback

Call back spreads are also referred to as call ratio back spreads, but I prefer to call them callbacks. With the callback, you buy two or more higher strike call options, and you sell one lower strike price call option or any other combination which leaves you delta neutral. How can this be neutral to the underlying market? Remember that when one buys call options these positions provide positive deltas, and when one sells call

101

options these positions provide negative deltas. What we must do is balance the deltas so that in combination they equal zero.

Suppose I buy two out-of-the-money call options which have a strike price higher than the prevailing market price. Suppose each option has a delta of 0.25. If I buy two of them, my total delta position will be a positive 0.50. If I then sell an at-the-money call, this will give me an equivalent short position with a delta of –0.50. Remember, at-the-money options always have a delta of 50/50. In combination, the two options I have purchased give me a delta position of +0.50 and the short call at the money gives me a delta of –0.50. Therefore, the overall delta position is zero and so delta neutral. This position is 'long' volatility because I am buying more options than I am selling. Thus, this position profits as volatility increases because the two options I have purchased are more sensitive to volatility changes than the single option I sold. As will be demonstrated, I am going to have a limited gain potential if the market falls and an unlimited gain potential if the market rises.

To show how this works, I will separate the components of the spread into trades already discussed. If I buy one out-of-the-money call and sell an at-the-money call, what is that? The answer is a bear call spread. Let us assume I have a bear call position. If the reader refers back to our trading strategy matrix Table 4.3 in Chapter 4, he will see that the bear spread is bearish on the market and neutral to volatility. I will split our two long calls in the callback into two sets of one apiece and combine one of these with the short call to create our bear spread. Then, with the other call option, I will add it to the bear call spread. What will be the net effect? Since buying a call has a bullish bias on the underlying position, and the bear spread has a bearish bias, in combination the bias relative to the underlying would be neutral. Regarding the volatility exposure, the long call is a buyer of volatility while the bear call spread is neutral. So in combination, the spread will be a net buyer of volatility. Thus, the callback spread will be neutral to the market but long volatility.

It would appear that the callback spread is purely a volatility spread because it is neutral to the market and long volatility. Why then am I calling this a 'leaning' volatility strategy? The reason is that at expiration the payoff profile will not be symmetrical as it was with the straddle or the strangle. The callback will profit more from the market going one way than the other. To see this better, the reader is referred to Figure 5.5 which is the buildup diagram for the callback spread.

We start off by combining a $6.00 call we have purchased with the $5.50 call we have sold. Suppose that when this trade was established, the underlying Soyabean futures market was at $5.75. So the $5.50 call we wrote is in-the-money and the $6.00 call we bought is out-of-the-money. As the reader can see in Figure 5.5, the payoff at expiration is displayed as a bear vertical spread similar to the one I discussed in Chapter 4. To determine the exposure now, I must look at the deltas. The $5.50 short call has a delta of –0.69 when its price is 35¾¢, and the $6 long call has a delta of +0.34 associated with a price of 11¾ ¢ . In combination, the bear spread has a delta position of –0.35. When we add the second long $6 call, we pick up another +0.34 delta. Thus, our overall exposure to the underlying Soyabean futures will be zero because the sizes of the positive and negative delta positions are exactly offsetting.

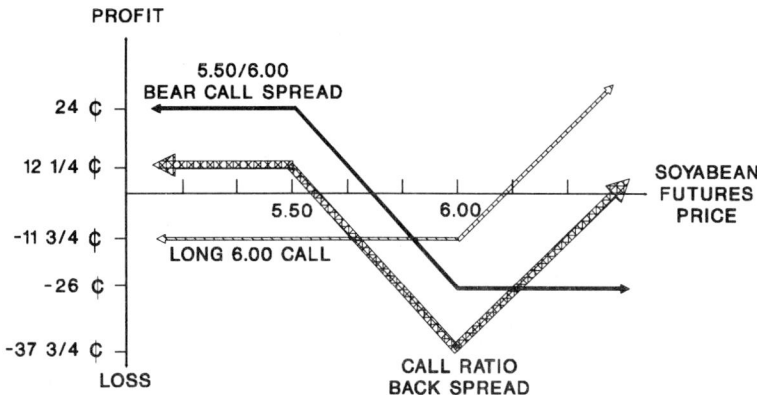

Figure 5.5 Call Ratio Back Spread

For this reason, the callback spread starts out as delta neutral at the current levels. The profit/loss of this trade at expiration is also displayed in Figure 5.5.

In that Figure, I have applied the graphing rules to determine the shape of the combined trade. To the left of $5.50, the bear call spread has a limited gain of 24¢ per bushel (the net premium received) and the $6 call has a limited loss of the 11¾ ¢ per bushel premium. The rule, when we have both a limited gain and a limited loss, is that their two payoffs will offset to some degree. So, below the $5.50 strike price, the callback spread has a limited profit of 12¼ ¢ per bushel. Between $5.50 and $6, the bear call spread has a loss potential that moves to the southeast one for one with an increase in the underlying Soyabean futures market. The $6 call we are holding has a limited loss over this range equal to the premium paid for it. So, we have a limited loss and an 'unlimited' (one for one) loss potential. In combination, an 'unlimited' loss will exacerbate the limited loss and the callback spread will therefore have a one for one loss potential over the range. The maximum loss potential is equal to 37¾¢. This can be determined by assessing the maximum loss potential for the bear call spread and adding the premium loss the 'extra' $6 call. For the bear spread, this loss is equal to 26¢ (the difference in the strike prices – 50¢ – minus the 24¢ in premium we received). The loss for the $6 call is an additional 11¾¢, and 26¢ + 11¾¢ equals 37¾¢.

Finally, to the right of $6, the $5.50/$6 bear call spread will have a limited loss while the $6 call will have an unlimited profit potential. Again, in combination the unlimited profit dominates the limited loss, and the callback spread has an unlimited upside profit potential with a breakeven price at $6.37¾. At this point, the intrinsic value for the $6 call will exactly offset the maximum loss potential for the strategy experienced at $6 (of 37¾ ¢ per bushel). Above $6.37¾, the strategy has an unlimited profit potential.

In summary, to the left (below $5.50) the callback has a limited profit, between $5.50 and $6 the callback has a loss potential experiencing the maximum loss of 37¾ ¢ per bushel, at $6 and above the breakeven price of $6.37¾ the callback has an unlimited profit potential. The spread is a 'leaning' volatility strategy because the trader would profit more if the market rallied than if it fell, so he is leaning his directional bias to the bullish side.

If one compares the callback profit/loss profile with that of either the long straddle or the strangle, one will notice that while the price volatility strategies are balanced to underlying movement profiting equally, the callback spread is 'leaning' to the upside.

So, the callback is a spread which is initially neutral to the market and a buyer of volatility. If, however, the market moves up, the callback has an unlimited profit potential and if the market falls the callback has a limited profit potential. Quite often, the downside can actually have a limited loss potential. However, in this example, the option premiums were such that this did not occur. The next example is another 'back' spread which will also provide both an unlimited gain potential on one side and a limited gain potential on the other side. The difference is that this 'back' spread will be the mirror image of the callback spread.

The Put Ratio Back Spread: the Putback

This leaning volatility spread is the putback spread. The putback is established when you buy two or possibly more puts and you sell one put, so that the combination is delta neutral. In this example, let us assume the Soyabean futures price is currently at $5.75, there are 68 days until the Soyabean options expire, the options volatility is 22 per cent and the short-term interest rate is 6.25 per cent. You buy two puts at a strike price of $5.50 and pay 11¢ per bushel for each (22¢ per bushel in total). These puts are out-of-the-money and each has a delta of –0.3. Then, you sell one put which is in-the-money with a strike price of $6.00 and receive back 36½ ¢ . The $6.00 put has a delta of 0.608. The total negative delta exposure is once again approximately equal to the positive delta exposure so the overall position is almost delta neutral (–0.008). This position profits as volatility increases because once again you are buying more options than you are selling. Secondly, you have a limited gain potential on the upside and an unlimited gain potential on the downside.

To see how this is created, we will once again break the spread into trades I have previously examined, and see how in combination the spread evolves. We split the two long $5.50 put options into two sets of one put each, and combine one of the long $5.50 puts with the $6.00 put we have sold. By selling the higher strike price put option 36½¢ and buying the lower strike price put option 11¢ , we have constructed a bull put spread. This is a credit bull spread as we will receive 25½¢ in premium back, and this maximum profit will occur at prices $6.00 or higher. The biases of a bull spread are neutral to volatility and bullish on the underlying market. Then we buy an additional put option at the $5.50 strike price and again have to pay 11¢ for it. This trade is a bearish position relative to the underlying market and bullish to volatility. In combination, the putback will be neutral to the market and bullish on volatility. But since the spread is almost delta neutral, how can it be a leaning strategy? Like the callback spread, the putback gains more on one side than on the other. In the case of the putback spread, this will occur on the downside. To see this, we must again view the strategy at expiration. In Figure 5.6, the putback spread is displayed.

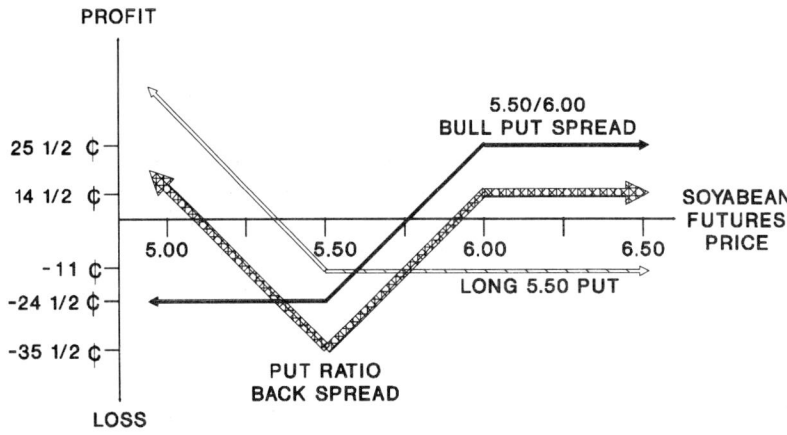

Figure 5.6 Put Ratio Back Spread

To the left of the $5.50 strike price, the bull put spread has a limited loss potential equal to 24½¢ and the long put option has an unlimited profit potential. Since the unlimited profit potential dominates the limited loss potential, the putback spread will have an unlimited profit potential when the market falls below the breakeven price of $5.14½. This breakeven price is equal to the lower strike price minus the maximum loss potential on the bull spread minus the premium paid for the 'extra' put ($5.50 – 24½¢ – 11¢). Between $5.50 and $6.00, the 'unlimited' gain potential on the bull put spread will dominate the limited loss on the put we purchased; so over this range, the putback will have an 'unlimited' profit potential. This will break even when the Soyabean futures price is equal to $5.85½. Finally, above $6.00, the bull put spread will have a limited profit potential and the $6.00 put will have a limited loss potential. When combined, over this range the limited profit and loss potentials will offset with a limited profit of 14½¢. Therefore, the putback started out almost delta neutral but if the market starts going down, it is going to have an unlimited profit potential. This is the reason we call the putback spread a leaning volatility trade; one holding such a position would rather see the market fall than rise.

Quite often, these spreads are created over time. Suppose I have purchased a bull spread, either a bull call or a bull put spread. The market moves up and I have a profit. I could simply take my profit and consolidate. But if my view has now changed and my bias has become bearish on the market and bullish on volatility, I can protect the profit in the bull spread and change the bull spread into a putback spread simply by purchasing another put. At that moment, I am delta neutral which means my exposure to the underlying position has been covered. In addition, the trade is now long volatility and if the market really collapses as volatility rises, the putback will profit where the bull spread would have shown a loss.

Where Ratio Back Spreads Fit in the Strategy Matrix

Callbacks and putbacks are somewhat difficult to categorise. Are they volatility trades or directional trades? The correct answer is that they are both. They are initially neutral to the underlying market but can become a buying or selling position depending on how dramatically the market moves. They are net buyers of volatility because you are buying more options than you are selling, so they are definitely bullish on volatility. We might be inclined to put them into our trading strategy matrix in the neutral volatility category, but we should instead review when a trader might use these trades rather than the long straddle or strangle. Traders would use a callback, for instance, if their view was that the market would rise, and they would also wish to be a buyer of volatility but not want to pay as much premium as would be required for an outright call option. Because the callback spread precisely meets this view, it would make more sense to place the callback into the strategy cell which is long on the market and long on volatility.

So, if the reader refers to our updated strategy matrix at the end of the chapter (Figure 5.18), he will see that I have placed the callback spread in this cell. The putback spread by a similar argument would be classified as a bearish directional view with a long volatility bias. So, we will put it into the same cell as the long put option. Thus, if traders have a bullish volatility bias and can form some sort of directional view, the callback can substitute for the purchase of a call option and the putback can substitute for a long put option.

This ability to evolve one type of strategy into another by adding an option or two is one reason why option markets provide such tremendous flexibility to the investment strategist. The addition of one simple trade can change the whole character of an existing strategy to meet a trader's revised views on both the underlying market and volatility. With these two trades I will conclude volatility buying strategies.

THE 'PURE' SELLING VOLATILITY STRATEGIES

Probably the most common uses for options in volatility trading are strategies which benefit from quiet times, strategies for static markets. Many option trading professionals make money from selling option premiums. Since options are securitised risk, some people think of them in a similar light to a casino. This is not strictly correct. Risk in an underlying market existed prior to the introduction of options. On the other hand, casinos create risk that did not previously exist in order to provide a vehicle for gambling. Nevertheless, the logic is similar when considering the selling of options. In casinos, the consistent winners over time are the gambling houses which sell the bets. In options, this can also be the case. Option sellers will win over time if they have the 'edge'. The edge is an important consideration in option trading and merits a slight digression at this point.

The 'edge' is the difference between theoretical option values and actual option prices. For example, consider the following gamble. Someone throws a die. What you will receive from the gamble is one dollar times whatever is on the top face of the die when it comes to rest. If it lands with one dot up you will receive one dollar and if it lands with six dots up you get six dollars. What is the theoretical value of the gamble? To determine this, we multiply the possible payoffs by each payoff's probability of occurrence and then add these together. So, in this case:

$$(\$1 \times \tfrac{1}{6}) + (\$2 \times \tfrac{1}{6}) + (\$3 \times \tfrac{1}{6}) + (\$4 \times \tfrac{1}{6}) + (\$5 \times \tfrac{1}{6}) + (\$6 \times \tfrac{1}{6}) = \$3.5$$

The theoretical price is \$3.5 but the house may wish to sell the gamble for \$4. This would mean the casino had an 'edge' of 50¢ on each throw. Thus, over time the difference between the amount the casino receives in bets and the amount it has to pay out will average to a profit of 50¢ . Of course, if the buyer of the gamble were able to buy it for \$3 then he would have the edge of 50¢ and this would be the amount he would expect to make on average if he repeated the gamble an infinite number of times.

In option dealing the same principle applies. The option seller sells options at prices higher than their theoretical value and option buyers do the reverse. In volatility selling strategies, trades are established to maximise the edge.

The volatility selling trades I am going to talk about in this section will include straddles, strangles, butterflies, and condors. Options sellers benefit from selling a volatility level which is currently higher than they believe it should be. When sellers do this, they are taking the edge.

Selling the Straddle

To understand selling volatility, the reader should follow the same steps we took for the buying volatility strategies. Consider the individual who sells a call option. He will have a short position relative to the underlying market. If he also sells a put option, this is a long position relative to the underlying market. So, if he combines these two trades, he will have a position that is neutral to the underlying market. The purest of the selling volatility trades is the straddle and one simply does the exact opposite of those trades which make up the long straddle. With the short straddle, I sell a call option and I sell a put option both on the same underlying position and maturity and with the same strike price, generally both at-the-money. Why sell at-the-money options? The simple reason is that the greatest time value for an option is when that option is at-the-money. Furthermore, the time value is the insurance component of the option premium and this is the amount the option writer expects to earn.

Option sellers make money in the same way as insurance companies; by selling premiums. Insurance companies receive a premium by assuming a risk for the policy holder. Such companies generally make a lot of money by collecting premiums and investing the proceeds. However, they can only sell their insurance against one side of the market. For example, they can sell insurance to pay if you die, or to protect against your house burning down. The insurance companies cannot sell an insurance policy against your not dying or against your house not burning down. But with options, you can sell somebody the right to sell, and sell somebody the right to buy; by definition, these two trades will offset each other to some degree. Option sellers therefore have an advantage when compared with insurance underwriters who can only sell insurance policies on one side of the market. Consider for a moment the short straddle. By selling both a call and put option at the same strike price, at least one of these options has to expire worthless, and potentially both could expire worthless.

Let us look at an example. Suppose you sell a $5.75 call option on Soyabean futures. The most you can make is the premium received and you have an unlimited loss potential. A short call is an equivalent short position that makes money when the market goes down and loses money when the market goes up. In addition, suppose you also sell a $5.75 put option. Again, the most you can make is the premium you received when the market rises, and you have an unlimited loss potential when the market falls. What will these options look like in combination? If we apply our graphing rules, it will look like the opposite of the long straddle. To the right of $5.75, one has a limited gain on the put and an unlimited loss potential on the call. To the left of $5.75, one has a limited gain on the call and an unlimited loss potential for the put. What is the graphing rule when you have an unlimited loss and a limited profit together? Unlimited is going to dominate the limited, so the short straddle will have an unlimited loss potential on both sides. However, you are going to make a substantial amount of money if the market finishes right at $5.75, the strike price for the options. The profit/loss profile for the short straddle can be seen in Figure 5.7.

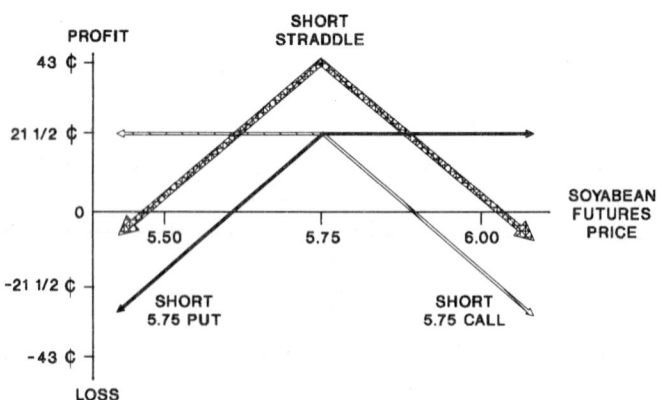

Figure 5.7 Selling a Straddle

This ability to profit from market prices staying in a range is unique to options trading. How many people have heard a dealer say 'I don't know where the market's going but, I tell you what, I guarantee that it'll be between $5.50 and $6.00 per bushel over the next month.' How can someone make money from this view? With the short straddle, you can profit if the market stays within a given range. It is a very effective strategy for making money in stable markets. It is like roulette: someone bets on the reds and someone bets on the blacks. At least one of them will lose and the house will profit from that fact.

So, you receive premiums from both buyers. If both options are priced at 21½¢ per bushel, you will receive a total of 43¢ inflow, and are going to make money anywhere in the range from $5.32 to $6.18 (plus or minus 43¢ from $5.75). Your maximum profit will be 43¢ if the market finishes at $5.75. The best thing about selling straddles is that one earns so much from time decay. As Figure 5.8 indicates, time decay accelerates, with the greatest gain occurring over the last 30 days. Volatility sellers often try to sell straddles during this time period of heaviest time decay. Prior to this time, for example 60 days, the time decay is much less and – given the risk the straddle seller must assume – it is often not worth considering.

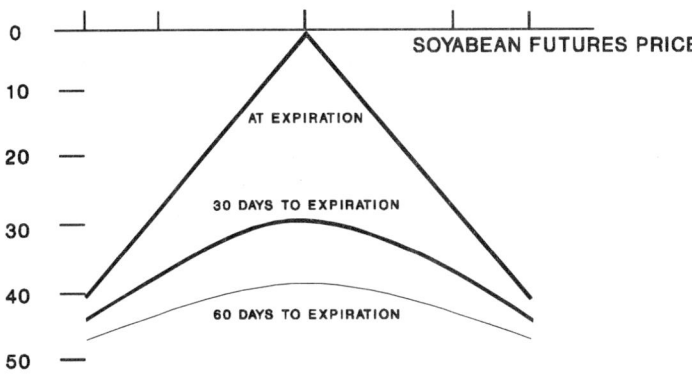

Figure 5.8 Value of Short Straddle at Different Points in Time

Selling the Strangle

Another way to sell volatility, which I personally prefer to selling the straddle, is to sell a strangle. Straddles are problematic because they are only delta neutral at one point. If I am trying to maintain a delta neutral position with the straddle, when the market starts moving around I have constantly to readjust my position to remain hedged. This gamma risk has proved to be the number one cause of grey hair in options dealers. Many dealers prefer a position which may not make as much money but is easier to manage; that is, positions which remain delta neutral over a wider range and do not require the same degree of revision. The strangle provides these kind of benefits. My maximum profit is spread over a much wider range.

A short strangle is easy to understand if you recall the long strangle and remember you are doing exactly the opposite transaction. You sell the out-of-the-money call which is a short position and you sell an out-of-the-money put which is a long position. You establish this trade on the same underlying, the same maturity, and at strike prices which are out-of-the-money options, equidistant from the prevailing underlying market price. Suppose the underlying market is trading at $5.75; the first thing I will do is sell the $6.00 call. I receive 11¢ for it. Next, I sell a put option against it to balance the exposure to the underlying position. I will sell the put option at $5.50 and receive 11¢ per bushel for it. Because these options are equally distant from the current futures price, they will have roughly the same premium and the same delta. The total premium received is 22¢ .

How will the combined short position look? Using our graphing rules we would say to the left of $5.50, the $6.00 call has a limited gain potential and the $5.50 put has an unlimited loss potential. So, the unlimited loss potential will dominate. Between $5.50 and $6.00, we have a limited gain on both the options, so they add up for a limited gain. Above $6.00, the $5.50 put has a limited gain and the $6.00 call has an unlimited loss potential. In combination, the short strangle has an unlimited loss potential. As the reader can see in Figure 5.9, the strangle seller will earn his maximum profit of 22¢ if the market finishes anywhere between $5.50 and $6.00. Suppose the market ends up at $5.75. In these circumstances both the $5.50 put and the $6.00 call expire worthless and the strangle seller retains the entire premium inflow. In fact, they will expire worthless anywhere over the range. So, between the strike price levels, he will have a flat return. Above $6.00, he will have an unlimited loss potential and below $5.50 another unlimited loss potential.

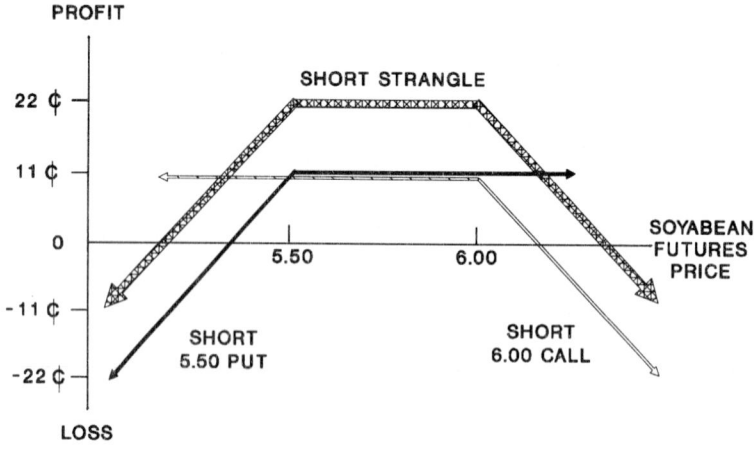

Figure 5.9 Selling a Strangle

Generally, when you are trying to sell volatility, one of the most important considerations is to remain delta neutral. A major problem with deltas is that they change. Back in the chapter on advanced option pricing I discussed this and introduced the concept of the gamma which measures how much the delta changes. For both the straddle and the strangle, the initial slope of the position is zero, which implies that the delta is also zero. But at expiration, the straddle can only be delta neutral if the market finishes right at $5.75. The strangle, on the other hand, has a slope of zero anywhere from $5.50 to $6.00. So, the strangle is both delta neutral and gamma neutral. With strangles, because they are more gamma neutral than straddles, you do not have to revise the position continually to remain delta neutral. However, if the underlying market moves up or down close to your strike prices, things may start getting a little bit painful.

Let us go back to our strangle example. You have sold both options and received 11¢ for the $5.50 put and 11¢ for the $6.00 call. You will retain the 22¢ per bushel of premium everywhere between $5.50 and $6.00. Your upper breakeven level is equal to the upper strike price plus the premium you received or $6.22, and your lower breakeven is equal to the lower strike price minus the premium you received or $5.28. The most you can make is 22¢ the premium you received. As with the straddle, the strangle benefits from time decay but an interesting feature of the strangle is that the rate of time decay in the period from 60 days to 30 days is greater than for the straddle. The time decay characteristics of the strangle can be seen in Figure 5.10. While the amount you earn will be less, the rate of decay for out-of-the-money options is greater

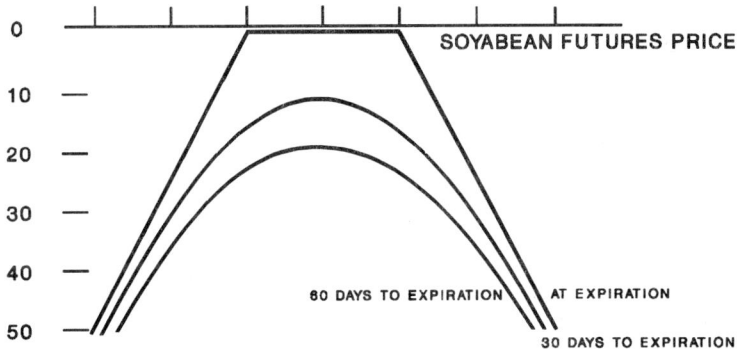

Figure 5.10 Value of a Short Strangle at Different Points in Time

than the rate of decay for at-the-money options. Quite often in a systematic volatility selling programme, one will first sell strangles at about 60 days until expiration and then, with 30 days to go, buy back the strangles and sell straddles to get the maximum benefit from time decay over both periods. In essence, one will choose which strategy to sell by seeing which has the greatest relative benefit of time decay for that particular period.

The good thing about selling straddles and strangles is that you make money from volatility decreasing and from time decay. If both occur you will have a double benefit. Time decay can become so important – especially as you approach expiration – that it can 'save' your position even if volatility increases. The time decay is so rapid that the increased volatility may not have a chance to be realised by an actual movement in the underlying asset. Often, by the time the market has moved the options have expired.

The major problem with both of these trades is the unlimited loss potential. There has been a large group of individual option traders who made quite a good living for many years by selling option volatility via straddles and strangles. Like a gambling house, they won almost all the time. But the probabilities are against them winning all the time. I have personally known people who have made money on almost every expiration for five years by selling straddles and strangles. Then, during one expiration, the unexpected happened and they lost all the money they had made for the previous five years. Remember, there was once a man who broke the bank at Monte Carlo and had a song dedicated to his feat (he later went on to lose it all)! Therefore, if one assumes an unlimited risk potential for a long enough period, eventually one will realise that loss.

Many conservative and low capitalised traders may still wish to sell volatility, but can only do so if they can limit their loss potentials. How is this achieved? The answer can be found with our graphing rules. The only way to cancel an unlimited loss potential is with an unlimited profit potential. I am now going to show you two more kinds of volatility selling strategies – called butterflies and condors – which allow you to limit your loss potential when selling volatility by applying this rule.

Buying a Butterfly Spread

With a butterfly, what you are doing is selling at-the-money options which have the highest time value, and buying out-of-the-money options as disaster insurance. Thus, you are selling the options with the greatest amount of time value and buying options with very low time value to eliminate the unlimited loss potentials on both the upside and the downside.

To construct the butterfly, you will combine strategies already discussed. You start off with a short straddle. This is created by selling the $5.75 call option and put option on Soyabean futures. Figure 5.11 displays what this looks like. Suppose you are unable to accept the unlimited loss potentials on the downside and upside. The only way to cancel an unlimited loss potential is with an unlimited profit potential. Therefore, you will buy options both on the downside and the upside to provide yourself with protection against the unlimited loss potential. Suppose you buy a $5.50 put and a $6.00 call. To the left of $5.50, the $5.75 put you sold has an unlimited loss potential and the $5.50 put you purchased has an unlimited profit potential. If we use our graphing rules, we can see that these two will cancel, yielding a limited loss potential for the combined trade. Between $5.50 and $5.75, the $5.50 put has a limited loss and the $5.75 put has an unlimited profit, so the unlimited will beat the limited and the combined trade over this range will profit up to $5.75. Between $5.75 and $6.00, the $5.75 call has an unlimited profit potential while the $6.00 call you purchased will expire worthless with a limited loss. Again, the unlimited will dominate the limited, so the combination has an unlimited profit potential over this range. Finally, above the

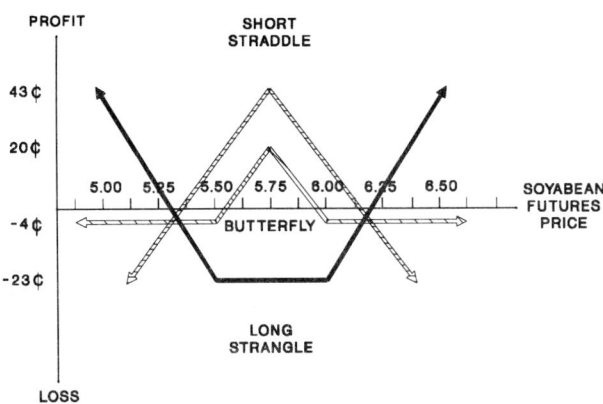

Figure 5.11 A Butterfly Spread

$6.00 strike price, the $6.00 call has an unlimited profit potential and the $5.75 call you sold has an unlimited loss potential; both puts will expire worthless. So, the unlimited profit potential and the unlimited loss potential cancel each other.

In summary, the butterfly strategy has a limited loss to the left of $5.50, a northeastern sloping unlimited profit potential to $5.75, a northwestern sloping unlimited profit potential from $5.75 to $6.00, and a limited loss potential to the right of $6.00.

A butterfly is a short volatility strategy that makes money from both volatility decreasing and from time decay. In this case, the most you can lose is determined at the initiation of the strategy, thus giving it a limited loss potential. Butterflies are superb trades for under-capitalised traders who wish to sell volatility but cannot accept the unlimited loss potential associated with straddles and strangles. The profit potential has been reduced because the disaster insurance options had to be purchased, but if the market does move dramatically, these small traders will suffer a limited loss instead of being wiped out. Consider October 1987, the great stock market crash. The people who did not come back after the crash were those who sold straddles. They had risked the unlimited loss potential for the chance of a little extra profit. Many of those who survived were individuals who remained disciplined and continued to establish strategies with limited loss potentials like the butterfly trade. Whenever you have small dealers or speculators selling strangles or straddles, they are courting big trouble. I have seen the proverbial 'market wise' dentists lose everything by establishing positions with unlimited loss potentials. Straddles and strangles should only be undertaken by market professionals who can withstand the possible loss potentials.

Butterfly spreads are also brilliant from a time decay standpoint, especially in the last 30 days. They decay at an extraordinarily rapid pace over this period, so are ideal trades by which to reap the rewards of heavy time decay without having to assume an unreasonable amount of risk. Figure 5.12 displays the time decay characteristics of the butterfly. I would strongly recommend people to trade butterflies when they first start selling volatility, until they become more comfortable with the risks of an unlimited loss potential strategy.

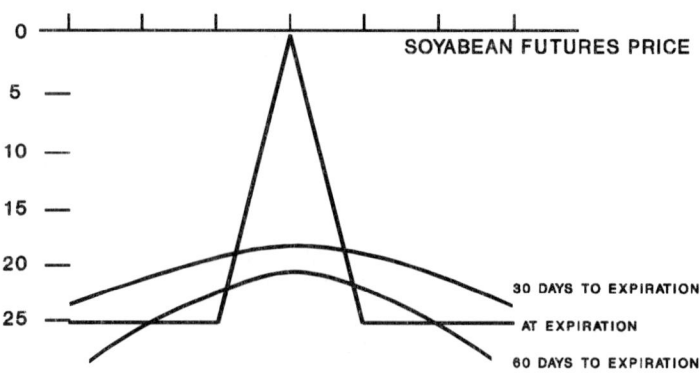

Figure 5.12 Value of a Butterfly at Different Points in Time

Buying a Condor Spread

The last pure volatility selling trade I am going to discuss in the following paragraphs is a variation on the same theme. This trade is called the condor. With a condor, you are selling options near the prevailing underlying price and buying options further out-of-the-money to protect yourself, similarly to the butterfly. The difference is that you are selling the first out-of-the-money put option and the first out-of-the money call option rather than the at-the-money options. As with the butterfly, to protect against the unlimited loss potentials, you are buying a deeper out-of-the-money put and a deeper out-of-the-money call. If you balance it correctly with the same underlying position and maturity, the positions should be approximately delta neutral.

To show how the condor is constructed I will once again use trades previously discussed. Suppose you start with a $5.50/$6.00 short strangle. This means you sell the $5.50 put and the $6.00 call with the market trading at $5.75. Then, to offset the

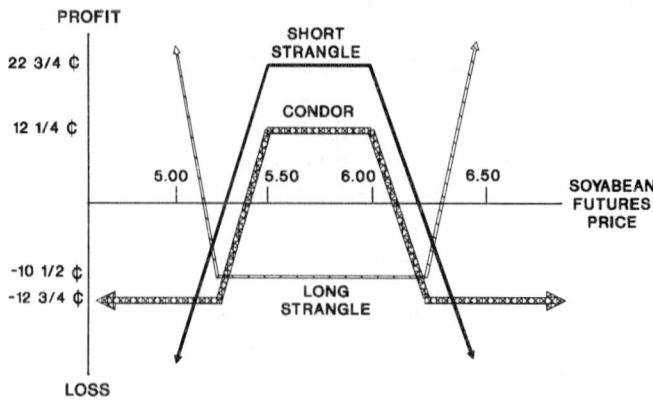

Figure 5.13 A Condor Spread

unlimited loss potentials, you purchase options which provide unlimited profit potentials. So, you are buying deeper out-of-the-money options at strikes of $5.25 (put) and $6.25 (call). That is, you are buying the further out-of-the-money strangle. Figure 5.13 displays the buildup profit/loss graph for this combination trade. Below $5.25, you have an unlimited profit potential on the $5.25 put and an unlimited loss potential on the $5.50 put and, because unlimited profits and losses cancel, the combination will have a limited loss potential. Between $5.25 and $5.50, the $5.50 put has an unlimited profit potential and the $5.25 put has limited loss; so, the unlimited profit dominates here. Between $5.50 and $6.00, all the options expire worthless, providing a limited gain overall. Between $6.00 and $6.25, the $6.00 call has an unlimited profit potential and the $6.25 call has a limited loss potential, so the unlimited dominates the limited. Finally, above $6.25, the $6.25 call has an unlimited profit potential and the $5.75 call has an unlimited loss potential; they will offset, leaving the condor with a limited loss potential.

Condors are one of my favourite short volatility trades because they are both delta neutral and extremely gamma neutral with a limited loss on both sides. The problem with condors is that you rarely make any money with these trades since the out-of-the-money options you are selling rarely bring in much premium. Compounding this problem is the fact that very elaborate condors can become what are known as 'crocodile' spreads. These are trades with so many parts that the brokers take their many pieces of flesh in the form of bid/offer spreads, the net effect being as if the condor had been eaten piecemeal by a crocodile.

Condors are often evolved over time and are not established at the same moment. Unfortunately, this involves the risks of legging, as discussed before. Legging in this context, though, is different from the legging techniques previously examined. This trading technique is not based on greed but rather on a disciplined approach to risk reduction. Condors are usually established either by market makers (who do not have to give up the bid/offer spreads when establishing the positions), or by traders who build the position over time (establishing each component at levels which will produce a reasonable profit).

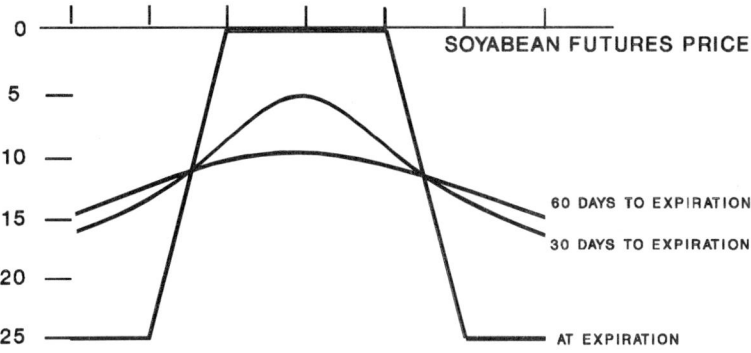

Figure 5.14 Value of a Condor at Different Points in Time

The way condors are generally evolved begins with a strangle being sold. Suppose you sell a strangle at 60 days prior to expiration, it works fairly well, and at 30 days to expiration you decide – instead of taking off the strangle – to limit your losses by buying the further out-of-the-money options (which should at this point be very inexpensive). For the last 30 days you are going to get extremely rapid time decay on any remaining time value in the options, all with a limited loss. The time decay characteristics of the condor can be seen in Figure 5.14. So, unless you are a market maker, setting up a condor is essentially an evolutionary process. Thus, condors are as much an example of a disciplined trading routine as they are of a trading strategy. One should always take the opportunity to limit one's loss potentials whenever possible. Only when your loss potentials are limited can one go to sleep at night knowing that the morning will not bring dreadful positions with dreadful losses.

Comparison of the Pure Volatility Selling Strategies

At this point, I will compare the profit and loss profiles of all four strategies I have discussed. The reader can see these displayed in Figure 5.15. The straddle offers the maximum return from selling premium with the profit peaking at the strike price of both options, in this case $5.75. The straddle has an unlimited loss potential on both sides. Our strangle provides a flat maximum return between $5.50 and $6.00 but also has an unlimited loss potential on both sides. The $5.50/$5.75/$6.00 butterfly provides a peaked return like the straddle, however the maximum profit is reduced owing to the purchase of the out-of-the-money options which are required to limit the loss potential. So the butterfly is essentially an evolution of the straddle. The condor is in the same way an evolution of the strangle. The condor has a flat pattern of maximum returns with limited risks on both sides, and it makes the smallest maximum profit. Obviously, if you are trying to earn the highest possible profit you sell a straddle, but the market must finish exactly at your strike price. Strangles are the second best money maker and will make their money over a very wide range. Unfortunately, they also

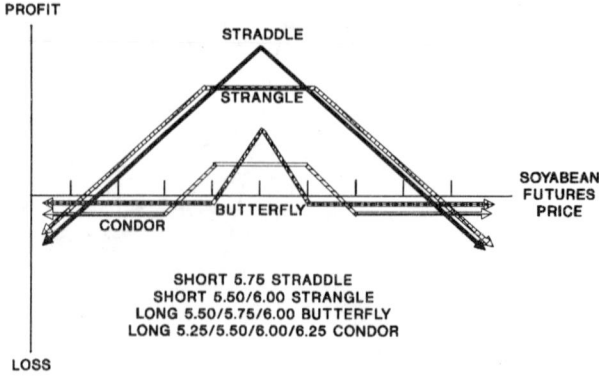

Figure 5.15 Graphical Comparison

have an unlimited loss potential on both sides. The butterfly has the next highest profit potential but again you have to have the market finish exactly at the middle strike price. If you are wrong, the butterfly's potential is a small price to pay for cutting off the unlimited loss potentials. Finally, the lowest money maker is the condor, which gives you a wide range for the maximum profit and a limited loss.

For a disciplined, systematic volatility selling programme, the sequence might proceed as follows. Start off by selling a strangle 60 days to expiration. At 30 days either turn it into a condor or sell the butterfly for the last 30 days. If you really have courage, over this last 30 days you could also sell the straddle.

Where Pure Volatility Selling Strategies Fit into the Strategy Matrix

These positions are all initiated as delta neutral positions. That is, you do not know whether the market is going to go up or down. You would prefer that over the period it goes nowhere, if possible. Because you are selling premium, you have a position which will also benefit as volatility decreases. So, we can go back to our trading matrix in Table 5.2. Since these trades are neutral to the market and sellers of volatility, we will put them into the middle right cell of the strategy matrix. For all these trades, time decay works in your favour and so does a decrease in volatility.

The choice of which of these strategies to use depends on whether you can accept a limited or an unlimited loss potential. These trades are pure volatility trades because they are neutral to the underlying market when they are established and will get hurt equally if the market goes up or down. They are not leaning in any way, shape or form: they are essentially neutral. With these trades you are simply trying to benefit from a decrease in volatility.

LEANING VOLATILITY SELLING STRATEGIES: THE RATIO SPREADS

Volatility trades called 'leaning volatility trades' have a bias or preference for which direction the market may move. The most common of these are known as put ratio spreads and call ratio spreads.

The Put Ratio Spread

A put ratio spread is the exact opposite to the putback spread I discussed previously. The putback spread is created when you buy two or more puts and sell one at a lower strike price. As the reader will recall, the putback is initially delta neutral but long volatility since you are buying more options than you are selling. With the put ratio spread, you will sell more options than you are buying. If the exact opposite of the putback spread is done, then you will sell two or more put options and buy one put. As with the putback spread, there is a preference for where the market will go. With the putback (which is the opposite of this strategy), the trader has an unlimited profit

117

potential on one side and a limited profit or bias on the other. The putback buyer loses most if the market finishes in the middle. Since the put ratio spread is on the opposite side, he will have exactly the opposite profit/loss payoff. So, he will have a limited profit or loss on one side and an unlimited loss potential on the opposite side, and the maximum profit if the market finishes in the middle. Because you are selling more options than you are buying, the put ratio spread is a position that will benefit if volatility decreases. To demonstrate why the position has limited loss if the market goes up and an unlimited loss potential if the market goes down, we will once again combine option strategies (and the premiums) and use our graphing rules to determine the profit/loss profile of the combined position.

Let us go back to our previous example with the put ratio spread. If you are selling this spread, you are selling two of the $5.50 put options and buying one of the $6.00 puts. Again, you will split the two puts you have sold into two sets of one each. When you combine a short $5.50 put option with a long $6.00 put, this position is a vertical spread. When you buy the higher strike option this means that the spread is a bear spread. As the reader will recall, a bear spread is a bearish position relative to the underlying Soyabean futures market and neutral to volatility. Then, you sell another put option at the strike price of $5.50. What are the views when you sell a put? Short put positions are bullish on the underlying Soyabean futures market and sellers of volatility. So in combination with the bear spread, you will have a position which is neutral to the underlying position and bearish on volatility. This trade is used when your view is that volatility is going down and the market is going to be stable. Why is this trade a leaning trade? Because while it is initially delta neutral, the payoffs of the strategy at expiration are not symmetrical. On one side is a limited loss and on the other an unlimited loss potential. So the put ratio spreader would prefer that the market move one way rather than the other. The best thing would be for the market to remain stable. But if things go wrong, the put ratio spreader is not indifferent to where the market goes. He wants the market to rise rather than fall. This is best seen in the payoff diagram of the put ratio spread at expiration (see Figure 5.16).

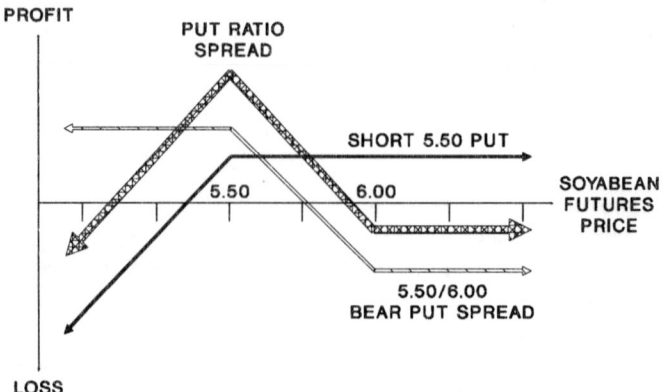

Figure 5.16 Put Ratio Spread

In Figure 5.16, the bear put spread is displayed with the additional short put. To the left of the lower strike price, $5.50, the bear put spread has a limited profit potential and the short put has an unlimited loss potential. The rule is: when we combine an unlimited loss with a limited gain, the unlimited loss will dominate. Therefore, the combination has an unlimited loss potential below $5.50.

Between the $5.50 and the $6.00 strike prices, the bear put spread profits one for one with the decrease in the underlying market. The northwestern slope is an unlimited profit potential for this range. The $5.50 put(s) will expire worthless over this range with a limited profit potential equal to the premium received. When one combines the unlimited profit on the bear spread with the limited profit on the short put, the overall slope for the put ratio spread will still slope to the northwest and we will call that 'unlimited'. Above $6.00, both the bear put spread and the $5.50 short put position have limited potentials. In our example, the bear put spread has a limited loss and the short puts provide a limited profit. So these will offset. If the put premium received was greater than the cost of the bear put spread, then this combination will have a limited profit. However, in this example the premium received was less than the cost of the bear put spread; thus, the combined strategy has a limited loss over this range.

Overall, the put ratio spread has an unlimited loss potential to the downside, makes the greatest profit if the market is stable, and has a limited loss on the upside. Because we are selling more options than we are buying, we make money from volatility going down. If we are wrong and the market fails to remain stable, we hope that if it moves, it moves to the upside where we have a limited loss potential. This trade is 'leaning' because we do care where the market goes; we want it to go up if it moves at all. Therefore, the put ratio spread, while initially neutral to the underlying market, is leaning to the upside. The ideal situation for the put ratio spread is for time decay and a decrease in volatility to accompany underlying market stability.

The Call Ratio Spread

The other leaning volatility selling strategy is the call ratio spread, which is the opposite of the callback spread. What you do here is to sell two or more higher strike price calls and buy one lower strike price call, and balance the number of options to be delta neutral. Like the put ratio spread, you achieve a volatility selling strategy which is initially delta neutral but has a preference for market movement. In this case, the call ratio spread has a limited loss potential to the downside and an unlimited loss potential on the upside.

To be able to see these characteristics, I will display how the call ratio spread is created graphically in Figure 5.17. Again, we create the spread by selling two call options and buying one. As with the put ratio spread, we separate the two short calls into two sets of one and combine one with the long call. By buying the lower strike price call and selling a higher strike price call, this will give us a bull call spread. The bull call spread has a bullish bias on the underlying market and is neutral to volatility. Then, we sell an additional call option at the higher strike price. When we sell a call,

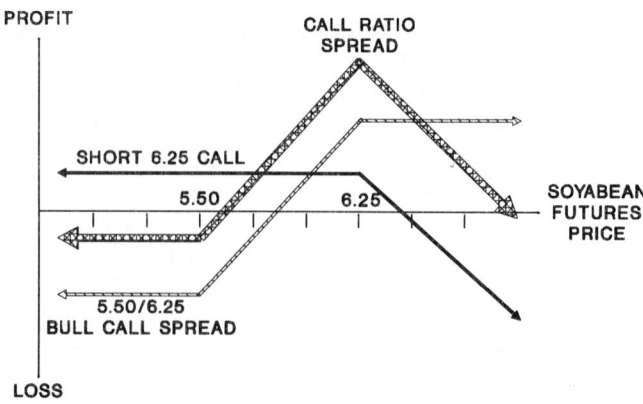

Figure 5.17 Call Ratio Spread

the view is bearish on the market and also bearish on volatility. Therefore, in combination with the bull call spread, the call ratio is now neutral to the market but bearish on volatility.

Establishing call and put ratio spreads is very often an evolution of more simple strategies. For example, say I put on a bull spread, the market has gone up, and I have made my profit objective. Now my view changes: I wish to benefit from the market retracing to the downside, and from volatility decreasing. If I sell the higher strike price call option, I will achieve both objectives and turn the bull spread into a call ratio spread.

In Figure 5.17, one can see how this occurs. To the left of the $5.50 strike price, the $5.50/$6.25 bull call spread will expire worthless with a loss limited to the premium paid for the spread. The $6.25 call option I sold also expires worthless, meaning that I earn the premium which is a limited profit. In combination, the limited loss and limited profit offset and, in this case, provide a limited loss.

Between $5.50 and $6.25, the bull call spread profit/loss profile is moving at a northeastern slope which we call an unlimited profit potential. The extra $6.25 call also expires worthless over this range and in combination the unlimited profit dominates the limited profit. So, the call ratio spread also moves in the northeastern direction, indicating an 'unlimited' profit potential over this range.

Finally, to the right of $6.25, the bull call spread has a flat or limited profit and the extra $6.25 call has an unlimited loss potential. In our graphing rules, the combination of an unlimited loss potential with a limited profit potential means that the unlimited will dominate. So, the call ratio spread has an unlimited loss potential to the upside and on the downside I will have a limited loss potential.

Since the call ratio spread also benefits from time decay, I have yet another positive element which should help the trade turn a profit. The optimal event would be for the market to remain at the current level and time decay to earn the profit. This is the perfect way to get the remaining profit out of a bull spread in the last 30 days prior to expiration when time decay is at its greatest.

However, there is no law requiring one to keep the unlimited loss potential for this trade indefinitely. Often, traders will turn a bull spread into a call ratio spread and then, if the market falls a little, buy another call at an even higher strike price, above the higher strike previously purchased. By adding this long call, which has cancelled the unlimited loss potential on the upside, and in combination, the trade has now been made a butterfly. If the trader is disciplined, he might be able to create a butterfly which has no loss potential and therefore no risk. But this once again requires legging the spread over time and can be extremely risky until all the trades are in place. Once the trades are placed, though, the combination can potentially be risk-free.

Where Ratio Spreads Fit into the Strategy Matrix

Ratio spreads are initially neutral to the underlying market but the extra short call or put positions can turn the ratio spread into either a buying or a selling position. They lean one way or the other, with a preference for where the market might go. With ratio spreads, you believe that if the market does move it will move to one side rather than to the other. With this view, you cut off the unlimited loss potential on that one side. The reason why professional traders use this trade frequently is because it is often possible to build up strategies like condors or butterflies for a more reasonable risk/reward tradeoff by starting with simple trades and adding more positions at opportune points. Traders use ratio spreads because with these trades they are not giving up all the theoretical edge initially (and the bid/offer spreads). They are assuming the risk that if they are wrong it will be on one side. Of course, this entails the assumption of risk. But professional option dealers make their money from assuming intelligent risks and covering them quickly if they are wrong. Ratio spreads are ideal trades for this kind of trading philosophy.

In conclusion, for the reasons outlined above, call ratio spreads start out initially neutral to the underlying market but have a directional bias to the downside rather than to the upside. Therefore, we will assign these trades a bearish bias on the underlying and, because we are selling more options than we are buying, also assign the call ratio

VIEWPOINT ON THE SOYABEAN MARKET

		BUYER	SELLER	NEUTRAL
VIEWPOINT ON VOLATILITY	BUYER	BUY CALL OPTION CALL BACK SPREAD	BUY PUT OPTION PUT BACK SPREAD	BUY STRADDLE BUY STRANGLE
	SELLER	SELL PUT OPTION PUT RATIO SPREAD	SELL CALL OPTION CALL RATIO SPREAD	SELL STRADDLE SELL STRANGLE BUY BUTTERFLY BUY CONDOR
	NEUTRAL	LONG FUTURES BULL SPREAD	SHORT FUTURES BEAR SPREAD	

Table 5.2 Option Trading Strategy Matrix

spread as bearish on volatility. Thus in our strategy matrix (Table 5.2), we will place call ratio spreads in the middle cell of the table along with the short call option. By a similar argument, we will categorise the put ratio spread as an equivalent 'long' underlying position with a selling volatility bias. Therefore, it will be placed in the same cell of the strategy matrix as the short put. With this final entry, we have filled up eight of the nine cells in our matrix. The only cell that is left to fill is the lower right-hand cell when the trader has both a neutral viewpoint on the underlying market and on volatility. I will cover these trades in the next chapter.

As indicated at the beginning of Chapter 4, options trading allows the strategist a tremendous amount of flexibility in his choice of which strategies to use. Remember, in the typical market only three things can be done: buy, sell, or sit still. But with options, applying these three possible viewpoints on all the factors which determine an option's prices will allow the strategist an almost infinite number of trading strategies. In the strategy matrix, I have expanded the realms of the possible to 18 and haven't finished yet. There is in fact no limit to the possible trades that can be created using options.

THE DIFFERENCE BETWEEN TRADING FUTURES AND OPTIONS

The principal difference between option trading and trading an underlying futures or spot market is that when trading the underlying market it is like guerrilla warfare. You buy and sell quickly. In guerrilla warfare, you kill one guy at a time and sometimes he kills you. Option trading is more like a well thought out military strategy. You develop a campaign plan, deciding what you want to do and when to do it. Then you decide how best to achieve the objectives arising from your views and develop contingency plans for revising the strategy if things do not work out the way you planned. Once you have established the strategy, you sit back, leave it and let it work. These strategies will work as time decay, volatility movements, and the spreads change. Once the market has moved, you can do one simple transaction and evolve the strategy into something else. So the difference between guerrilla warfare and a long-term military strategy is rationale and discipline. Options dealing, especially with volatility strategies, allows you to use these virtues to their best effect.

[1]   However, since the rate of time decay for the strangle may actually be greater than the straddle for various periods prior to expiration, the quantity of money that will be lost is less.

6: Option Arbitrage

This chapter discusses option arbitrage, the last category of option trading strategies, where one has a neutral view on the underlying market and on volatility. In most markets, this would preclude any activity but with options, opportunities may still exist to profit. These opportunities include calendar spreads, 'delta neutral' trading, and put/call parity arbitrages like conversions, reversals, and box trades.

By way of examples, I will use the option on Eurodollar futures traded at the International Monetary Market of the Chicago Mercantile Exchange (IMM). The futures prices are actually an index level which is calculated by subtracting from 100.00 the expected annualised three-month London InterBank Offer Rate (LIBOR) for US dollar time deposits in London. So, if the expected three-month LIBOR is 6.5 per cent, then the Eurodollar futures price is equal to 93.50 (which is $100 - 6.5$). The underlying value of the contract is $1,000,000 in a hypothetical deposit and the minimum movement in the value of the futures contract is 0.01 points (or $\frac{1}{100}$ of an interest rate percentage point). This minimum movement – which is called a 'tick' – is worth $25 because $\frac{1}{100}$ of an interest rate percentage point for a $1,000,000 deposit with a three-month time horizon will equal this amount

$$(0.0001 \times \$1,000,000 \times 90 \ days / 360 \ days = \$25)$$

Table 6.1 outlines the contract specification for this option.

TRADING UNIT.	1 EURODOLLAR TIME DEPOSIT FUTURES CONTRACT
CONTRACT MONTHS	MARCH, JUNE, SEPTEMBER, DECEMBER
LAST TRADING DAY	2nd LONDON BUSINESS DAY BEFORE 3rd WEDNESDAY OF CONTRACT MONTH
MINIMUM PRICE MOVEMENT (TICK SIZE)	0.01 IMM INDEX POINT, EQUAL TO $25
EXERCISE PRICE INTERVALS	0.25 (E.G. 89.75, 90.00, 90.25)
TRADING HOURS	7:30 - 14:00 (NEW YORK TIME)
EXERCISE	ANY TRADING DAY. THE FUTURES POSITION IS EFFECTIVE ON THE TRADING DAY FOLLOWING EXERCISE, AND IS MARKED-TO-MARKET TO THE SETTLEMENT THAT DAY.

Table 6.1 Options on Eurodollar Futures (IMM)

The interesting factor about this contract is that it moves exactly inversely to the movement in interest rates. For example, if LIBOR rises then the Eurodollar futures price will fall (and vice versa). The options on Eurodollar futures allow the buyer or seller to deal in interest rate insurance. They can pay a premium to assure either borrowing insurance (a put on Eurodollar futures) or investment insurance (a call on Eurodollar futures). This highly successful contract has led to the development of similar futures and options contracts on deposits in Deutschmarks, Sterling, Yen, Lira, French Francs and a wide variety of other currencies. The simple index format has also proven to be a winner as the general format has been copied worldwide. The cash settlement feature of the Euro futures and options has made settlement easy and free from manipulation. Thus, the option on Eurodollar futures is ideal for explaining option arbitrage.

THE TYPES OF ARBITRAGE STRATEGIES

Arbitrage in the purest sense is buying and selling the same thing for a differential in price at the same moment. It has to be exactly the same thing; not a spread, not slightly different, not a 'relative value' trade. You buy gold and you sell gold; the same purity of gold from two different people at two different prices. This is arbitrage. In options, arbitrage includes trades which fit this definition and are referred to as pure arbitrage trades. Other option strategies fall under the category of arbitrage without having the risk-free element that arbitrage implies. These kinds of 'arbitrage' are either isolating for the time decay element in an option, or buying and selling mispriced volatility. The pure arbitrage strategies involve creating synthetic positions that are dealt against the actual positions to lock in any price discrepancies. In this chapter, I will examine all these kinds of trades, beginning with the less 'pure' strategies.

CALENDAR SPREADS

The first category of 'arbitrage' I will examine is the calendar spread, which is essentially a time decay strategy. Calendar spreads are similar to vertical spreads in that you buy a call option and sell a call option, or buy a put option and sell a put option. But this time, both options have the same strike price. How can this be? If you buy a call option and then sell the same strike call option then will you not have wiped out your position? This is true; it is a complete offset if you buy and sell the same option series. In a calendar spread, one will buy and sell options with the same strike price but for different maturities.

If I buy a call for December Eurodollar futures and then sell a call for September Eurodollar futures at the same strike price, then I have a position that is offsetting to some degree relative to the underlying Eurodollar time deposit market; but it is in a position that will benefit from various factors, not the least of which is time decay. If

I buy a long-dated option, over the period of its life the time value will initially decay slowly and then accelerate as it approaches expiration.

Suppose on 1 July 1991, the September Eurodollars futures is trading at 93.50 and the December Eurodollar futures is also trading at 93.50. I buy a 93.50 December call option. Over the time period from 1 July to 16 September (the expiration of the September Eurodollar option), the time decay for the December call option will be relatively slow, and then from 16 September to 16 December it will accelerate. Then, suppose on 1 July I also sell a September 93.50 call. For the time period between then until the September expiration (16 September), the time decay will be very rapid. At the expiration of the September contract, the September 93.50 call will have no time value at all, its value will only consist of its intrinsic value. In this case, if I buy options which have a very slow time decay and sell options with a rapid time decay over that same time period, I should be able to benefit simply from this time decay discrepancy. When one does this, it is called buying or going long the calendar or time spread.[1]

Let us now look at an example with numbers. On 1 July, the December 93.50 call I bought might be worth 44. If the Eurodollar futures market remains at the current level of 93.50 by 16 September 1991, the December call should then be worth about 32. The loss on this call from time decay would therefore be 12. If I sold the September 93.50 call for 30, and the market finishes at 93.50, the option will be worth nothing. So, by selling the September 93.50 call, I am essentially playing the time decay game; expecting stable markets to exist but purchasing the longer-dated December option to limit my loss potential. The time decay loss of 12 on the December call will be more than offset by the time decay profit of 30 on the September call yielding an overall profit of 18. Therefore, if I buy long-dated options before they experience rapid time decay and sell short-dated options during the period of their most rapid time decay, I can gain from the passage of time if markets remain static.

This sounds too good to be true. How can it be? Well, on 16 September, the December call option I bought will still have the two components of an options price: intrinsic value and time value. This means that the option price relative to the underlying Eurodollar futures market price will have a curved slope leading up to the

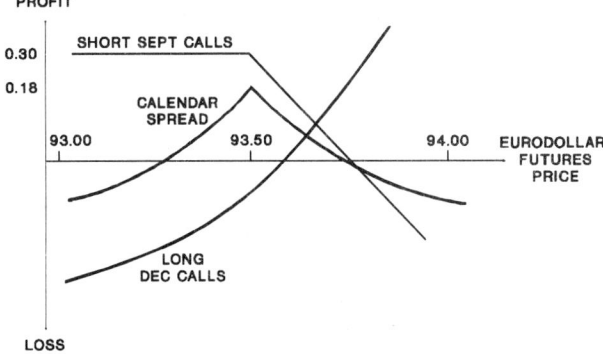

Figure 6.1 Calendar Spread on 16 September

northeast. If I sell a September call option against it, this call option will have no time value in September. Its price will be made up entirely of intrinsic value. Hence, its profit/loss profile will be the typical 'hockey stick' diagram for an option value at expiration. This can be seen in Figure 6.1.

On 16 September, both 93.50 call options values will contain intrinsic value, but the December call will additionally have time value. Thus, relative to the Eurodollar futures price, the unlimited intrinsic value profit potential on the December call should offset the unlimited intrinsic value loss potential on the September call. The combined position should flatten out. Figure 6.1 displays the profit and loss diagram for this trade.

As the reader can see, when you combine the two call options you will get a payoff that looks similar to a curved butterfly. It is curved with a limited loss on the downside and curved with a limited loss on the upside, and will make money if the market remains at the current level. The pure effect of time decay earns the profit. The reader may also notice that the profit/loss profile for this trade looks remarkably like the time value graph in the option pricing chapter (Figure 2.11b). This is because this trade is isolating for the time value of the December option. If the market finishes at 93.50 and both calls are at-the-money, then the total profit will be 30 – 12 or 18. This is the expected amount you make from this trade. The loss potential is 14, the premium outflow when you bought the spread (44 – 30). So, you are risking 14 to make 18, which is a risk/reward approximately risking seven to make nine in the best case.

The reader will note that this is not a pure arbitrage trade because the trade can experience losses. A true arbitrage involves no risk. The calendar spread is really a fairly low-risk trade that attempts to benefit from the different rate of time decay occurring for long-dated and short-dated options. By both buying and selling the same kind of options (calls or puts), the loss potential from the movement of the Eurodollar futures is limited and the volatility exposure is less than that of a single option purchase or sale.

A disadvantage of calendar spreads is that while initially your view on volatility might be neutral, you will become 'long' volatility as the short-dated option approaches expiration. The reason for this is that the December option will still have a positive volatility exposure when the September option expires with no volatility exposure at all. Therefore, your position will be exposed to the level of December volatility at the September expiration, at which point you will have to sell back the December option. If the market is stable and volatility has not fallen, then you should make the 18 from time decay. As calendar spreads benefit most from this time decay, most traders establish calendar spreads in the 30 days preceding the short-dated option's expiration, expecting stable markets and stability regarding volatility. Calendar spreads are a useful alternative to a butterfly since they provide an even greater benefit from time decay.

However, if volatility increases (decreases), the December option will be worth more (less) than the expected 32 and the profit from the trade will be more (less) than 18. Increases in volatility often occur when traders roll their long call option positions from the shorter maturity to the longer maturity to continue their directional view. As traders do this, the demand increases for the longer dated options and their prices increase. This higher demand – which means higher prices – will be reflected as a higher implied volatility in the longer-dated options. This can be a very good strategy to adopt near the point where people roll their buying positions, usually within the last 30 days before expiration. Calendar spreads, because they are composed of both buying and selling options, limit the loss to the net premium paid out. They also benefit from time decay and will profit from volatility either remaining stable or increasing.

Another potential problem for option calendar spreads is the intra-month spread relationship between the September and December futures. If you are going to establish calendar spreads with options, you must make a prediction on what will happen to the price relationship between the September and December underlying futures markets. For instance, if you buy a call in December and the December futures price increases, you make money from that fact. If September happens to fall at the same time, then the call option you sold will also profit. However, if the opposite occurs and the September contract rises as the December futures falls, the change in the intra-market spread will hurt this long call options calendar spread. Generally, this spread is determined by subtracting the price of the deferred futures contract (December) from the price of the nearby futures contract (September).

To take advantage of this change in the intra-month spreads, you can construct a calendar spread with either calls or puts depending on what you project will occur to the intra-month spread relationship. You buy longer maturity puts and sell shorter maturity puts when you expect that either the spreads will remain constant or will widen out (the nearby futures price minus the deferred futures price). To benefit from the spread falling, you could buy the deferred call and sell the nearby call. Call calendar spreads and put calendar spreads possess a similar profit/loss profile. But, the call calendar spread benefits more from a decrease in the intra-month spread and vice versa for the put calendar spread. Therefore, in the analysis of calendar spreads, the trader must have a view on the underlying Eurodollar futures market, volatility *and* the intra-market spreads. As always, time decay and the liquidity of the options markets must also be considered.

Another consideration when establishing calendar spreads is that the prices for the deferred and nearby futures may not be the same. Suppose that in our above example, the December and September futures prices were not at the same level; this would complicate the establishment of the calendar spread. The standard technique for implementing a calendar spread is to buy and sell at the same strike price. However, when the underlying Eurodollar futures prices are different, a better technique is to choose strike prices which are the same relative to each Eurodollar futures price. If I sold the at-the-money September call option, I would sell the 93.50 call because the September Eurodollar futures was trading at around that level for this period. But the 93.50 call strike price may not be the at-the-money call for the December underlying futures because the December futures might be trading at 93.00. Therefore, for the December option series, it makes more sense to buy the 93.00 call option which is the at-the-money option for that particular Eurodollar futures position. Likewise, if I sold the first out-of-the-money September call option, then I would go to the next contract month, December, and buy the first out-of-the-money call option. Often, and especially in the share market, calendar spreads are established at the same strike price. For options on Eurodollar futures, you should establish the calendar spreads not necessarily at the same strike price but at strike prices which have the same relationship to the prevailing Eurodollar futures market. Frequently, the December Eurodollar futures price will be different from the September Eurodollar futures price, so the strike prices to choose in the calendar spread should also be different.

DELTA NEUTRAL TRADING

The second category of options arbitrage that I will discuss is again not a 'pure' arbitrage but a technique for profiting from an incorrect estimation of the market's volatility. This category of volatility 'arbitrages' is known as delta neutral trading. When Black and Scholes and others developed their pricing models, a critical assumption they had to make was that equilibrium option prices could only exist if no arbitrage were possible. For example, if you could hold a position which provided an equivalent payoff to an option contract by borrowing money to buy the underlying asset, then the value of this equivalent portfolio should be equal to the price of the option. If this is not the case, someone can create a risk-free strategy by borrowing to buy the underlying asset and selling options against it or selling stock short, investing the proceeds in interest bearing securities and buying options.

One of the breakthroughs in the Black and Scholes research was the determination of the proper hedge ratio to use to create a risk-free strategy. This hedge ratio – later christened the delta – determined the proper amount of underlying positions needed to be 'equivalent' to an options position. While a number of their fundamental assumptions seem erroneous – such as that no transaction costs exist, and that markets move perfectly – Black and Scholes' formula is remarkably robust. Furthermore, it allows traders not only to identify divergences existing between options markets and the underlying Eurodollar futures markets, but also provides the tools (in the form of deltas) necessary to benefit from these discrepancies. Reliance on such pricing models is the essence of delta neutral trading.

As a review, option deltas are variable. Their value depends on whether the option is an equivalent long position or a short position, and what the relationship of the option strike price is to the Eurodollar futures market price. For equivalent short positions, deltas vary from minus one (for options which are deep in-the-money) to zero (for options which are deep out-of-the-money). For equivalent long positions, they can also vary between zero and positive one. At-the-money options always have deltas of 0.50/ –0.50. Deltas are the measures of relative risk to the underlying Eurodollar futures position which the volatility arbitrageur will use to hedge both underlying and options positions.

To create the hedge ratio from the delta, you simply divide the number of the Eurodollar futures positions you intend to trade by the delta. If a delta for a particular option is 0.67 and you intend to hedge using one of the Eurodollar futures position, you divide 1 by 0.67 and get 1.5. This indicates that for every one Eurodollar futures, you would require 1.5 of that particular strike price option to establish a risk-free position. Since one cannot trade half an options contract, you have to round up until both the number of Eurodollar futures trades and options are integers, assuming that the ratio stays the same. If we multiply this hedge ratio by two then we will get three; this means you would require three options for every two trades in the underlying market, i.e. a ratio of 1.5. If an option has a delta of 0.33, one underlying position divided by 0.33 gives a hedge ratio of three. This indicates that you must trade three options for every Eurodollar futures contract to create a hedged portfolio. Therefore, one technique to determine the hedge ratio is to divide one by the delta and find the nearest integer mix that is equal to that ratio.

Now that the review is over, let us look at a few practical examples of these theoretical concepts. Suppose I bought ten contracts of the Eurodollar futures, the delta position overall would be positive 10. To hedge the position, I would have to acquire offsetting negative deltas. Suppose I chose to use at-the-money call options. If I sold call options, they would provide me with offsetting negative deltas and the exposure of each option is equal to –0.50. So, how many calls must I sell? Ten underlying positions divided by 0.5 yields 20. Therefore, selling 20 at-the-money call options would result in a delta neutral position. When I sell the calls, the call buyer pays me a premium. So, with a volatility of 25 per cent, 90 days until expiration, and the current Eurodollar futures price at 93.50, each 93.50 call would result in an inflow of 32 basis points. The profit/loss profile for this strategy can be seen in Figure 6.2 at various points in time prior to the expiration of the options.

If this position is really a hedged position, then any losses or gains on the call option side will be the same amount I gain or lose on the futures side. If the price of the Eurodollar futures goes down to 93.40, then I will lose 10 points on my 10 long Eurodollar futures contracts for a total loss of 100 points. The option price will drop from 32 points when the market was at 93.50 to 27 points now that it is at 93.40. Thus,

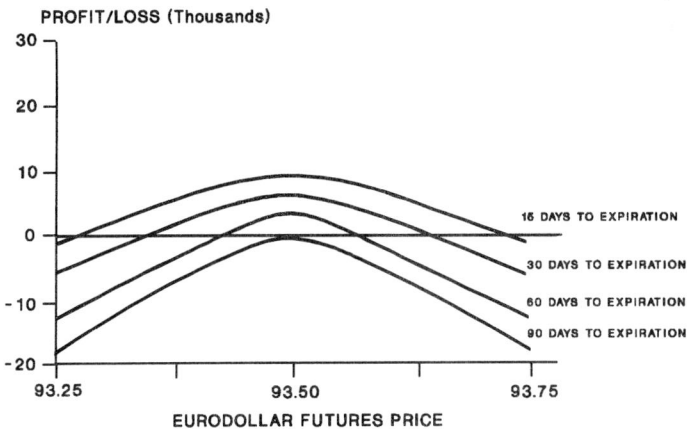

Figure 6.2 Delta Neutral Trading by Writing Calls

I have a gain of 5 points times 20 contracts yielding an overall profit of 100 on the options side. Since I have a loss of 100 on the Eurodollar futures and a gain of 100 on the options on Eurodollar futures, the total position is neutral to changes in the price of the underlying asset. As this example illustrates, for small changes in the price of the underlying market, a delta neutral position is indeed immunised.

The problem with deltas is that they change as the price of the underlying market changes. So, at the new price of 93.40, the 93.50 call options are no longer at-the-money but are now out-of-the-money. Thus, their delta has risen above –0.50. At the new price of 93.40, the short 93.50 call options now have a delta of –0.468. Therefore, we must determine the new hedge ratio to retain our risk-free position. The ten futures contracts divided by 0.468 will yield a hedge ratio of 21.37 options. Since we are unable to sell 0.37 of an option, we must round to the nearest integer which indicates that we will sell an additional call option at the new price of 27 basis points. This extra call option will bring us back approximately to delta neutral. In total, this will give us 21 short call options against the ten long futures.

But suppose the price of the Eurodollar futures market then rises to 93.65. What is now the effect on the rebalanced delta neutral position? You originally bought the ten futures contracts at 93.50. With the market at 93.65, you make 15 basis points on each of the ten contracts for a total profit of 150 basis points. You are short 21 options, one was sold at 27 basis points and 20 were sold at 32 basis points. At 93.65, the 93.50 call option is now worth 40 basis points; so the single call we sold for 27 basis points has a loss of 13 basis points, and the 20 we sold at 32 basis points will lose 8 points per option. In total, we lose 173 basis points on the short option position. This overall position now has a net loss of 23 basis points because the loss on the adjusted option position exceeds the profit on the underlying Eurodollar futures position.

Therefore, as one can see from this example, the problem with delta neutral trading is that when the Eurodollar futures price changes, the hedger must continually re-adjust his position to remain neutral. The delta neutral hedger had to sell an additional 93.50 call option when the underlying market fell to 93.40 and then as the market went back up he should have bought it back at 93.50. Furthermore, as the futures market continued to rise, additional calls should have been bought back at a loss to remain neutral.

In conclusion, the problem with delta neutral trading is that you will have mismatches whenever the market price changes unless you continually revise your hedged position. Thus, delta neutral hedging only works for very small price changes in the underlying position and requires continuous revision of the hedged position. However, if the Eurodollar futures market stays in a fairly tight range, delta hedging will work. If you continuously rebalanced the hedged portfolio, then and only then could you achieve a delta neutral hedge which is immune to movements in the underlying Eurodollar futures markets. Such continuous rebalancing is impractical. Therefore, if the Eurodollar futures market rallies up, you rebalance, and then the market proceeds to collapse, you are going to have losses instead of profits since the hedge will now be unbalanced. However, if you have strong instincts for where the market will eventually settle, you may decide to run these positions with the original hedge ratio. This strategy contains the implicit acceptance of an overall position which may become mismatched but might be neutral at expiration.

Given the problems in remaining delta neutral, why would anyone do this? One reason is that you expect the actual market volatility to be less than the volatility implied in the option's price. So you sell the implied volatility because you consider it to be overvalued, but remain hedged to overall movements in the underlying market price. You are 'arbitraging' volatility by gaining more from the drop in the volatility embedded in the options time value than you are giving up in the expected rebalancing costs to remain delta neutral. So this is not a true risk-free arbitrage but is rather a volatility trade with a risk that the actual volatility may increase more than the level of the implied volatility which has been sold.

Theoretically, this should work. However, the assumptions this strategy is based upon do not hold true in the real world. For example, the Black and Scholes pricing model and the delta hedge ratio assume continuous markets allowing instantaneous revisions to the number of underlying or options positions held, all with no transactions costs. The basic problem is that the deltas for these two kinds of assets (underlying markets and options) do not behave in the same way as the price of the underlying market changes. The underlying Eurodollar futures contract always has a delta of 100 per cent which does not change. Option deltas are more fluid and variable. Many delta neutral traders who combine the underlying Eurodollar futures market with options often find that it is like trying to hit a bowl of jelly with a hammer. As the fixed hammer hits, the jelly simply squirts away. Because of this, many 'volatility' arbitrageurs hedge their option positions with other options which also have fluid deltas. This often reduces the 'gamma' risk, which is the change in deltas. Unfortunately, a reduction of the expected profit from the 'volatility arbitrage' may occur because option premiums must often be paid to achieve this neutrality.

Delta neutral positions occur whenever the overall deltas of the equivalent long positions are equal to the overall deltas of the equivalent short positions. With a number of strike price series available, the possible combination of options and underlying assets which will be delta neutral is almost infinite. Since all delta neutral strategies have a net delta equal to zero, these strategies also have a slope in their profit/loss diagrams which for instantaneous changes in time will be near zero. When the position is initiated, the delta neutral position profits solely from either a change in volatility or from time decay. To remain absolutely neutral to the underlying market is critical, for only then can one isolate the volatility and time decay factors.

If we return to our delta neutral strategy of buying ten Eurodollar futures and selling 20 calls, we find that, at expiration, we make our maximum profit if the market ends up at the option strike price. This can be seen in Figure 6.3. In fact, the final profit/loss profile of this delta neutral spread resembles a short straddle. How can this be? We have sold 20 call options and bought ten of the underlying position, and a short straddle is produced when we sell ten 93.50 calls and ten 93.50 puts. We know that in this delta neutral strategy we have sold ten calls as well as another ten calls, which means that

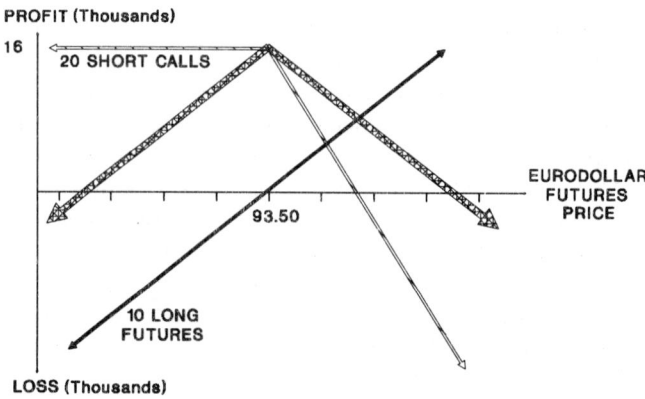

Figure 6.3 Delta Neutral Trading by Writing Calls

we have 20 short calls. It is easy to spot the short ten calls, but where do the short ten puts come from? For the answer, we must return to put-call parity:

$$C - P = F - E$$

Now, if we combine a long position in the Eurodollar futures market with a short call, we have a trade known as a covered call write. If the reader refers back to the chapter on advanced option pricing (Chapter 3), he will remember that this position is equivalent to a short put. By selling ten call options and buying ten Eurodollar futures contracts, we achieve exactly the same payoff as selling ten put options. Therefore, by buying ten futures and selling 20 calls, we have a position equivalent to selling ten calls and selling ten synthetic puts which has the same payoff as a short straddle.

Another method of achieving a delta neutral position might be to buy ten of the underlying Eurodollar futures at 93.50 and pick up negative deltas by buying put options. To determine the correct number of puts to hedge, we divide the number of Eurodollar futures by the delta of the put options. Suppose we use the 93.50 put option which is at-the-money with a delta of –0.50. If we buy these puts, each one provides a negative delta position of –0.50. Suppose we have purchased ten of the underlying Eurodollar futures. Dividing these by –0.50 our hedge ratio once again turns out to be 20 options. Suppose we buy them at a price of 32 basis points. At the prevailing market price of 93.50, we will have a position that is delta neutral. However, this time we have established a position which benefits from volatility increasing.

Essentially, we are buying low implied volatility and selling expensive actual volatility. Consequently, we will suffer from time decay. If we establish this trade with 90 days until expiration and volatility does not increase or the market price fails to move within 30 days, we should lose about $150 in time value per option. If nothing happens by expiration, we expect to lose the entire $800 in premium we have paid per option (32 ticks × $25 per tick). Therefore, we want the actual market volatility to be higher in this period than the volatility implied in the option. If this occurs, we will make money from this volatility discrepancy by selling the put options at a price higher than the price we paid for them. As the reader can see in Figures 6.4 and 6.5, the position is displayed at various points prior to expiration and at final expiry. Initially the profit/loss of the strategy is flat (a slope of zero) at the current market price of 93.50. However, the strategy does bend to the northeast and prices rise and bend to the northwest as prices fall. In fact, it looks like a big 'smile'. At expiration, the strategy resembles something quite different. It looks identical to the long straddle I discussed in the last chapter.

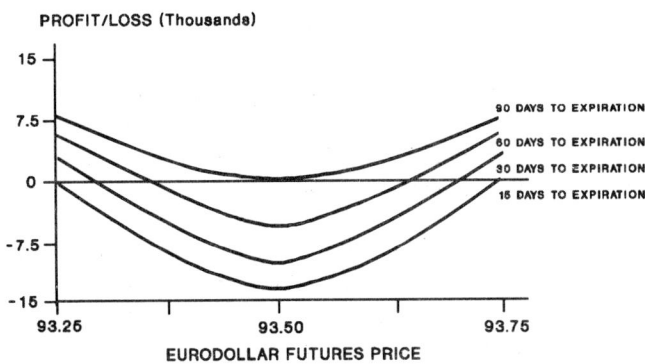

Figure 6.4 Delta Neutral Trading by Holding Puts

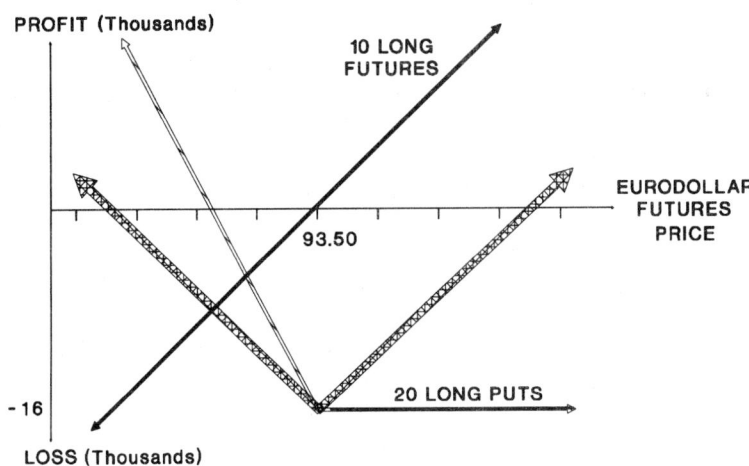

Figure 6.5 Delta Neutral Trading by Holding Puts

The reason that this payoff resembles a long straddle is that we have once again created a synthetic position. The logic is similar to the one used for the creation of the synthetic short straddle we discussed above. As before, we can separate the 20 long puts into two sets of ten. We then combine the long ten Eurodollar futures with ten of the long put options. Applying put-call parity, we know that long underlying positions combined with long puts produce synthetic long call options. Therefore, we have bought ten actual put options and purchased ten synthetic call options which gives us the same payoff as a long straddle. So, this delta neutral position is really just a long straddle in disguise.

Why trade a synthetic straddle when you could trade the actual straddle? Let us say you want to buy a straddle and no one is making a market in calls, but a number of market makers are offering to sell puts. Since it is impossible to buy calls, you could still buy your straddle by buying ten of the underlying Eurodollar futures and 20 puts. You are able to purchase a synthetic straddle which you were unable to establish in the normal way. This ability to create synthetic option strategies is critical in assuring that fair option pricing exists; otherwise arbitrage would take place. These trades help keep option prices in line.

Two practical considerations in doing these delta neutral volatility 'arbitrages' are: the liquidity in the Eurodollar futures and options markets; and the transactions costs involved in the implementation. Very often, these trades can be difficult to establish. Both the options and futures trades must be filled at the same moment and in practice this does not always occur. In addition, when the delta neutral trader is establishing the trades, he must give up the bid/offer spread on both the futures and the options. Not surprisingly, this can result in the reduction of the total profit of the trade.

PURE ARBITRAGE STRATEGIES

Finally, there is a category of trades which are pure arbitrages. These allow the arbitrageur to profit from options being mispriced. These trades have 'locked in' returns which offer a risk-free return. The ability to create synthetic options positions implies that if at any time options prices become mismatched, the trader will buy the underpriced position and sell the equivalent overvalued position; these trades are true arbitrage trades.

In this final section, I am going to examine how to create synthetic positions with options, compare them with actual positions, and – if any discrepancies exist – show how to lock in these deviations to make a risk-free return. Although the next few pages will review what we previously discussed in Chapter 3, I believe it will be worth the reader's while. The essence of true options arbitrage is contained in the put-call parity equation and only with a clear understanding of this can the reader really grasp arbitrage.

Let us first consider how to create a synthetic long futures position. When I buy a call I secure the right to buy. If I sell a put, I am obliged to buy. If I combine these two, what do I get? Remember how in the first chapter I claimed that to create options, all one needs to do is take a long position in any underlying market and split that position into two parts: a good part and a bad part. In this case, if I create options from the underlying Eurodollar futures, all I have to do to create a synthetic long Eurodollar futures position is to recombine the options. So, by buying a call on Eurodollar futures and selling a put on Eurodollar futures (both at the same strike price), I will produce the same profit and loss profile as buying the actual Eurodollar futures.

In the United States, this technique is often used to create synthetic futures contracts for markets where only options contracts exist. I did this to create Ginnie Mae (Government National Mortgage Association) futures on that particular security. These were created on an over-the-counter basis when I bought a call on the particular security and sold a put on that same security at the same strike price. The combination was a futures contract on the specific security. In any market, if calls and puts are available, it is possible to create futures contracts. By buying the call option and selling the same strike price put option, a long futures position has been produced. The reader is referred back to the discussion in Chapter 3 on put-call parity for a more thorough coverage of why this is the case.

Now that we have identified the synthetic long underlying Eurodollar futures position, we will also identify the synthetic strategies which are equivalent to the long call and the short put. Assume we wish to purchase a call option. We may want to evaluate whether it is fairly valued. One way to check this is to examine the price of the actual call and compare it with the price of a synthetic call with the same strike price. First of all, we must determine what a call option is equal to. We find the answer with the put-call parity formula: $C - P = (F - E)$. If we add a P to both sides of this equation, it will now read:

$$C = (F - E) + P$$

Thus, the call price must be equal to buying the underlying Eurodollar futures market and buying a put option. How would we create a synthetic short put? Essentially, we are asking what is a minus P equal to? If we subtract a C from both sides of the put-call parity equation, which implies selling a call, we get:

$$-P = (F - E) - C$$

So, a synthetic short put has to be equal to buying the underlying market and selling a call option. Whenever a call or put option price gets out of line, you can create a synthetic option that will provide exactly the same payoff and can be used to deal against the mispriced option to lock in the discrepancy.

What are synthetic selling positions? To create synthetic short positions all you need do is take our put-call parity equation and multiply it by minus 1. The new equation now reads:

$$-C + P = -(F - E)$$

If you sell a call option and buy a put option, the position is equivalent to selling the underlying Eurodollar futures. Thus, when you combine the right to sell and the obligation to sell, this produces a short position in the underlying futures.

To create a synthetic long put you take the negative put-call parity formula and simply add a C to both sides, in other words, buy a call option. The equation now reads:

$$P = -(F - E) + C$$

This implies that if you are short the underlying futures and buy a call, you will have a position which must be equal to the price of the put option. The most you can lose if you buy an option is the premium paid. So, what is the most you can lose on the purchase of a synthetic put option? It is equal to the premium paid for the actual call option. If the actual put option premium and the synthetic put option premium ever diverge, you can close the differential by buying the actual option and selling the synthetic. Therefore, for 'no arbitrage' to exist, there must be no difference between the prices of synthetic puts and actual puts.

Finally, how do we create a synthetic short call? With the negative put-call parity equation, we subtract a P from both sides of the equation. This cancels the $+P$ on the left and adds a $-P$ on the right. The new equation reads:

$$-C = -(F - E) - P$$

This implies that if we are short the underlying position and short a put, we will have exactly the same position as being short a call.

Practical Applications of Synthetic Transactions

If a particular trader buys a Eurodollar futures and then buys a put option to protect it, what is the net effect of this transaction? The answer is a synthetic long call. Suppose he establishes this trade and the price of the futures rises. He may then wish to close out his position and take his profits. One way he could do this would be to sell back the put and sell the underlying Eurodollar futures. An alternative, which is much simpler, would be to sell a call at the same strike price as the put and he has synthetically closed out the position (without having to sell the underlying position). In the put-call parity equation it would then read:

$$0 = (F - E) + P - C$$

In literal form, zero is the difference between buying the underlying Eurodollar futures, buying a put and selling a call.

Consider instead the trader who implements a cover call write. In this trade, he buys a Eurodollar futures and sells a call against it. Suppose he also decides he wants to cover the position. He will have to buy back the call, and the liquidity for this option

EURODOLLAR SEPTEMBER 1991

TERM	77 DAYS				VOLATILITY RATE	25.50 PERCENT 6.25 PERCENT
						STRIKE PRICES
FUTURES		93.00	93.25	93.50	93.75	94.00
93.40	CALL	0.55	0.39	0.26	0.15	0.09
	DELTA	(0.663)	(0.546)	(0.420)	(0.296)	(0.189)
	PUT	0.15	0.24	0.35	0.50	0.68
	DELTA	(0.324)	(0.441)	(0.567)	(0.691)	(0.798)
93.45	CALL	0.58	0.42	0.28	0.17	0.10
	DELTA	(0.685)	(0.571)	(0.445)	(0.319)	(0.207)
	PUT	0.14	0.22	0.33	0.47	0.64
	DELTA	(0.301)	(0.416)	(0.542)	(0.668)	(0.780)
93.50	CALL	0.62	0.44	0.30	0.19	0.11
	DELTA	(0.708)	(0.596)	(0.470)	(0.342)	(0.226)
	PUT	0.12	0.20	0.30	0.43	0.60
	DELTA	(0.279)	(0.391)	(0.516)	(0.644)	(0.761)
93.55	CALL	0.65	0.47	0.32	0.20	0.12
	DELTA	(0.729)	(0.621)	(0.496)	(0.367)	(0.246)
	PUT	0.11	0.18	0.27	0.40	0.56
	DELTA	(0.258)	(0.366)	(0.491)	(0.620)	(0.741)
93.60	CALL	0.69	0.51	0.35	0.22	0.13
	DELTA	(0.750)	(0.645)	(0.522)	(0.392)	(0.268)
	PUT	0.10	0.16	0.25	0.37	0.53
	DELTA	(0.237)	(0.342)	(0.464)	(0.595)	(0.719)

Table 6.2 Minerva Consulting Eurodollar Option Evaluations September 1991

may have 'dried up' (especially if it is deep in-the-money). However, the put option which at that point is deep out-of-the-money may still be trading. By purchasing the put option, the position will be completely covered:

$$0 = (F - E) - C + P$$

These synthetic transactions add considerable flexibility to hedgers.

For market makers and arbitrageurs, these same transactions are referred to as conversions, reversals, and box trades, rather than as synthetics. These trades are essential to efficiency in the options market. The first of the strategies I will examine is the conversion.

When people trade options as market makers, to facilitate fair pricing and arbitrage, many dealers refer to sheets of theoretical option prices. These sheets provide the fair value of options for a given set of strike prices and for a given range of underlying Eurodollar futures prices. They allow the market maker an overview of all option prices for a given volatility and for a given interest rate factor. Table 6.2 provides an example of such a worksheet. For example, one can read across from the current market price of 93.50 on the left column and down from the strike price of 93.25 to see that the 93.25 call option is worth 44 basis points when the Eurodollar futures price is at 93.50. What happens if the futures price rises to 93.60? One can read across from 93.60 on the further left column to see that the 93.25 call should rise in value from 44 to 51 basis points. This is a change of seven basis points, which implies a delta of about 70 per cent (70 per cent of the movement in the Eurodollar futures price). One will also notice that below the call premium on the sheet is a delta of 0.645. Thus, the option price did change roughly in line with the delta's prediction. We can also look at the 93.50 options which are at-the-money. The 93.50 put option will have a theoretical price of 30 basis points when the Eurodollar futures market is trading at 93.50. If the market moves up or down, how much should the option price change? Below the price of 0.30 one can see that the delta is 0.516. If the market price falls from 93.50 to 93.40, the new value of the put will be 35 basis points. So, the theoretical option price has risen from 30 to 35, which is a profit of five basis points. As predicted by the delta, for a market move of ten basis points, the option only moved by five basis points which is 50 per cent of the movement in the underlying Eurodollar futures.

With these price sheets in hand, market makers can review at a glance what is happening to all the available option series. Many dealers will also have three or four different sheets with different volatilities in case the volatility changes during the day. On the Eurodollar futures, it would be reasonable to have three separate sheets at 25 per cent, 25.5 per cent, and 26 per cent volatility to complement a trader's market making activities. Basically, what a market maker does during a typical trading day is to use his price sheets as an indication of what theoretical option values should be at certain levels. They are constantly comparing the theoretical values on the sheets to actual market prices both to revise their volatility estimates and to spot arbitrage opportunities.

THE CONVERSION ARBITRAGE STRATEGY

If you looked on the screen and spotted a bid on the 93.50 Eurodollar futures call at 30, and an offer on the 93.50 Eurodollar futures put at 28, you would glance at your sheet and see that both should be at 30 when the market is trading at 93.50. The call is fair valued and the put is undervalued.

What should you do if something is undervalued? Buy it. But then you have a position exposed to changes in volatility and sensitive to time decay. So, let us close up the trade and eliminate all risk. Since you have bought the actual put, you must sell a synthetic put. This is accomplished by selling a call and buying the underlying Eurodollar futures. This trade is commonly known as a conversion.

You have to do all three trades in the batting of an eye: buy the 93.50 put, sell the 93.50 call and buy the Eurodollar futures. If you don't, others will see it and close the discrepancy, taking the profit themselves. It is like seeing a $20 note on the ground; you'd better pick it up quickly before someone else sees it and grabs it.

But is this trade truly an arbitrage? Let us see what could happen at expiration. If you have truly closed the trade, you can then consolidate it, knowing that irrespective of where the market price finishes you will make an arbitrage profit. What are the three things that could possibly happen by the expiration date? The answer is: the market could fall, rise, or stay the same.

Let us first assume that the market falls to 93.00 at expiration. You bought the underlying market at 93.50, and it is now worth 93.00. Therefore, you are going to lose 50 basis points on that. But remember, you purchased the put option which gives you the right to sell at 93.50. With the market at 93.00, you will exercise your put with an inflow of 50 basis points. This exactly offsets the 50 basis points which you lost on the position in futures. So, no loss or gain here. What about the call option you sold? With the market at 93.00, the call option buyer will let his option expire worthless.

You are therefore going to receive the entire 30 basis points in premium paid to you for the call option. Then you must deduct the 28 basis points you paid for the 93.50 put. The net effect if the market finishes at 93.00 is an inflow of 30 basis points in option premium minus your payment of 28 basis points plus a squared position which has no profit or loss (futures/put offset). This sums up to two basis points in profit.

What happens if the Eurodollar futures market ends up at 93.50 at expiration? The put option is the right to sell at 93.50, and if the market is also at 93.50, the put will expire worthless and you will lose the 28 basis points you paid. The short call option is the obligation to sell at 93.50, and if the market is sitting at 93.50 the call also expires worthless; in this case, providing an inflow of 30 basis points in premium. Finally, the underlying is also at 93.50 and it settles at that level with no profit or loss. The net inflow is equal to two basis points. That seems to work if the market finishes at 93.50, but could it not finish higher than 93.50?

Suppose the market does finish above 93.50. You have bought the underlying Eurodollar futures at 93.50 and the market is now at 94.00, so your profit on this trade is 50 basis points. What about the 93.50 put option you purchased? With the market at 94.00, you will abandon the put option allowing it to expire worthless and losing the 28 basis points you paid for it. But the call holder has the right to buy from you at 93.50, and with the market at 94.00, he will do so. Since you are obliged to sell it at 93.50, you will lose 50 basis points; exactly equal to the 50 basis points you made by buying the underlying futures. However, you will still earn the premium of 30 basis points the call buyer paid to you less the 28 basis points in premium you paid, so once again the net profit from the arbitrage will be two basis points. Whenever option prices get out of line, one can knock them back into line using the put-call parity principles underlying the conversion.

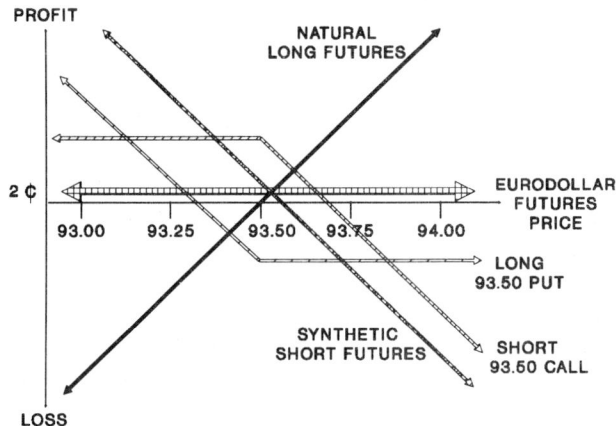

Figure 6.6 Conversion

What you have done with this conversion is to create a synthetic short underlying Eurodollar futures position by purchasing the put option and selling the call at the same strike price. You also covered the synthetic by buying the actual underlying Eurodollar futures market.

We will now see how these arbitrages are produced using our graphing rules. In Figure 6.6, we have all the positions displayed. To the left of 93.50, there is an unlimited profit potential for the long put option and a limited gain potential for the short call option. What is the rule? Unlimited dominates limited, so the combination gives you an unlimited profit potential. To the right of 93.50, you have an unlimited loss potential on the short call option and a limited profit potential on the long put option, so what is going to happen? The unlimited loss on the call is going to overwhelm the limited loss on the put and we end up with a position that has an unlimited loss potential. Overall, this is the same payoff as selling a Eurodollar futures contract. All you need to do to eliminate all risk is to establish an offsetting trade which has exactly the opposite profit/loss profile. The opposite trade is obviously to buy the underlying Eurodollar futures market. The arbitrage occurs because you are buying the natural underlying position at a fair price and selling the synthetic at an overvalued price, locking in a risk-free return as demonstrated above. This profit is 'locked in' no matter where the market price finishes at expiration.

These transactions, as one might imagine, do not happen very often and when they do, they exist only momentarily. But the same thing can be said about finding a $20 note on the street: it doesn't happen very often, but when you see one lying there you certainly pick it up.

Will these trades work in an illiquid market, though? If you can complete all three components of this transaction, the answer is yes. That is, once you lock these trades in, you do not have to trade again to realise your profits. Liquidity becomes irrelevant.

As the reader may begin to see, arbitrage keeps market prices efficient. Options arbitrageurs are basically the 'fair price police' that step in and keep prices in line. Without them, options markets would be no better than a free-for-all, and option pricing theory would become unmanageable.

THE REVERSAL ARBITRAGE STRATEGY

The second kind of arbitrage trade we will discuss is the reversal (which is also known as a reverse conversion). In this trade, suppose that a 93.50 call option is offered at a price of 27 basis points, and the 93.50 put is bid at 30 basis points. What are you going to do? Buy the undervalued call, sell the fairly valued put, and finally sell the underlying Eurodollar futures. Now that is done, let us see what can happen to the combination of trades at expiration. As before, if the arbitrage profit is earned no matter where the underlying Eurodollar futures market finishes, you can declare this trade to be risk-free.

Let us assume that the market remains unchanged at 93.50. The call and the put both have strike prices of 93.50, and since the market is also at 93.50, both options expire worthless. The profit and loss on the underlying Eurodollar futures is also zero because it is unchanged from the level at which you sold it previously. The only cashflows that occur comprise the 27 points you paid for the call option and the 30 basis points you received back from the put option you sold. So, if the market finishes at 93.50, you will collect the three basis points differential between the option prices.

What happens if the market goes down? If the market goes down to 93.00 and you sold the Eurodollar futures at 93.50, you can buy it back at 93.00; realising a profit of 50 basis points. Unfortunately, someone has purchased a put option from you which allows them the right to sell the underlying to you at 93.50. With the market at 93.00, the put holder will exercise and you will have to pay him the 50 basis points right back. What about the call you purchased? Since you possess the right to buy at 93.50, and the market is below that, you will abandon it, allowing it to expire worthless. So once again, the futures profit covers the option's loss and you paid 27 basis points for the call and received 30 for the put. Thus, you are also going to earn those three points even when the market price falls.

The last thing which can possibly happen is for the market to finish above your strike price. If this happens, finishing at 94.00, and you have sold the underlying Eurodollar futures market at 93.50, you are going to have a loss of 50 basis points. The put option holder will let the option expire worthless because it is out-of-the-money. Finally, the call you have bought gives you the right to buy at 93.50. When the market is at 94.00, you will have inflow of 50 basis points which covers the outflow on the futures position. Again, you have a premium outflow of 27 basis points on the call and a premium inflow of 30 basis points from the put. Since the intrinsic value is covered, you still earn the three points which were the initial divergence in the option premiums.

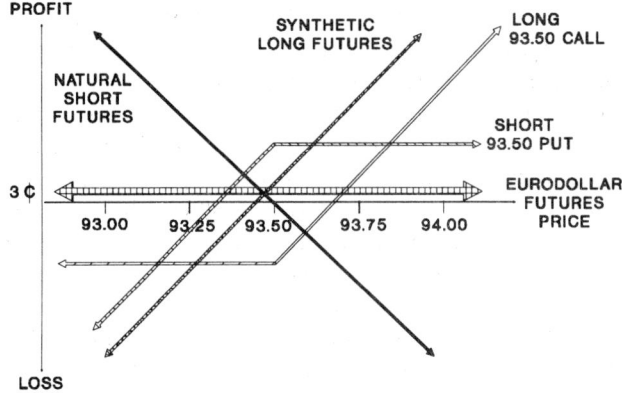

Figure 6.7 Reversal

141

In this example, I have shown how to create a synthetic long Eurodollar futures by buying a call and selling a put. Because the options prices were mispriced, this allowed us to create a synthetic long position that was cheaper than an actual long position in the Eurodollar futures market. To eliminate the risk from holding this position on an outright basis, we hedge your exposure by selling an actual Eurodollar futures contract. In combination, these positions are risk-less, producing a three basis point arbitrage profit. Figure 6.7 displays how this trade is formed and why it is risk-less. This trade is known as the reversal.

THE BOX ARBITRAGE STRATEGY

What happens if it is impossible to trade the underlying Eurodollar futures market? This can occur when you do not have Eurodollar futures markets or if a Eurodollar futures market does exist but is illiquid. This situation occurs in the share market where buying or selling shares forward in time is difficult. As long as there are other option strike prices trading, you can employ options alone to close the arbitrage and this trade is referred to as a box trade.

So, back to our price sheet in Table 6.2. I will now concentrate on both the 93.50 and the 93.00 strike price options on Eurodollar futures. At the 93.00 strike, the call option value is 62 basis points when the market is at 93.50 and the put is valued at 12 basis points. The 93.50 strike price call and put options are both priced at 30 basis points. With these sheets in hand, you look at the screen and notice somebody has made a mistake, offering the 93.50 put option at 26 basis points when it should be worth 30. So, you buy this put for 26 basis points and sell the same strike price call at its fair price of 30 basis points. As outlined above, this will produce a synthetic short Eurodollar futures position. Now to close the arbitrage, you need a long underlying Eurodollar futures position. If no long Eurodollar futures position is available, you can simply create a synthetic long position by buying another call and selling another put. But instead of using the 93.50 strike prices, you will use the 93.00 strike price options to create the synthetic long Eurodollar futures position. By doing this trade with options at different strike prices, you will have four separate trades which will lock in an arbitrage, assuming that only the 93.50 put is mispriced.

Suppose you bought the 93.00 call and sold the 93.00 put, with both the right to buy and the obligation to buy at 93.00. You have created a synthetic long futures position at 93.00. By buying the 93.50 put and selling the 93.50 call, with both the right and obligation to sell at 93.50, you have a synthetic short position at 93.50. If you bought the futures at 93.00 and sold it at 93.50, you would have a gain of .50. So, with this trade, you are guaranteed a 50 basis point inflow. Now, you must determine how much it has cost to establish this trade. By selling the 93.00 put for 12 basis points and selling the 93.50 call for 30 basis points, you have a premium inflow of 42 basis points. For the 93.00 call you must pay 62 basis points, and for the 93.50 put you must pay 26 basis points. This is a total outflow of 88 basis points. The net outflow is therefore 46 basis points (88 − 42 basis points) for the box and you expect to receive 50 basis points back.

Do you really lock in the four basis points of arbitrage? Again, what could happen at expiration? The markets could finish below the lower strike price, at the lower strike price, in between the strike prices, at the higher strike price or above the higher strike price. I will now go through all five possible situations at expiration and prove that the profit of four basis points will be earned in each possible case.

If the market price finishes below the lower strike price, say at 92.75, you have bought the 93.00 call and sold the 93.50 call, both of which expire worthless. What about your two put options? You bought the right to sell at 93.50 and when the market finishes at 92.75 will exercise this option, receiving 75 points back. Unfortunately, someone else has purchased a 93.00 put from you which gives him the right to sell at 93.00. With the market at 92.75, you will have to pay out 25 basis points. The difference between these cashflows is an inflow of 50 points. This, minus what you paid for the spread initially (46 points), yields a profit of four points. So, in the first case, you do indeed make your four basis points.

What happens if the futures market finishes right at 93.00? Again both calls expire worthless and the put you sold at the 93.00 strike price also expires worthless. However, the put you purchased at the 93.50 strike price is worth 50 basis points which is an inflow. This − less the 46 basis points you paid for this spread − is a net inflow of four basis points. Therefore, in the second situation, you also earn your expected profit.

What about the third case? Suppose the market finishes between the 93.00 and 93.50 strike prices at 93.25. You bought the right to buy at 93.00 and also the right to sell at 93.50. If the market is at 93.25, you will exercise both options and pull in 25 on each (a total inflow of 50 basis points). What about the options you sold? One is the right to buy at 93.50, and because that call is out-of-the-money, it will expire worthless. The other option is the right to sell at 93.00, and this put option is also out-of-the-money, expiring worthless. Therefore, you have an inflow of 50 points less the 46 points you paid − a profit of four points once again. So in the third case, you also earn your expected arbitrage profit.

In the fourth case, the futures market finishes at 93.50. Both the 93.00 and the 93.50 put options expire worthless. In addition, the 93.50 call option you sold is worthless, so you have no inflow or outflow on that option. But the 93.00 call you purchased is in-the-money by 50 basis points, which is an inflow of 50 basis points on this trade. Since your initial premium outflow was 46 basis points, the profit of four basis points is again earned.

Finally, when the futures market finishes above 93.50, the reader can rest assured the arbitrage works here too. If the market finishes at 94.00, you have the right to buy at 93.00 which you will exercise to realise an inflow of 100 basis points. However, you also sold a call option at 93.50. With the market at 94.00, the holder will exercise, calling away from you the underlying asset for a loss of 50 points. So, the net inflow is 50 points. As far as the put options go, at 94.00, both puts expire worthless. Since the spread cost you 46, and you have a 50 points inflow on the options, the net profit

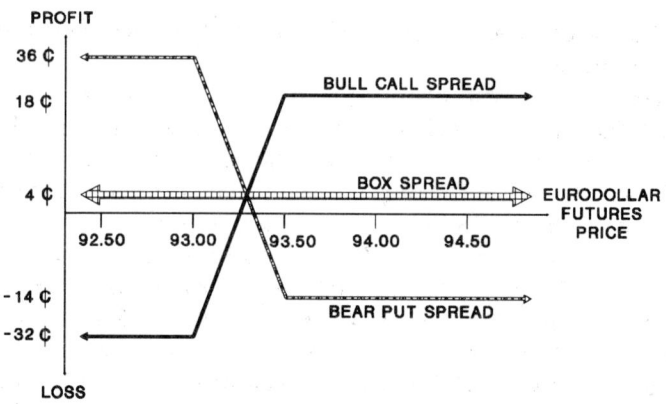

Figure 6.8 Box Spread with Bear and Bull

is four points in this final situation. Therefore, no matter where the market finishes at expiration, you will earn the four basis points of the 'locked in' arbitrage.

The box demonstrates that it is not necessary to deal in the underlying market to arbitrage option prices. However, one must be sure of sufficient liquidity in the options market to place all these trades simultaneously.

We will now look at the box spread graphically. The reader will notice that I examine the box trade in terms of the equivalent option strategies constructed. This can be seen in Figure 6.8.

If you sell the 93.00 put and buy the 93.50 put, this is simply a vertical spread. In Figure 6.8 we can see this. When one establishes a vertical spread by buying the higher strike price put option, this strategy is known as a bear put spread. On the call option side, you bought a 93.00 call and sold a 93.50 call. When one establishes a vertical spread by buying the lower strike call option, this is a bull call spread. This can also be seen in Figure 6.8. What happens when you combine a bear spread with a bull spread with the same strike prices? To the left of 93.00 the limited profit potential on the bear spread and the limited loss potential on the bull spread cancel. Between 93.00 and 93.50, the unlimited potential on the bear spread and unlimited potential on the bull spread cancel. And finally, above 93.50, the limited loss potential on the bear spread and the limited profit potential on the bull spread also cancel. So, the whole position is exactly offsetting: you earn the arbitrage profits no matter what happens to the price of the underlying market.

Some complications do exist for this trade if people exercise early. At the IMM, early exercise can occur and cause problems if option contracts and the underlying assets do not expire on the same day. If such exercises occur (most commonly in the share market), these positions must be financed until expiration (which is where bankers come in). But because everything at the IMM does settle at the same moment and cash settlement occurs, financing of option premium is minimal and the box trade is a relatively pure extension of put-call parity.

WHERE THE ARBITRAGE STRATEGIES FIT INTO THE STRATEGY MATRIX

In conclusion, option 'arbitrage' strategies are neutral to the underlying market and for the most part neutral to volatility, with the exception of calendar spreads (which become long volatility at the expiration of the short-dated option) and delta neutral trading. Delta neutral trading is not a pure arbitrage trade but is usually an extension of volatility trading. This is why many people consider it as 'volatility arbitrage'. So back to our trading strategy matrix that has been filled by now. In Table 6.3, all these trades will be placed into the cell in the lower right corner.[3]

If you have no view on the market, and you have a neutral view on volatility, the categories of trades that you might wish to consider include calendar spreads, delta neutral trading (if you think that the volatility is mispriced) and pure option arbitrage. This last category of strategies works most effectively when prices get out of line.

As promised, options provide the dealer with a tremendous amount of flexibility. If one can form views on both the underlying market and volatility, then the use of our trading matrix should assist the trader to find that particular trade which will maximise his expected profits given the dual view on the underlying market price and volatility. All the trader needs to do is to refer to the strategy matrix in Table 6.3 which identifies the appropriate strategy for a given set of views.

VIEWPOINT ON THE EURODOLLAR MARKET

		BUYER	SELLER	NEUTRAL
VIEWPOINT ON VOLATILITY	**BUYER**	BUY CALL OPTION CALL BACK SPREAD	BUY PUT OPTION PUT BACK SPREAD	BUY STRADDLE BUY STRANGLE
	SELLER	SELL PUT OPTION PUT RATIO SPREAD	SELL CALL OPTION CALL RATIO SPREAD	SELL STRADDLE SELL STRANGLE BUY BUTTERFLY BUY CONDOR
	NEUTRAL	LONG FUTURES BULL SPREAD	SHORT FUTURES BEAR SPREAD	CALENDAR SPREAD DELTA NEUTRAL SYNTHETICS CONV/REVERSAL BOXES

Table 6.3 Option Trading Strategy Matrix

---

[1] One can also sell a calendar spread by selling the deferred contract month and buying the nearby month. However, I will not discuss that strategy in this book. The reader should be able to envisage how the 'short' calendar spread will look by turning Figure 6.1 upside down.

2 We will recover ground here previously seen in Chapter 3. In that chapter, the emphasis was on the theoretical foundations of the option markets. In this chapter, I have chosen to use exactly the same examples but with the emphasis on practical applications.

3 We could just as easily put delta neutral trading in the long or short volatility cells in the strategy matrix. However, since these trades are really long or short straddles, they are already in those cells. We chose to include delta neutral trading in the arbitrage cell because it is based on volatility 'arbitrage'; in reality effective delta neutral trading is simply maximising the trader's theoretical edge.

7: Option Hedging Strategies

In this chapter I will examine the applications of options for hedging fixed income securities. Across the globe, futures and option contracts on Bonds, Gilts, or Bundesanleihen have proved to be among the most successful of all derivative products. In this chapter I will examine the first and most successful of the Government Fixed income derivative markets: the US Treasury Bond futures and options markets traded at the Chicago Board of Trade (CBOT).

Let us review the T-Bond futures and the option on T-Bond futures which are traded at the CBOT. Their price will be in percentage of the par value for a hypothetical 8% coupon 20-year US Treasury Bond with a face value of $100,000. The quotations are in full points ($1000) followed by thirty-seconds ($\frac{1}{32}$). For example, if the futures price equals 80–16, this indicates that the value of the contract is 80 per cent of $100,000 (or $80,000) plus $\frac{16}{32}$ of a per cent which is $\frac{1}{2}$ per cent of $100,000 (or $500). So the cash price is $80,500. The option on T-Bond futures is quoted in a similar fashion, except that in addition to the full points for the option premium, the following numbers after the '-' are in sixty-fourths ($\frac{1}{64}$). So if a particular option is quoted at 1-40, this means the cash price for the option is 1 per cent of $100,000 (or $1000) plus $\frac{40}{64}$ of 1 per cent which is 0.625 of 1 per cent (or $625). In this example, the total price for the option would be $1625. Furthermore, the tick size (the minimum value of the movement) for the futures is $31.25 ($\frac{1}{32}$ per cent × $100,000) and for the option

TRADING UNIT	1 CBOT U.S. TREASURY BOND FUTURES CONTRACT (FACE VALUE $100,000 OR MULTIPLE THEREOF)
CONTRACT MONTHS	FRONT MONTH OF CURRENT QUARTER PLUS NEXT 3 CONTRACTS OF THE REGULAR QUARTERLY CYCLE (MARCH, JUNE, SEPTEMBER AND DECEMBER)
LAST TRADING DAY	12:00 PM LAST FRIDAY PRECEDING BY AT LEAST 5 BUSINESS DAYS THE LAST BUSINESS DAY ONE MONTH BEFORE THE FUTURES EXPIRATION
MINIMUM PRICE MOVEMENT	1/64 OF A POINT ($15.625)
EXERCISE PRICE INTERVALS	2 POINTS PER T-BOND FUTURES CONTRACT (80, 82, 84, ETC.)
TRADING HOURS	DAYTIME HOURS 7:20 - 14:00 EVENING HOURS 17:00 - 20:30 OR 18:00-21:30 DAYLIGHT SAVINGS TIME
EXERCISE	ANY BUSINESS DAY PRIOR TO EXPIRATION BY 18:00 CHICAGO TIME. AUTOMATIC EXERCISE OCCURS IS ON THE LAST TRADING DAY, THE OPTION IN I-T-M BY AT LEAST 2 POINTS
EXPIRATION	10:00 AM ON THE FIRST SATURDAY FOLLOWING THE LAST TRADING DAY

Table 7.1 Options on US T-Bond Futures (CBOT)

on T-Bond futures is $15.625 ($\frac{1}{64}$ per cent × $100,000). Table 7.1 outlines the contract specification for the options on T-Bond futures. The ultimate asset underlying the option is a US Treasury Bond that is closely tied to the T-Bond futures contract, and the option represents the obligation either to buy or sell this US Treasury Bond in the month following the expiration of the option.

BASIC CONSIDERATIONS IN DESIGNING A HEDGING STRATEGY

When considering how to construct an effective hedging strategy, a helpful analogy is a scale. Consider the old-fashioned scales with plates on opposite sides of a fulcrum. The scale operates by balancing weights on the two sides. To balance the scale, whatever is on one side must be matched with an equal weight on the other. When hedging, the first thing to do is to find which 'side' one is on (either a long or short position), and determine the size of the exposure. Then, on the opposite side, one establishes a position which offsets it with an equivalent exposure. The goal of the hedged portfolio is to neutralise the original exposure or to restructure the pattern of returns. Therefore, when the original position loses money the hedging position gains a profit of exactly the same amount. Furthermore, when the hedging position loses money the original position earns exactly the same amount. Thus, as the price of the original asset changes, the hedged portfolio will experience no profit or loss and is considered risk-free.

In hedging, three points must be established:

1. The size of the exposure;

2. Whether the exposure is long or short;

3. A position in the intended hedging instrument which is exactly opposite to points 1 and 2.

For example, suppose I am long a physical T-Bond on one side of my 'scale'. To hedge the risk of this position I must either sell short physical T-Bonds, sell T-Bond futures or utilise options strategies which have a selling equivalency to the underlying market. Similarly, hedgers may have a short position relative to the underlying US Treasury Bonds market and so require equivalent long positions in derivative products to manage these risks.

Early in this book, I identified the two kinds of options equivalent short positions and the two kinds of equivalent long positions. This chapter will examine when a hedger might use all these options strategies in a hedging programme. Specifically, I will show how the purchase of calls or puts reduces the risk of an exposure to the US Treasury Bonds market. I will also cover when a hedger might sell calls or puts to increase yields and cushion his loss potentials. In addition, one of these examples will compare and contrast in some detail an options hedge with a futures hedge. The aim

CASH STATISTICS

FUTURES STATISTICS

SECURITY		PRICE	YIELD	C. FACTOR	DECIMAL GROSS BASIS
UST 7 1/2	11/15/16	87-31	8.679	0.9463	25.3
UST 7 1/4	05/15/16	85-18+	8.671	0.9200	28.3
UST 8 7/8	08/15/17	101-29+	8.686	1.0946	34.6
UST 8 3/4	05/15/17	100-23+	8.677	1.0811	36.4
UST 9 1/4	02/15/16	105-16+	8.701	1.1327	37.3

**SEPTEMBER
T-BOND FUTURES**

CURRENT PRICE : 92-04

DELIVERY DAY:
(108 DAYS)   30/9/91

OPTIONS ON FUTURES STATISTICS

SEPTEMBER T-BOND FUTURES EXPIRATION

	PRICES [1]		PRICES [1]
90.00 SEPT. CALL	2-58	90.00 SEPT. PUT	0-43
92.00 SEPT. CALL	1-40	92.00 SEPT. PUT	1-23
94.00 SEPT. CALL	0-49	94.00 SEPT. PUT	2-30
96.00 SEPT. CALL	0-20	96.00 SEPT. PUT	4-00

[1] WITH 63 DAYS UNTIL THE EXPIRATION OF THE OPTIONS (ON AUGUST 16th),
A 6.25% INTEREST RATE AND A 10.5% VOLATILITY

Table 7.2 US Treasury Bond Market Conditions; Cash, Futures and Options, June 14, 1991

of this chapter is to show the reader the realm of the possible so that he can determine when options hedging would be most appropriate to his situation.

MARKET CONDITIONS: 14 JUNE 1991

To compare and contrast the hedging strategies mentioned above, I will take a particular point in time, present a set of market conditions, and show the reader how hedgers with different objectives might choose the most appropriate hedging strategy. The market scenario is on 14 June 1991, and is presented in Table 7.2. In this table, the current September T-Bond futures price is 92-04/32 and the current prices and yields are presented for a variety of US Treasury Bonds. In addition, I have included a few statistics that are critical in determining the relationship of these US Treasury Bonds to the T-Bond futures and options markets. Shortly, I will examine these numbers in more detail to allow the reader an overview of how the cash, futures and options markets are integrated. Also in Table 7.2, there is a variety of T-Bond call and put options with strike prices of 90, 92, 94 and 96; these will be the universe of tools I shall apply to the various hedging situations.

THE RELATIONSHIP BETWEEN US TREASURY BONDS AND T-BOND FUTURES

While the reader is studying the table, he may wonder what is meant by numbers under the headings *C. Factor* and *Decimal Gross Basis*. These numbers provide an insight into the relationship between each of the five US Treasury Bonds and the T-Bond futures. To delineate this relationship, I must first explain the conceptual framework for T-Bond futures. Options on T-Bond futures are derived from the underlying T-Bond futures market, as we have previously discussed. In the case of T-Bond futures, they are derived from the US Treasury Bonds market.[1]

In Table 7.2, five deliverable US Treasury Bonds are listed. The reader may ask, 'But which one underlies the T-Bond futures?' The answer to this question is: the US Treasury Bond which is cheapest to purchase and subsequently to deliver into the T-Bond futures (at the expiration of the T-Bond futures in September). To determine which US Treasury Bond is cheapest to deliver, we will need to digress slightly and examine the mechanics of T-Bond futures.

To simplify matters, let us only consider two of the US Treasury Bonds in Table 7.2, the 7½ per cent coupon T-Bond maturing on 15 November 2016 (hereafter referred to as the 7½ per cent) and the 7¼ per cent coupon T-Bond maturing on the 15 May 2016 (henceforth called the 7¼ per cent). The reader will notice that the 7½ per cent is priced at 87-31/32 and the 7¼ per cent is priced at 85-18+/32.[2] The concept of 'cheapest to deliver' means that when there is a choice between a number of US Treasury Bonds for delivery into a T-Bond futures contract, the one which is cheaper to purchase and ultimately to deliver will underlie the futures. At first glance, the one that might appear cheaper is the 7¼ per cent because its price is lower. However logical this may seem, this is not necessarily the case. Cheapest to deliver is defined by the net cost. The net cost is equal to what you actually receive when you sell the US Treasury Bond via the futures market minus the price you had to pay to purchase the T-Bond. Obviously, if you delivered instruments into the futures market with low coupons, the price would be low as well. Unfortunately, what you receive back upon delivery is also low. If cheapest to deliver simply means the most inexpensive to purchase, then the US Treasury Bond underlying the T-Bond futures would always be the one with the lowest coupon. However, this is not the case.

To correct for the fact that the range of deliverable US Treasury Bonds may all have different coupons, the CBOT provides a conversion factor system to make all these securities equivalent to the 8 per cent standard of the futures contract. To make all US Treasury Bonds of the maturity range years to years attractive to deliver into the T-Bond futures contract, an adjustment is made to the T-Bond futures price to take into account that the coupon of the US Treasury Bond delivered might be different from the 8 per cent which is the basis of the T-Bond futures contract. This adjustment is achieved by multiplying the T-Bond futures price by a conversion factor which is provided by the CBOT. The reader can see that these factors are listed in Table 7.2 for a variety of deliverable US Treasury Bonds under the column titled *C. Factor.* For example, the 7½ per cent conversion factor is 0.9463, while the 7¼ per cent conversion factor is 0.9200. This means that the 7½ per cent instrument is roughly 5.4 per cent (1.0 minus 0.9463) less valuable than an 8 per cent 20-year maturity T-Bond futures, and that the 7¼ per cent instrument is about 8.0 per cent less valuable. To determine the cheapest to deliver, we must consider what will be the net cost of buying a particular US Treasury Bond and then delivering it into the futures. What we receive upon delivery (at the futures expiration) is the closing futures price times the conversion factor, and what we pay is the current price of the US Treasury Bond.

As of 14 June 1991, what would be the net costs for these two T-Bonds if we purchased them and then delivered them into the September futures at the current futures price of 92-04/32? If we bought the $7\frac{1}{2}$ per cent, the price would be 87-31/32 per cent of par. Since the par value underlying the T-Bond future is $100,000, the amount we would have to pay to deliver this US Treasury Bond into one T-Bond futures contract would be $87,968.75 (87-31/32 per cent of $100,000). At the T-Bond futures delivery, if the current futures price remained unchanged, we would be paid 92-04/32 per cent multiplied by $100,000, multiplied by 0.9463. This would result in a payment of $87,177.89 upon delivery of this security into the T-Bond futures. A loss would result equal to $790.86. This loss can also be expressed in terms of T-Bond futures prices (as a percentage of the par value) which for the $7\frac{1}{2}$ per cent T-Bond is equal to 25.3/32 ($790.86/$31.25 per basis point). If the reader refers to Table 7.2, he will see that under the column *Decimal Gross Basis*, the number 25.3 appears for the $7\frac{1}{2}$ per cent coupon US Treasury Bonds. This corresponds exactly to our 25.3 calculated above. What about the $7\frac{1}{4}$ per cent T-Bonds? If we purchased this security, the current cost is 85-18+/32 per cent of par. By selling the T-Bond via the futures market, we agree to receive 92-04/32 per cent multiplied by $100,000 and 0.9200 (at the futures delivery date of 30 September). This translates into a cash inflow of $84,755 minus today's price for the $7\frac{1}{4}$ per cent T-Bond of $85,578.13, which results in a net loss of $823.13. In price terms, this is equal to 26.3/32 ($823.13/$31.25 per basis point). Again in Table 7.2, under the *Decimal Gross Basis* column, the number 26.3 corresponds to this loss for the $7\frac{1}{4}$ per cent T-Bond. In conclusion, the $7\frac{1}{2}$ per cent T-Bonds loses $790.86 and the $7\frac{1}{4}$ per cent T-Bonds loses $823.13 by purchase and subsequent delivery into the September T-Bond futures. It is easy to see that between these two securities, the $7\frac{1}{2}$ per cent T-Bonds are cheaper to deliver because of their smaller loss. A brief overview of this example is provided by Table 7.3.

The 'cheapest-to-deliver' US Treasury Bond is determined by using this methodology for each of the potentially deliverable T-Bonds. The security, which has the smallest loss upon delivery into the futures contract (or in some cases which

EXAMPLE

SECURITY	CASH PRICE	FUTURES PRICE	x	CONVERSION FACTOR	=	ADJUSTED FUTURES PRICE	
UST 7 1/2 OF 11/15/16	87-31	(92-04	x	0.9463)	=	87.1779	87-05+
UST 7 1/4 OF 05/15/16	85-18+	(92-04	x	0.9200)	=	84.755	84-24

SECURITY	CASH PRICE	−	ADJUSTED FUTURES PRICE	=	BASIS
UST 7 1/2	87-31	−	87-05+	=	25+/32
UST 7 1/4	85-18	−	84-24	=	26/32

SINCE 25+/32 ‹ 26/32
THE UST 7 1/2 % T-BOND IS CHEAPER TO DELIVER

Table 7.3 Cheapest T-Bond to Deliver

provides the largest profit) is the 'cheapest to deliver' US Treasury Bond. Under the column *Decimal Gross Basis*, this loss is standardised in basis points. Therefore, the cheapest to deliver T-Bond also has the smallest decimal gross basis. In Table 7.2, the cheapest to deliver US Treasury Bond is the 7½ per cent coupon of 11/2016 (25.3/32s), followed closely by the 7¼ per cent coupon of 05/2016 (26.3/32s) and then by the 8⅞ per cent coupon of 08/2017 (34.6/32s).

On 14 June 1991, the September futures price was at 92-04/32. The basis values indicate the number of basis points which the T-Bond futures is at a discount to these deliverable US Treasury Bonds. This means that when we adjust the futures price for the coupon of a particular US Treasury Bond, say the 7½ per cent T-Bond, the actual futures price of 92-04/32 is lower than the 7½ per cent T-Bond price adjusted to the 8 per cent standard. Furthermore, the current T-Bond futures price is below all the futures adjusted cash prices.[3]

Why would anyone buy a US Treasury Bond and then sell futures to hedge if the net effect is a loss? The reason is that when one hedges a US Treasury Bond with a short T-Bond futures contract, the combination of transactions provides a new pattern of returns that is fundamentally different to the initial position in the US Treasury Bond. What we need to do is not compare the hedged position with the unhedged US Treasury Bond but rather compare the hedged position with some other security which has exactly the same cashflows. Only in this way can we assess the true performance of the hedged position. When we sell T-Bond futures to hedge our holdings in US Treasury Bonds, we agree to sell that security in the future. In this example, if we do deliver the security into the futures market in 108 days time (14 June to 30 September), the period of time for holding the T-Bond is only for this period. If we hold the US Treasury Bond unhedged, our expected return is equal to the yield. However, this depends on holding the security until its final maturity in 2016, and yield to maturity also assumes that the coupons received will be reinvested at the same yield. Furthermore, this means that we are willing to accept the risks of holding that security for 25 years. Suppose instead that our exposure to US Government debt was only for 108 days, as is the case with the short T-Bond futures hedge. We would no longer expect to make the yield associated with 25-year securities but rather the yield for a 108-day maturity security. When we sell our US Treasury Bonds using the T-Bond futures market, at delivery, we will actually surrender the security and be paid cash for it. If we consider the period of exposure, we have reduced our exposure to US Government interest rates to 108 days. Therefore, the short T-Bond futures hedged position has cashflows which are identical to investing in a short-term US Government paper with a maturity of 108 days. If the short-term US Government interest rate from 14 June to 30 September were lower than the yield for the longer maturity US Government instruments (which it was for this period equal to 6.25 per cent), we would also expect to have a lower yield on a short T-Bond futures hedge since it provides exactly the same pattern of cashflows. Thus, relative to the original investment in the US Treasury Bonds, we are surrendering a portion of our yield. The way the reduction in yield occurs is for the cash equivalent T-Bond futures price to be lower than the current cash market prices. Thereby, the hedger is selling the T-Bond futures at a level that is lower than the current (adjusted) prices in the cash market. This loss of, for example, 25.3 basis points for the 7½ per cent T-Bond, simply equilibrates the 25-year securities' return with that of a 108-day investment. The amount of the futures discount is a function of the short-term interest rate for 108 days, the coupon rate for the instrument, and the current price for the cheapest to deliver security.

HEDGING EXAMPLE 1: BUYING T-BOND FUTURES VERSUS BUYING CALL OPTIONS TO HEDGE A US TREASURY BOND PURCHASE

Our first hedging example compares the use of futures contracts and call options to hedge an anticipated purchase in the US Treasury Bonds market. Our scenario involves a money manager in the US who has offered his services to a corporate pension fund. Ten million dollars is in the pension fund, and the corporation has stipulated that it wants a minimum yield of 8.5 per cent for 25 years. The money manager has identified the 7¼ per cent US Treasury Bonds maturing in May 2016 as the instrument that would be most appropriate. This security can be seen in Table 7.2. At the time of the scenario, June 1991, this instrument had an 8.671 per cent yield. However, the pension fund will not choose who will manage the money before the board of directors meets in two weeks. The money manager is concerned that within these two weeks, yields may have dropped below the target. A problem arises because he may have agreed to provide a rate of 8.5 per cent and if yields have decreased by the time the board meets and agrees to retain him, he might be unable to provide this yield at that point. The money manager has identified two kinds of risk he is facing:

1. The underlying market risk from a possible drop in yields;

2. The contingent risk that he may not be chosen by the pension fund directors in two weeks' time.

His market risk is one-sided; that is, yields might fall below the 8.5 per cent return he has agreed to provide. The contingent risk is that he may not be awarded the funds. Thus, he needs one-sided protection that will only pay off if yields fall. He also needs to be able to cancel his protection if his services are not retained.

Hedge Ratio Determination

The first problem our money manager has is to determine the size of his exposure. Given the situation outlined above, he knows that the money he might be responsible for is $10,000,000. The second problem he has is to find out which side of the market his exposure is on. The easiest way to determine this is to see what happens to his profits and losses as the price of the securities at risk changes.

In this scenario, if yields increase and the price of US Treasury Bonds falls, the money manager will be better off, assuming of course that he is awarded the funds to manage. For example, if the yields for the appropriate T-Bonds rise to 9.5 per cent and he has promised to provide an 8.5 per cent yield, then the money manager will be able to pocket the difference. However, if yields fall and US Treasury Bonds prices rise, the money manager could be in trouble. Consider the situation where the yields drop to 8.0 per cent. The money manager has promised to provide an 8.5 per cent yield and can only purchase securities which offer an 8.0 per cent yield. Unless he can find another security with a higher yield he will be losing 0.50 per cent per year for 25 years, which would be unacceptable. When the T-Bond market falls, he makes an additional profit, and when the T-Bond market rises he will experience losses. This position is equivalent to a short position in the US Treasury Bonds market. To hedge this exposure, the money manager must establish a long position in T-Bond futures or an equivalent long position using options on T-Bond futures.

So far, I have covered short T-Bond futures hedges. When one is holding a US Treasury Bond and is selling T-Bond futures to protect the value, the return for the hedge is equal to the short-term interest rate. As I discussed, a basis loss occurs for the short futures hedge which reduces the yield on the US Treasury Bonds holding to equal the yield of short-term US Government paper. What about the individual who places a long T-Bond futures hedge? He is buying T-Bond futures which are at a discount to the cash T-Bond market. So, he expects to have a profit as the T-Bond futures rises to equal the cash market at expiration. In conclusion, in a normal yield curve environment, where longer maturity yields exceed shorter maturity yields, the long T-Bond futures expect to make a profit from the convergence of the futures to the cash market. This is exactly opposite to the situation of the short T-Bond hedge I discussed previously.

However, the final problem which our money manager faces is determining the proper number of futures or options to use for his hedge. There exist many methodologies for the estimation of hedging ratios. These run from the simple – such as using the par values of the securities – to the esoteric, such as multi-factor duration techniques. For our purposes, I will choose a 'middle' approach, which is to divide the par value of the hedged instrument by the par value of the underlying futures and multiply it by the conversion factor, which equates the value of that security to the 8 per cent hypothetical T-Bond futures. While this technique is a 'rough and ready' approach, it is fairly accurate when applied to the cheapest-to-deliver T-Bonds that a short future contract holder would presumably select to deliver.[4] If the reader finds the 7¼ per cent T-Bond in Table 7.2, he will see that the decimal gross basis is only 26.3, which is slightly higher than the cheapest to deliver (the 7½ per cent T-Bond at 25.3). Therefore, both T-Bonds are practically equal in terms of attractiveness for delivery, and the money manager can treat the 7¼ per cent T-Bond as though it were the cheapest to deliver, applying the conversion factor hedge ratio scheme outlined above.

The actual hedge ratio he will use is determined by dividing $10,000,000 by the par value of the T-Bond futures – which is $100,000 – and then multiplying this result by the conversion factor of the 7¼ per cent T-Bond (which is 0.9200). This will result in a hedge ratio of exactly 92 T-Bond futures to cover his exposure.

T-Bond Futures Hedge Results

What effect will be had by the money manager's hedge of buying 92 T-Bond futures? As yields go down and the T-Bond futures prices rise, the 92 September T-Bond futures will provide profits which will offset the loss incurred by the increased price he will have to pay for the US Treasury Bond. Essentially, he will have locked in the prevailing yield of 8.671 per cent for the 7¼ per cent T-Bond, plus a profit from the futures basis converging from its current discount up to the cash market. If the market remains at present yields, the futures price should slowly converge to the level of the cash market and at expiration the basis (the difference between the cash and futures prices) should be zero. But during the two-week time horizon for the hedge, the money manager will not expect to earn the entire basis but a proportion of it which is related to the number of days the hedge is maintained. This will amount to an expected profit of 3.4 basis points in the futures price for the two-week period.[5] In terms of yields, this amounts to an additional profit of 0.01 per cent which will make it even easier to meet his 8.50 per cent target on his cash T-Bonds.[6] If the yields increase by 33 basis points by 28 June, while he will be able to get a higher 9.000 per cent rate (8.67 per cent plus 33 basis points) on the 7¼ per cent T-Bond, unfortunately this will be erased by the loss on the long futures contracts since the T-Bond futures market will fall when yields rise. Furthermore, if the yields decrease instead, he will have a loss on the US Treasury Bond position which will be exactly offset by the profits on the T-Bond futures, and will 'lock in' the 8.68 per cent yield that is equal to the prevailing yield for the security at the beginning of his hedge plus the convergence profit on the futures basis he expects to earn over the period. The money manager has therefore created a position which will be immune to changes in yields for his US Treasury Bonds. The logic of the futures hedge is that when one side makes money, the other side loses exactly the same amount. Thus, his achievable yield is fixed at 8.68 per cent, plus or minus any divergences in the cash/futures basis relationship.

Table 7.4 displays the hedged results by buying futures as a substitute for buying the 7¼ per cent US Treasury Bonds, and assumes that the money manager is awarded the management of the entire $10 million. If yields fall to 8.00 per cent the money manager has to pay $635,937.50 more for the purchase of the T-Bonds. The futures hedge makes $644,000. The money manager will close out the 92 long futures contracts (by selling 92 September T-Bond futures) and this cash amount will be credited to his account. He will then withdraw these funds and apply them to the purchase price of the T-Bonds. The hedge position was able to cover the increased cost of the T-Bond purchase as well as provide an additional profit of $8062.50.[7] So, the long futures hedge protected the position when a decrease in yields occurred.

	ASSUMING THE MANAGER IS CHOSEN AND PURCHASES THE 7 1/4 % T-BOND PROFIT / LOSS TABLE ON 28/6/91				
YIELDS ON 28/6	8.00 %	8.34 %	8.67 %	9.00 %	9.50 %
MARKET PRICE OF 7 1/4 % ON 14/6	85-18+	85-18+	85-18+	85-18+	85-18+
MARKET PRICE OF 7 1/4 % ON 28/6	- 91-30	- 88-20	- 85-18+	- 82-23	- 78-21
CHANGE IN PRICE FROM 14/6	(6-11+)	(3-01+)	0	+ 2-27+	+ 6-29+
$ LOSS ON $10,000,000	($635,937.5)	($304,687.5)	$ 0	$285,937.5	$692,187.5
SEPT T-BOND FUTURES 28/6	99-04	96-17	92-07	89-04	84-22
SEPT T-BOND FUTURES PRICE AS OF 14/6	- 92-04	- 92-04	- 92-04	- 92-04	- 92-04
CHANGE IN PRICE FROM 14/6	+ 7-00	+ 3-13	+ 0.03	(3-00)	(7-14)
NUMBER OF CONTRACTS	x 92	x 92	x 92	x 92	x 92
FUTURES PROFIT/LOSS ($31.25 PER POINT)	$644,000	$313,375	$8,625	($276,000)	($684,250)
OVERALL HEDGE RESULT	$8,062.5	$8,687.5	$8,625	$9,937.5	$7,937.5
YIELD EQUIVALENT	8.68 %	8.68 %	8.68 %	8.68 %	8.68 %

Table 7.4 T-Bond Futures Hedge

Unfortunately, if yields had risen to 9.50 per cent, while the money manager would have been able to buy the T-Bonds at a price which was $692,187.50 cheaper, the long futures position would have had a loss of $684,250 and wiped most of this out. In this case, when the money manager closed out the 92 futures contract, he would have had to pay the $684,250 to settle his account. As the reader can see, at all yields from 8.0 per cent to 9.5 per cent, the futures hedge achieves a yield equivalent close to the money manager's expected rate of 8.68 per cent, and in this rate is the profit between $8062.50 and $9937.50 from the futures convergence.

T-Bond Call Options Hedge Result

Let us now consider a simple option hedge that entails buying call options with a strike price of 92-00/32, instead of buying futures. The same hedge ratio of 92 is used for the options because the asset underlying the option is a T-Bond futures contract. In order to achieve the limited loss payoff and unlimited profit potential we are looking for, we always use the same hedge ratio as we would with the underlying asset.[8]

Purchasing calls provides a 'floor' price, assuring the money manager that he will be able to buy his T-Bonds at a price which will provide the yield he is looking for. Consider the cash side: when yields increase, the physical T-Bonds will be cheaper to buy. Because futures move in lockstep with the cash market, the futures would also be cheaper; probably below the options strike price. Thus, the call options would then be out-of-the-money. If it were expiration they would expire worthless and that would be the end of the story. If yields decrease, the 7¼ per cent T-Bonds becomes more expensive and the futures prices also increase potentially above the strike price of the call. In this case the call options would then be in-the-money and the proceeds from selling them would offset the increased cost for the T-Bonds. If the date of consolidation was at the options expiration, the options position would provide the same profits as buying 92 T-Bond futures contracts at a price of 92-00/32 and this is a fully covered hedge. However, we are not holding the options until expiration and will remove the hedge in only two weeks' time. At that point, the proceeds of the options hedge will depend upon the option price. On 28 June, there will be 49 days remaining until the expiration of the option. At that point, the 92-00/32 options price will contain both intrinsic value and time value. Thus, the results of the hedge will depend not only on what happens to the underlying T-Bond market but also on what happens to volatility and the time decay impact on the time value component of the option's price.

As with all options strategies, the premium must be carefully considered. In this example, we must pay 1-40/64 points (see Table 7.2). This limited premium expense implies that when the T-Bond market falls, we can walk away from the option with a fixed and known loss. If the drop in the market is accompanied by an increase in volatility, then it might actually result in a profit (most certainly a reduction of the loss). The reader is referred back to the explanation of Figure 2.17 (p. 38) which describes how this could occur. Nevertheless, the hedger knows the worst case scenario. In combination with the unlimited gain potential on the physical T-Bond position, the known and fixed premium loss allows the hedged position to have an unlimited gain potential to the downside (for prices), and this is reflected in Table 7.5. The logic behind this is that if the 7¼ per cent T-Bond is cheaper in the market, the hedger will not need the insurance offered by the call. However, if T-Bond prices rise, he will use the insurance benefits of the call to allow him to purchase the T-Bond at an acceptable level.

Table 7.5 displays the hedged results achieved by buying the 92 call options, and assumes that the money manager is awarded the management of the entire $10 million. If yields fall to 8.0 per cent, the new price for the 7¼ per cent T-Bond will be much higher (equal to 91-30/32), and the September T-Bond futures price will also have risen to 99-04/32. The 92-00/32 call option is deeply in-the-money and is worth 7-6/64. The mechanics of the hedge would require the money manager to sell his call options on 28 June, receiving the premiums listed in the table. He would include the proceeds

ASSUMING THE MANAGER IS CHOSEN
AND PURCHASES THE 7 1/4 % T-BOND
PROFIT / LOSS TABLE ON 28/6/91

YIELDS ON 28/6	8.00 %	8.34 %	8.67 %	9.00 %	9.50 %
MARKET PRICE OF 7 1/4 % ON 14/6	85-18+	86-18+	85-18+	86-18+	85-18+
MARKET PRICE OF 7 1/4 % ON 28/6	- 91-30	- 88-20	- 85-18+	- 82-23	- 78-21
CHANGE IN PRICE FROM 14/6	(6-11+)	(3-01+)	0	+ 2-27+	+ 6-29+
$ LOSS ON $10,000,000	($635,937.5)	($304,687.5)	$ 0	$285,937.5	$692,187.5
SEPT T-BOND FUTURES PRICE OF 92.00	99-04	95-17	92-07	89-04	84-22
CALL OPTION ON 28/6	7-6/64	3-52/64	1-33/64	25/64	1/64
PRICE OF 92.00 CALL OPTION ON 14/6	- 1-40/64	- 1-40/64	- 1-40/64	- 1-40/64	- 1-40/64
OPTIONS PRICE CHANGE	+ 5-30/64	+ 2-12/64	(7/64)	(1-15/64)	(1-39/64)
NUMBER OF CONTRACTS	x 92	x 92	x 92	x 92	x 92
OPTIONS PROFIT/LOSS ($15.625 PER 1/64)	$503,125	$201,250	($10,062.5)	($113,562.5)	($148,062.5)
OVERALL HEDGE RESULT	($132,812.5)	($103,437.5)	($10,062.5)	$172,375	$544,125
YIELD EQUIVALENT	8.52 %	8.56 %	8.66 %	8.87 %	9.31 %

Table 7.5 T-Bond Options Hedge

(or losses) from the sale of the options to the $10,000,000 awarded by the pension fund and then purchase the 7¼ per cent T-Bonds. If he sold the 92 call for 7-6/64, then after deducting the initial premium payment of 1-40/64, his net profit would be 5-30/64 points for the 92 options or a gain of $503,125. The increased cost for the 7¼ per cent T-Bonds of $635,937.50 is substantially covered by the option's gain of $503,125. However, the options missed the mark of a perfect result by $132,812.5. The options contracts failed to keep pace with the movement in the T-Bonds because of two factors:

1. The time decay occurred over this period for the options;

2. Option price movements will be less than 100 per cent of the price change in the underlying owing to the delta factor.

In this case, while the yield achieved has been reduced to 8.52 per cent, it is still above the 8.50 per cent yield promised to the pension fund.

If yields had increased instead, the price of the T-Bonds the money manager intends to purchase would be cheaper. Unfortunately, the options prices would have fallen as well. So he would once again sell the options back to the market and get what he could. The difference between what he paid for the options and what he can sell them for is deducted from the savings of the cheaper T-Bonds to provide him his profit. If yields rise to 9.00 per cent, the 7¼ per cent T-Bond is $285,937.50 cheaper and the loss on the option premium is $113,562.50. So, he can still provide the yield he promised and pocket the difference of $172,375. If, instead, he decided to pass all these gains to the pension fund, then the realised yield could be increased to a 8.87 per cent yield. Furthermore, if yields rise to 9.5 per cent, the 7¼ per cent T-Bond will be $692,187.50 cheaper with the options position losing almost all its premium value. However, even with the $148,062.50 options premium loss, the money manager is ahead by $544,125. Again, if he passes this on to his client, the yield will be increased to 9.31 per cent. If

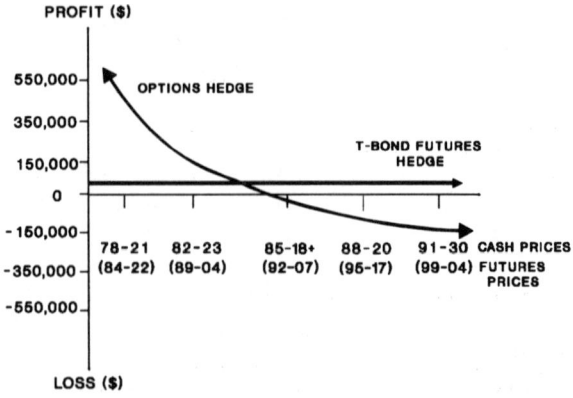

Figure 7.1 Hedge Comparison; T-Bond Futures versus T-Bond Options

the money manager had instead sold T-Bond futures at these levels, he would have locked in the 8.68 per cent yield. Therefore, in two weeks' time, the options hedge would allow the money manager a 'floor' yield of 8.52 per cent and the chance to make significant profits if yields should rise and the T-Bond be cheaper to purchase. The comparison of the T-Bond futures and options hedges can be seen graphically in Figure 7.1.

So far, we have looked only at the hedge, assuming that the pension fund capital would be awarded to the money manager. If we examine the hedged positions with the assumption that the board of directors rejects the services of the money manager, then we see a very different picture.

Comparison of T-Bond Futures and Call Options Hedges if the Cash Market Exposure does not Materialise

Suppose the contract is not awarded on 28 June. The money manager would have to lift the hedged position and – depending upon the prevailing yields and the hedging strategy he chose – have a profit or loss on the strategy.

The Impact of the Open T-Bond Futures Contracts
The hedge which is now unmatched is equivalent to an exposed position in either T-Bond futures or options. Let us consider the implications of our money manager not being awarded the pension plan funds for the futures hedged position he has established. If he bought the futures at 92-04/32 and the underlying T-Bond market did not change, then his now exposed position would experience a slight gain from the convergence. He could get out of his position with a small profit. But if the futures market increased, he would make a substantial profit of perhaps $644,000 on the futures contract if yields dropped to 8.00 per cent. (At that point the T-Bond futures price would be 99-04/32.) If the market went the other way, he would face equally

ASSUMING THE MANAGER IS NOT CHOSEN

PROFIT / LOSS TABLE ON 28/6/91

YIELDS ON 28/6	8.00 %	8.34 %	8.67 %	9.00 %	9.50 %
SEPTEMBER T-BOND FUTURES PRICE 28/6	99-04	95-17	92-07	89-04	84-22
SEPTEMBER T-BOND FUTURES PRICE 14/6	- 92-04	- 92-04	- 92-04	- 92-04	- 92-04
CHANGE IN FUTURES PRICE	+ 7-00	+ 3-13	+ 03	(3-00)	(7-14)
NUMBER OF CONTRACTS	x 92	x 92	x 92	x 92	x 92
FUTURES PROFIT/LOSS	$644,000	$313,375	$8,625	($276,000)	($684,250)

Table 7.6 T-Bond Futures Hedge

substantial losses. This can be seen in Table 7.6 (which contains the same numbers as Table 7.4 without the impact of the 7¼ per cent T-Bond). In the worst case, he would suffer a loss of $684,250 for an 83 basis point increase in yields for the T-Bond market. (At a 9.50 per cent yield the T-Bond future price would be 84-22/32.) Since he has an unlimited loss potential and an unlimited gain potential with the futures contract, he faces a significant exposure to interest rates and changes in T-Bond futures prices.

The Impact of the Open Call Option Positions

Let us now compare this with the call option hedge. If the contract to manage the funds is cancelled two weeks later, our money manager can simply sell the call option back to the market (like cancelling an insurance policy and receiving the outstanding premium back). When he sells it, he will be paid the two components of an option's value: the intrinsic value and the time value. Table 7.7 displays the value of the call options in this circumstance. (Again, like Table 7.6, Table 7.7 has the same numbers as Table 7.5. The only difference is that the cashflows for the 7¼ per cent T-Bond have been removed.) To determine how much cash he will receive back, the value of the call is multiplied by 92 (contracts) at each appropriate futures price level. Since he initially paid $149,500 (92 contracts $\times$ $15.625 per ¼ point $\times$ 104^9 of the ¼4s), his net profit or loss on the options hedge will be the amount he retrieves less this amount that he paid on 14 June. If yields increase to 9.50 per cent or decrease to 8.00 per cent, the profit/loss on the option is in a range between a $503,125 profit and a $148,062.50 loss. As can be seen in Table 7.6, the uncovered futures hedge has a much larger gain and loss potential with a loss at the 9.50 per cent yield at $684,250. On the other side, when yields fall to 8.00 per cent, the futures position picks up $647,000, which is $143,875 more than the options position at the same level ($647,000 – $503,125). In fact, the option losses start levelling out very quickly to a loss amount limited by the premium expense. Figure 7.2 displays graphically the profits and losses of both the T-Bond futures hedge and the T-Bond options hedge if the manager is not

ASSUMING THE MANAGER IS NOT CHOSEN

PROFIT / LOSS TABLE ON 28/6/91

YIELDS ON 28/6	8.00 %	8.34 %	8.67 %	9.00 %	9.50 %
SEPT. T-BOND FUTURES PRICE 28/6	99-04	95-17	92-07	89-04	84-22
PRICE OF 92.00 CALL OPTION ON 28/6 [1]	7-6/64	3-52/64	1-33/64	25/64	1/64
PRICE OF 92.00 CALL OPTION ON 14/6	- 1-40/64	- 1-40/64	- 1-40/64	- 1-40/64	- 1-40/64
OPTIONS PRICE CHANGE	+ 5-30/64	+ 2-12/64	(7/64)	(1-15/64)	(1-39/64)
NUMBER OF CONTRACTS	x 92	x 92	x 92	x 92	x 92
OPTIONS PROFIT/LOSS ($15.625 PER 1/64)	$503,125	$201,250	($10,062.5)	($113,562.5)	($148,062.5)

[1] THE OPTION PRICE WAS DETERMINED THEORETICALLY USING 49 DAYS TO EXPIRATION AND A VOLATILITY OF 10.5 %.

Table 7.7 T-Bond Options Hedge

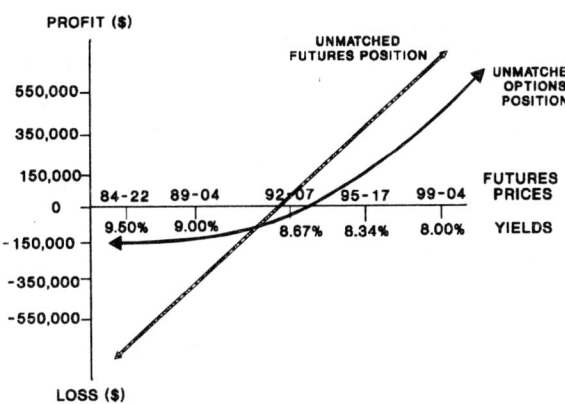

Figure 7.2 Unmatched Futures Position

chosen to manage the funds. Therefore, if the money manager's services are not retained and he used an options hedge, he faces a maximum loss potential of $148,062.50 while the futures position could lose more than four times this amount in the worst possible scenario.

Comparison of T-Bond Futures and T-Bond Options Impacts

One can see that the options hedge does not only have a limited loss and unlimited gain potential, but also does not experience as much profit or loss compared to hedging with the T-Bond futures. An unmatched T-Bond futures position has an unlimited loss potential while an unmatched option position has a limited loss potential. Thus, *a priori*, the money manager should prefer options over futures for this hedging situation. Effective hedging is the minimisation of the expected change in net wealth. Clearly, in this case the options strategy minimises the risk for the money manager.

Quite often, options are ideal for reducing the risk of contingent situations. For example, currency options are often used when a corporation is bidding on a project abroad. These options provide protection in case the project is not secured and no foreign exchange receipts result. If the project is awarded, the option has insured the value of the foreign exchange position. Another contingent application is for corporations that purchase or sell raw materials without knowing the exact quantity of raw materials required. They may use futures to lock in the amount they know they will need, and use options for the remainder. Whenever a contingency is involved in a hedging situation, the hedger should look at options as the appropriate hedging tool.

HEDGING EXAMPLE 2: BUYING A PUT OPTION ON T-BOND FUTURES TO PROTECT THE VALUE OF A US TREASURY BOND

Another time when it is appropriate to buy options to hedge is to protect the value of underlying assets already held. Suppose I have purchased a US Treasury Bond and I want to protect its value. What I need is an insurance policy on the price of the security. As we discussed in Chapter 1, purchasing an option is similar to an insurance purchase. Furthermore, buying a put option can be thought of as 'selling price' insurance. So, buying put options can be an effective tool to protect a long T-Bond position against a decrease in its price by providing the right to sell at an appropriate level.

What would we expect the profit/loss profile of the put hedge to resemble? At the end of Chapter 3, we combined a long position in \$/£ forward (futures) with a long put option. The result was a new synthetic security. To jog the reader's memory: we determined the composition of this synthetic security by applying the put-call parity formula. We were able to prove that when we combine a long underlying position ($F - E$) with a long put ($+P$) the resulting payoff is identical to a long call ($+C$). So, when we hedge the holding of an asset with a put option, the payoff should resemble a long call with the maximum loss potential occurring when the underlying market price is equal to or less than the strike price. Therefore, the breakeven point is the price in the underlying futures equal to the strike price of the put plus the put option premium. At that point, the increase in the value of the underlying futures is sufficient to offset the cost of the put option, and above that is an unlimited profit potential. Let us go through a simple example.

Suppose the T-Bond futures is trading at 92-00/32 and we have purchased one futures contract. If we also bought a 92-00/32 put option and paid 1-27/64s for it, what would the payoff of this put hedging strategy be at the expiration of the option? If the T-Bond futures market finishes at 91-00/32, the futures position will have lost one full point and this will be exactly offset by the one full point in intrinsic value for the put. After the 1-27/64s premium has been taken into account, the net effect of the hedge is a loss of 1-27/64s in premium. If the T-Bond futures market remains at 92-00/32, there will be no profit or loss on the futures and the put option will also expire worthless. Again, the net effect of the hedge is a loss of the put option premium of 1-27/64s. If the T-Bond futures ends up at 93-14/32, then there is a profit of 1-14/32s on the long futures contract and again the 92-00/32 put option will expire worthless. After the 1-27/64s premium (which is equivalent to 1-13+/32) has been deducted, the net result of the position is that the put option expense has been covered by the movement in the underlying asset. This price is known as the breakeven point for the put hedge. If the T-Bond futures market rises to 94-00/32, then the long futures contract will have a profit of two full points, the put expires worthless and – after deducting the put option premium – the net profit is 37/64s (which is equivalent to 18+/32s). The reader will recognise that this is exactly the same payoff as a long 92-00/32 call.

Complications of Using Options on T-Bond Futures to Hedge a US Treasury Bond

When one hedges a US Treasury Bond with options on T-Bond futures, the situation becomes more complicated. The hedge involves the use of a derivative of another derivative. That is, the underlying for options on T-Bond futures is the T-Bond futures, and the underlying for the T-Bond futures is a US Treasury Bond (which we may be interested in hedging). Therefore, to evaluate properly a T-Bond futures option hedging strategy, we must first compare the option strategy to its underlying (the T-Bond futures) and adjust that comparison for the relationship between the T-Bond futures and the underlying US Treasury Bond.

Suppose we are holding $10 million in par value of the 7½ per cent US Treasury Bonds maturing in 2016. Again it is 14 June (the prices for this security can be seen in Table 7.2) and the 7½ per cent US Treasury Bond also happens to be the cheapest to deliver into the futures market with a current yield of 8.679 per cent. Suppose too that we believe yields will increase by 16 August (the expiration of the September T-Bond futures options for the September 1991 delivery) and that we expect the value of these T-Bonds will decrease by then. However, we are unsure about when the yields may increase, and concerned that an increased volatility in the T-Bond market may occur instead. If this is the case, then it is possible that yields might fall instead of rising. In a highly volatile and uncertain market, we might want to limit our exposure and still be able to profit if the T-Bond market happens to rally. Thus, we purchase put options to establish a floor value for the T-Bond position and still retain the upside potential.

Since the options we can use (in Table 7.2) are offered at four separate strike prices, we have the opportunity to vary the degree of protection we want to receive and the price we will have to pay for it. For example, suppose you purchased collision insurance for your car and could choose between policies with no excess or one with a large excess (also known as a deductible). The one with no excess will cost more because the entire risk is passed off to the insurance broker. If, instead, you chose the insurance with a large excess, you are assuming part of the risk. Therefore, the insurance with an excess would be less expensive. A similar situation occurs when one is deciding which strike price to choose when hedging. Purchasing an at-the-money strike price put option is like purchasing an insurance policy with no excess, and the out-of-the-money strike price put options are more like purchasing an insurance policy with an excess. The more risk one assumes, the lower the cost of the insurance or of the option.

Choosing At-the-Money or Out-of-the-Money Puts

Referring back to Table 7.2, I will concentrate on the 90-00/32 and 92-00/32 put options. The premium for the 90-00/32 put is 43/64s and the 92-00/32 put is priced at 1-23/64s. Let us consider what these options offer us. One is the right to sell at 90-00/32 and the other is the right to sell at 92-00/32. The market is presently trading at 92-04/32. If I buy the right to sell at 90-00/32, then I do not get any protection until the futures market falls below 90-00/32. Therefore the 'excess' on this put 'insurance' will be more than two full Bond points. If I buy the 92-00/32 put, there is only an excess of 4/32. This is because the 92-00/32 is barely out-of-the-money and if the T-Bond futures price falls, the intrinsic value of this put option will thereafter increase one for one. Hence, the 92-00/32 put provides almost immediate coverage (relative to the T-Bond futures). This is the reason why it is more expensive than the 90-00/32 put which has a 2-04/32 point excess. Which option will I choose? Given the expectation that T-Bond futures are more likely to fall, I will be more conservative and purchase the put option with almost no excess (the 92-00/32 put).

Hedge Ratio Estimation

Since I have decided to purchase the 92-00/32 put option to hedge the exposure, I must now determine the proper hedge ratio. To do this for the $7\frac{1}{2}$ per cent T-Bond, I would divide the par value of the holding – which is $10,000,000 – by $100,000, and multiply the result by the conversion factor of 0.9463. The result is a hedge ratio of 94.63 contracts. Unfortunately, I cannot purchase 0.63 of an option contract, so I must either either 94 or 95 puts. The choice of which number to use will decide upon my view of whether it is more likely the market will fall or rise. Since the view is that it is more likely prices will fall for T-Bonds and that volatility may increase, I will choose to buy 95 puts and be slightly overhedged.

Conversion of the Option on T-Bond Futures to an Option on the US Treasury Bond

Having determined the hedge ratio, I will determine where the maximum loss occurs for the hedge and where the hedge breaks even. Since the ultimate underlying security is the $7\frac{1}{2}$ per cent T-Bond, I must then convert all our prices from the 8 per cent T-Bond futures standard to the levels of the $7\frac{1}{2}$ per cent T-Bond. To convert the put option on T-Bond futures to the level of the $7\frac{1}{2}$ per cent T-Bond, I simply multiply the strike price by the conversion factor for the $7\frac{1}{2}$ per cent T-Bond. When I do this, the 92 strike price is equivalent to a price of 87-02/32 for the $7\frac{1}{2}$ per cent US Treasury Bonds (92 × 0.9463). To determine the breakeven price for the put hedge, I first determine the breakeven for the put hedge relative to T-Bond futures. This is equal to the strike price of 92-00/32 plus the 1-23/64s in premium expense. (Remember that the long put hedge is equivalent to buying a call option.) So, the breakeven price for the put hedge in T-Bond futures terms is 93-12/32, and this translates to a price of 88-11+/32 for the $7\frac{1}{2}$ per cent T-Bond.

It is interesting to note that the 92-00/32 put option is at-the-money relative to the September T-Bond futures (which is currently at 92-04/32). However, when I convert the 92-00/32 put option into an equivalent 7½ per cent T-Bond price, the strike price of the option is now out-of-the-money. That is because the 92-00/32 strike price for the T-Bond futures is equivalent to an 87-02/32 strike price for the 7½ per cent T-Bond; and with the current 7½ per cent T-Bond price at 87- 31/32, the put is out-of-the-money relative to this security. The reason this has occurred is that the underlying T-Bond futures is at a discount to the cash US Treasury Bonds market, since short-term interest rates are lower (6.25 per cent) than the yields for the US Treasury Bonds (8.679 per cent) on 14 June. As discussed earlier, the short T-Bond futures hedger gives up this convergence loss so that the proceeds of the hedge are equal to the equivalent investment in short-term US government paper. Since the put option is a substitute strategy for selling the T-Bond futures, it will also be exposed to this convergence loss. Therefore, the put hedger will not only lose the premium he must pay, but will also lose an additional amount equal to the price differential between the T-Bond futures underlying the put and the 7½ per cent instrument to be hedged.

Hedge Results of the Put Purchase

Having converted the put option on T-Bond futures to a 7½ per cent equivalent, I can now examine the profit/loss profile of this hedge at the expiration of the put. Figure 7.3 displays the payoffs for the put, and the profit and loss profile for the 7½ per cent T-Bond on an unhedged basis. To assist the reader in comparing the levels of the 7½ per cent T-Bond and the T-Bond futures, I have included both the prices for the 7½ per cent T-Bond and the equivalent in the T-Bond futures. (The numbers directly above the x axis represent prices for the 7½ per cent, and the prices underneath in parentheses are the T-Bond futures prices.)

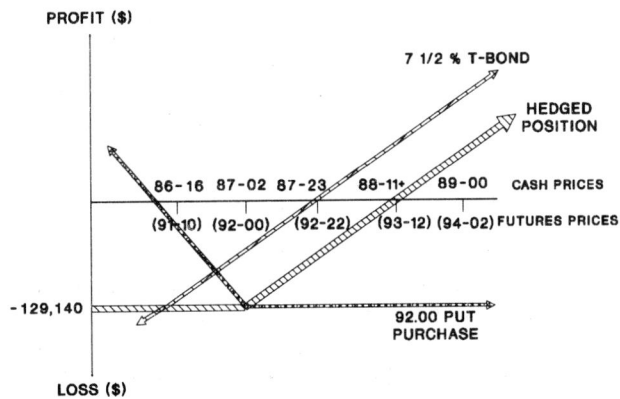

Figure 7.3 Hedging with a Put Option

The reader can see that the put option hedging does not provide immediate protection, but only after the 7½ per cent T-Bond has fallen to a price of 87-02/32. Below this level, the hedge has a limited loss of $129,140.63. The breakeven is at a 7½ per cent price of 88-11+/32 and the profit potential thereafter is unlimited. The hedged position, as expected, looks similar to a long call option. I forego some of the upside potential by paying an option premium, but the most I can lose is the premium paid.

When the market price of the 7½ per cent T-Bond decreases, I have an unlimited loss potential if the position is unhedged. This can be seen in Figure 7.3. However, the put options allow me to sell the security at a fixed price and thereby limit the loss for my holding of the 7½ per cent T-Bond. Thus, I am limiting the risk of falling markets without sacrificing the opportunities of rising markets.

HEDGING EXAMPLE 3: SELLING CALL OPTIONS ON T-BOND FUTURES AGAINST A US TREASURY BOND TO REDUCE RISK AND ENHANCE YIELDS

Having discussed hedging positions with short T-Bond futures and long put options, I will now examine another strategy for protecting a long position in US Treasury Bonds; this is to sell call options against the position. This is probably the most popular option hedging strategy used by institutional investors worldwide. It is commonly called covered call writing because you sell a call option and, at the same time, are holding the assets needed in case the option is exercised against you.

In this example, let us suppose an American institutional investor is holding 25 million dollars in the 8⅞ per cent T-Bond maturing on 15 August 2017. The price for this security is 101-29/32 (which can be found in Table 7.2). The basis for this security is 34.6, which is only slightly higher than the basis for the cheapest to deliver 7½ per cent T-Bond (at 25.3). Therefore, once again, the investor might consider this security to have a similar relationship to the underlying T-Bond futures as does the 7¼ per cent T-Bond and, for his purposes, consider it to be the cheapest to deliver T-Bond. The prevailing yield of this T-Bond is 8.686 per cent.

This time, the holder of the 8⅞ per cent T-Bond expects the T-Bond market to be stable over the period from 14 June to 16 August. Since his view differs from the one taken in the previous example, another strategy has to be employed. Suppose the investor's objective was to enhance the yield on his holdings and reduce the risk caused by an increase in yields. Since he has a long US Treasury Bonds position on one side, he must establish a short position on the other side. Of the three alternative short positions, the long put would be inappropriate given the investor's objectives. This also applies to a short futures hedge because it would reduce his risk but also reduce his yield (remember on 14 June, the futures is at a discount). So the only hedging strategy left is to sell a call option. The investor knows that he will be paid a premium and that if the call expires worthless, it will enhance his yield. Furthermore, if he is expecting the T-Bond market to be stable over the summer period, the chances that the call will be exercised are fairly small, especially if its strike price is currently out-of-the-money. Referring to the investor's view, selling a call would meet his objectives.

The Choice of the Call Option Strike Price to Sell

With the T-Bond futures market trading at 92-04/32, the investor looks at the four available call options in Table 7.2 and asks himself: 'Which one should I sell?' If he is correct in his predictions, market stability occurs and he sells the 90-00/32 call, he can be fairly certain that he will be exercised upon and will either have to offset the position in the T-Bond futures market or ultimately deliver his T-Bond. But he may not want to sell his T-Bond; he may only want to increase its yield over this period. If this is the case, the 90-00/32 strike price call would not meet his needs. What about the 92-00/32, 94-00/32 and the 96-00/32 strike price calls? The 92-00/32 call will provide a premium inflow of 1-40/64s, the 94-00/32 call will provide an inflow of 49/64s and the 96-00/32 call will only yield 20/64s. So, it would appear that if his goal is to maximise his yield, then the 92-00/32 call would be the best choice. However, the investor must be aware that he gives up all the profit potential above the strike price of the option when he sells a call option against his T-Bond. This means, if the call is exercised, he will experience losses that directly offset any gains achieved by a favourable change in the price of his T-Bond. The choice of the strike price is quite simple; the investor must choose a strike price that is equal to where he believes the market will end up on the expiration date of the option. In this example, the investor really expects no movement in the market and that the futures will finish at the current levels to slightly higher. Considering this, he decides to sell the 92-00/32 call option and receives a premium of 1-40/64s per option.

Hedge Ratio Determination

So far, the investor has determined the most appropriate strategy and which strike price to use. Now he needs to estimate the correct hedge ratio. Once again, the $7\frac{1}{2}$ per cent and the $8\frac{7}{8}$ per cent T-Bonds are almost equally cheap to deliver. This allows him to determine the hedge ratio using the simple conversion factor formula. The correct hedge ratio is the par value of the T-Bond holdings ($25,000,000) divided by the par value of the T-Bond futures ($100,000) and multiplied by the conversion factor for the $8\frac{7}{8}$ per cent T-Bond (1.0946). This will result in a hedge ratio of 273.65 call options. Again, it is not possible to sell 0.65 of one option, so the investor will round to the nearest integer and sell 274 of the 92-00/32 call options. With each option worth 1-40/64s, he will have a total premium inflow of $445,250 (274 contracts $\times$ $15.625 per $\frac{1}{64} \times$ 104 64s).

Results of the Covered Call Hedging Strategy

If the T-Bond futures market ends up equal to or less than 92-00/32 in 63 days, he will retain all the premium as income. If the T-Bond futures market increases above 92-00/32, his income will depend on how much the futures price will have risen. If the T-Bond futures rises to 93-20/32, he will break even on the hedge relative to his unhedged position. Above that, he will have a maximum income equal to the call option premium he was paid, and a yield lower than the one he would have achieved without hedging. Again, this goes back to the basics of options discussed in Chapter 1. Figure 7.4 presents the profit/loss profile for the covered call writing relative to a long position in the 8⅞ per cent T-Bond at the expiration of the options. In this figure, the prices above the x axis are again the equivalent 8⅞ per cent prices, with the associated T-Bond futures prices immediately below in parentheses.

Suppose the long position in US Treasury Bonds was established when the T-Bond futures was trading at 92-04/32. You have sold a call option and bought the underlying. As prices fall, the unlimited loss potential of the underlying T-Bond dominates the limited gain potential of the call option. Thus, the net effect is an unlimited loss potential for both positions. If prices rise, the covered call write position has a limited gain potential with the most you can gain on the hedge being equal to the premium paid to you for the call. In summary, the hedged position makes money when the futures market increases and loses money when the market decreases with a limited gain potential and an unlimited loss potential.

Upon careful consideration of the hedged position's payoff diagram, the reader might wonder how a short call option could end up looking 'backwards'. The reason is that the combined portfolio has an identical payoff structure to that of selling a put, which also makes money when the market increases and loses as the market falls. In fact, it is hardly surprising if one recalls the put-call parity formula discussed in Chapter 3.

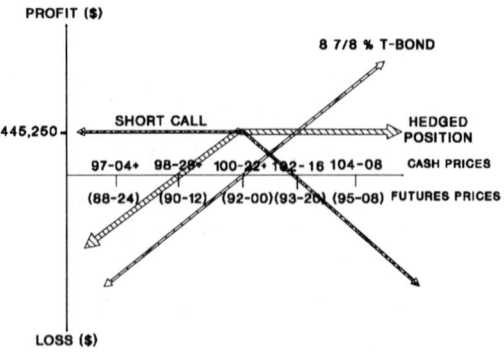

Figure 7.4 Covered Call Writing Results

The Risks of the Covered Call Hedging Strategy

With the covered call hedging strategy, considerable risk still exists. One might step back at this point and say: 'I thought the objective in hedging was to eliminate the loss potential'. Since covered call writing still retains an unlimited loss potential, how can it be considered hedging? Well, is the covered call position any worse than holding the underlying US Treasury Bonds position unhedged? Both have an unlimited loss potential. The difference is that the covered call hedge brings in a premium which serves as a buffer to losses as prices fall.

For example, suppose the market drops from 92-04/32 to 90-16/32. The position has lost 1-20/32s on the underlying T-Bond futures. As the market goes from 92-04/32 to 90-16/32, the call options that were sold against the position expire worthless and the inflow of 1-40/64s in option premium will exactly offset that loss. If the market decreases further, you continue to lose on the underlying position but by selling the call you are 1-40/64s better off than you would have been otherwise. The cost of this buffer is the foregone opportunity if the market instead increases. However, since there might be up to six actively-traded T-Bond option strike prices that one can choose from when selling the calls, the hedger has an equally wide range of possible payoff structures that can emphasise downside protection or upside opportunities. Figure 7.5 displays the possible payoffs to a covered call writing programme using out-of-the-money, at-the-money, and in-the-money call options.

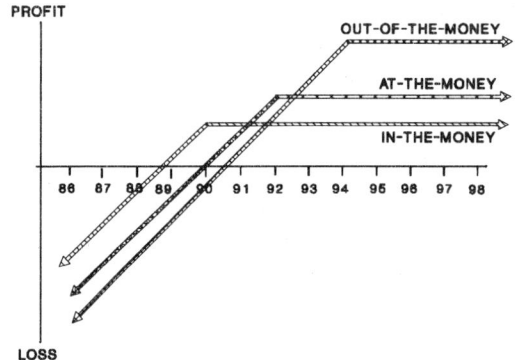

Figure 7.5 Alternative Covered Call Writing Results

Performance of the Covered Call Hedging Strategy

How would this strategy perform? When these options were sold, the 8⅞ per cent T-Bonds were at a yield of 8.686 per cent. Let us suppose that yields had actually increased slightly to 8.70 per cent at the expiry of the options in the middle of August 1991. The prices of the T-Bonds therefore remain basically unchanged (101-25/32). The futures market would have a current price of 92-11/32 which means that 92-00/32 calls would finish in-the-money. Since they have expired in-the-money, the options

$$\text{RETURN} = \text{INTEREST} \begin{array}{c} + \\ - \end{array} \begin{array}{c} \text{BOND} \\ \text{RETURN} \end{array} \begin{array}{c} + \\ - \end{array} \begin{array}{c} \text{OPTION} \\ \text{RETURN} \end{array}$$

$$= \frac{\$382{,}962.30 - \$35{,}156.25 + \$351{,}062.50}{\$25{,}476{,}562.50} * \frac{365}{63}$$

$$= 15.89\%$$

Figure 7.6 Formula for Determining Return for Covered Call Writing Strategy

will be exercised and the hedger will have to fork over the intrinsic value of 11/32s (which is equal to 22/64s). He has also experienced a small loss of 4+/32s on the cash position. Consequently, if the T-Bond holder had remained unhedged, he would have achieved an 8.686 per cent yield. By selling the 92-00/32 call options against his holdings he was given the opportunity to increase his realised yield. The formula to estimate this return can be seen in Figure 7.6.

In this formula, the return for a covered call writing strategy is calculated by first estimating the interest received on the particular instrument. In our case, it is for 63 days on an 8⅞ per cent coupon for $25 million ($382,962.30). The next step is to subtract the loss on the US Treasury Bonds position (how it actually changed in value) of $35,156.25 and then add the option premium retained at expiration which equals $351,062.50. Finally, this sum is divided by the value of the underlying US Treasury Bonds holdings at the beginning of the period. By converting it to an annualised basis (365 days divided by 63), one finds that a 15.89 per cent yield has been achieved for the holding period.

The way this strategy works is similar to the way casinos make money. Those who are selling call options against their holdings are basically providing a 'bet' to speculators. These speculators are paying for the right to possess what they do not have. However, over the long term, does the casino or the gambler make more money? The casino, of course, because the casino has what the gambler wants: money. So if you hold the assets, you can act like the casino and speculators will pay you for the chance of a big payoff. Considerable research has shown that you can consistently increase your returns and reduce your risk by writing call options against your holdings.[10]

HEDGING EXAMPLE 4: SELLING PUT OPTIONS IN ANTICIPATION OF THE PURCHASE OF A US TREASURY BOND

In this final section of Chapter 7, I will discuss another possible hedging strategy which is to sell put options. This is considered a hedging strategy when the investor has a short position in the T-Bond market. As was the case with the call buyer, the investor may not actually have sold short the security but might have a position where he will profit or lose from market movements as if he were short. The classic example of this is someone who anticipates buying a US Treasury Bond at some point in the future. When he sets his cash aside in anticipation of a purchase and sells put options to protect himself, the hedging strategy is referred to as cash secured put writing.

Imagine the following situation. The yield for the 9¼ per cent US Treasury Bond is currently at 8.701 per cent on 14 June and you are interested in buying this T-Bond. However, you believe the yields will improve to 9.10 per cent shortly. If you bought this T-Bond today and yields did increase, you would experience a capital loss on your investment. Therefore, you decide not to buy now but to wait. One thing you could do is put in an order with your broker to buy the T-Bond for you when the yields rise to 9.10 per cent, and keep you money in deposits until the time your order is filled. But suppose, instead, you decided to make use of the T-Bond futures market to achieve your 9.10 per cent yield. With a few calculations, it is easy to determine that at a 9.10 per cent yield the T-Bond futures price should be around 90-00/32. So you could place an order to buy the T-Bond futures at 90-00/32 (with the current price at 92-04/32) and hope for the best. However, this is the equivalent to putting in an order to buy the cash market. Another thing you could do is assume the obligation to buy the T-Bond futures at 90-00/32 and, if you play your cards right, someone will pay you a premium for agreeing to do so. Is this too good to be true? Well, no. You have just sold a 90-00/32 put option.

Remember that when you buy a put option, you pay a premium and receive the right to sell. The put seller receives this premium and is obliged to buy from the put buyer upon exercise. If you are certain that you wish to buy at a 9.10 per cent yield (or a futures price of 90-00/32), then the short put can be a clever alternative to placing your purchase order.

Results of the Cash Secured Put Writing Hedging Strategy

The profit/loss profile for this strategy can be seen in Figure 7.7. The reader will see that the payoff for the cash secured put writing strategy looks remarkably like the payoff for selling a 'naked' call (that is an uncovered call). You will see that the combination of a short put with a short position in the underlying will provide the same payoff as selling a call option.

Cash secured put writing works particularly well when the yield curve environment is inverted. That means short-term interest rates are higher than longer maturity yields. Let us look at a hypothetical situation in the US. Suppose an investor could receive a 10.00 per cent return on short-term money market instruments. At the same time, the best he could achieve in the longer end of the T-Bond market would be an 8.701 per cent yield. He may not wish to invest in long-term debt that only offers an 8.701 per cent return at this time, but he might be willing to buy T-Bonds if he could receive a 9.10 per cent yield. Furthermore, suppose he feels the yields for the T-Bond market will rise for a while but eventually drop. In these circumstances he would invest all

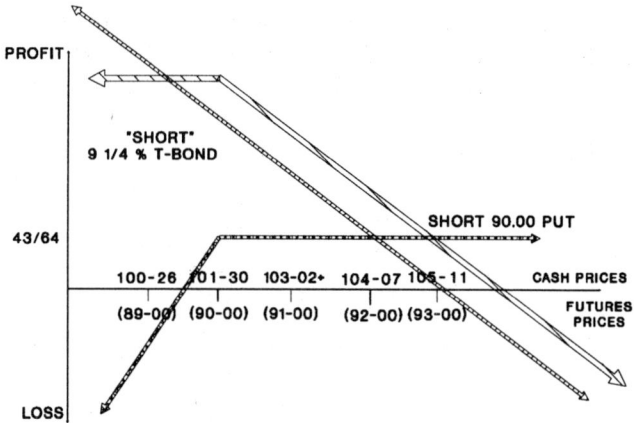

Figure 7.7 Cash Secured Put Strategy

his funds in the money markets and then enhance the yield on his short-term instruments by selling the 90-00/32 put options. If rates increase above the 9.10 per cent threshold, the put options he has sold will be exercised and he will have to buy T-Bonds at the more attractive yield of 9.10 per cent. On the other hand, if yields remain below that 9.10 per cent level for T-Bonds his investment will earn 10 per cent for the investment period plus an additional 43/64s for each put option he sells (see Table 7.2 for the 91-00/32 put price).

As long as the yield curve remains inverted, the short-term investment will be preferred. However, if the yield curve returns to its normal shape this will probably be associated with an increase in longer maturity yields. His put options will oblige him to purchase a long-term T-Bond with a very attractive yield, with the additional benefit of the put option premium income. Therefore, he can receive money for agreeing to buy the underlying at the yield in which he was interested in the first place.

SUMMARY

The purpose of this chapter has been to show the reader how to utilise a variety of hedging objectives to choose the most appropriate futures or options hedging strategy. I have presented detailed examples of hedging by purchasing both call and put options, and of how investors can sell options to increase yields and reduce risks. While it is possible to construct other hedging strategies using combinations of different option strike prices, these four basic hedging strategies should be enough to get the hedger ready to use options to reduce the risks of dealing in any underlying market.

[1] By definition, then, options on T-Bond futures are a derivative of a derivative.

[2] When a 32nd price for a Treasury Bond has either a '-' or a '+' associated with it, that means the price is midway between that 32nd and the next lower or higher 32nd. For example, a price of 85-18+/32 means 85 per cent of the par value plus 18.5/32. This is also equal to 37/64s. If

the price were 85-18-/32, then this would be equal to 85 per cent of par plus 17.5/32. Thus, 17+/32s is equal to 18-/32s and is also equal to 35/64s. The convention is to not use '-'s in the quotes but rather '+'s or 64ths.

3   To determine the future price equivalent of a particular US Treasury Bond, one simply applies the following formula: Current US Treasury Bond Price/Conversion factor.

4   See Allan M. Loosigian, 'Interest Rate Futures and Option Strategies in Fixed-Income Portfolio Management', *The Financial Analyst's Handbook,* ed. Sumner N. Levine, 2nd Edition, Homewood, Illinois, Dow Jones-Irwin, pp.1450-51 (1988)

5   Since the basis for the 7¼ per cent T-Bond is 26.3 basis points and this should converge to 0 basis points in 108 days, he can do a simple linear extrapolation to see how much the basis should have dropped in 14 days. The specific formula would be basis/days to futures delivery times the number of days for the hedge. In this example, 26.3/108 days times 14 days equals 3.4 basis points.

6   To determine the yield effect of the 3.4 basis point convergence profit on the futures, we determined the yield for a futures contract with an 8 per cent coupon, a maturity of 20 years and at a price of 92-04/32. The yield was 8.85 per cent. Then, we changed the futures price to 92-07+/32 (including the 3.4 basis points in convergence gain) and re-evaluated the yield. The new yield was 8.83 per cent. Note that when yields go down prices will rise.

7   This result is mostly due to the positive convergence of the T-Bond futures of 3.4 basis points over the two-week period. If one multiplies $3.4 \times \$31.25 \times 92$ the result is $9775.

8   A thorough discussion of why one uses the same hedge ratio for the options as one would with T-Bond futures will follow in Chapter 8 with the delta hedging example.

9   The reason why it is 104 64s is that 1-40/64 is equal to 64/64 + 40/64 which equals 104/64.

10 A short and sweet paper the reader may wish to refer to is John W. Labuszewski, 'Using Dynamic Covered Calls to Enhance Yields', *Futures,* Vol.XVIII, No.8, pp.42-45 (August 1989).

8: Option Portfolio Applications

This chapter discusses the potential portfolio applications of options. It differs from the previous chapter in emphasis. There I examined options in a tactical light: how one can use call options as substitutes for the purchase of an underlying asset (a US Treasury Bond); how to buy puts to speculate on declines; how to sell call options to enhance yields by expecting volatility to decrease; and how to write cash-secured put options in anticipation of a better price in the underlying market. In this chapter, I will place more emphasis on the strategic applications of options in portfolio management. The options contracts I use to explain these concepts include the Standard & Poors 100 (S&P 100) Stock Index option traded at the Chicago Board Options Exchange (CBOE), and options on the Standard & Poors 500 (S&P 500) Stock Index futures traded at the Index and Options Market (IOM) of the Chicago Mercantile Exchange. In addition, I will examine the use of the S&P 500 Stock Index futures also traded at the IOM. The contract specifications for all these contracts can be seen in Tables 8.1a, 8.1b and 8.1c.

When one thinks of portfolio management, the underlying assets which probably come to mind are shares since most of the breakthrough research on portfolio theory applied to stocks.[1] The conclusion of these seminal papers was that the best way (in terms of expected risk and return) to invest in stock markets was to buy the entire market. To facilitate the measurement of the movement of the entire stock market, Stock Indices were constructed which measured either the entire stock market or a representative subset of that market. To understand why Stock Index futures and options are among the most actively traded of all derivative products, we must first understand the concepts of index construction[2] and later examine the basics of portfolio theory which underlie these products.

BASICS OF STOCK INDICES

A Stock index is a measure of the value of a group of stocks. Stock indices are compiled and published by various sources, including securities markets. An index may be designed to be representative of the stock market as a whole, of a particular broadly based sector, or of a particular industry. It is ordinarily standardised relative to a 'base' period when the index was first created. For example, suppose a new 'value-weighted' index were created today with the total value of the component stocks (market prices times the number of shares outstanding) equal to $25 billion. The publisher of the index assigns an arbitrary index level of, let's say, 500. He does this by dividing the

TRADING UNIT	$100 TIMES THE CURRENT VALUE OF THE INDEX
EXPIRATION MONTHS	EACH OF THE FOUR NEARBY MONTHS
EXPIRATION DATE	FIRST SATURDAY FOLLOWING THE THIRD FRIDAY OF THE EXPIRATION MONTH
PREMIUM QUOTATIONS	DOLLARS AND FRACTIONS PER UNIT OF THE INDEX. EACH PREMIUM POINT REPRESENTS $100. THE MINIMUM FRACTION IS 1/16 (FOR SERIES TRADING IN FIRST 4 NEARBY MONTHS) AND 1/8 FOR ALL OTHER LONGER MATURITIES
EXERCISE PRICE	FIVE POINT INTERVALS TO BRACKET THE CURRENT VALUE OF THE INDEX

Table 8.1a S&P 100 Index Options (CBOE)

TRADING UNIT	ONE S&P 500 FUTURES CONTRACT
EXPIRATION MONTHS	ALL TWELVE CALENDAR MONTHS
LAST DAY OF TRADING	MARCH, JUNE, SEPTEMBER, DECEMBER: THURSDAY PRIOR TO THE THIRD FRIDAY. OTHER 8 MONTHS: THE THIRD FRIDAY
MINIMUM PRICE MOVEMENT (TICK SIZE)	0.05 INDEX POINTS • $25.00 PER CONTRACT
EXERCISE PRICE INTERVALS	5.00 POINTS
TRADING HOURS	8:30 - 15:15 (CHICAGO TIME)

Table 8.1b Options on S&P 500 Index Futures (CME)

TRADING UNIT	$500 TIMES THE CURRENT VALUE OF THE INDEX
EXPIRATION MONTHS	MARCH, JUNE, SEPTEMBER, DECEMBER
LAST DAY OF TRADING	THURSDAY PRIOR TO THE THIRD FRIDAY OF THE CONTRACT MONTH
MINIMUM PRICE MOVEMENT (TICK SIZE)	0.05 INDEX POINTS • $25.00 PER CONTRACT
EXERCISE PRICE INTERVALS	N/A
TRADING HOURS	8:30 - 15:15 (CHICAGO TIME)

Table 8.1c S&P 500 Index Futures (CME)

value of the stock portfolio today ($25 billion) by the value at the base period (which is also today $25 billion) and multiplies this result by 500. If the market value of the component stocks in the index rose tomorrow by 2.5 per cent to be worth $25.625 billion, then the new value of the index would be $25.625 billion/$25 billion × 500 or a new level of 512.50. Thus the index level would rise by the same amount (2.5 per cent) as the value of the underlying portfolio.

This base may be adjusted from time to time to reflect such events as changes in the capitalisation, or to maintain continuity as stocks are added or deleted from the index group. These changes are generally made to assure that any changes in the index level will result only as a result of price changes occurring from trading.

There is a variety of ways to calculate stock indices. The most popular indices referred to by institutional investors (like the Standard & Poors Stock Indices) are 'value weighted'. This means that the market prices of the stocks included in the index are each multiplied by the number of shares outstanding. Because of this method of calculation, changes in the stock prices of larger corporations will generally have a greater influence on the level of the index than the price changes of smaller corporations.

Another popular method for index construction is the 'price weighted' index. These indices simply sum the prices of the component shares and divide by the value of the shares in the base period. Popular price indices include the Dow Jones Industrial Average, the Nikkei Dow Index and the Major Market Index (which trades as a futures and options contract at the Chicago Board of Trade and elsewhere). These price indices allow each stock in the index to have more or less equal impact on the level of the index, and are often preferred to the 'value weighted' ones by traders who place more importance on price changes.

The final kind of stock index construction is known as a 'geometric weighted' approach. These indices are based upon the percentage changes in either the 'value' or 'prices' of their component shares. The percentage changes of each of the components are summed and then multiplied by the level of the index in the previous period to provide the index value today. These have proved to be the least popular of stock indices used by either institutional investors or traders. The Value Line index (which underlies futures and option contracts at the Kansas City Board of Trade) is an example of a 'value' weighted geometric index and the Financial Times 30 is an example of a 'price' weighted geometric index.

STOCK INDEX FUTURES CONTRACTS

The most popular stock index futures contracts on US equities is the Standard & Poors 500 Stock Index futures traded at the IOM. However, at the beginning of 1991, 39 stock index futures or options contracts were offered in 17 countries (19 of which trade in the US). This contract is equal to $500 times the futures price of the S&P 500 Stock Index. For example, with a price of 300.50, the value of one futures contract would be $500 × 300.50, or $150,250. At the expiration of the futures contract, the final futures settlement price is set equal to the level of the cash S&P index on that day. The S&P 500 futures price will generally follow the movement of the underlying index, but the level will usually be different until the final day when they are exactly equal. The advantage of participating in the stock market with S&P 500 Stock Index futures rather than the actual stocks is that the position can be established in the futures market with only a margin payment, while the excess funds can remain in more liquid assets such as deposits. Furthermore, the transaction costs involved in trading futures can be as little as 10 per cent of the cost in purchasing (or selling) an equivalent amount in the cash market.

On the final settlement date for the S&P 500 futures, no delivery of shares occurs but rather there is a cash transferral equal to the difference between the level of the cash index and the level at which the futures contract was originally established. This procedure, called 'cash settlement', assures liquidity and efficient settlement of the contracts. Compared with the physical delivery of the T-Bond futures discussed in the previous chapter, there is no 'cheapest to deliver' into the Stock Index futures. The only underlying the hedger or trader need consider is the stock index itself. The contract specifications for the S&P 500 futures can be seen in Table 8.1c.

Options on Stock Index Futures Contracts

Also traded at the IOM are options on S&P 500 Stock Index futures. These contracts are the right but not the obligation of buy or sell an S&P 500 futures contract any time before the option expires. Exercise of the option prior to expiration will result in an S&P 500 futures contract position being assigned to the holder on the next business day (and the writer will be assigned an opposite position in the S&P 500 futures). This was discussed in detail in Chapter I with the COMEX gold option. At the expiration of the option contract, cash settlement also occurs as it does for the futures contract. The cash inflow for the call option holder will be equal to the amount the cash S&P 500 Index is above the call's strike price (if the Index is equal to or less than the call strike price, no cash is transferred). The cash inflow for the put option holder will be equal to the amount the S&P 500 Index is below the put's strike price (if the Index is equal to or greater than the put strike price, no cash is transferred). The contract specifications for the option on S&P 500 futures is displayed in Table 8.1b.

Options on Stock Indices

Index options are very similar to stock options and are traded in essentially the same manner. The most popular of the options on a US stock index is the S&P 100 Stock Index option traded at the Chicago Board Options Exchange (CBOE). The underlying index is similar to the S&P 500 index. The S&P 100 index includes the stocks of those corporations which are roughly the 100 largest in the S&P 500. The major difference between stock options and stock index options is how exercise is handled. When the

S&P 100 Stock Index option is exercised, the settlement is made by the payment of cash and not by the delivery of stock. The assigned writer is obliged to pay the exercising holder cash in an amount equal to the difference between the current level of the S&P 100 Stock Index and the exercise price of the option times $100. The difference between options on stock indices and options on stock index futures is that upon exercise, the holder of the option on the stock index receives cash and the holder of the option on the stock index futures receives a position in the futures market. The contract specifications for the S&P 100 Stock Index option can be found in Table 8.1a.

Now that I have introduced the products, I will devote considerable space to the concept of risk and return and the rationale for stock index trading generally. In addition, I will examine how options and futures on stock indices allow the portfolio manager to restructure the patterns of his portfolio returns and control his risks. I will also explain some of the most popular portfolio applications of options on stock indices, namely the 90/10 money market and the 90/10 *plus* strategies, zero cost options, portfolio insurance and delta neutral strategies. Finally, I will conclude the chapter with examples of possible portfolio payoffs associated with the most popular futures and options hedging strategies. The first topic I will discuss is a popular call option buying strategy, known as 90/10.

The 90/10 Money Market Strategy

The 90/10 strategy is the name often applied to an investment in interest-bearing securities (typically short term) and the purchase of option contracts in some underlying market. The expression '90/10' comes from the convention of allocating 90 per cent of the investor's assets in risk-free money market instruments and 10 per cent in options.

Consider the case of a US portfolio manager who finds that short-term rates are particularly attractive in the current environment and believes the stock market is poised for a rally. He may wish to invest in short-term money market rates which are presently high and at the same time benefit if the stock market stages a dramatic increase. His objective is to earn the high short-term interest rates, but also to have the option to benefit from the potential capital gain associated with an increase in the value of the stock market.

Suppose that he has $10 million to invest on 19 June, the yield on six-month money markets is at 10 per cent and the price of the cash S&P 500 Stock Index is 376.65. The December S&P 500 futures is trading at 383.00 and a variety of options are available for the December S&P 500 futures. For this scenario, see Table 8.2 where the 375 call is priced at 19.25, the 380 call at 16.65, the 385 call is priced at 14.30, and the 390 call at 12.20. Four options give him the right to buy the December futures at prices of 375, 380, 385 and 390 (Table 8.2).

As discussed before, the rationale for this strategy is to benefit from the expectation that the stock market will rally dramatically in the next six months. However, because short-term interest-bearing securities are presently more attractive than the dividend

	YIELDS
6 MONTH MONEY MARKET RATE	**10.00%**
S&P STOCK INDEX	**376.65**
DEC S&P 500 FUTURES	**383.00**
	PRICES
DEC 375.00 CALL	**19.25**
DEC 380.00 CALL	**16.65**
DEC 385.00 CALL	**14.30**
DEC 390.00 CALL	**12.20**

Table 8.2 90/10. Market Conditions (June 19)

yield for the S&P 500 stocks (about 4.5 per cent), the investor will place the bulk of his funds there. Thus, the portfolio manager will place 90 per cent of his $10 million on the money market at ten per cent in a deposit which matures in six months on 19 December. With the remaining ten per cent, he will purchase call options on December S&P 500 futures.

Suppose that he chooses to purchase call options with a strike price of 385. With the $1 million allocated to the purchase of options, he could purchase 139 options giving him the right to purchase $26,757,500 worth of S&P 500 futures (the strike price of 385 × $500 × 139). The investment of $9 million in a ten per cent money market security will provide a return to the investor of the $9 million plus interest which in total is $9,450,000 in six months. The worst that can happen to the calls is that they expire worthless. So the investor knows the minimum value his portfolio can have in this worst case. He could vary the allocation mix to be somewhat different from 90 per cent/10 per cent. Suppose he places 95.24 per cent of his funds in money market deposits, and with the remaining $476,000 he purchases the 385 call options. He can still purchase 66 options which give him the right to buy $12,705,000 worth of S&P 500 futures (the strike price of 385 × $500 × 66). In this case, the money market security will provide a cash inflow of $10 million on 19 December, and no matter what happens to the stock market he will have guaranteed recouping his initial investment. This strategy is the basis for guaranteed investment funds. In addition, he would have the right to hold a position greater than the magnitude of what he would hold by placing all of his funds in stocks in the S&P 500. By varying the allocation ratio devoted to options from ten per cent to 0 per cent, he can achieve a minimum payback on this investment strategy of between $9,450,000 and $10,500,000.

The 90/10 *Plus* Strategy for Options with Futures Style Margining

At a number of exchanges (for example the Sydney Futures Exchange), the ability to margin the call options purchase means that the 90/10 strategy is even more advantageous; and I will rename it the 90/10 money market *plus* strategy.

In a traditional 90/10, 90 per cent of the assets are placed in a money market instrument, and ten per cent remains. At the exchanges with futures-style margining of option premium, the option is not paid up front, but the position is margined and one pays the premium ultimately at expiration. These exchanges allow one to use a variety of interest-bearing securities as the basis for margin. These instruments generally include short-term Government paper and sometimes Government Bonds. Theoretically, one could place the entire $10 million in one of these instruments and leave it at the exchange as the basis for purchasing the options. For example, our investor could place all the dollars in one of these instruments that matures in six months that provide a ten per cent yield, and know with certainty that on the 19 December $10,500,000 would be returned. The clearing house would treat this as an initial margin payment and guarantee the position. Therefore, because all the money would be in a ten per cent investment, the investor could simply use the interest earned to purchase options, leaving the principal of $10 million untouched.

With the $500,000 earned in interest, he could buy a packet of options. For example, if such futures-style margining were available at the IOM, the number of 385 call options purchased would be 70 (an additional 4 options), equivalent to $13,475,000 worth of S&P 500 futures. In the worst case, if the options expired worthless, he would get back his $10 million. If the stock market actually rallied, the S&P 500 futures price would increase, leaving a leveraged position in S&P 500 futures; any profit from this would be added to his holdings. As, at the futures-style margined exchange, the option premium is ultimately paid at expiration when the instrument pays its interest, the portfolio manager knows *a priori* his cashflows. So, the investor looking to implement a 90/10 strategy should see if the exchange he is dealing on allows this extra bonus. However, for the IOM this feature is not possible, so we will return to the original strategy of the 90/10.

Results of the 90/10 Call Option Buying Strategy

If the investor decides that he wants to apply the 90/10 strategy *and* guarantee the return of his initial endowment, he will not use a 90 per cent/10 per cent allocation ratio but will choose instead a 95.24 per cent/4.76 per cent allocation ratio. As was shown above, this will assure that $10 million will be returned regardless of what happens to the stock market by December. The result on 19 June is that the investor is guaranteed the preservation of his capital and, irrespectively, will recover his $10 million. In addition, he has the chance to buy the S&P 500 Index at a price of 385 for 66 contracts. These 66 contracts would be equivalent to $12.70 million worth of S&P 500 futures. The profit/loss profile for this strategy can be seen in Figure 8.1. As you

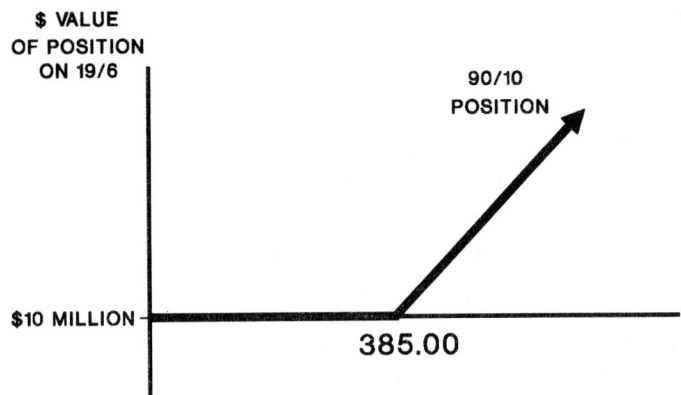

Figure 8.1 Profit/Loss Profile

can see in this graph, regardless of what happens to the level of the stock market, the portfolio will be worth $10 million.

However, imagine that the stock market does rally above 385, which implies that the options are in-the-money. Since the options are in-the-money and thus have a delta close to 1, the investor has the equivalent of $12.70 million worth of S&P 500 futures. This is a considerable amount of leverage, especially since his capital is guaranteed. Any profit above the $10 million position would have to come from its highly levered position in the options on the S&P 500 futures.

What else could the investor do to achieve a similar levered position? Well, he could have chosen the strategy of buying the equivalent in S&P 500 futures and also placing a US Government security with the clearing house of the IOM for his margin requirement (futures contracts can be margined with such securities). Again, this position would provide the $500,000 in interest and no option premium would be required, but he would face an unlimited loss potential from an unfavourable move in stock prices. (If stock prices decreased, the S&P 500 futures would also decrease and his loss potential be unlimited.) In Figure 8.2, this strategy is compared with the 90/10

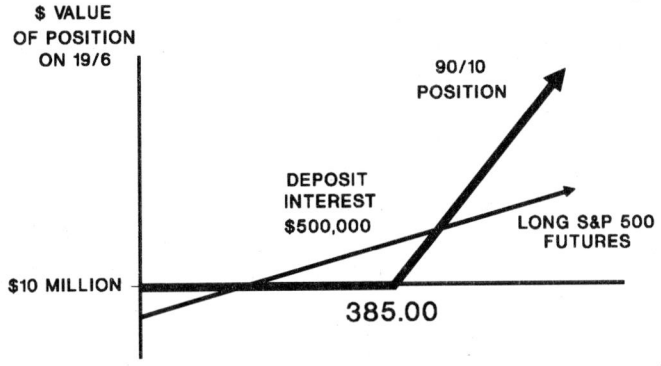

Figure 8.2 Profit/Loss Profile

strategy. The reader can see that the futures strategy is only better off by the $500,000 interest earned but the loss potential is unlimited.

What about the strategy of simply placing the investment in the stock market? In this case, if the dividend rate is only 4.5 per cent, then the investment will earn over the period $225,000 in dividends. Once again, the loss potential is not limited and, as with the S&P 500 futures, it could be substantial.

Furthermore, with the 90/10 levered position, if the underlying S&P 500 market increases, the position has 1.370 times more 'punch' than simply purchasing the S&P 500 Stock portfolio. If the market remains at the same level, buying the underlying instrument and getting the dividends, or just buying the futures contract and leaving the endowment in deposits earning ten per cent (which provides the margin coverage, earning $500,000) would be the more profitable alternatives. But with the levered position of the 90/10 strategy, if the market moves then this strategy wins on both sides. If the stock market falls by 19 December, the investor lets the options lapse and can reinvest the $10 million dollars that he gets back at what may be a high money market rate without incurring the capital loss of the alternative strategy of buying the S&P 500 stock index. If the stock market rallies, he has a position that is 1.370 times the size of his initial investment and will profit from the advantageous movement by this same multiple. Thus, the 90/10 strategy gives him the preservation of his capital and increased leverage. Therefore, it is easy to see why this strategy is extremely popular among portfolio managers worldwide.

The Zero Cost Options Hedging Strategy

Another important and interesting use of options in portfolio management is to create profit/loss payoffs which are flat for certain levels of the underlying asset and fully exposed for other levels. One example of this kind of contingent hedge is the popular zero cost option. A zero cost option is a combination of two options. The primary selling point of this strategy is that people do not pay any premium to pick up the limited loss benefits of a long option hedging strategy. To do this they must give up another option. This technique involves buying and selling options in such a way that the premium inflow and the premium outflow offset each other. These strategies are also known as hedge wraps, collars, range forwards, or cylinders.

I learned of a situation where this trade occurred when I was trading options in London. A certain Japanese institution was concerned about its exposure to the US dollar. They were interested in purchasing a currency option to cover this risk but were loath to pay a premium. They called their favourite currency broker and asked for help. The Japanese indicated a concern that the exchange rate for yen for dollars might fall below 125 yen per dollar. The current exchange rate was 130 yen per dollar. So, the broker determined the price for a 125 yen/dollar put options and informed the Japanese institution of the cost. The broker could tell from his client's voice that the cost of the option was prohibitive. Being a smart broker, he suggested that the cost of the option could be reduced if the Japanese were willing to 'give up' some of the unlimited profit potential if the dollar strengthened. The suggestion fell on responsive ears and he asked the Japanese client what was the upper limit that they believed that yen per dollar could attain within the life of the option. They felt that 135 yen/dollar was an acceptable ceiling. With this bit of information and the request by the Japanese client to reduce the premium expense as much as possible, the broker set to work.

His proposed strategy was to sell a 125 put option to his client and purchase back from the client a 135 call option. This would reduce the cost of the put options for the client because the positive cash flow from selling the call option would be credited back to the client's account and to some degree offset the cost of the put option.

Having calculated the fair values for the put and call, and then calling a market maker to verify that deals could be done at those levels, the broker found to his delight that the call option was worth $75,000 more than the put. If he purchased the 125 put and sold the 135 call, the market maker would pay the broker this amount.

The broker then called back the Japanese client and informed him that not only could the cost be reduced, but that the cost of both transactions would exactly offset; so the client could get the 125 put option 'for free'. The delighted client agreed at once to the transaction and the broker consummated the trades.

What occurred was that the Japanese client was so eager to reduce his premium expense that he actually accepted a hedging strategy which was a $75,000 'loser'. The broker, on the other hand, pocketed the $75,000 and made his first down payment on a new Porsche.

This situation is not uncommon. Such strategies of premium reduction are often most advantageous to brokers or market makers and can be disadvantageous to the client. Nevertheless, if a client can determine the fair prices of the options, and make sure that the broker gives him these prices, this type of strategy can make a lot of sense.

Suppose you are long a diversified portfolio of stocks that tracts the S&P 100 index underlying the options at the CBOE, and you decide to purchase a S&P 100 put option to protect yourself. Of course, this will cost you a premium. To reduce the cost of the put, you could sell a call option against it. Generally, these trades are done with strike prices that are out-of-the-money. The zero cost hedger must simply find which strike prices have options with equal premiums. The net effect of this strategy is that the hedger will hedge his downside risk by limiting his upside potential. Let us go through an example with the S&P 100 options to see how this might work.

Zero Cost Option Hedging Strategy with Options on the S&P 100

Suppose on 12 June 1991, an investor wishes to protect his holdings of $5 million worth of US stock. The current price for the S&P 100 Index is 358.66. The short-term interest rate is 6.10 per cent and the dividend yield for shares in the S&P 100 is equal to 4.5 per cent. As I discussed in Chapter 3, the critical price is not the current price but the expected forward price. To determine the arbitrage free forward price on the last trading day of the options (16 August 1991), one simply multiplies the current stock index level by 1 + (the interest rate − the dividend yield)[# of days/365]. This will provide a forward price for the S&P 100 Stock Index on 16 August of 359.63. The portfolio manager wants to protect himself with options on the S&P 100 but he must find two series of puts and calls that have exactly the same premium. Table 8.3 shows the range of S&P 100 options available on 12 June. He finds that the 350 put is offered at 6 3/8s and the 365 call is priced at 6 3/4s. He decides to purchase an out-of-the-money 350 put option to protect himself. It is out-of-the-money by about 8.66 index points relative to the current index and 9.63 index points relative to the estimated forward price. These options will cost him 6 3/8s index points in premium per option. The number of options he should purchase will be equal to the size of his holdings $5 million divided by the contract value of this option. Each option allows him the right to sell the index at a price of 350 and the contract multiple is $100. Therefore, each 350 put option gives him the right to sell $35,000 worth of stock. In total, we divide $5 million by $35,000 and come up with a hedge ratio of 143 options he must purchase. His total premium expense is 6 3/8 × $100 × 143 contracts or $91,162.50. In order to fund that cash outflow, he sells the August 365 call which is trading at 6 3/4s. The hedge ratio for the number of these he should sell is determined by dividing $5 million by $36,500 and this yields 137 contracts. The total amount of money he receives back is equal to $92,475. So in fact, the zero cost option in this example has produced a small inflow of $1312.50. With this strategy, the hedger expects either a dramatic drop in the stock market or a slow increase in the market, the latter being the more likely case. Figures 8.3a and 8.3b represent all the transactions plotted individually and the composite result. As the reader can see in Figure 8.3a, the 350 put option will offset the loss potential of the underlying stock portfolio when the market falls below 350. Above 365, the profit potential for the stock portfolio is 'cut off' by the sale of the 365 call. In between these strike prices, the stock portfolio is unaffected by the options. The net effect represented in Figure 8.3b looks remarkably like the bull spread I discussed in Chapter 4.

MARKET CONDITIONS (JUNE 12)

S&P 100 INDEX	358.66
SHORT TERM INTEREST RATE	6.10%
DIVIDEND YIELD (SHARES S&P 100)	4.50%
S&P 100 FORWARD PRICE	359.63

AUG 350 PUT	6 3/8
AUG 355 PUT	8 3/8
AUG 360 PUT	10 3/4
AUG 365 PUT	12 1/8
AUG 350 CALL	15 7/8
AUG 355 CALL	12 7/8
AUG 360 CALL	10 3/8
AUG 365 CALL	6 3/4

Table 8.3 Zero Cost Options Strategy

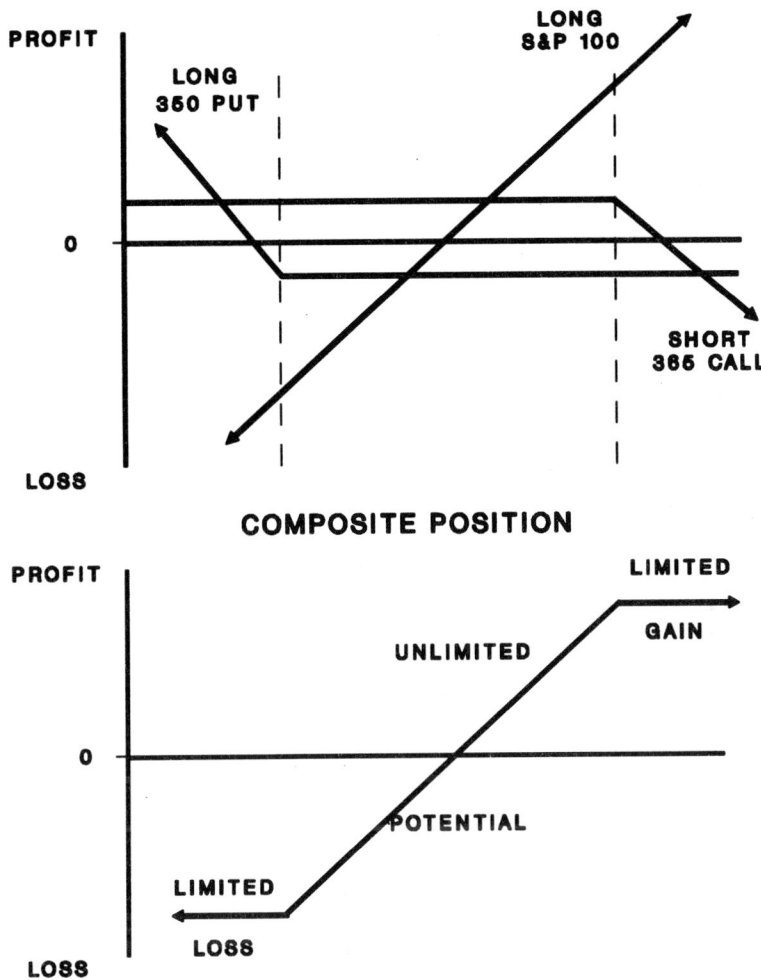

Figures 8.3a & 8.3b

This strategy has cut off the upside profit potential in exchange for cutting off the downside loss potential. On the other hand, if the hedger had used a short S&P 500 futures position to hedge, then he would have locked in the current level without any chance to profit if prices rose. Thus, the zero cost option strategy enables the hedger to choose a tradeoff between being completely hedged if the price of the stock market falls, and unhedged in the range between the lower strike price to the higher strike price.

185

Comparison of the Zero Cost Options Hedge with a Futures Hedge

Let us compare in more detail the zero cost option hedge with S&P 100 options to a S&P 500 futures hedge. The futures hedge will have no loss potential and no gain potential, because it is an instantaneous and a fully hedged position. The futures hedge is established with only a margin payment that can be established with interest-bearing securities. Thus, I will claim that a futures hedge is also 'zero cost'. For the zero cost option strategy, I will also have no cost but with this hedging strategy my limited loss potential only occurs at levels at or below the strike price of the option I have purchased. My position is unhedged above that level until the underlying market price reaches the level of the strike price for the option I have sold. Therefore, this strategy has a little downside risk and a little upside potential. If the market does drop dramatically I will still retain a fully hedged position.

If one expects a dramatic decrease in the stock market to occur and an equally dramatic drop in the S&P 100 or S&P 500 indices, then the best hedging strategy is to sell S&P 500 futures. If you expect a major rally in the stock market to occur, then the best course is not to hedge at all. However, as I have stated earlier, clairvoyance is not one of the pillars of modern financial theory; so, given that there is risk, what is the best thing to do? With the zero cost option, the position is hedged at the level of 350 for the S&P 100 or below. Between 350 and 365, you retain the good and bad features of your underlying stock market portfolio. Should the stock market slowly drift up then you make money on this position, and should it dramatically fall you have a predetermined maximum loss potential.

If you wish to use this strategy, it is critical that you determine what the fair prices are for the options. The aim is to cover what you plan to pay in premium with what you will receive back. Remember the story about the Japanese client; many brokers make considerable money with this strategy by relying on their clients' naivety. Many clients who do not fully understand how options work will refuse to pay a premium. The broker will then provide the client with this kind of strategy for 'free' when the client should have been paid a premium. The brokers will instantly cover their position and make a risk-free profit.

PORTFOLIO INSURANCE

The next topic to discuss is portfolio insurance. I shall examine both a dynamic asset allocation portfolio insurance method using a dynamic trading strategy in a stock portfolio and S&P 500 futures, and compare this with purchasing put options on S&P 500 futures.

BASIC CONCEPTS IN PORTFOLIO THEORY

To discuss portfolio insurance properly, and to understand the rationale for stock indices, we need to go back to the basics of portfolio theory: the tradeoff between risk and return. The classical risk/return tradeoff assumes that the more risk you take the more return you will expect. Furthermore, the risk of a particular investment will be defined by its variance of return, which is the square of the standard deviation.[3] Finally, with a portfolio of more than one asset, the risk of the portfolio will be defined by the proportion invested in each asset multiplied by its particular risk and the correlative relationship that asset has with other investments in the portfolio. Suppose that the capital market is composed of two kinds of assets: risky assets (like the stock market) and risk-free assets (like short-term pure discounted Government paper), and that we are interested in assessing the risk of this two asset portfolio. The formula for the expected return for this combination is the proportion invested in each asset multiplied by each asset's expected return. For example, let us assume we have as our two assets a stock portfolio which we expect to make 12.5 per cent on in the investment horizon and a risk-free US Government Treasury Bill yielding seven per cent and we decide to invest 50 per cent in each. Then the expected return will be 0.50×12.5 per cent + 0.50×7 per cent for an overall expected portfolio return of 9.75 per cent.

The risk, as stated above, will depend on the risk of each security, the proportion invested in each and their correlations. The formula for the standard deviation of this two asset portfolio is:

$$\sqrt{x_1^2\, \sigma_1^2 + x_2^2\, \sigma_2^2 + 2x_1\, x_2\, p_{12}\, \sigma_1\, \sigma_2}$$

In this formula, the x_1 is the proportion invested in the risky stock portfolio, the x_2 is the proportion invested in the risk-free deposit, σ_1^2 and σ_2^2 are the variances of each of these assets. Respectively, σ_1 and σ_2 are the standard deviations for these assets and p_{12} is the correlation coefficient which indicates how these assets' returns move together.

Now imagine a portfolio investment strategy which is 50 per cent in the risky stock portfolio and 50 per cent in the risk-free assets. Given that the σ^2 (variance) of the risk-free asset is zero, what is the risk of the entire portfolio? If one looks at the above formula for the portfolio standard deviation, one will see that the σ_2 (or the σ_2^2) appears in both the second and third term. If this value is set to zero, then the total portfolio risk is simply defined as $\sqrt{x_1^2\, \sigma_1^2}$. Once one takes the square root, the equation reads in English that the portfolio risk is equal to the proportion invested in the stock portfolio multiplied by its standard deviation. Unfortunately, the expected return for the stock portfolio is not that easy to estimate; however, it is possible to determine the expected return for the stock market by looking at historical returns or by subscribing to the numerous forecasting services. In this example, my trusty investment advisor provided the input of 12.5 per cent. Where does one get the expected standard deviation? If the reader goes back to Chapter 3 and looks again at the concept of implied volatility, he will see that this is the expected standard deviation for the underlying asset. Therefore, the options market plays a critical role in providing expectations of what risk will be over a particular investment horizon (until the expiration of the options contract). With these bits of information, we can determine easily what we expect to gain on this simple portfolio and what the risk is expected to be over its life.

The Foundations of Portfolio Insurance

As the investor changes the allocation percentages between the risk-free asset and the risky asset, he can either reduce his risk (and hence his expected return) or increase both. When he has invested 100 per cent in the risk-free asset, his standard deviation or volatility is zero and his expected return is seven per cent. If he invests 100 per cent of his asset in the stock portfolio, his expected return is 12.5 per cent and his standard deviation can be estimated by the implied volatility for the stock portfolio options that expire at the date of his investment horizon. Let us assume that this implied standard deviation (volatility) is 15 per cent per year. With these numbers, we can estimate the price of the risk. By being fully invested in the stock portfolio as opposed to the risk-free asset, he picks up an additional 5.5 per cent in yield. For this pickup, he must assume an additional 15 per cent risk, so the 'price of risk' is 5.5 per cent/15 per cent or 0.37 percentage points in return for each one per cent in additional risk he takes.

These concepts were fundamental to the development of the hedging strategy known as portfolio insurance. Basically, portfolio insurance works by the portfolio manager dynamically shifting his asset allocation mix between the risk-free asset and the risky asset as the price of the risky asset changes. When the risky asset's price rises, the investor places more of his investment there. Conversely, as the risky asset's price falls, the investor shifts his investment to the risk-free investment. Simply said, this implies that when the stock market rises, you buy more of it (using the proceeds of selling a proportion of your risk-free asset); and when the market falls, you sell out of the stock portfolio (putting the proceeds into the risk-free asset). This strategy is an attempt to achieve downside portfolio protection and provide for an unlimited profit potential as the value of the stock portfolio rises. Let us stop here and consider what the portfolio manager is trying to achieve. He wants a limited loss potential and an unlimited profit potential. What does that sound like? It is exactly the same rationale as that for purchasing an option.

Thus, as the market starts to go up, you shift your allocation base to those riskier assets; and as markets are falling you shift out of them and into risk-free assets where you are guaranteed a risk-free rate. How does this strategy actually work? Generally, the investor starts out with 50 per cent in risky assets at a current market price and 50 per cent in the risk-free asset, such as short-term deposits. As the market for risky assets starts to fall, the investor will at certain predetermined points (commonly referred to as trigger points) sell a percentage of his stock portfolio and place the

RESULT: MARKET FALLS

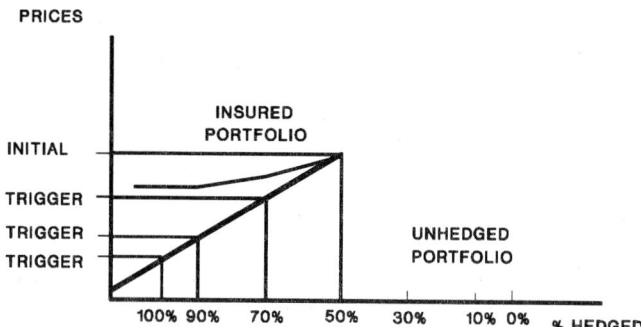

Figure 8.4 Initial Position: 50% Hedged

proceeds on deposit. For example, if the market price of the stock portfolio drops from its current level by five per cent, the portfolio manager sells 20 per cent of his stocks. His allocation percentages would then be 40 per cent in stock and 60 per cent in the risk-free asset. If the stock market falls another five per cent, he sells another 20 per cent of his stocks. At this point, 30 per cent of his holdings are in stock and 70 per cent in the risk-free asset. This process continues as the stock market falls until at some point the portfolio manager is completely out of stock and completely invested in the risk-free investment. Figure 8.4 displays the profit/loss profile for this dynamic allocation strategy as the price of the stock market falls. As the reader can see, the loss potential is limited at some point. However, until the position is fully hedged, the portfolio will incur losses from having to wait for the trigger points at which the portfolio insurer will sell the falling stock.

If, on the other hand, the stock market rises, the process is reversed. For example, imagine that stock prices rise by five per cent. The portfolio manager will sell a proportion of his holdings in the risk-free security and use the proceeds to buy more

RESULT: MARKET RALLIES

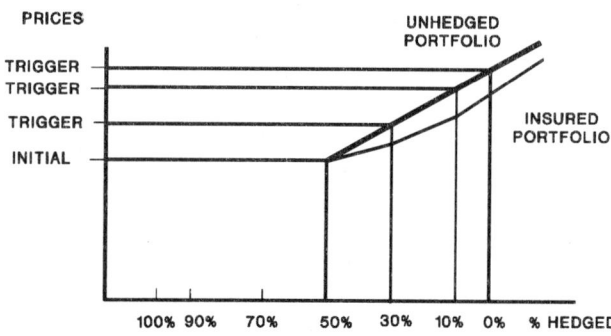

Figure 8.5 Initial Position: 50% Hedged

189

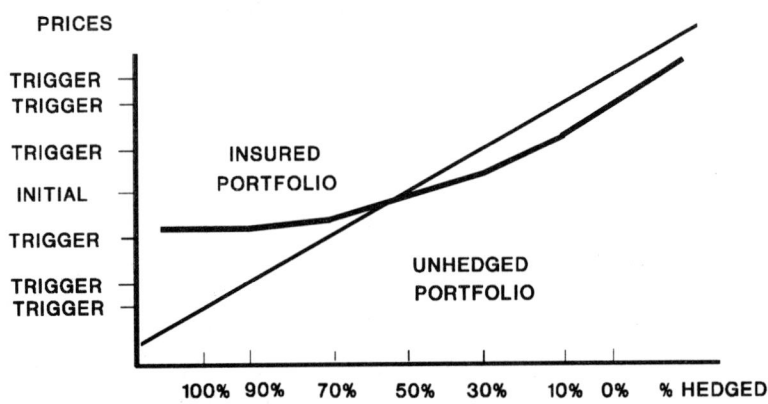

Figure 8.6 Combined Position

stock. At this point, his allocation percentages will be 60 per cent in stock and 40 per cent in the risk-free asset. Again as the stock market continues to rise, this process is repeated until he has invested entirely in stock. The profit/loss diagram for this strategy is shown in Figure 8.5.

Finally, let us combine these two graphs to see how the strategy appears over the entire range of possible stock market prices. This is done in Figure 8.6. The reader can see that the profit/loss profile for this strategy looks remarkably like that of a call option prior to expiration. It is a call option with both intrinsic and time value. The reader who researches the original Black and Scholes paper will realise that this is the expected outcome, for the Black and Scholes model was solved using just such an allocation process to determine the fair value of the call option. By shifting between the risky asset and the risk-free asset, they were able to create a portfolio which mimicked the payoff of a call option. Since they were able to determine the values for the risky asset and the risk-free asset in their 'equivalent' portfolio, they were also able to determine the call option's price. Their fundamental problem was to determine the amount of each asset to hold in order to create that equivalent portfolio. Here enters the heat transfer equation which provided them with the proper hedge ratio to create that equivalent portfolio. We now know this statistic as the delta.

Going back to our example, the portfolio insurer initially placed 50 per cent of his investment in the risky stock portfolio. The reader may recall that, in Chapter 3, 50 per cent figured quite prominently with the delta concept. When an option is at-the-money, the delta is always 50 per cent. It is not simply an accident that the asset proportion for the risky stock is also 50 per cent. Consider a case where the underlying stock price falls. In the portfolio insurance scheme, the hedger will systematically reduce his holdings (and the associated exposure) in the stock portfolio. This is exactly what happens to the delta of the call option: the call option's relative exposure (which is the delta) to the underlying stock market falls as the price of the stock market falls. Furthermore, at some point, the call option's delta will be zero, so too the portfolio insurer's holdings in the stock market. When the underlying stock prices rise, the delta of the call will also rise. Likewise, the insured portfolio will increase its exposure in the stock portfolio until there is a 100 per cent exposure in this risky asset. Essentially, portfolio insurance is the creation of a synthetic call option on the risky asset (in our case a well diversified US stock portfolio) by dynamically trading the underlying stock market.

The Relationship between Portfolio Insurance and Options

Basically, this describes the manner in which portfolio insurance is supposed to operate. But what happens in practice? To see if the technique actually fulfils its promise, we should review the assumptions upon which the strategy is based. As I stated earlier, the aim of portfolio insurance is to replicate a Black and Scholes call option. Since this is the case, the assumptions underlying portfolio insurance and Black and Scholes call options are the same. Therefore, we will review the assumptions of the Black and Scholes options pricing formula to understand better the potential flaws of portfolio insurance.

Two of Black and Scholes' most fundamental assumptions are: markets trade continuously (without transaction costs); and the market variance is constant. Since portfolio insurance is based upon these same assumptions, these conditions must also hold for portfolio insurance to work. Are these assumptions correct? In the US stock market (and almost all other markets except foreign exchange), the market does not trade around the clock (although selected stocks like IBM do). Furthermore, we know that the risk of the stock market (measured by the volatility) is not constant. So it is clear that these assumptions are incorrect.

The important question then becomes: what are the implications for portfolio insurance (and indeed option markets) if the fundamental assumptions underlying it are violated? For instance, suppose you wanted to apply portfolio insurance to a particular US stock portfolio. This would require continuously shifting your asset allocation between short-term US money market instruments and the stock portfolio. To work truly, the transaction costs involved would have to be extremely low and the portfolio manager have access to these markets on a 24-hour basis. We know that this is not the case. The high transaction costs alone would quickly reduce the profit potential for this strategy. In addition, the volatility of the stock markets is certainly not stable. The reader can verify this fact by looking at Figure 2.15 in Chapter 2 for the IBM stock. In that table, we see that stock volatility varies considerably over time. Why then do so many portfolio managers worldwide use portfolio insurance when the two most fundamental assumptions underlying its use are flawed?

Reasons for the Use of Portfolio Insurance

There are a number of possible reasons for the use of this strategy in portfolio management. I believe that three are pre-eminent. Initially, this potentially dangerous strategy is veiled behind the term 'portfolio insurance' and insurance has the connotation of risk reduction. Therefore, an aggressive portfolio manager might be able to have the strategy approved by the investment committee of his financial institution by claiming that this strategy will 'insure' the portfolio. Secondly, portfolio insurance is a technique for trading volatility. If one expects the actual market volatility to be less than the volatility implied in options prices, one can create an 'option-like' position for a smaller expected cost. In addition, if the market fails to move at all (implying that the realised volatility is much lower than was expected), then the insured portfolio will not lose anything; while if this situation occurs for the purchase of an option, the portfolio manager will suffer the loss of the premium. Finally, the introduction of alternative securities which have greater liquidity and lower transactions costs (compared with the cash stock portfolio) might make this strategy feasible. With the introduction of the S&P 500 futures at the IOM, such an alternative security became available. With S&P 500 futures, the portfolio insurer simply substitutes a short S&P 500 futures position instead of selling the stock portfolio. He will also buy the S&P 500 futures when he wants to increase his exposure to the risky stock market.[4]

Portfolio Insurance with Stock Index Futures

Even when using S&P 500 futures, one is still attempting to create a synthetic call option. It is most probable that in order to work this will require a large number of transactions in S&P 500 futures. Imagine that a particular S&P 500 futures contract became illiquid at the IOM, or that the stock market moved when the IOM was closed. These scenarios could be disastrous to the portfolio insurance strategy because they would make it impossible to rebalance the portfolio mix continuously. In addition, even if the IOM were open and trading fairly active, if other portfolio managers were using the same strategy at the same trigger prices, they would join you, doing the same trades at the same time. So, when the market rose, you would be buying with everybody else, and when the market fell, selling with everybody else. Even with only 15 per cent of futures trading volume associated with this kind of strategy (as is the estimates with the S&P 500 Stock Index futures in the US), this 'herd' effect could be destabilising. For example, whenever the market fell, portfolio insurance strategies would by definition sell *more*, causing the market to fall further and so trigger more portfolio insurance selling until the whole process spiralled out of control. While the jury is still out on the causes of the 1987 stock market crash, there can be little doubt that these kinds of dynamic 'hedging' strategies played a role.[5] Thus, in some markets, it appears that portfolio insurance is a key element of the market dynamics, and this has certainly proved to be the case with the US stock market. Nevertheless, while the liquidity is adequate on the IOM, the coverage cannot extend around the clock and the risks of overnight moves in the stock market make this strategy unsuitable. This has spurred the Chicago Mercantile Exchange (and a number of worldwide exchanges) to set up a 24 futures market which has been christened GLOBEX. This new development may substantially reduce the risk of overnight moves in the stock market for portfolio insurers.

However, why should the investor consider dynamic portfolio insurance given its chequered track record (the crash of 1987 is just one example)? Since the allocation ratio in the dynamic strategy is defined by the delta of a hypothetical option, why try to replicate an option using a dynamic asset allocation strategy when one could go directly to the options market? Let us now see how put options on S&P 500 futures can provide a purer insurance protection to the portfolio manager.

Portfolio Insurance with Put Options on S&P 500 Futures

In the options market, when you buy a put option you purchase the guaranteed right to sell at a specific price level. The put option hedge has a limited loss and an unlimited profit potential. Therefore, like portfolio insurance, you can eliminate the risk of your stock position when the market goes down. When the stock market goes up, the option is ignored, allowing you to have an overall position similar to the insured portfolio. In fact, this portfolio is truly insured. You pay your 'stock insurance premium' to achieve a hedged position. The profit/loss profile for the put option 'portfolio insurance' can be seen in Figure 8.7.

If one thinks about it logically, the Black and Scholes fair value of the put is the cost of the equivalent portfolio which tries synthetically to recreate it using something like a portfolio insurance scheme. Given the high transaction costs in the US stock market and the fact that the US stock market, S&P futures and options contracts do not trade 24 hours; it is best to leave this kind of synthetic options creation to those arbitrageurs who are willing and able to accept this risk. The individual portfolio manager could be doomed to failure by attempting to create his own synthetic put option.

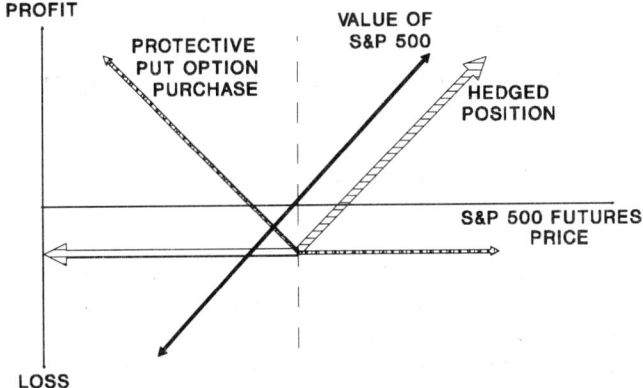

Figure 8.7 'Portfolio Insurance' with Put Options

	PERCENT OF STOCK PORTFOLIO
REAL PUT OPTIONS	
- 2% ONE WAY COMMISSION - 1% ONE WAY SPREAD GIVE UP - 6 TRADES PER YEAR	0.48%
SYNTHETIC PUT OPTIONS	
A) FUTURES - $30 ROUND-TRIP COMMISSION PER CONTRACT - $25 SPREAD GIVE-UP - TURNOVER OF 2.5 TIMES PORTFOLIO VALUE	0.18%
B) CASH/STOCK TRANSACTIONS	0.56%

Table 8.4 Comparison of Portfolio Insurance Costs

If the portfolio manager does try to insure his portfolio using the put option, at least he will know what the additional cost would be. Nevertheless, before deciding on a put option to insure his portfolio, he should compare the cost of the put option with the expected costs of the dynamic cash or futures strategy. In a study completed by Salomon Brothers in 1985, these costs were compared. Table 8.4 displays the costs for hedging a US stock portfolio with a variety of portfolio insurance schemes.

Cost Comparisons of Various Portfolio Insurance Techniques

The traditional method of dealing in the cash market to implement a portfolio insurance strategy had the greatest cost of 0.56 per cent of the stock portfolios value per year. The second most expensive was the purchase of put options on stock indices, which cost 0.48 per cent. The cheapest alternative was using stock index futures contracts, which cost only 0.18 per cent. However, the reader must be careful when drawing conclusions about future performance. The 1987 crash and the 1989 mini-crash demonstrated just how vulnerable the dynamic strategy can be.

The Fallacy of Delta Hedging a Stock Portfolio

In this section, I will cover delta hedging with options. This strategy can be considered an extension of the concept of portfolio insurance I have just discussed. The difference between these two techniques is that portfolio insurance is the dynamic trading of futures contracts in an attempt to replicate an option, while delta hedging is the dynamic trading of options to attempt to replicate the strategy of selling stock index futures.

Returning to Chapter 3, the reader will recall that the delta is the hedge ratio of the options relative to its particular underlying asset. For options on stock index futures (like the S&P 500 traded at the IOM), the underlying asset is the S&P 500 futures. If, for example, the delta of a particular option on a S&P 500 futures is 0.60, when the futures rises by ten basis points, the option will only rise by six basis points. The implication for the hedger seems obvious. If the hedger buys one option to hedge his exposure of a $2 million cash stock portfolio and the market price falls, then he will be underhedged. Assuming that the stock portfolio moves exactly like the S&P 500 futures, if the cash stock portfolio drops in value by $10,000, the options profit will not necessarily be equal to that amount. If the option's delta is 0.5, then the gain will only be $5000. The only way that the option will provide 'full' protection is if the delta of that option is 1.0.

Some authors (and a lot of brokers) use this fact to argue for increasing the number of options in the hedge ratio to take into account the delta factor. However, I find this logic to be fundamentally flawed and will attempt to prove this presently.

Suppose that a hedger decided to hedge a particular stock portfolio and was considering the available alternative instruments. He could go short S&P 500 futures, buy put options or sell call options on the S&P 500 futures. However, the hedger wishes to have a limited loss potential and an unlimited gain potential since he is uncertain about where the market may go. Of the two bearish options strategies, the long put hedge will fit the bill. As a hedger, buying the put is the more conservative strategy. In fact, hedging by buying options is, as I have said, in many ways comparable to buying stock market price insurance.

Suddenly, the hedger faces a dilemma. He remembers that the put option will not exactly offset gains or losses of his underlying stock portfolio owing to the delta, and therefore he considers delta-weighting the hedge ratio. This seems logical, especially since many people – myself included – refer to the delta as 'the hedge ratio'. *Beware!* Do not fall into the common trap of misinterpreting the delta and its appropriateness to the hedger. The delta tells you how many options you must have to replicate a *single S&P 500 futures position*. So, by delta-weighting your hedge ratio of put options, you simply create a 'short' futures equivalent position. The delta-weighted put options position will benefit (or lose) from a drop (or rise) in the futures price exactly as if it were a short futures position.

For example, if you have an at-the-money option the delta will be approximately 0.5. So, you would need two of these options to get the same effect as one future contract. Our hedger would therefore need to buy two at-the-money put options to equal one short futures. If the hedger needed ten short futures contracts to hedge his cash market position, and instead decided to create the equivalent hedge by buying puts, he would have to buy 20 put options. These 20 put options will mimic ten short futures contracts both when the market falls and when it rises.

Surely the reader can see that this is madness. The delta neutral hedger must not only pay twice as much transaction costs to establish the hedge but must also pay the premiums for the 20 options. These premiums will most probably be extremely expensive. If the hedger sold the ten S&P 500 futures contracts, his transactions costs would be cut by half and there would be no option premium to pay. In addition, as I discussed above (with portfolio insurance), the futures hedge can be considered costless since only a margin is required (and the funds used for margin can earn interest). This fact alone begs the question: why pay so much in option premium to duplicate what is essentially an almost costless futures contract? The answer is that one should shy away from this kind of hedging technique. You should use options in a hedging programme because you want the option to act like a futures contract when you need protection, and act like nothing when you do not need protection. Options allow the hedger insurance benefits only if he uses them correctly. Use the options for their own unique protection characteristics; do not try to reconstruct a futures contract with them.

So, what is the correct hedge ratio to employ when using option contracts? The answer is to use the same number of options contracts as one would use if they used the S&P 500 futures underlying the option contracts. In this example, since we would use ten short S&P 500 futures contracts to hedge, we should also buy ten put options on S&P 500 futures if we decided to hedge.

The reader may still be wondering what his profit and losses will be if the underlying market falls and he is only holding ten put options. It is true that the option profits will not completely offset his loss in the underlying asset *initially*. However, at the expiration of the option contract, he will be fully hedged if the market has fallen below the strike price of the option, and fully unhedged if the market price is above that level. The key concept is to compare the options hedge over the long term; this means at the expiration day of the option. The hedger will have paid a premium, but this is simply the cost of insurance. The delta neutral strategy outlined above can double this insurance cost. Therefore, delta neutral hedging can be thought of as a short-term hedging strategy. Clearly, in the long run it does not make sense and can actually increase the risk. Taking the example outlined above, if my true underlying exposure were ten S&P 500 futures (equivalent) and I buy 20 put options, at expiration, my position could potentially be overhedged by a factor of two if the options finish in-the-money. Options are not the ideal instrument for short-term hedging except when a contingent situation is involved. If one wishes to cover a short-term exposure with complete coverage, futures contracts make much more sense.

Comparison of Alternative Hedging Strategies for the Holder of a Stock Portfolio

In this final section, I will compare the alternative hedging strategies available to the portfolio manager. These hedges include: remaining unhedged (which really is not a hedging strategy but most portfolio managers seem to do this); buying puts on stock indices; selling calls on stock indices; or hedging with stock index futures. For this analysis, we assume that the stock market can do one of three things: fall, stay the same or rise. Given these possible states of the world, we will compare the three most popular hedging strategies and rank them in terms of hedging effectiveness.

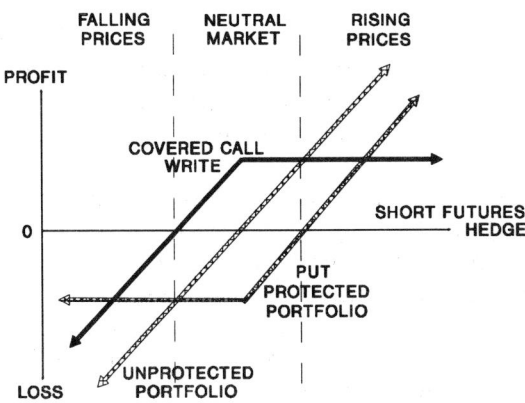

Figure 8.8 Alternatives for Portfolio Protection

Assume that one is holding a well diversified US stock portfolio which has a high correlation to the S&P 500 Stock Index. If a decrease in stock prices occurs, what are the results of the three hedging strategies? With a S&P 500 futures hedge, the protection is immediate and the hedging costs are trivial. Remember that you can establish a margin with interest-bearing securities and when futures prices fall, your margin account (a short futures' position) will always have a positive cash balance. So, the value of the stock portfolio is maintained at the level at which the S&P 500 futures contract was sold. This can be seen in Figure 8.8 on the left side of the diagram. The put option hedge provides a 'floor' level of protection but is only effective if the stock market drops dramatically. The short call position has a limited profit potential and if the market decreases by more points than the premium received, the losses start to mount. Finally, the unhedged position has the worst performance of all with an immediate loss potential that exceeds the previous three hedging strategies. We will

RANKING			
	BEARISH	*NEUTRAL*	*BULLISH*
SELL FUTURES	1	2	4
BUY PUTS	2	4	2
SELL CALLS	3	1	3
UNHEDGED	4	3	1

WHERE 1 IS BEST AND 4 IS WORST

Table 8.5 Comparison of Alternatives for Portfolio Protection

rank the efficiency of these strategies as follows: the best in a bearish market is to sell the S&P 500 futures; the second best is to buy the put option on either the S&P 500 futures or on the S&P 100 Stock Index; the third is to sell the call option on either of these indices; while the last is to remain unhedged. This ranking can be seen in Table 8.5.

What about the situation of market stability? If you have this expectation, you might be inclined to remain unhedged. If you did this, then your profit would be equal to the dividends you were paid for that period and you would have no adverse impact from price changes. If instead you sold the futures, there would be no benefit from a movement in the market price. For this hedge, your return would be equal to the short-term interest rate needed to 'carry' the stock portfolio until the futures delivery.[6] If the short-term interest rate is substantially higher than the dividend yield (which it generally is), then the futures hedge would be superior to simply holding the cash and your return equal to a short-term money market instrument.

If instead of these strategies you sold a call option on a stock index (or the futures), then you would receive a premium in addition to the dividend income on the stock portfolio. This profit is maximised over a range extending from the current market price and higher. To the downside, the covered call strategy will still profit until that point where the premium received has been exhausted and the hedge is at the same profit and loss point as the short futures hedge. What about the put option purchase? In the stable state of the world, the premium is lost and the net position has the worst performance. The profit/loss profiles for these hedging strategies can be seen in the centre of Figure 8.8.

The ranking for these four alternatives in a stable market is as follows: the best strategy is to sell the call option on the stock index; when interest rates are higher than dividend yields, number two is to hedge the stock portfolio with a short S&P 500 futures contract; the third best choice is to remain unhedged; where the dividend yields are higher than the returns on interest-bearing security, remaining unhedged is superior to the S&P 500 futures hedge; and the worst alternative is to buy the put option on the S&P 100 Index or on S&P 500 futures. These rankings can also be seen in the centre column of Table 8.13.

Finally, if the market rises dramatically, what are the comparative results of these four strategies. If one remained unhedged and the market rallied, then this position would do the best of all. Unfortunately, the portfolio manager must be aware that he is taking an unlimited risk position. If he protects the stock portfolio by buying a put option on an S&P index, he is still going to enjoy an unlimited profit potential but will only realise a profit after the movement in the market has been sufficient to cover the premium paid. Now consider the covered call position. When the portfolio manager sells the call option, the most he can ever make is the premium paid. Therefore, when the market rises the covered call hedge has a limited participation. Finally, what about the short S&P 500 futures hedge? In this situation, this is the worst choice because the portfolio manager cannot participate at all in the profits associated with the market increase. Once again, the profit/loss profiles for these strategies when the market rises can be seen in the right-hand portion of Figure 8.8. In our ranking of these strategies, in a rising market we will choose being unhedged as the best alternative, the put option purchase as second, the covered call writing strategy as third, and the short futures hedge as the least promising. Table 8.5 lists on the right-hand column this final ranking for the possible approaches.

The reader might find it interesting that in none of the possible states of the world will the put option purchase be the best alternative. Why does anyone purchase a put option to hedge an asset? The reason is that people cannot be certain that the market will fall, remain stable or rise. Therefore, in a world dominated by uncertainty, insurance exists to provide protection against the unforeseeable. Puts are also ideal if you anticipate markets going down and then coming back over a given period of time. You might then want to establish a minimum acceptable level to protect yourself and still benefit if eventually the market rises to higher levels. In an uncertain world where you expect a high degree of volatility, then a put option will give that floor to your potential losses (see Figure 8.8) and allow you to benefit if the market does rally above current levels. If you buy a put and the market remains stable you lose the premium. Is that any reason for not buying a put? If it is a valid reason, then the same logic could be applied to your home fire insurance. If you knew with certainty whether your house was going to burn down in any given year, then the optimal strategy would be simple: either go uninsured if you know your house will not catch fire or sell the house before it burns down. If the world were so contrived, insurance would have no purpose. However, with house fires and market prices, uncertainty does exist and therefore options exist.

I would like to finish this chapter by providing a few guidelines to stock portfolio managers who may wish to include S&P 500 futures and options in their risk management strategies. The first step in designing a hedging programme with either futures or options is to determine what the long-term objectives of the portfolio manager are. These could include maximising return, assuring the stability of the principal or perhaps increasing the cashflow over an investment period. Secondly, the portfolio manager must make some judgments about what will happen to the stock market in general, to interest rates and finally to the volatility of the market. Next, given this view, he must construct an optimal strategy using combinations of cash, futures and options to benefit most from these views. Thereby, he should place special attention to the fact that if his views are uncertain, options may be the appropriate instrument to use (see the first example in Chapter 7). Finally, the portfolio manager must evaluate the performance of his hedging strategies over time, making sure to evaluate the performance relative to his initial assumptions and views. As his viewpoints change, he must revise his portfolio accordingly.

The portfolio manager who is allowed to use S&P futures and options will face a situation similar to that of a carpenter who is first introduced to a drill or a keysaw. It is true that it was possible to make holes in a piece of wood before the advent of the drill or keysaw, but the introduction of these tools has made the job more efficient and accurate. Thus, the use of S&P futures and options will provide a similar benefit to the astute stock portfolio manager.

1   The first of the major papers on portfolio theory was Harris M. Markowitz, 'Portfolio Selection', *Journal of Finance*, 7, pp.77-91 (March 1952). In addition, the reader is referred to the groundbreaking work on the Capital Asset Pricing Model (CAPM) by William F. Sharpe, 'Capital Asset Prices: A Theory of Market Equilibrium under Conditions of Risk', *Journal of Finance*, 19, pp.425-42 (September 1964); and J. Linter, 'The Valuation of Risk Assets and the Selection of Risky Investments in Stock Portfolios and Capital Budgets', *Review of Economics and Statistics*, 47, pp.13-37 (February 1965).

2   The following section which explains the basics of stock indices draws extensively from the publication *Characterisitics and Risks of Standardised Options* published by the Options Clearing Corporation, pp.32-34.

3   If one assumes the Capital Asset Pricing Model, then the risk of a particular asset is its risk relative to the portfolio of all assets, and this is called the Beta. For a thorough and simple introduction to these concepts, the reader should read Richard Brealey and Stewart Myers, *Principles of Corporate Finance*, 2nd Edition, McGraw-Hill, Chapters 7, 8 and 9 (1984).

4   For a good introduction to the use of futures in hedging a stock portfolio, the reader is referred to Robert W. Kolb, *Understanding Futures Markets*, Scott, Foresman Co., (1988).

5   For an interesting review of the effect of portfolio insurance and other kinds of programmed trading strategies on the 1987 stock market crash, the reader is referred to: Well Fargos Investment Advisors, *Anatomy of a Decline: The Role of Index-Related Trading in the Market's Records Fall* (9 November 1987).

6   The reader is referred to Darrell Duffies, *Futures Markets*, Prentice-Hall (1989) for a thorough discussion of the expected gains that accrue from a short futures hedge.

9: Risk Management of Options

In this chapter, I will address the risk management of options dealing and – using a popular computer risk analysis programme – help the reader see how option market makers evaluate and control the risks of their portfolios.

A BRIEF HISTORY OF OPTION MARKETS

Options are among mankind's oldest instruments for managing risk. For example, there are references to option contracts in Ancient Greece. Aristotle indicated in *Politics* that a certain philosopher named Thales the Milesian 'gave deposits for the use of all the olive presses in Chios and Miletus, which he hired at a low price because no one bid against him. When the harvest time came, and many wanted them all at once and of a sudden, he let them out at any rate which he pleased, and made a quantity of money.'[1] Throughout ancient times, options were struck between merchants, mostly for the management of commodity price risk. In the Renaissance, although many Italian banks were offering option-like products, options became particularly infamous from their association with the Dutch tulip bulb mania. After this time, more abuses of options occurred in London and later in the US where 'bucket shops' specialised in offering unsecured options.[2] While most of these abuses were due to the lack of financial backing, fundamental problems also existed in the pricing of these securities and the risk management of those who underwrote the contracts.

WHY OPTIONS MARKETS HAVE GROWN EXPONENTIALLY SINCE THE 1970s

Though financial options of various types have been in use for a long time, it is only since the mid-1970s that they have become actively traded on a large scale. Their surge in popularity has occurred primarily for three reasons.

First, Professors Fischer Black and Myron Scholes (then at the University of Chicago) developed a formula for pricing options that not only allowed people to determine a particular option's fair values, but also to regulate those values through arbitrage. While Black and Scholes are 'household names' in the financial world, it is a little known fact that much of the groundwork for their model was done by Louis Bachelier in 1900.[3] Unfortunately, this brilliant Frenchman was unable to consolidate his work into a comprehensive, all-encompassing formula which actually worked. If he had done so, Paris might very well now be the centre for the trading of world options instead of Chicago.

The second reason was the security provided through the introduction of options contracts on regulated exchanges where the contracts had the financial backing of the clearing house. The inauguration of the Chicago Board Options Exchange in 1973 meant that, for the first time, option contracts were standardised, regulated and could easily be purchased or sold by the general public through stock brokers. This revolution was so successful that in less than 20 years over 40 exchanges have opened worldwide to trade option contracts.

The third reason that the level of options trading has grown so dramatically since the 1970s exists in the strident advances made through computerisation in the business world. Computers and computer programmes are essential to option trading because of the complexities involved in dealing with simultaneous multiple option contracts and the constant needs to analyse, change and update complicated trading positions.

Apart from dealing, the computer is vital to the formulation of market strategies, and especially essential in maintaining an integrated approach to risk management. There has been a proliferation of risk management computer software systems over the last few years to meet this need. For our purpose of understanding options risk management, I have chosen to use the Risk Analysis Program (commonly known by its acronym, RAP) written by Dr. David Emanuel.[4] I have used this program since its introduction in 1984 and have used the latest revisions of RAP (2.7) for the analytical illustrations in this chapter.

AN OPTION RISK ANALYSIS COMPUTER PROGRAM

With any risk analysis package, the primary task must be to evaluate the overall risks of all positions held in the underlying asset as well as for all options on this asset. The ideal system should not only determine the implied volatilities of a position, but also compare actual option prices with their theoretical values, evaluate time decay, and assess all potential exposure, especially volatility, for the period of the trade. The system should also be flexible enough to permit the creation of custom-designed contracts modeled on both exchange-traded instruments and over-the-counter instruments such as rights issues or warrants.

In this chapter, I will examine the risk management of option contracts using Live Cattle futures and options traded at the Chicago Mercantile Exchange (CME).

First, we need to understand what these contracts represent. The price of the Live Cattle futures is the number of US dollars per hundred pounds of Live Cattle delivered at various points in the Midwest of the United States. The quantity delivered is equal to 40,000 pounds of Live Cattle. The minimum price change for the futures is 2.5¢ per hundred pounds (or 0.025¢ per pound) or a dollar amount of $10.00 (0.025¢ × 40,000 pounds). Thus, if the price for the Live Cattle futures is 72.92, then this means that the contract value is equal to $29,168. The option on Live Cattle futures is quoted similarly, except that it is in cents per pound instead of dollars per hundred pounds.

TRADING UNIT	**ONE LIVE CATTLE FUTURES CONTRACT (40,000 POUNDS)**
CONTRACT MONTHS	**FEBRUARY, APRIL, JUNE, AUGUST, SEPTEMBER, OCTOBER, DECEMBER**
LAST TRADING DAY	**LAST FRIDAY THAT IS MORE THAN 3 BUSINESS DAYS PRIOR TO FIRST BUSINESS DAY OF DELIVERY MONTH**
MINIMUM PRICE MOVEMENT (TICK SIZE)	**0.025 CENTS PER POUND ($10 PER CONTRACT)**
EXERCISE PRICE INTERVALS	**2 CENTS PER POUND (E.G. 72, 74, 76, ETC.)**
TRADING HOURS	**9:05 - 13:00 (CHICAGO TIME)**
EXERCISE	**BY 19:00 UP TO AND INCLUDING THE LAST TRADING DAY**

Table 9.1 Options on Live Cattle Futures (CME)

The minimum tick size for the option is also 0.025¢ per pound. Table 9.1 outlines the contract specification for the options on Live Cattle futures. The ultimate asset underlying the option is 40,000 pounds of Live Cattle that must be delivered in the month following the expiration of the option.

Contract Definitions in the Program

For the futures and options seminars I present, the RAP is an integral part of our risk management module. For this purpose, I have created a contract in the RAP specifically for CME Live Cattle contracts. This contract file can be seen in Table 9.2. To analyse options on Live Cattle futures, I first need to define this contract in the

```
First Menu for Editing Contracts.  Parameters to be used are shown below
Type Y to change parameters.  Use up and down arrows to move up and down
 Do you want to change these current parameter values? <y/n>
Quote format for futures(cash) price is                     DDD.DD
Editing contract for LIVE CATTLE
Quote format for option price is                            DDD.DD
Quote format for strike price is                            DDD.D

Quoted futures(or cash) price is actual futures price times        1
Quoted option price is actual option price times                   1
Quoted strike price is actual strike price times                   1

Futures(or cash) contract value is actual futures price times     400
Option contract value is actual option price times                400
Premiums are paid up(Chicago)or margined like futures(LIFFE) Premium(Chicago)
Interval(decimal) between adjacent strikes(can be ignored)is        2


Second Menu for Editing Contracts.  Parameters to be used are shown below
Type Y to change parameters.  Use up and down arrows to move up and down
 Do you want to change these current parameter values? <y/n>
Option pricing model for this contract is                  American
This contract is based on (Futures or Physical security)   Futures
Dividend(or convenience) yield in percent per year               0
This only has relevance for Physical security options

Annual volatility of underlying contract in percent             10
Range of annual percent volatility changes(+ or -) to scan       1

$ range in value of one futures(cash)contract to scan + or -    560
You might want to use the contract margin for these ranges
$ range in intermonth spread relationship to scan + or -        420
No changes are permanent until you back up the SYSTEM file
```

Table 9.2 Live Cattle Futures Option Contract

203

program. This requires us to include all the elements in the Live Cattle options contract definitions. This includes how the underlying is quoted, what the underlying size is and how the margining system functions.

In Table 9.2, the reader can see that the contract definition is actually split into two parts. In the top portion of the table, the first selection determines how the Live Cattle futures and options will be quoted. These contracts are both listed in decimal format with DDD.DD indicating that prices can have a maximum of three numbers to the left of the decimal point and two numbers to the right. The string of three '1's indicates that each Live Cattle futures and options contract is for only one underlying. For both the Live Cattle futures and options contracts, the value is actually 400 times the prices quoted in the market ($ per 100 pounds). Therefore the contract value of the August Live Cattle futures is really equal to the price per 100 pounds × 400 which is equal to cents per pound × 40,000 pounds of Live Cattle. Consider the following example: the Live Cattle futures price is $74.0. To determine the contract value, we simply multiply $74.0 by 400 to give us the actual value of $29,600. The next line down indicates that the premiums for Live Cattle future options have the Chicago system where one must pay the premium for an option upfront. This is important for the pricing and risk evaluation of Live Cattle futures and options. The Live Cattle options strike prices are quoted in cents per pounds 2¢ intervals between the strike prices. Therefore, at the bottom of the first page of the contract definition, there is a line for increments of the option strike prices and this is 2. This allows for the strike prices to have 2¢ intervals (although, as RAP indicates, this can be ignored).

The top of the second page of the contract definition indicates that the option has an American-style option feature, meaning it can be exercised anytime until maturity. Since the option is based upon a futures contract, we must select that type of underlying asset. Since the Live Cattle options on the CME are not on a physical security, the underlying asset (futures) has no interest, coupon or dividend yield; this is why the dividend or convenience yield is set to 0. If instead you were evaluating options on physical Live Cattle, then you would have to include the convenience yield for Live Cattle (i.e. Calves).[5] The annual volatility is a default value that we can change later in our analysis. For the Live Cattle contract I have set the default volatility to 10 per cent. The next line allows us to set the size of the possible volatility movements that could occur in a single day. When doing options risk analysis we want to know what can happen for a particular overnight movement in volatility of perhaps 1 per cent. So, I enter into RAP a figure of 1 per cent as the range of how high or low the market volatility could move overnight. Thus, if the current Live Cattle futures volatility is 10 per cent, then we want to know what could happen if tomorrow the volatility either increased to 11 per cent or decreased to 9 per cent.

The next line down allows us to determine a range of possible Live Cattle futures price movements overnight. The figure $560, for the range of the futures (cash) to scan + or − , indicates that when we do our risk management, we will assume that the underlying Live Cattle futures market can move at most $1.40 overnight. This $1.40 range is calculated by dividing the $560 by the contract multiple of 400 which gives us 1.4. This means that if the Live Cattle futures contract is trading at $74.0, the RAP assumes that for risk management purposes, the market cannot move below $72.6 or above $75.4 in a single day. Finally, the bottom line of the second page of the Live Cattle futures contract definition indicates how much the spread could change *between* Live Cattle futures contract months. For example, if we purchased August 1991 Live Cattle futures and sold October 1991 Live Cattle futures, we have a risk that these contracts will not move together. The spread relationship could change overnight. In the RAP, all positions and all maturities are combined into a single risk analysis. To do this, it is unwise to assume that the various maturities will always change in the same degree. Therefore, the $420 indicates the amount that the relationship between various Live Cattle futures months could change overnight. The $420 translates to a change of $1.05 in a single day ($420/400). For example, let us say that the August 1991 Live Cattle futures is trading at $72.92 and the October 1991 Live Cattle futures is trading at $75.17. At these levels, the spread between these contracts is a positive $2.25. RAP assumes that if the spread changes overnight it cannot fall below plus $1.20 or rise above plus $3.30. These amounts for the overnight movements on the Live Cattle futures and the spreads are drawn from the margin requirements for the Live Cattle futures position ($560) and a Live Cattle futures spread ($420) established at the CME (as of 10 June 1991).

Adding Expiration Dates and Strike Prices into the Program

Once we have defined our Live Cattle futures and options contracts in the programme, the next step is to add the maturities for these futures and options contracts. This can be seen in the top of Table 9.3. After this step, we now need to add the strike prices against which we wish to evaluate the options. These values appear at the bottom of Table 9.3. With these steps completed, we can now enter the futures and options positions on a spreadsheet and do our risk analysis simulation.

```
        LIVE CATTLE Hypothetical date is  10 Jun 1991

        Contract      Options  Days until    Futures  Days until
         Month        Expire (Expiration)    Expire (Expiration)
        Aug 1991    26 Jul 1991 (   46)    2 Aug 1991 (   53)
        Oct 1991    26 Sep 1991 (  108)    4 Oct 1991 (  116)
        Dec 1991    21 Nov 1991 (  164)    6 Dec 1991 (  179)
```

```
     1 is # for DM    2 is # for SF    3 is # for BP    4 is # for JY
     5 is # for SP    6 is # for ED    7 is # for LC    8 is # for LH
     9 is # for TB   10 is # for XDM  11 is # for XBP   12 is # for XSF
    13 is # for XJY  14 is # for FC   15 is # for PB    16 is # for CD
    17 is # for LB   18 is # for AD   19 is # for US    20 is # for NK
    I need the contract # please      7Strikes(decimal)in spreadsheet for this con
    tract (Max # is  25) are:-
        72.00000000       74.00000000       76.00000000       78.00000000
        80.00000000
    I need the strike price(decimal) to add or drop
    Use a + price to add, a  - price to drop. Type <Esc> to ABORT
```

Table 9.3 Maturities and Strike Prices

A Live Cattle Option Sample Trade Entry Spreadsheet

Table 9.4 displays a sample Live Cattle futures and options spreadsheet for a position entered on 10 June 1991. Let us take a few sentences to describe what the spreadsheet is showing us. Listed at the top of the sheet are the maturities for the Live Cattle futures. Notice that only August 1991, October 1991 and December 1991 are available. The maturity dates actually say 2 Aug 91, 4 Oct 91 and 6 Dec 91. These reflect the maturity dates of the underlying Live Cattle futures. The reader can see in Table 9.1 that the options on Live Cattle expire on the last Friday that is more than three business days prior to the first business day of the delivery month of the underlying futures contract. As the reader can appreciate, this is very complicated, but fortunately is already taken into account in the program (as can be seen from a quick review of Table 9.3). Below the maturities, the reader sees a series of *Call & Put* repeated across the chart. These display the available calls and puts for each of the entered maturities. On the left side of the matrix, one sees the word *Futures* and below that *QTY* and *PRC*. These show the quantity of various futures contracts held and the respective prices of those instruments. Below these lines, the reader will see *Strikes*. These represent the strike prices for the options we will be evaluating. The first strike, immediately below the word *Strikes*, is $72.0. To the immediate right and below, the reader will again see *QTY* and *PRC*. Again this means that all $72.0 options – both calls and puts – will be in this row along with the quantity held and the price associated with the relevant transaction. Below these lines the sequence is repeated for $74.0, $76.0, $78.0, and $80.0. These will be all the options and futures contracts necessary to build our sample market maker's portfolio. Since our spreadsheet is now established, we can travel around the spreadsheet and enter the actual market prices or quantities held for the various kinds of assets.

FUTURES	2 Aug 91		4 Oct 91		6 Dec 91					
QTY										
PRC	72.92		75.17		76.22					
STRIKES	CALL	PUT	CALL	PUT	CALL	PUT	CALL	PUT	CALL	PUT
72.0 QTY										
PRC	1.70	0.78	3.80	0.73		0.70				
74.0 QTY										
PRC	0.65	1.73	2.30	1.15		1.13				
76.0 QTY										
PRC	0.20	3.23	1.20	2.00	1.90	1.73				
78.0 QTY										
PRC	0.05	5.11	0.60	3.33	0.93	2.70				
80.0 QTY										
PRC	0.03		0.20		0.43					

Table 9.4 Sample Live Cattle Futures Options Spreadsheet

		LIVE CATTLE POSITIONS								
FUTURES	2 Aug 91		4 Oct 91		6 Dec 91					
QTY										
PRC		72.92		75.17		76.22				
STRIKES	CALL	PUT	CALL	PUT	CALL	PUT	CALL	PUT	CALL	PUT
72.0 QTY										
PRC	1.70	0.78	3.80	0.73		0.70				
74.0 QTY	-10			-10		5				
PRC	0.65	1.73	2.30	1.15		1.13				
76.0 QTY		15	15	-15		-25				
PRC	0.20	3.23	1.20	2.00	1.90	1.73				
78.0 QTY			25		-20					
PRC	0.05	5.11	0.60	3.33	0.93	2.70				
80.0 QTY			25							
PRC	0.03		0.20		0.43					

Table 9.5 Sample Portfolio

Entry of a Sample Portfolio of Live Cattle Options into the Spreadsheet
Table 9.5 shows a sample portfolio duly entered. Suppose that the nearby Live Cattle futures is trading at a price of $72.92.[6] We have bought 15 of the $76.0 August puts. So the reader should read down from '2 August 91' and 'PUT' until on the left he sees '76.0' and 'QTY'. He will see a 15 here and below it the price of the option of 3.23. Also, we sold ten calls at $74.0 strike price. To find that, the reader should read down from the '2 Aug 91' and 'Call' column heading until on the left is '74.0'. He will see on top of this cell a – 10 and below it a 0.65. This shows that the quantity held is minus ten, which means ten have been sold, at a price of $0.65.

As the reader scans the spreadsheet in Table 9.5, he will see that a wide variety of positions are held. For example, in the October Live Cattle futures we have purchased 15 of the $76.0 call (at a price of $1.20), 25 of the $78.0 calls (at a price of $0.60) and 25 of the $80.0 calls (at a price of $0.20). We have also sold ten of the October $74.0 put options at $1.15 and 15 of the $76 put options at $2.00. The current price of the August Live Cattle futures is $72.92 and the October Live Cattle futures is $75.17. In the December maturity, we have sold 20 of the $78.0 calls (at a price of $0.93), bought five of the $74.0 puts at $1.13 and sold 25 of the $76.0 puts at $1.73. In addition, all the closing prices for the options are listed. An empty QTY (quantity) cell shows that we have no positions there and where we have entered numbers, we actually have positions. Again, the numbers below each quantity are the prices at which we bought or sold each particular instrument.

Comparison of Market Prices with Theoretical Prices

After entering the prices we make a comparison of the theoretical prices versus actual market prices and see if there are any discrepancies. For this purpose, the RAP program displays a spreadsheet showing the market prices and the theoretical prices. This can

```
Press M to proceed  Variable Sigma&Interest Rate LIVE CATTLE 10 Jun 1991
                  72.92          75.17          76.22
               2 Aug 1991     4 Oct 1991     6 Dec 1991
STRIKES       CALL    PUT   CALL    PUT   CALL    PUT
 72.0 Mkt     1.70   0.78   3.80   0.73          0.70
     Theory   1.61   0.70   3.61   0.48   4.44   0.29
      Delta .633770-.36013.786279-.20321.855964-.13499
      Gamma .003358.003348.001774.001717.001471.001317
 74.0 Mkt     0.65   1.73   2.30   1.15          1.13
     Theory   0.66   1.73   2.24   1.08   2.90   0.72
      Delta .354785-.63918.615879-.37070.706931-.27536
      Gamma .003331.003342.002308.002291.002084.002021
 76.0 Mkt     0.20   3.23   1.20   2.00   1.90   1.73
     Theory   0.20   3.26   1.24   2.06   1.70   1.49
      Delta .142495-.85352.424493-.56188.521454-.45817
      Gamma .002019.002064.002373.002385.002401.002395
 78.0 Mkt     0.05   5.11   0.60   3.33   0.93   2.70
     Theory   0.04   5.10   0.61   3.40   0.89   2.63
      Delta .040189-.96184.253295-.73532.335686-.64555
      Gamma .000775.000901.001943.001990.002204.002252
 80.0 Mkt     0.03          0.20          0.43
     Theory   0.01   7.08   0.26   5.04   0.41   4.12
      Delta .007961-1.     .129900-.86431.186291-.80138
      Gamma .000195       .001286.001391.001625.001750
```

Table 9.6 Market Prices and Theoretical Prices

be seen in Table 9.6. It also determines the deltas, the relative risk of the option to a full long position in the underlying market, and the gammas.

These functions are most useful in options risk management software for they show whether the options dealt are overvalued or undervalued relative to their theoretical value. This is an important theoretical edge RAP can give to those dealing. The reader may refer to the chapter on volatility trading (Chapter 5) for a more extensive discussion of how to use this theoretical advantage. For the $74.0 put option that we sold at a price of $1.15, the theoretical price and market price are divergent. The actual market price is $1.15 in the table but immediately below it is the theoretical price of $1.08. Therefore, if our volatility estimate (of 10 per cent) is correct, we expect to make a profit from mispricing of at least 0.07¢ per pound. The delta for this option is −0.37070, thus giving it the same risk as being short 37 per cent of one futures contract. Its gamma – the amount by which the delta will change for a given one basis point move in the underlying – is 0.002291. Thus, as was stated in Chapter 3, the gamma for an out-of-the-money option is fairly low.

Comparison of Gamma Values Across Strike Prices and Maturities

The highest gamma values are for options that are at-the-money and closest to maturity. If the reader looks carefully at Table 9.6 for the $72.0 and $74.0 calls and puts on August Live Cattle futures, he will see the highest gammas. These are 0.003358 and 0.003348 for the $72.0 series and 0.003331 and 0.003342 for the $74.0 series. If one remembers that gamma is simply a measure of how close the option is to its strike price and maturity date, then the concept of gamma is a snap. The closer it is to the strike price, and the closer it is to maturity, the higher the gamma. The reader will also notice that some of the deltas in the table have positive values and some have negative values. RAP assigns a minus sign to the deltas of put options (because they are short positions), and a plus sign to the deltas of call options. This is consistent when one recalls the relative exposure one has to the underlying market when buying put or call options. However, the reader will recall that when one sells put or call options, the exposure is reversed. To take this into account, RAP applies a simple mathematical rule to assure that buying a put (or selling a call) is a short position and that selling a put (or buying a call) is a long position. This is achieved in a two-step process in the program. Initially, if a position is purchased then the quantity bought will be entered in the QTY cell in the spreadsheet as a positive number. Furthermore, if a position is sold then the quantity sold is represented by a negative number in the appropriate QTY cell. To determine the exposure of each position, RAP will multiply the quantity in that QTY cell by the delta for that option. For example, the exposure of a single short put is estimated by the product of – 1 that is entered in the QTY cell and the negative delta factor estimated by the program. Thus, the exposure of the short put becomes positive relative to the underlying market because a negative number multiplied by another negative number results in a positive number. So, if we sell three put options with a delta of – 0.5, the relative risk is – 3 × – 0.5 or a +1.5 delta.

Determination of the Implied Volatilities

The RAP program can determine the implied volatility for every option that has been entered into the spreadsheet. At any point in time – in this case 10 June 1991 – RAP simply synthesises the option's prices, their individual striking prices and the current price of the underlying market to calculate instantaneously the implied volatility for each option. Table 9.7 displays the implied volatilities for the Live Cattle futures options in the spreadsheet. For example, RAP assesses that the $74.0 call and put options for the August Live Cattle futures both have an implied volatility of 10.69 per cent and that the $74.0 option series for October futures has a lower volatility of 10.40 per cent. As the reader can see, the volatilities do vary across the strike prices. Generally, the out-of-the-money options have a higher implied volatility. There can be several possible explanations for this effect. First, these options do not trade as actively as the at-the-money options and market makers do not have the same high degree of liquidity to get rid of these out-of-the-money options. Therefore, they charge

Please press the M key to continue LIVE CATTLE   10 Jun 1991
FUTURES PRICE

STRIKES		72.92 2 Aug 1991		75.17 4 Oct 1991		76.22 6 Dec 1991	
		CALL	PUT	CALL	PUT	CALL	PUT
72.0	PRC	1.70	0.78	3.80	0.73		0.70
	VOL	11.64	11.53	11.59	12.02		11.18
74.0	PRC	0.65	1.73	2.30	1.15		1.13
	VOL	10.69	10.70	10.40	10.43		10.33
76.0	PRC	0.20	3.23	1.20	2.00	1.90	1.73
	VOL	10.75	10.07	9.75	9.63	8.99	9.19
78.0	PRC	0.05	5.11	0.60	3.33	0.93	2.70
	VOL	10.98	11.14	9.94	9.41	8.19	8.35
80.0	PRC	0.03		0.20		0.43	
	VOL	12.69		9.25		8.11	

Table 9.7 Implied Volatilities

more for these options because of that liquidity risk. Another explanation is that if the market did decrease to the level of the out-of-the-money strike prices, then the volatility will probably have increased. To counter this potentiality, some market markers use the volatility they would expect to have if the market moved to the level of their strike price. Finally, it could be that the assumptions underlying the popular option pricing models, such as Black and Scholes, are violated. There is considerable evidence that the returns for many markets cannot be characterised by a lognormal distribution but follow a bizarrely shaped distribution called leptokurtic. This means that dramatic upward or downward movements in markets occur more often than predicted by a lognormal distribution.[7] My feeling is that all these factors contribute to volatility differing across strike prices. The important question then becomes: what is the use of theoretical pricing models if these discrepancies occur? The answer to this question was covered extensively in Chapter 3. If the reader recalls the aeroplane analogy, option pricing models programs such as RAP are the gauges which provide information and should not be used as exclusive substitutes for looking out of the window. The option market maker recognises that volatility, and hence option prices, do not always conform to theory. However, theory does allow a framework within which he can recognise obvious deviations and thus take advantage of them.

Evaluating the Risks of the Option Portfolio

The next thing we need to determine is the risks inherent in an entire portfolio of Live Cattle futures and options. As was pointed out in Chapter 3, to see the entire picture it is necessary to look at the net delta, gamma, vega, and theta positions consolidated for all the trades in our options portfolio. Table 9.8 displays a printout with just these statistics. As one looks at it, in the upper half on the left he will see Net FUTURES and below that Net # Calls and Net # Puts. Immediately to the right of Net FUTURES, he will see 0 (no position). Below that he will see a − 10 for the net number of calls

```
Press M to proceed                          LIVE CATTLE 10 Jun 1991

                  2Aug91   4Oct91   6Dec91   AllMths

Net FUTURES       0        0        0        0
Net # Calls       -10.     65.      -20.     35.
Net # Puts        15.      -25.     -20.     -30.

Net Delta         -16.350  28.0826  3.36377  15.0956
Net Gamma         -.00234  .057637  -.09388  -.03858
Net Zeta          -.02093  1.54053  -3.1395  -1.6199
Net Theta         -5.0065  71.4342  -73.367  -6.9395

FUTURES PRC       72.92    75.17    76.22
DAILY SIGMA       0.50     0.48     0.39
ANNUAL SIGMA      10.750   10.000   8.000
INTEREST RATE     6.250    6.350    6.500
```

Table 9.8 Delta, Gamma, Vega and Theta

and 15 for the net number of August puts. As I stated in Chapter 3, option risk is not only defined by the number of contracts purchased or sold; another critical factor is the delta. The reader can see the net delta impact of all these positions if he looks further down the table to the immediate right of net delta. Here, he will see that the net delta of all the August positions is – 16.350. Thus, relative to August Live Cattle futures, the overall impact of the trade he has established has the same underlying price risk as being short 16.4 August Live Cattle futures. Below this is the gamma for the August position and it is – 0.00234. This indicates how much the delta for the entire August position will change if the price of the underlying Live Cattle futures changes by one basis point. The reader will note that in this case the gamma is negative, indicating that when the market rises, the delta of the overall position will also become less positive or more negative; and that when the Live Cattle futures price falls, the overall exposure to the underlying market will become more positive.

Below the gamma value for the August futures and options portfolio, one can see more numbers. The first is the net zeta. This is the same derivative that we call the vega. The numerical value for the zeta (vega) is – 0.02093. This indicates the amount of $1000 that will be earned or lost for every one per cent increase or decrease in volatility. With the present level of volatility at 10 per cent, if it increased to 11 per cent and everything else remained unchanged, one would expect to lose $20.93 on the August trades. The number below this is the net theta. This indicates how much one will make or lose on the position from time decay as a single day passes. For the August Live Cattle futures and options positions, we expect to make $5.0065 from 10 June to 11 June (a minus sign means we profit and a plus sign means we lose). Finally, below the 'Greeks' are some useful statistics. These include: the futures price used in the estimation; the daily sigma (standard deviation) for the futures; and the annual sigma (the volatility) used in the analysis.

The reader will recall that we also have positions in our options 'book' (another name used by market makers for their option portfolio) which should be evaluated relative to the October Live Cattle futures. Thus, in the middle column of Table 9.8, we can see the same net positions, deltas, gammas, zetas and thetas for the October expiration. The overall delta for October is 28.0826. This shows that, in total, the options we have dealt with a October expiration have the same risk as buying 28 October Live Cattle futures contracts. The gamma here is a positive 0.057637 indicating that the changes in the delta of the position will be positively related to the movement of the October futures. Finally, the zeta (vega) and the theta are both positive (at 1.54053 and 71.4342 respectively). The interpretation of this is that we are net buyers of volatility in October and will, therefore, lose from time decay.

In addition, we also have trades for the December expiration. Thus, in the third column of Table 9.8, we can see the same net positions, deltas, gammas, zetas and thetas for the December expiration. The overall delta for December is 3.36377. This shows that, in total, the options we have dealt with a December expiration have the same risk as buying 3.4 December Live Cattle futures contracts. The gamma here is – 0.09388, indicating that the changes in the delta of the position will be inversely related to the movement of the December futures. Finally, the zeta (vega) and the theta are both negative (at − 3.1395 and − 73.367 respectively). The interpretation of this is that we are net sellers of volatility in December and will, therefore, benefit from time decay.

The column furthest to the right indicates the exposures across all months. The exposures of the August contracts will either be additive or offsetting when combined with the October and December positions. Therefore, the delta exposure of 15.0956 indicates the combination of August, October and December deltas. The reader will no doubt notice a slight mathematical deviation; this is due to assumptions RAP makes about the spread relationships between August, October and December futures. This number indicates that the entire portfolio of transactions will have the same gains and losses from movements in Live Cattle futures as holding approximately 15 Live Cattle futures. As the reader can also see, the rest of the 'Greeks' are aggregated in this column as well. In conclusion, this tool measures the relative risks both generally and specifically within each month.

A critical point to remember is that if one is short 20 calls or even 1000 calls, neither is the real measure of the risk. The real measures of risk are the derivatives. For example, relative to Live Cattle futures the delta position is the true exposure to the underlying market. By adding the deltas for all the months, we can determine the total risk of the 'book' relative to a given underlying futures contract.

Back again, what is our volatility risk for the entire position? The answer is the zeta (vega). This gives us a measure of the amount of dollars we will make in thousands from a one per cent move in the volatility of the market. If the volatility moves up one per cent and we are short in it, we will lose $1619.90 (−1.6199 × $1,000). Conversely, if volatility moves down by one per cent we will make $1619.90.

What will happen to the future and options portfolio as time passes? With theta, we have the amount of time decay that will occur. From today until tomorrow, we expect to make $6.9395. Overall, we are short volatility across all maturities, so there the time decay will help us.

GRAPHING THE RISKS OF THE OPTION PORTFOLIO

All these numbers are extremely helpful in assessing the risk of a portfolio of derivative products. However, to get a real grasp on the situation, nothing beats a graph. Let us examine a graph of all the risks at once. With the RAP, we can take a five-dimensional risk management problem (delta, gamma, vega, theta and intra month spreads) and reduce it to a simple two-dimensional graph. Essentially, what the program does is re-evaluate our entire portfolio of derivative products – including different maturities – as though it were composed only of transactions in the futures contract month closest to expiration. This can be seen in Table 9.9.

The total risk analysis graph is a plot that indicates the exposure relative to the nearest futures contract of the entire portfolio. Furthermore, it measures what our position expects to make overnight if the market stays at present levels or if the nearest futures contract either rises or falls (up to our maximum amount of $1.40). The reader

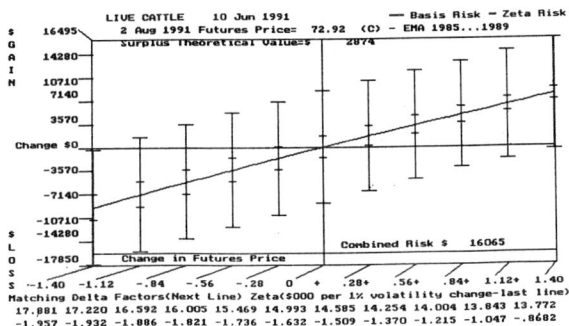

Table 9.9 Risk Analysis Graph

can see that this portfolio looks remarkably like buying a futures contract. In fact, if you return to Chapter 1 and review Figure 1.2 you will be hard pressed to see any difference. Thus, if the market starts rallying, this position will make substantial profits. In fact, if the August Live Cattle futures price goes $1.40 higher, which would then be $74.32, they would make around $7140. Unfortunately, if Live Cattle futures price falls by $1.40, then worth $71.52, the portfolio would lose almost $8500 and the career of our market maker would probably be over forthwith.

Remember that the delta is the slope of an option or a portfolio of options, relative to the underlying market. The angle of the curve is therefore equal to the delta at that point. To aid analysis, the reader will find the deltas for this portfolio at the bottom of the plot. They are immediately below the line which reads 'Matching Delta Factors (Next Line)'. At the current price for August Live Cattle futures, in the middle of the line, the delta is 14.993.[8] Again, as we saw in Table 9.8, this indicates that the position is approximately equivalent to long 15 August Live Cattle futures contracts. Unfortunately, a problem with deltas is that they can change. (See Chapter 3 for more detail.) So if one looks at the furthest left and the furthest right delta factors, one sees the delta changes are equal to 17.881 deltas when the market falls by $1.40, and to 13.772 deltas when the markets rises by $1.40.

As the market moves up, the position becomes less long and as the market falls it becomes more long. This is because the gamma for this position is negative. Unfortunately, gamma is almost as unstable as the delta is. Fortunately, programs such as RAP exist because these plots are the only way to determine accurately what the impact of gamma changes will be.

I have repeatedly stressed how important volatility is to the pricing of options. It is also consistent to stress that measuring the volatility exposure is equally important in the risk management of these securities. In addition, the plot displays the volatility risk of the portfolio but in a very subtle way. If the reader looks closely at the profit and loss line for the portfolio, he will notice little 'I's appearing on top of it. This result is especially marked on the left side of the diagram. What these little 'I's indicate is the plus and minus range within which the portfolio value could be given a movement of volatility by one per cent up or down. If the volatility remained at current levels, then the change in the portfolio's value would simply be a function of the movement in the underlying market price and would therefore lie on the line. If, however, the volatility happens to move in one's favour, then that result would be a compounding or at least have an ameliorating impact on the effects of the futures price change. Again, as with the deltas, the volatility sensitivity numbers are listed in the line at the very bottom of the plot. These zeta (vega) numbers indicate the thousands of dollars one would gain or lose from a one per cent move in the level of volatility. Notice that the volatility impact is also not constant but changes as the underlying market price moves. At the current futures price of $72.92, the zeta (vega) is – 1.632. However, if the market drops by 1.40¢ per pound (which is the same as $1.40 per 100 pounds), the zeta (vega) rises to – 1.957. This shows that one will lose more than $1,957 for every one per cent increase in volatility at that point because the minus sign indicates that the position is short. When you consider what would probably happen to volatility if the market did fall 1.40¢ overnight, you would be safe to bet that such a market move would have to be associated with a dramatic increase in volatility.

Finally, do we not have positions in different months as well? By making everything equivalent to August Live Cattle futures, are we not making an assumption that the October Live Cattle futures and options will move in a lockstep manner? The answer to both of these questions is yes. So, to examine this risk, another 'I' is added and it is the larger 'I' that is compounded onto the volatility 'I'. This risk measure indicates what – if the spread between August, October and December Live Cattle futures changes by the maximum amount we have specified (1.05¢ per pound) – would be the incremental effect on the profit or loss of the portfolio. If the change in the spreads helps us, this will be treated as an additional profit. This would occur if the August Live Cattle futures fell and the October and December futures instead rose. The lower portion of the 'I' indicates an adverse move in the spread. So, in review, the little 'I' is the volatility range for profit and loss and the bigger 'I' indicates the incremental impact from the spreads also changing in addition to the maximum volatility move. Therefore, when one looks at the lower left-hand corner of the plot in Table 9.9, this is the worst case scenario. The loss of $17,850 occurs when 'Murphy's Law' applies: the market has fallen by the maximum amount, volatility has risen by one per cent, and the spread between August, October and December Live Cattle futures has also moved against the strategy.

We now have our delta positions at various market levels and our exposure to volatility. We can also see clearly when we make and lose money and, if everything goes wrong, what our maximum loss potential will be. The number in the lower right quadrant of the plot is titled the Combined Risk. This number for the portfolio is $16,065. This designation was devised by the Chicago Mercantile Exchange to determine the margin they would require for the trader to maintain these positions with the clearing house. The Combined Risk is basically a 95 per cent confidence interval on everything going wrong. While the Combined Risk figure does not tell you the absolute worst case scenario, it is useful because at a 95 per cent level these numbers provide us with a workable general risk measure. The final number in the graph that has not yet been explained is the 'Surplus Theoretical Value'. This indicates the theoretical edge the portfolio has over the theoretical prices for the futures and the options trades we have established. In this example, the portfolio has an edge of $2874 relative to the theoretical prices of the securities in that portfolio.

APPLICATIONS OF COMPUTER RISK ANALYSIS PROGRAMS FOR THE MANAGEMENT OF LIVE CATTLE OPTION PORTFOLIOS BY MARKET MAKERS

The reader may be interested in how this applies to the real day-to-day management of an options 'book'. When I set up two dealing operations, I had to determine from the management control standpoint how the traders were going to be monitored and controlled. The manager must have an accurate risk management system that will help him determine the risk limits for his traders. Ideally, he should get a simple graph or table that measures the maximum amount a trader could lose and what the maximum exposure or delta position would be overnight. The manager could then determine how far the market could move overnight, how much volatility could change and how the spread between futures months could move. With these initial parameters set, back office staff would then update the system daily with current market data from the day's transactions. Reports would then be generated for both the individual trader's accounts and in consolidation. In our department, both traders and their managers received a copy of these reports. Traders were then restricted to trading within prescribed limits for loss potential and deltas (sometimes gammas and vegas too). When I traded, my limits were five deltas (futures) long or short overnight and a maximum loss potential of no more than $15,000. Within these constraints, I could construct any combination of trades that I saw fit.

HOW TO REDUCE THE RISK OF THE LIVE CATTLE OPTION PORTFOLIO

Let us pretend that this sample Live Cattle options 'book' is my personal portfolio and that I have the same limits as when I traded in Chicago. The steps I would take to hedge the position would be to consider first what possible trades would bring me back within limits and reduce my risks. Since the position is extremely 'long' and exposed to the spreads between months, I will have to gain negative deltas to offset the risk and attempt to cover the intramarket risks. Well, what are the possible equivalent short positions? These equivalent short positions include short futures, buying puts or writing calls. The choice of which strategy to use will depend upon my view on volatility (this was discussed extensively in Chapter 5). Suppose that my view on volatility is neutral. If the reader returns to the strategy matrix in Chapter 5, he will find two potential strategies which are both short on the underlying market and neutral to volatility: short the underlying futures and a bear spread. Upon flipping a coin, I decide to buy 16 August Live Cattle futures, sell 28 October Live Cattle futures and

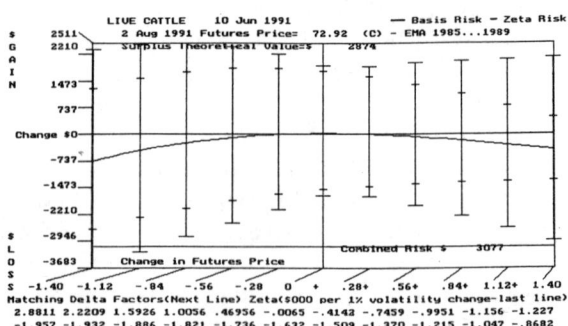

Table 9.10 Risk Analysis Graph of the New Portfolio

sell 3 December Live Cattle futures contracts. The reason I do not simply sell 15 August (or October) Live Cattle Futures is because I also want to reduce my spread risk. By reducing the delta risk in each maturity to as close to zero as is possible, my overall delta is still zero and the risk within each maturity is zero as well. By doing this, my net futures contracts sold still equals 15 short futures (short 28 Octobers, short 3 Decembers and long 16 Augusts) but the risk between months has also been minimised. Table 9.10 displays the risk of this new portfolio. The first thing the reader should notice is that the plot has flattened considerably. Only when the market moves up or down by more than 28¢ does the position lose its neutrality in delta terms.

What about the loss potential and the delta limits? The reader can run his finger across the delta line at the bottom of the plot and see that at no point does the position exceed three deltas, so this is now within the limits. What about the loss potential? The Combined Risk factor is now $3077. Therefore, this position is now within limits. Still, the position has considerable risk. If this were my own portfolio, I would try a wider range of hedging strategies until the loss potential was minimised.

Regardless of the computer systems one chooses, it is critical to realise the computational complexity in dealing options. In this chapter, I have demonstrated one system which provides 'gauges' critical to option risk management. Without some system to price and manage the risks of options, I strongly recommend the reader to abstain from active option dealing.

---

[1] Aristotle's *Politics*, Book 1, Chapter 11, Jowett translation. This example of early Greek options was first referred to in Gary Gastineau's book, *The Stock Options Manual*.

[2] See Gastineau's book for a lively description of the stock options markets prior to the 1970s.

[3] Louis Bachelier, 'Théorie de la Speculation', *Annales de l'Ecole Normale Supérieure*, 17 pp.21-86 (1900). English translation by A.J.Boness in *The Random Character of Stock Market Prices*, ed. Paul H. Cootner, pp.17-78. Cambridge, Mass, MIT Press (1967). (Thank goodness for the translation.)

4 David Emanuel worked as an economist at the Chicago Mercantile Exchange from 1984 to 1985, the experience of which he used in developing RAP. Apart from this program, Dr. Emanuel is well known for his expertise in the field of warrants.

5 Ha, Ha, got you! Cattle don't pay dividends or coupons, the only time this feature is used is for option on physical stock, or Bonds.

6 These prices are actual CME prices as of 10 June 1991.

7 See A. Larson, 'Measurement of a Random Process in Futures Prices', *Food Research Institute Studies*, Vol.I, No.3, pp.313-24 (November 1960).

8 The difference between this aggregate delta and the aggregate delta in Table 9.8 lies in the fact that the October and December deltas are being discounted by the interest rate to make them equivalent to August deltas. See RAP manual.

10: OTC Interest Rate Options

So far in this book, I have discussed only options that are traded at organised markets. In the 1980s a whole new option market developed to address the unprecedented interest rate, commodity and currency risks that were associated with a variety of economic shocks. These products were not offered at an organised marketplace but were instead offered directly by financial institutions to clients. They became known as over-the-counter (OTC) options. The principal differences between exchange-traded options and OTCs are that the former are more actively traded but not very flexible (a restricted range of maturities and strike prices), while OTCs offer tailor-made terms but often with a lower liquidity or at a higher cost.

These products were particularly popular in the management of interest rate risks and they include OTC options on fixed income instruments (like Bonds), Interest Rate Guarantees, Interest Rate Ceilings, Floors and Collars, Options on Interest Rate Ceilings and Floors, Options on Interest Rate Swaps (Swaptions), and a variety of exotic options like Average Rate options (Asian options) and Maximum/Minimum Rate options (Look back options). In this chapter, I will discuss each of these in turn and show the reader how these customised products relate to the concepts I have previously discussed.

OTC OPTIONS ON BONDS

Of the available interest rate OTC options, options on fixed income securities, portfolios, or loans have been among the most popular. Of course, options have long been associated with fixed income securities with the embedded call features that many Bonds have. A call feature typically gives the issuer of the Bond the right to buy the Bonds back from the holders at a price specified at the issuance of the Bond and for a certain period. The holder of a callable Bond essentially has a position which is 'long' a Bond and 'short' a call option on that Bond. If the reader refers to Example 3 in Chapter 7, he will note that when one combines a long position in a Bond with a short call the payoff to the portfolio is identical to a short put option. Thus, the issuer of the callable Bond, by symmetry, must have a position which is similar to buying a put option on Bonds.

Quite often, these call (or put) features will be decoupled from the underlying Bond and sold separately as OTC Bond options. Probably, the most interesting recent example of this technique has been in the German market where the German Government issued Bundesanleihen (Government Bonds) which are called

Schuldscheindarlehen, and include a put feature allowing the buyer to sell the security back to the German Government after one, two and three years. A number of Investment Banks purchased these securities and then stripped off the put option feature, selling them into the market as OTC Bundesanleihen options (actually as Swaptions, which I will discuss later in this chapter).[1] Of course, this is done quite often in all fixed income markets and has proved a solid money maker for a number of Investment Banks.

In addition to the creation of OTC Bond options by stripping embedded options away from an existing Bond, many market makers have also offered 'new' options by writing the options and hedging the risks with the underlying security. What exactly is an OTC Bond Option? Typical conditions for an OTC Bond option can be seen in Table 10.1. An OTC Bond option is a negotiated (sometimes called 'bespoke') option flexible with regards to the terms of the contract. The terms that can be negotiated include the underlying instrument (i.e. a particular fixed income instrument), the size of the underlying amount (subject to a minimum amount), puts or calls with either European or American (or a variety of other) exercise features, a completely flexible maturity (generally out to one year) and settlement that can be either by physical delivery or cash settlement upon exercise.

Why would one want to deal with an OTC Bond option when exchange-traded options on Bonds are so liquid? The answer is flexibility. The terms of an OTC Bond option are totally negotiable while the exchange-traded option on Bond futures (or on a physical Bond) are not. Therefore, the OTC Bond option allows the user an instrument which will exactly meet his trading or hedging needs without having to incur the risks of 'cross-hedging' an exposure with another instrument and taking on what is known as the 'basis risk'.[2] Furthermore, the hedger will not have to accept yield curve risks or the risks of hedging a time period which is mismatched with the maturity of an exchange-traded option.

SIZE	SUBJECT TO A MINIMUM OF $1,000,000 NOMINAL BONDS
PUT OR CALL	THESE CAN ALSO BE EITHER "EUROPEAN" OR "AMERICAN" STYLE
STRIKE PRICE	ANY PRICE IS AVAILABLE EXPRESSED IN TERMS OF THE CLEAN PRICE OF THE BOND
EXERCISE/ EXPIRY DATE	WITH A DURATION UP TO 5 YEARS
SETTLEMENT	THIS CAN EITHER BE FOR DELIVERY OF THE SPECIFIC BOND OR FOR THE CASH DIFFERENCE, IN WHICH CASE THE SETTLEMENT PRICE WILL BE THAT OF THE CASH MARKET FIXING ON THE DAY OF EXERCISE

Table 10.1 Conditions for an OTC Bond Options

DOWN-AND-OUT CALLS AND UP-AND-OUT PUTS

A good example of the kind of customisation offered with OTC Bond options is the availability of specialised structures in the OTC market, known as down-and-out calls and up-and-out puts. Down-and-out calls provide the holder with the same rights as a normal call option except that the option is cancelled if the underlying Bond price reaches a predetermined level below current prices. When cancellation occurs, a rebate (or refund of premium) is often paid to the holder. Because of the potential limited life for down-and-out calls, their price can be significantly below the price of a normal call option. Up-and-out puts provide the holder the same rights as a normal put option except that the option is cancelled if the underlying Bond price reaches a predetermined level above current prices. Again, when this occurs, the holder is paid back a refund of the portion of his initial premium expense.

What is the rationale for down-and-out and up-and-out options? For option buyers, the cost can be significantly lower than that of an outright call or put option. But the principal attraction of these exotic options are for option writers. For option writers of OTC Bond options (that are not simply split off from a Bond issue), significant risk occurs when hedging the options with the underlying security. The writer will employ some sort of 'delta neutral' hedging technique as was outlined in Chapter 6. The reader will recall that significant risk occurs from the change in the deltas as the price of the underlying market moves (the gamma risk). The situation could occur with a normal call option that the price of the underlying market falls, and the hedger would then have to sell a portion of the underlying Bonds (he had previously purchased to hedge the calls). Of course, this would be at a loss. If he did so and then the underlying price rallied back to the previous levels, he would have to buy back the Bonds and again establish the previous hedged position. If then the underlying price fell again, then once again the writer would lose on the Bond hedge without being able to realise the gain on the reduced theoretical value of the call option. To allow the writer the ability to realise the profit on the reduction in the call price when the underlying market price falls, the down-and-out feature allows the writer to cancel the option, realise his gain on that side which will offset the loss on the hedge with the underlying Bond. Thus, the down-and-out feature makes writing of options less risky to those who sell OTC options on Bonds.

Another nice feature for holders of OTC Bond options is the flexibility in the settlement of these contracts. For example, with exchange-traded options on fixed income securities, the general rule is that the premium for the option must be paid immediately upon the purchase of the option. With OTC Bond options, other settlement procedures are available in addition to the immediate payment of premium. For example, the premium can be margined until the expiration of the option and added to the final purchase price of the Bond (assuming the OTC option is a call option and is exercised).[3] But in most circumstances, the margin for delayed option premium payment is covered by drawing upon credit lines agreed between the counterparties. Often, collateral – in lieu of margin – will be requested when the exposures exceed the agreed credit lines.

WHY CLIENTS AND BANKS DEAL IN OTC BOND OPTIONS

In review, the key features that induce clients to purchase OTC Bond options include: customisation of the instrument, size and strike price, no basis risk for hedgers, maturities for OTCs are longer than for exchange-traded options, easier delivery mechanisms for OTCs, a choice of the exercise style, the ability to margin option premiums and finally overall flexibility in the structure of the agreements.

The reasons why financial institutions offer OTC options include: the basic need to meet their individual client's needs and the ability to learn more about their customers' businesses. In addition, by offering OTC Bond options to a variety of clients, a Bank can set up its own kind of 'clearing system' and match customers against each other. Also, these OTC options can create additional commissions and add to their core Bond selling activities by the combination of Bond sales and option sales. Finally, involvement in OTC option trading can help the bank to anticipate movements in the cash Bond markets. If they find that an order imbalance occurs in the options market (more buyers than sellers) then research in the US markets has shown that the option markets lead movements in the cash market by 15 to 30 minutes.

EXAMPLES OF APPLICATIONS FOR OTC BOND OPTIONS

I will now examine a number of applications of OTC Bond options for customers. Let's say that an investor plans to buy a particular Bond (perhaps a new issue) and has a particular level where he would wish to sell it out. This being the case, he can initiate a Buy-Write strategy, where he buys the Bond and writes a call option on that Bond to the bank at a strike price equal to the level the investor wishes to sell the Bond. Then, if the Bond price rises to his level, the investor will sell his Bond via the option exercise and if the market fails to rally, he will be able to retain the OTC Bond option premium. In addition, an investor can use OTC Bond options as substitutes for the purchase of a particular security. (The reader will recall this being discussed in Example 1 of Chapter 7.) The difference with the OTC Bond option is that the buyer knows which security he will actually purchase upon exercise; and with options on T-Bond futures, he will receive upon exercise a T-Bond futures contract which at delivery will allow him to buy the 'cheapest-to-deliver' US Treasury Bond which may not be the instrument he wishes ultimately to purchase. The third example of customer use of OTC Bond options concerns the foreign investor who might wish to benefit from the movement in the US Treasury market, but does not want to place the bulk of his available funds in US dollars. The OTC Bond option will allow him, for a small premium payment, a chance to choose exactly the security he wishes to purchase (or sell) with a minimum exposure to the US dollar. Furthermore, if the exchange rate between his currency and the US dollar moves in his favour (as does the level of the US Treasury security), then he will have a double benefit amounting to a combined fixed income option and a currency option. A final example of customer use of OTC Bond options is for those traders who may want to be short a particular Bond but for various reasons are unable to borrow that particular Bond to sell short. By buying OTC put options and selling OTC call options on that same security at the same strike price, they will have created a synthetic short selling position in the security.[4]

PRICING OF OTC BOND OPTIONS

The pricing of interest rate options is easily the most difficult topic I will attempt to explain in this book. The main reason for this is that the ultimate underlying factor driving the value of Bonds or other interest-bearing securities is the interest rate itself. While stocks or commodities can be assumed to follow a random walk, interest rate movements are much harder to model. In addition, a Bond price will not simply be a function of one interest rate but as many interest rates as that Bond has cashflows. For example, a ten-year US Treasury Bond will pay coupons biannually, and after ten years the principal. So in total, the Bond has 20 dates where cash is paid to the holder. To determine the value of the Bond today, we simply take all these future payments and discount them back to present value, sum them up and we have the Bond price.

The problem becomes which interest rate or rates to use. If one argues that a coupon Bond is simply a set of (in this example, 20) pure discount Bonds, then each of the 20 cash payouts should be discounted to present value by their own particular interest rate. Quite often this is called the 'Zero Coupon' interest rate because each of the 20 cashflows can be thought of as a Bond that pays no (and therefore a Zero) coupon.

So we determine each of the interest rates for the individual cashflows, and probably find that they are at different levels. This is generally the case and the name academics have for this effect is the 'Term Structure of Interest Rates'. Most practitioners call this effect the (zero coupon) yield curve. The problem with pricing options on Bonds is that one is not pricing a derivative security (an option) of just one underlying security but rather an option on a portfolio of underlying securities (the individual cashflows); and each of these 20 'sub-securities' may have a different underlying level, volatility and lifetime. So, to price the option on the portfolio of cashflows (the coupon Bond), one must provide a lot more information than would be required for a simple option that could be priced by the Black and Scholes model. In fact, one needs to incorporate the entire term structure of interest rates and somehow assess how this could change over the life of the option. Furthermore, the Bond price itself will change over time as it moves closer to its maturity. Consider the following: the volatility of a Bond is simply some sort of summation of the volatilities of each of the individual cashflows that make it up. As these cashflows are paid up (coupon payment dates), these elements of volatility drop from the Bond's volatility because they are no longer uncertain (they are already sitting in your pocket). So as one would expect, a Bond's volatility slowly drops over time as it approaches maturity. What a mess!

To address these issues and obtain a price for a Bond option, basically two approaches have been proposed. The first adapts the basic Black and Scholes model and tries to incorporate the changing Bond variance as the Bond approaches its final

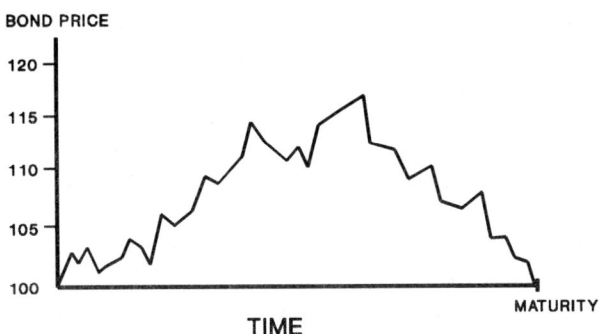

BOND PRICE

TIME

MATURITY

Figure 10.1 Brownian Bridge for a Bond

maturity. These models include Merton's Debt option model, the 'Brownian Bridge' model of Ball and Torous, and the Schaefer and Schwartz Duration model. The other approach is to tackle the problem by trying to estimate the movements in the overall term structure of interest rates and the most famous of these models is the Ho and Lee model.

The Black and Scholes is immediately thrown out of the running because it assumes a constant volatility and while that might make sense for one security, it certainly won't work for a portfolio of different securities each of which has a different volatility. Returning to the analogy of the Black and Scholes model as discussed in Chapter 2, the basic model is as good as a Nikon camera, but the problem with Bond options is one needs a 'movie camera' to record a number of pictures almost simultaneously and not just a single frame. The first model which tried to take in a 'broader picture' was supplied by Robert Merton in 1975.[5] The solution Merton found to the problem of pricing Bond options entailed specifying the Bond (return) volatility. This included the average expected volatility over the life of the option along with a correlation term between short-term interest rates and long-term rates. Later in this chapter I will present another model which essentially does this for the pricing of Options on Swaps.[6]

The second revision of the Black and Scholes model for Bond options came from Ball and Torous in 1983.[7] What they did was question the Black and Scholes assumption about Brownian motion. Their argument is that a Bond price cannot just wander around aimlessly (like the random walk of a drunk). We know that when a Bond is first issued, if the coupon is equal to the prevailing yield for comparable Bonds of the same maturity, its initial price will be 100 (par). At maturity it will also be at 100 (par) as the last payment of the principal is made. Between these dates, however, the Bond can vary around as it pleases. Their term for this is 'the Brownian Bridge', and can be seen in Figure 10.1. In that graph, the Bond starts at 100 (on one side of the 'river') and varies around until it returns to 100 (on the other side of the 'river') at maturity. With this revised assumption for how Bond prices move, they essentially used the Black and Scholes approach to price Bond options. The problem with the Brownian Bridge approach is that it also assumes a constant proportional variance over time. This implies that as the bond approaches maturity, the volatility increases to infinity. However, we know that exactly the opposite happens as the number of cashflows (that cause the Bond to be volatile in the first place) are paid off and cease to add to the total volatility of the Bond.

The final approach I will discuss for pricing options on Bonds by adjusting the Bond's volatility is the Schaefer and Schwartz Duration model.[8] Schaefer and Schwartz decided to assume that the risk of a Bond is related to its duration.[9] The problem with this model is that duration is like an option's delta; it can change when interest rates change. Furthermore, the duration concept assumes that the term structure of interest rates can only change in one way: the same amount for the maturity of each interest rate. So, if interest rates rose by one per cent from seven per cent to eight per cent for the 90-day interest rate, then they would also change by the same one per cent for the 20-year interest rate from perhaps nine per cent to ten per cent. If interest rates fail to follow this pattern, then the approach will not work.

To take into account the fact that interest rates do not always change by the same amount across the term structure, another approach was tried; that of trying to model the possible changes in the whole term structure of interest rates. The first of these models was presented by Ho and Lee.[10] What they did, rather than try to model the volatility of one or more interest rates to determine the term structure of interest rates, was begin with the term structure as it is (at the point when they have to price the option) and ask how could the entire thing change? By assuming that the term structure is that way for a reason; that the market has determined it should look that way (and that no arbitrage trades are possible), they simply try a variety of different term structure patterns and see what happens. The way they do this is to apply the Binomial approach outlined in Chapter 3. Over time, the term structure can twist upwards or downwards or become flatter with certain probabilities. With the expected movement in the term structure taken into account, then it is a simple matter to evaluate each of the individual sub-bonds in the overall coupon Bond and the sum of all these mini-options is the price of the option on the coupon Bond. Unfortunately, one of the problems with the Ho and Lee model is that their assumptions allow the possibility of negative interest rates (which is clearly impossible).

With so many models to choose from, which one should the practitioner choose to price options on Bonds? Of the approaches outlined above, the Ho and Lee model seems to be in vogue but it is very complicated and assumes the trader can feed in variables about the expected movements in the term structure. Another simpler approach has already been presented in Chapter 3. In the discussions of the correct pricing model for currency options, I presented the argument of Mark Garman that all options can be seen as options on the future price of the asset. If this is so, then it is a simple matter to determine the future price of the Bond and then apply the trusty Black (1976) model for options on futures. In a recent book[11] it was shown that there is almost no difference between the result of the Ho and Lee model and the Black (1976) model for options on future Bond prices. Essentially, all these complicated option formulas are trying to estimate what the Bond price will be at the expiration date of the option (the future price), and then determine the option price. As with the currency options in Chapter 3, why not just estimate the forward price of the Bond yourself and then apply a simple model to determine the option's time value component? For many traders (including myself), simplicity seems to win out and they will estimate their own future price for the Bond and then apply the Black (1976) model to price the option on it.

INTEREST RATE GUARANTEE AGREEMENTS

Interest Rate Guarantee Agreements are simply interest rate insurance policies for a single floating interest rate exposure. IRGs generally come in two varieties: borrower and lender options. In this market, the equivalent of a put option on rates is called the Lender option (LO), as it benefits as rates fall; and the Borrower option (BO) is the equivalent of a call option on rates since it benefits as rates rise. The underlying asset for this contract can either be an interest rate such as the Prime Rate or the London InterBank Offered Rate (LIBOR), or a forward contract on interest rates. These forward contracts on interest rates are OTC futures and they are commonly known as Forward Rate Agreements (FRAs).

An FRA is an arrangement between a financial institution and a client which allows the client to fix interest costs for a specific future period. The interest rate to be paid on a nominal deposit of a specified maturity on that future date is agreed upon at the consummation of the transaction. At the maturity of the FRA, if rates have risen above the agreed rate, the seller of the FRA will pay an amount in cash that will remedy the buyer for his increased interest expense. If rates are below the agreed rate, then the buyer will have to compensate the seller. With the FRA, no principal is exchanged, only the difference between the agreed-upon rate and the interest rate on the maturity date. As the reader may see, an FRA is almost identical to a Eurodollar futures contract. The differences are: a Eurodollar futures contract is standardised for dates (IMM dates) and amounts ($1 million contract size) and the FRA is customised; a Eurodollar futures price is 100 minus the interest rate level, while the FRA is simply the interest rate level; and finally, Eurodollar futures must be margined every day and FRAs generally have no such margining requirement.

Therefore, if FRAs are simply OTC Eurodollar futures, then Interest Rate Guarantees (which are options on FRAs) must simply be OTC options on Eurodollar futures. Since this is the case, the pricing of these products must be identical to that of the option on Eurodollar futures. The major difference in the pricing of Interest Rate Guarantees arises from the fact that they tend to have a European exercise feature. Thus, the method for estimating the theoretical price for European Interest Rate Guarantees is determined by using the simple Black (1976) model for futures, with the underlying price the FRA rate for the expiration date of the Interest Rate Guarantee. If the Interest Rate Guarantee is American-style, the Binomial approach could be used. The reader is referred back to Chapter 3 for the actual formulae for these models.

OTC interest rate options, like Interest Rate Guarantees, are based upon the annualised interest rates rather than upon price indices like options on futures. The premiums for these options are also in terms of annualised percentage terms and, as with futures options, the cash price for the option is equal to the price in percentages (basis points) times the value of each 0.01 per cent point (1 basis point). Because most OTC interest rate options cannot be exercised early (European-style), there is no problem associated with what is actually delivered upon exercise. At the final maturity date of the option (a lender option for example), the writer of the option will simply pay the holder of the Interest Rate Guarantee in cash the difference between the strike 'rate' for the IRG and the market reference rate. This will only occur if the reference interest rate (like LIBOR) is below the strike 'rate'. If the reference interest rate is higher, no cash is paid and the option expires worthless.

An example of the use of an Interest Rate Guarantee would be a borrower who must insure his next rollover of his floating rate funding. He would choose to purchase a Borrower Option (BO) to protect himself. Table 10.2 outlines the current market dynamics for the hedger. He finds that the current six-month LIBOR is 6.5 per cent and he wishes to lock in this rate in nine months' time. The strike rate is 6.5 per cent and the amount of the exposure is $20 million. Since the BO is a European-style option, it is important to determine what the expected six-month LIBOR will be in nine months' time (the forward rate) and this can be determined with a 9 vs. 15 FRA. This quote format for FRAs indicates that the beginning of the borrowing or lending exposure begins in nine months' time and finishes in 15 months' time. Thus, this would represent a six-month borrowing in nine months' time. This rate is 6.75 per cent. To see better when the exposures occur, Figure 10.2 displays the period of exposure the option covers and the actual borrowing period. The cost of the option is 0.50 per cent or $50,000 (50 basis points × 50 $per 6-month LIBOR basis point per $1,000,000 × $20,000,000). At the expiration of the BO, the holder receives either nothing (if the six-month LIBOR is below 6.5 per cent) or the difference between the then six-month

OPTION TYPE:	EUROPEAN
UNDERLYING INTEREST RATE:	6 MONTH $ LIBOR
EXPIRATION DATE:	9 MONTHS (274 DAYS)
STRIKE LEVEL:	6.5%
FACE VALUE:	$20,000,000
CURRENT 6 MONTH $LIBOR INTEREST RATE:	6.5%
COST OF OPTION	0.50%

Table 10.2 Interest Rate Options

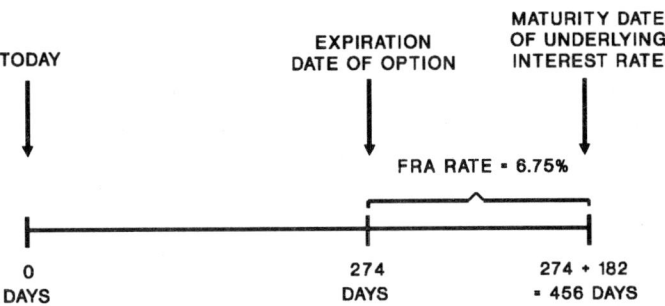

Figure 10.2

LIBOR and 6.5 per cent × 182/360 × $20,000,000. Suppose that on the expiration date, six-month LIBOR is equal to eight per cent. Then, the holder of the BO will either be paid $151,667 (8 per cent – 6.5 per cent) × 182/360 × $20,000,000 at the end of the borrowing period or the present value of this amount on day 274. Then the borrower must actually borrow in the market at eight per cent at that point, however the $151,667 he has received from the BO writer will reduce his interest payment accordingly.

The net effect of the BO hedge will be an interest expense of $808,889 borrowing at eight per cent (8 per cent × 182/360 × $20,000,000) minus the inflow on the BO of $151,667 plus the premium he had to pay upfront for the BO of $50,000. In total, his interest expense is equal to $707,222 ($808,889 – $151,667 + $50,000) or a rate of seven per cent six-month LIBOR ($707,222/$20,000,000 × 360/182). As expected, his worst case result is equal to his strike rate of 6.5 per cent + the 0.50 per cent in premium he paid for the BO.

INTEREST RATE CEILING, FLOOR AND COLLAR AGREEMENTS[12]

The incredible interest rate variability in the early 1980s led many borrowers and investors to seek protection for their streams of floating rate payments. A perfect product for these needs was the Interest Rate Cap Agreement which would limit either the variable rate interest expense of a borrower or the variable rate return for an investor. This OTC product thus 'capped' the exposure and hence the name 'Cap Agreement'. An Interest Rate Cap Agreement is a contractual arrangement where the Grantor (seller) of the Agreement has an obligation to pay cash to the Holder (buyer) if a particular interest rate exceeds or is less than a mutually agreed level at some future points in time. The two most basic forms of the Interest Rate Cap Agreement are Floor and Ceiling Agreements.

The Ceiling Agreement allows the holder to establish a maximum interest rate level for borrowing (on a floating basis) over a given period. If interest rates rise above the Ceiling rate, the holder receives cash to offset exactly the additional interest expense incurred at the now higher interest rate. If rates fall, the holder will be able to borrow at a rate below the ceiling rate. In this case, he receives nothing from the grantor. He might regard the Agreement as an interest rate insurance policy that has simply lapsed unused.

The Floor Agreement allows the holder to establish a minimum rate level for his floating rate deposits over a given period. If interest rates fall below the floor rate, the grantor reimburses the holder for the shortfall in interest income. If rates exceed the floor rate, the holder receives nothing from the grantor but can place his deposit at a higher market rate.

Collars (sometimes known as fences) are simply a combination of these two transactions. Collars allow the holder to establish a maximum (or minimum) interest rate level for borrowing (or investing) over a given period. In addition, the holder has sold a Floor Agreement which limits the gain from any fall in interest rates. If Interest rates exceed the ceiling rate, he receives cash from the grantor which (in cashflow terms) allows him to borrow at that rate. If interest rates are below the ceiling rate, then he can borrow at the more favourable rate until rates reach the level of the Floor Agreement he sold. At that rate and below, he must pay cash to the grantor which (in cashflow terms) locks in his minimum borrowing rate. The reason why Collars exist is because the cost can be substantially less than for a Ceiling Agreement. Basically, the rationale for the Collar is exactly the same as that for the Zero Cost Option strategy outlined in Chapter 8. The premium cost is reduced by giving up the unlimited profit potential.

By far the most popular of the Interest Rate Cap Agreements are the Ceiling Agreements. Therefore, Interest Rate Caps are used mostly by those who borrow at variable rates and are at risk from rates having changed by the time they roll over their borrowing. Take the example of a borrower funding himself for a three-year period with three-month LIBOR (the London Interbank Offered Rate in this case for US dollars). He may be concerned that over the next three years, when he must roll over his borrowing in three month increments, rates will rise. He may also have in mind a target LIBOR which, if exceeded, could cause him major problems. For this borrower, the appropriate Interest Rate Cap Agreement would be a Ceiling.

A potential user of a Floor Agreement would be a Bond portfolio manager who wants to limit his downside exposure on a floating-rate Bond portfolio to falling interest rates. He could either switch to a fixed-rate investment or purchase a Floor as an investment insurance policy. Of the two kinds of Agreements, Ceilings are much more popular among institutional clients.

When a Cap Agreement is purchased by the holder, a premium must be paid to the grantor. Thus, an Interest Rate Cap Agreement is similar to an option. As with an option, the holder of the Agreement must pay a premium upfront to enjoy its beneficial conditions and not be bound by the detrimental facets.

On the other side, the grantor is unsure when the agreement is reached whether or not a payout will occur. However, assuming that interest rate 'returns' are distributed comparably to other asset returns, he can use standard option pricing methodologies to help him determine the value of the agreement, gain an indication of the probability of payout, and quantify the risk of the position.

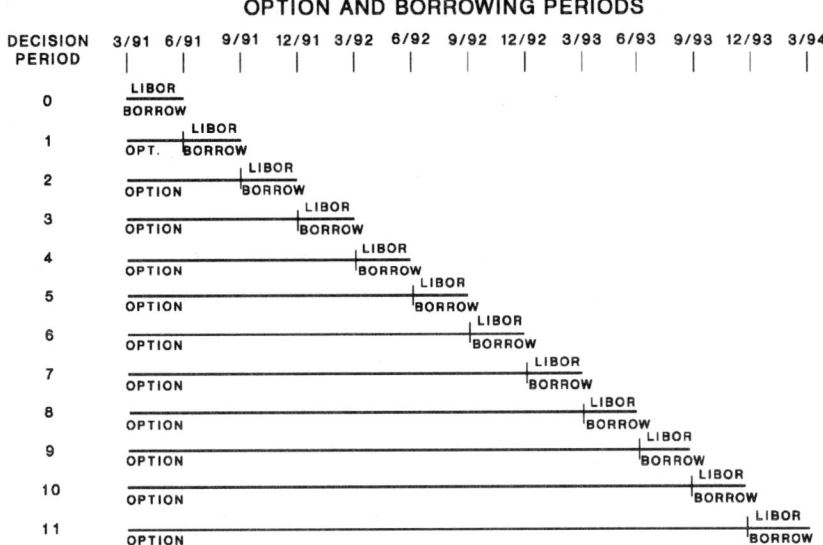

OPTION AND BORROWING PERIODS

Figure 10.3 Structure of a 3 Year LIBOR Cap-Rate Ceiling Agreement

Given that Cap Agreements are similar to options, would this Ceiling holder be buying a three-year option on interest rates? The answer is yes and no. What he is buying is a strip of European options (similar to Interest Rate Guarantees) that expire on the day each quarter during the three-year period that he rolls over his borrowing at the then prevailing LIBOR. Essentially, the Ceiling Agreement guarantees him a maximum rate for all his LIBOR rollovers.

Figure 10.3 outlines this process. It also shows the buyer of a three-year Ceiling Agreement starting in March 1991 actually acquiring eleven (11) options on three-month LIBOR. The horizontal lines to the right of the hatchmark, which have LIBOR BORROW associated with them, indicate the periods of his actual borrowing. The horizontal lines to the left of the hatchmark, which have OPTION underneath them, represent the term for each rollover option. The price he must pay for the Ceiling Agreement is simply the sum of the premiums for each of the eleven options.

Pricing of the Ceiling Rate Agreement

Payouts of a Ceiling Rate Agreement on three-month LIBOR are determined by the levels of three-month LIBOR at a specific future point in time. To value the Cap Agreement today, we must somehow determine the projected future levels of three-month LIBOR. In other words, we need futures prices of three-month LIBOR for the duration of the Cap Agreement.

If the term of the Cap Agreement is three years or less, and if the dates on which the Cap payout is determined correspond to the maturities of LIBOR futures contracts (Eurodollar futures) traded in Chicago, Singapore and London, all one has to do is

229

OPTION EXPIRATION PERIOD	DAYS TO MATURITY	EURO$ FUTURES PRICE	IMPLIED* EURO$ RATE	STRIKE PRICE	RISK-FREE # INTEREST RATE	VOLA- TILITY	OPTION PREMIUM	DELTA FACTOR
JUN 1991	91	93.21	6.79	8.00	5.84	14.50%	0.01	0.012
SEP 1991	182	92.84	7.16	8.00	6.13	14.50%	0.06	0.146
DEC 1991	273	92.38	7.62	8.00	6.58	14.50%	0.22	0.355
MAR 1992	364	92.20	7.80	8.00	6.57	13.70%	0.32	0.425
JUN 1992	455	91.92	8.08	8.00	6.66	13.70%	0.49	0.512
SEP 1992	546	91.68	8.32	8.00	7.12	13.50%	0.64	0.562
DEC 1992	637	91.43	8.57	8.00	7.36	13.40%	0.80	0.601
MAR 1993	728	91.39	8.61	8.00	7.40	13.00%	0.83	0.594
JUN 1993	819	91.28	8.72	8.00	7.50	13.00%	0.90	0.596
SEP 1993	910	91.18	8.82	8.00	7.62	13.00%	0.97	0.594
DEC 1993	1001	91.01	8.99	8.00	7.75	12.50%	1.07	0.584

* 100 − EURODOLLAR FUTURES
# U.S. TREASURY BILL
RATE FOR THE EXPIRATION PERIOD

QUARTERLY CAP PRICE Σ OP • 6.30
QUOTED CAP PRICE 1.575

Table 10.3 Pricing of a 3 Year Cap-Rate Ceiling Agreement

subtract the Eurodollar futures price from 100 to determine expected LIBOR for the Cap Agreement. If the Cap Agreement is for a longer term (sometimes up to ten years), or payouts are determined on a day other than the maturity of the futures; one must consult the Forward Rate Agreement market or do a forward/forward calculation using long-dated LIBOR deposit rates to determine the expected three-month rate. Returning to our example of a three-year Cap Agreement starting in March 1991, let us assume that payout is determined on the expiration of the Eurodollar futures. Table 10.3 displays actual (LIBOR) Eurodollar futures prices as of 18 March 1991 and the implied LIBOR rates (100 minus futures price). We can use these future rates as elements in determining the value of our individual LIBOR options that by summation make up our Ceiling Rate Agreement price. But first we must determine the other variables that we will need to price the individual options. The variables depend upon which option pricing model we select.

We have established that, since the separate LIBOR options can only experience cashflow from the grantor to the holder on a single day (expiration), they can be thought of as European options. We have also established that the expected future LIBOR will be equal to 100 minus the Eurodollar futures price. Thus, to price these LIBOR options we will use Black's (1976) model for pricing European options on futures.

This model requires five variables to be supplied: time to expiration (or payout determination date); the price of the underlying futures (or expected future LIBOR); the strike or exercise price (Cap Rate level); the risk-free interest rate for the time period of the option; and the variance of the return on the underlying (or the square root of this variance which is the 'volatility').

Table 10.3 displays these variables for each of the eleven options that comprise the value of our Ceiling. We have assumed that the buyer wanted a Ceiling with a strike price of eight per cent. The price of the Ceiling Rate Agreement is the sum of the individual LIBOR option premiums; in this case, 630 (three-month) LIBOR basis points, or $15,750 per million dollars borrowed. In our example, the Ceiling Rate Agreement was for a $20 million worth of borrowing and would have cost $315,000.

HEDGING A CEILING RATE AGREEMENT WITH EURODOLLAR FUTURES & OPTIONS

The holder of the Ceiling Rate Agreement is paying the grantor to assume his interest rate risk. A critical element in the price the grantor makes is how the string of OTC options will be hedged. How does the grantor hedge the risk of interest rates rising? In our example, if three-month LIBOR is above eight per cent, the grantor could hedge by then taking an opposite position in Eurodollar futures or LIBOR FRAs, with a 1:1 hedge ratio. In this case, selling $20 million worth of Eurodollar futures at 92.00 for each LIBOR rollover would do the trick (or buying $20 million worth of FRAs for each of the eleven dates).

However, if LIBOR at any rollover point is less than 8.00 per cent, no futures or FRAs are required, implying a hedge ratio of zero. Thus the grantor cannot tell *a priori* if he needs to hedge or not. Because the hedge/no hedge decision is based upon probabilities, he can only be sure that the proper hedge ratio is somewhere between 0 and 1.

So, how does the grantor arrive at a precise calculation of the hedge ratio he requires? In our estimation of the value of the Ceiling Rate Agreement, we used the Black (1976) futures options pricing model. In Chapter 3, Figure 3.7 shows the formula and Figure 3.13 a few of the partial derivatives of the model. Since we used the Eurodollar futures as the underlying price input – or rather 100 minus Eurodollar futures – we can, through differentiation, determine how the value of the individual option changes for a given change in the futures price. If we know this relationship, we can adjust the number of futures (or FRAs) in our hedge to offset exactly gains of losses in the value of the options comprising our Ceiling Rate Agreement (for a given change in underlying LIBOR rates).

The derivative we want is dc/dF, commonly referred to as the delta. The delta derivatives of the Black model for both calls and puts appear in Figure 3.13. As Black points out on page 177 of his 1976 paper, '[this delta derivative determines] the size of the short position in the futures that makes the combined position riskless.' Thus, the proper hedge ratio for each Eurodollar futures month (or FRA) is the delta for that LIBOR (component of the Ceiling Rate Agreement) that expires at the expiration of the particular Eurodollar futures month. This hedge ratio can be seen in the delta factor column of Table 10.3.

For example, if our Ceiling grantor were to hedge the agreement with futures, he would sell December 1993 Eurodollar futures equal to 58.4 per cent of the principal amount of the Ceiling Rate Agreement then remaining (because the delta for that single option is 0.584). So, if the principal amount at the time to be rolled over was $20 million, then the grantor would now sell approximately 12 December 1993 Eurodollar futures to hedge the value of the agreement from changes in the expected LIBOR interest rate for that date. (Actually, he would sell 11.68 futures if that were possible.) He would repeat this technique for each Eurodollar futures contract month that corresponds to a particular LIBOR option. If perfect divisibility of futures contracts existed, the Ceiling Rate Agreement grantor could achieve a riskless hedged position with futures (relative to changes in the present levels of interest rates). This hedging strategy using deltas is what I have previously referred to as delta neutral hedging.

Risks of the Hedged Positions

Traditional wisdom states that hedging involves the exchange of price (or interest rate) risk for basis risk. The basis risk, or the relationship of the changes in the cash price and futures price, is generally less than price risk, especially if the cash and futures prices move together (often measured by a correlation statistic). Since this basis risk has now become the primary risk of a futures/cash hedged position, the hedger manages his hedge by managing the basis risk. However, when hedging interest rate Cap Agreements or options with futures, there are additional risks beside the basis risk. These additional risks can be summarised as the risk of the deltas and the risk of changing variance in the underlying market.

A major problem of hedging options or option-like instruments with futures is that the magnitude of an options position varies while the futures (or FRA) magnitude is fixed. The delta-neutral hedged position is only 'hedged' at a single point (as I discussed in Chapter 6). If the underlying futures price (or interest rate) changes, the risk dimension of the options can become larger or smaller relative to the futures while the risk of the futures position is unchanged. As these option deltas change, the 'hedge' no longer exists and revisions must be made to the number of futures sold for the position to remain neutral. Thus, the hedger faces an additional risk of changing deltas.

This risk can also be quantified through the differentiation of the Black model. It is simply the second derivative of the option price relative to the underlying, commonly referred to as the gamma. The formula for this derivative is also given in Figure 3.13. Because the risk dimension of the futures is impervious to such changes in the levels of the underlying markets, an effective futures hedging strategy must include monitoring and revision. This will involve transaction costs that must be considered by the hedger.

Another alternative for hedging options on LIBOR is to use other options on LIBOR: exchange-traded options on Eurodollar futures, other Interest Rate Cap Agreements, or Interest Rate Guarantee Agreements. The intuition behind this approach is that it is best to cover a contingent liability (or asset) with another equally contingent asset (or liability). In reality, the only truly perfect hedge for a Cap Rate Agreement is to cover it with exactly the same Cap Rate Agreement. However, this reduces the grantor to the role of a broker and limits his profit potential accordingly. If the grantor chooses to hedge his risk by purchasing options, he must pay a premium, but he will offset underlying market risk and minimise the impacts that the market dynamics have on deltas. Thus, with options, the hedger can achieve both delta neutrality and gamma neutrality, but at a price.

Another advantage of options (relative to futures) for hedging Interest Rate Cap Agreements concerns the effect that changing market variances have on the value of these Agreements. Cap Agreements and options increase (or decrease) in value when the variance of the underlying increases (or decreases), while futures values are not determined by the variance. Again, hedging option-like instruments with futures creates a mismatch that cannot be protected against.

This variance risk can also be quantified through differentiation of the Black model; this derivative appears in Figure 3.13 as vega. The only way to offset variance risk is to hedge with assets whose value is sensitive to changes in the level of variance in exactly the opposite way. Thus, buying options for the same maturity, strike price and underlying asset will be the only exact hedge for the variance risk (and delta/gamma risk) associated with selling options.

Unfortunately, if the grantor of the Ceiling Rate Agreement decided he wished to do this by using the options on Eurodollar futures market, he would find it impossible because options failed to trade out as far as December 1993 (in March 1991). In fact, past the first contract expirations, no options are actively traded. So, how can the Ceiling grantor hedge a string of LIBOR option risk extending out eleven quarters with only the first two nearby (June 1991 and September 1991) Eurodollar options? The answer entails making all the various options positions directly comparable to one standard.

In Figure 10.4, additional derivatives for the Black (1976) model are presented that make the deltas and gammas equivalent to either a spot price or a nearby futures. Therefore, to hedge multiple option maturities with a single option maturity, one must

DELTA DERIVATIVES

TO MAKE DELTA EQUIVALENT TO SPOT, Sp

$$\alpha C / \alpha Sp = \exp^{-rt} \times \exp^{ht} \times N(d_1)$$

$$\alpha C / \alpha Sp = \exp^{-rt} \times \exp^{ht} \times [N(d_1) - 1]$$

TO MAKE DELTAS EQUIVALENT TO NEARBY FUTURES

$$\alpha C / \alpha NF = \exp^{-rt} \times \exp^{h} \left(\tfrac{t-t \text{ NEARBY}}{\text{FUTURES}} \right) \times N(d_1)$$

$$\alpha C / \alpha NF = \exp^{-rt} \times \exp^{h} \left(\tfrac{t-t \text{ NEARBY}}{\text{FUTURES}} \right) \times [N(d_1) - 1]$$

WHERE h = THE IMPLIED HOLDING COST RATE

GAMMA DERIVATIVES

CALLS & PUTS $= \exp^{-rt} \times \exp^{(-d_1^2/2)} / (F \times S \times \sqrt{2\pi t})$

TO MAKE GAMMA EQUIVALENT TO SPOT, Sp

MULTIPLY ABOVE BY $\exp^{(2ht)}$

Figure 10.4 The Black (1976) Commodity Option Pricing Model. Derivatives Relative to Spot and the Nearby Futures

make all the deltas in the multiple maturity options equivalent to the single maturity and these derivatives will do it for you.

The volatility derivative, vega, is not sensitive to different maturities since it is assumed to move the same degree across time. Unfortunately, a new risk emerges: the spread risk between the maturities. When comparing nearby futures (or spot) to deferred futures, we must assume that the holding cost relationships remain unchanged. But as these holding cost relationships do change, they become a primary component of risk for the hedging strategy just outlined. The holding cost defines the implied relationship between spot prices and futures prices and also applies between futures months. The holding cost adjusted derivatives (rho) can also be seen in Figure 3.13. This is the intramonth risk that the Risk Analysis Program addressed in the last chapter.

To come full circle, when hedging cash markets with futures markets, one exchanges price risk for basis risk; when hedging options with futures, one exchanges price risk for gamma risk and volatility risk; and when hedging multiple maturity options with single maturity options, one exchanges price risk, gamma risk and volatility risk for spread risk.

The advent of Eurodollar (and deposit on other currencies) futures and options has provided the fundamental building blocks financial engineers require to develop OTC option products. The Interest Rate Cap Agreement is a classic example of how this has occurred.

OPTIONS ON CAP RATE AGREEMENTS – CAPTIONS AND FLOPTIONS

For a number of contingent hedging situations, a client may not require an option but rather an option to buy an option. This situation was outlined in some detail in the first hedging example presented in Chapter 7. To review that example, a money manager had to submit a bid to a pension fund to provide his investment services, and had to offer a particular rate to the client. He was at risk if the market rates (for a long-dated US Treasury Bond) changed. Furthermore, he had a contingent risk that his services might not be selected at all. In that example, it was shown that an option hedge was superior to a futures hedge if the bid was rejected. This situation occurs quite often in the Foreign Exchange markets and has led a number of financial institutions to offer a whole new kind of option contract which is an option on an option. As always, these institutions have come up with clever names for these options on options which are known as compound options. Typical names for foreign exchange compound options include the EXTRA (by Hambros Bank), the TTC (the Tender to Contract option by Barclays Bank) and the SCOUT (a Midland Bank product). Of course, many other names exist for these products and perhaps the more exotic the name the more the Bank can charge the customer for that option.

In the interest rate risk management area, the most popular of the compound options are the options to purchase a Ceiling Agreement or to buy a Floor Agreement. The option to purchase a Ceiling Agreement is known as a Caption (a Marine Midland trademark name) and the option to purchase a Floor Agreement is known either as a Floption or a Floortion. These products were created for those hedgers who face a contingent interest rate risk and are uncertain whether or not an interest rate exposure will occur.

A classic example of such a contingent interest rate risk would be for the firm which begins a takeover bid for another firm. To purchase a sufficient quantity of the target firm's shares, money would have to be borrowed. However, the takeover firm is uncertain if the regulators will allow the takeover process to proceed. During the period before the regulator's decision, the firm intending to initiate the takeover would be exposed to a rise in interest rates. To protect itself against the rise interest rates, and to address the risk that the takeover bid might not be allowed, an option on a Ceiling Agreement (a Caption) would be the ideal solution. However, Captions and Floptions can also be useful for firms with existing borrowing or lending exposures.

For example, Chicago and Northwestern Transportation Company wanted to protect itself against a rise in dollar interest rates on a two-year $800 million loan extension being used for project financing. The company was concerned that rates would rise, but if instead rates declined, the firm would have missed an opportunity for interest savings. Thus, Chemical Bank, New York was able to put together a Caption that provided the greatest flexibility for the company. In September 1989, Chicago and Northwestern executed a strip of European-style options with Chemical Bank to run over the two-year loan extension period. The strike levels were set at ten per cent and eleven per cent against six-month US dollar LIBOR; every six months from the beginning of September 1990, the company could elect to execute the Cap Agreement. The Caption was structured in two parts, with an upfront fee to purchase the Cap in the futures at today's prices and then the exercise price if the company elected to exercise the option. Overall, the caption premium amounted to 35-40 per cent of the value of the underlying Cap Agreement.[13]

While options pricing is difficult at best, the reader may imagine the pricing of options on options to be doubly difficult. This is not necessarily the case. The first academic to crack the problem of pricing compound options was Robert Geske of the University of California, Berkeley.[14] To solve this problem, Geske examined compound options on stock. The equity in a levered firm (that is, a firm that borrows money) can be viewed as a call option on the value of the firm. Just like a call option, the most you can lose is the amount you pay for the security and your profit potential is unlimited. The only difference between a stock price and an option price is that the stock's 'term to maturity' is assumed to be infinite (or at least for a very long time). Geske supposed that the value of firm could be estimated as 'V' and that the face value of the outstanding debt was 'A'. We will substitute 'V' for the price of the stock 'S' in the Black & Scholes formula, and substitute 'A' for the strike price of the option 'E'. So, if the value of the firm (like the stock price) is below the amount of money borrowed (the strike price of an option), the firm is worthless and bankrupt (and the option is out-of-the-money and also worth nothing).

$$c = VM\left(a_1, b_1; \sqrt{\frac{t_1}{t_2}}\right) - Ae^{-rt_2} M\left(a_2, b_2; \sqrt{\frac{t_1}{t_2}}\right) - Ee^{-rt_1} N(a_2)$$

WHERE:

$$a_1 = \frac{\ln(V/V^*) + (r + 1/2\sigma_V^2)\, t_1}{\sigma_V\sqrt{t_1}}$$

$$b_1 = \frac{\ln(V/A) + (r + 1/2\sigma_V^2)\, t_2}{\sigma_V\sqrt{t_2}}$$

$$a_2 = a_1 - \sigma_V\sqrt{t_1}$$
$$b_2 = b_1 - \sigma_V\sqrt{t_2}$$
$$t_1 = T - t$$
$$t_2 = T^* - t$$

V = UNDERLYING ASSET PRICE
A = STRIKE PRICE OF UNDERLYING OPTION
E = STRIKE PRICE OF THE COMPOUND OPTION
M = BIVARIATE NORMAL DISTRIBUTION
T = EXPIRATION OF COMPOUND OPTION
T* = EXPIRATION OF UNDERLYING OPTION
t = TODAY'S DATE
r = RISK-FREE INTEREST RATE
σ_V = VOLATILITY FOR UNDERLYING ASSET

V* IS THE STOCK PRICE SUCH THAT THE COMPOUND OPTION WILL BE AT-THE-MONEY AT EXPIRATION RELATIVE TO THE UNDERLYING OPTION

Figure 10.5 Compound Option Model

Prior to expiration (or closing down of the firm), time value must be added and this is done using a formula very similar to the Black and Scholes formula. This formula for the Geske model on compound options can be seen in Figure 10.5. Geske uses the value of the firm 'V' instead of 'S' and he assumes that the volatility of the firm's value (σ_V) is constant. Furthermore, he assumes that the amount of debt 'A' does not vary (just as the strike price E never varies). Finally, and this is the critical point, the volatility of the stock price S is negatively correlated with the value of the firm 'V'. That means that when the firm value decreases and it looks like the firm is going to go bankrupt, the volatility of the stock price will increase. Of course, the reverse would occur when the firm value increases.

In Figure 10.5, 'V' is the value of the firm, 'A' is the amount of debt held, 'E' is the exercise price of the option and the M() function is a cumulative probability of a bivariate normal distribution (that takes into account both the distributions of the stock price and the value of the firm and the correlation between the two). Essentially, the Geske model first evaluates the price of the stock (the option-like feature in the two left terms) minus the exercise price for the option in the furthest right term.

How does all this relate to Captions, Floptions and other compound options? Simply by substituting the value of the underlying asset (or string of options like a Ceiling Agreement) for 'V', the strike price (or rate) of the underlying option for 'A' and then including the strike price of the compound option for 'E', the Geske approach will easily evaluate the theoretical value for a compound option.[15] Another way to look at Caption pricing is as the expected change in the time value of the underlying Cap agreement over the life of the compound option. For example, the reader is referred back to the graphs of time decay in Chapter 2. In Figures 2.13a and 2.13b, the time decay expected for two particular option buying strategies are presented. Basically, a Caption is similar to the situation in Figure 2.13b. In that case, one buys a long-dated option (or a string of options in the Ceiling Agreement) and then sells the option back well before the expiration of the option. The expected value of the Caption should be equal to the time decay (that would occur over the life of the Caption) for the underlying option contract. In Figure 2.13b, the expected loss is equal to $2½ and would also represent the expected cost of the option on that option. Unfortunately, the graphs in Figures 2.13a and 2.13b will only look that way if all the other variables are constant. The rationale for the compound option pricing model is to take into account the fact that the shape of the curves in Figures 2.13a and 2.13b could deviate if the price of the underlying asset or volatility changes.

OPTIONS ON INTEREST RATE SWAPS[16]

A Swaption is the right, but not the obligation, to assume a position in an underlying Interest Rate Swap. Swaptions came about (as almost all OTC option products did) when financial institutions perceived that a derivative product niche existed, and that by offering these new products a reasonable profit might be made. Moreover, the first to market Swaptions would probably earn much more than just prestige. Unfortunately, any introduction had to wait until those intending to offer Swaptions could determine a 'fair' price that would adequately cover any risk assumed, and still provide a reasonable profit.

The Structure of Swaption Agreements

Before we can examine in depth how these OTC options work, it is necessary to define terms and clarify what Swaptions are: what do they promise and when? What is promised is a conditional acceptance of a position in an Interest Rate Swap of a predetermined maturity. It is important to remember that an Interest Rate Swap is an exchange of a fixed rate stream of payments (like a fixed bond rate) for a floating rate stream of payments (like a floating bond rate). The buyer of the Swaption has the right, but not the obligation, to accept the Interest Rate Swap and will rationally exercise the right only if doing so will be beneficial. If, relative to the strike 'rate' (instead of strike price) of the Swaption, the buyer would exacerbate a loss, the Interest Rate Swap Agreement is not taken. For this right, buyers pay sellers a premium. It is not surprising that when Swaptions are reduced to their most basic form, one discovers that they are simply options on Interest Rate Swaps.

The question, 'What is actually exchanged: a floating rate stream or a fixed rate stream?' is a source of confusion for many potential users of Swaptions. A comparable conundrum exists in foreign exchange options where a 'mirror' effect exists. For example, the right to buy Deutschemarks for US Dollars (calls) is exactly the same transaction as the right to sell US Dollars and receive Deutschemarks (puts). In Swaptions, the right to pay the fixed component of an Interest Rate Swap is identical to the right to receive the floating component (and vice versa). To simplify matters, in general, the Swaption market quotes on the *fixed* rate component of Interest Rate Swaps. Swaptions (as most options) come in two variables. Instead of calls (the right to buy) and puts (the right to sell), Swaption varieties are offered as *Receiver* Swaptions (the right to receive a fixed interest rate) and *Payer* Swaptions (the right to pay a fixed interest rate). However, we must remember that a Receiver Swaption on the fixed component is the same as a Payer Swaption on the floating side (and vice versa).

A Receiver Swaption allows the purchaser of the Swaption the right, but not the obligation to receive the fixed rate side of an Interest Rate Swap. The buyer of the Receiver Swaption benefits as interest rates fall because he guarantees the receipt of a fixed rate above the prevailing rate (funding it at what is now a lower rate). As interest rates rise, the Swaption buyer will ignore the Swaption because he can choose to receive a higher fixed rate in the market (that offsets his higher floating rate expense). The seller of the Receiver Swaption is obliged to pay the fixed rate of the Interest Rate Swap and receive the floating rate. This type of instrument will produce a payoff structure similar to a simple put on interest rates (or a call on a fixed income instrument).

A Payer Swaption allows the buyer the right, but not the obligation, to pay a fixed rate and receive the floating rate for an Interest Rate Swap. In contrast to the Receiver Swaption, as interest rates rise, the buyer can lock in an attractive fixed rate and when fixed rates fall (below the Swaption strike) the buyer can let the Swaption expire worthless. The seller of the Payer Swaption is obliged to receive the fixed side of the Interest Rate Swap and pay the floating. Payer Swaptions will produce a payoff structure similar to call options on rates (or put options on fixed income instruments).

Now that we know what is promised, it is important to ask: when does the exchange of the fixed for the floating actually occur, given the buyer wishes to exercise the Swaption? For most Swaption Agreements (hereafter referred to as 'standard' Swaptions) the 'clock' on the Interest Rate Swap begins at the point of exercise. This 'starting gun' feature allows the buyer to define the exact term of the Swap and the dates of interest exchange.

For example, a one-year Swaption on a five-year Swap would allow the buyer upon exercise to establish a fixed for floating position on a five-year Swap, beginning immediately. Future coupon exchange dates would be set relative to this exercise date. So, if a Payer Swaption exercised the contract for a five-year Swap on 1 April, he would be obliged to pay a fixed coupon (the strike 'rate' of the Swaption) every 1 April (or an appropriate business date near it) for the next five years and would receive floating interest payments on dates set relative to 1 April. If the Swaption buyer exercised instead on 15 April, all payments of fixed for floating interest would be on dates relative to 15 April. Therefore, at initiation of the agreement, both participants in the Swaption know they are dealing with a hypothetical Swap with a five-year term, but it is possible that neither know at the inception of the Swaption which dates the payments will occur or if the agreement will be used at all.

As one might surmise, if buyers could exercise Swaptions at any date prior to expiration, the sellers of the agreements may have to accept an undesirable Interest Rate Swap with 'broken dates'. These 'broken dates' can present a problem because the non-standardisation of dates makes secondary trading of the underlying Interest Rate Swap Agreements difficult (and subsequent laying off of the Swaption's risk) relative to Swaps exchanging coupons on dates that are standard.

Typically, standard dates are those dates on which a significant number of financial institutions rollover floating rate obligations. Often the settlement dates of Eurocurrency Futures contracts represent such standardised dates as hedgers roll hedged positions into the cash market.

This particular uncertainty leads most sellers of Swaptions not to allow buyers the ability to exercise Swaption Agreements early (American exercise feature). The vast majority of options offered by sellers only allow exercise on a single date (European exercise feature); which means that if the buyers exercise, the resulting Interest Rate Swap Agreement would have not only a known maturity, but would also exchange interest payments on standard dates. We estimate that 'standard' Swaption arrangements with European exercise features comprise almost 90 per cent of all Swaption transactions. The remaining ten per cent of Swaption transactions are primarily 'reversible' Swaptions.

Reversibles are based upon an existing Interest Rate Swap where the terms of coupon exchange, as well as the maturity of the Swap, are established at the inception of the Swaption. These differ from 'standard' Swaptions which are based on a hypothetical Interest Rate Swap. We find that reversible Swaptions are more likely to have an American exercise feature since the dates of exchange are predetermined and early exercise would not result in broken dates. However, European exercise features seem to be more prevalent for reversibles as well as standard Swaptions.

Swaptions versus Interest Rate Cap Agreements

Swaptions and Cap Agreements are both option derivatives of underlying cash market transactions. The Swaption allows the holder the right to pay (or receive) a specific fixed rate and receive (or pay) a floating rate for an agreed-upon term. The Swaption can only be exercised once into the underlying Interest Rate Swap. A Cap Agreement is the right to fix a series of individual interest payments. As was outlined above, the Cap Agreement is really a string of options for each borrowing point. Thus, the Cap Agreement tends to be more expensive because the holder has multiple exercise dates and during the life of the agreement can benefit if rates fall and limit his loss potential if at any point interest rates have risen.

The Logic Underlying Swaption Pricing

The theoretical pricing of Swaptions is remarkably simple, after one gets over the initial hurdle that the instrument is 'a derivative on a derivative'. Derivative markets imply that their tradable instruments are derived from another market and that they are 'substitutes' several steps removed from it. For example, an ultimate underlying 'market' could be the term structure of interest rates. Unfortunately, interest rates cannot themselves be traded directly. Securities such as fixed and floating rate bonds provide a market surrogate for this 'time value of money'. Interest Rate Swap

Agreements are second order derivatives because they are not directly tied to the underlying term structure, but rather they reflect the relative price of fixed versus floating rate bonds (which are one step closer to the ultimate term structure). Swaptions are one step further removed because they are derived from the Interest Rate Swap. In essence, Swaptions allow the buyer the right to 'bet' on the relationship between fixed and floating rate bonds, rather than on interest rates (or bonds) directly.

The initial challenge in any option pricing problem is to determine what underlies the option. If you exercise the option, what do you get and when do you get it? Once this problem has been cracked, the theoretical pricing problem is greatly simplified. As was outlined earlier, a Swaption allows the buyer the right to receive or pay the fixed rate on an Interest Rate Swap. So the first step is to identify the particular features of the underlying Interest Rate Swap and determine its rate.

In a recent article on Interest Rate Swaps,[17] the authors suggested that the Swap rate has three components: forward interest rates, transaction costs, and the credit risk inherent in the Swap transaction. Essentially they show that a Swap contract is 'fundamentally a series of forward contracts'.

To determine the fixed rate associated with an Interest Rate Swap, the forward rates for floating rate assets are treated like a string of cashflows and discounted back to present value at what amounts to a yield to maturity calculation. This 'yield' is the fixed rate in the Interest Rate Swap. In other words, Interest Rate Swaps reflect an equilibrium rate that would equate a floating rate stream of payments (bond) with a fixed rate stream of payments (bond) at the present date.

In addition, to assess the Swap rate, the market maker in the Swap must then take into account the prevailing bid/offer spread (determined by the supply/demand for liquidity) and incorporate any credit risk of the intermediary and/or the counterparties. As is common knowledge to most credit officers, this credit issue potentially opens a nasty can of worms.

One might suppose that options on Swaps would require all these elements to be considered plus additional option-related variables. Luckily, this is unnecessary because the rate associated with the Swap already includes these elements. If the option took into account the yield curve impacts, transactions costs and credit risk, this would then amount to double counting. The Interest Rate Swap already has these elements embedded in the rate. Our principal task is to determine the appropriate stochastic process driving the underlying Interest Rate Swap market. Once this is accomplished, a Swaption price can be determined by applying an appropriate option pricing model with the rate on the Swap as the 'underlying market' input into the model.

Another significant issue must be considered: when do you actually acquire the Interest Rate Swap? Consider a Swaption with a European exercise feature (as is the convention for the vast majority of Swaptions). The actual underlying asset for the Swaption is not the present Interest Rate Swap rate, but rather the 'forward' rate of the Interest Rate Swap for the expiration day of the Swaption. Now we have the problem of determining the 'forward' rate of an Interest Rate Swap. As pointed out above in our discussion of option pricing, the 'forward' rate of a Swap does not need to include all the elements necessary for the evaluation of the present Interest Rate Swap rate. All that is required is to apply a simple time value of money 'arbitrage' formula that is often used to determine forward/forward rates. In the Interest Rate Swap market, these transactions are common and referred to as forward Interest Rate Swaps.

Having determined the forward Interest Rate Swap rate, it might appear that the Black (1976) model for pricing options on forwards would be most appropriate, and indeed most market participants utilise this formula. However, it must be recognised that the Black (1976) model applies to commodity (futures) markets where the option contract allows for the exchange of *cash* for some commodity at a future date and the model assumes that interest rates are constant. In Swaptions, the option contract allows the exchange of a floating rate 'bond' for a fixed rate 'bond' and, therefore, the use of the Black (1976) model is inappropriate as the model explicitly assumes that interest rates must be constant. It seems that a more appropriate approach to the Swaption pricing problem is to determine the value of an option to exchange one asset for another. Margrabe has already solved this problem and has determined a closed form solution for estimation of European options.[18] The Margrabe model for pricing an option to exchange one asset for another is presented in Figure 10.6.

The reader can once again see that this option pricing model is almost identical to the Black and Scholes formula. The only difference this time is that there is no interest rate component (so we don't have to assume that interest rates are constant) and the strike price 'E' has now been replaced by B_2. B_1 is the value of a 'fixed' stream of payments and B_2 is the value of a 'floating' stream of payments. Thus with the Margrabe model, both the 'underlying' asset (B_1) and the strike price (B_2) are allowed to vary. The only trick to the Margrabe model is the volatility input. Here, because both assets can vary, the variance of both is important to the overall volatility of the Swaption. To determine the volatility input, one must assess the volatilities for both the assets and subtract from this the covariance between them (multiplied by 2). Thus, the reader will see that the formula for volatility in Figure 10.6 looks remarkably similar to the formula for the risk of a portfolio presented in Chapter 8. This is no accident because the Margrabe model (and indeed all option pricing models) is based

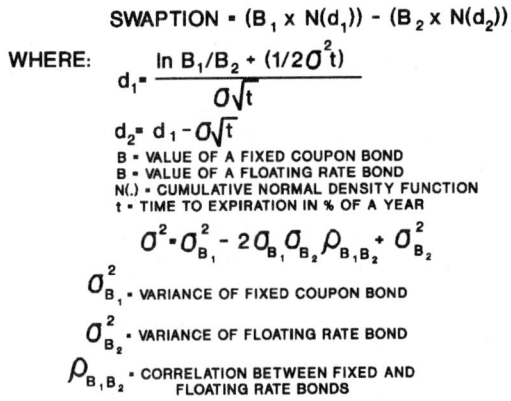

$$\text{SWAPTION} = (B_1 \times N(d_1)) - (B_2 \times N(d_2))$$

WHERE:

$$d_1 = \frac{\ln B_1/B_2 + (1/2\sigma^2 t)}{\sigma\sqrt{t}}$$

$$d_2 = d_1 - \sigma\sqrt{t}$$

B = VALUE OF A FIXED COUPON BOND
B = VALUE OF A FLOATING RATE BOND
N(.) = CUMULATIVE NORMAL DENSITY FUNCTION
t = TIME TO EXPIRATION IN % OF A YEAR

$$\sigma^2 = \sigma_{B_1}^2 - 2\sigma_{B_1}\sigma_{B_2}\rho_{B_1 B_2} + \sigma_{B_2}^2$$

$\sigma_{B_1}^2$ = VARIANCE OF FIXED COUPON BOND

$\sigma_{B_2}^2$ = VARIANCE OF FLOATING RATE BOND

$\rho_{B_1 B_2}$ = CORRELATION BETWEEN FIXED AND FLOATING RATE BONDS

Figure 10.6 The Margrabe Option Pricing Model

upon the concept of equivalent portfolio positions. For example, the Margrabe model for Swaptions assumes that one could create a portfolio with a stream of 'fixed' payments and another stream of 'floating' payments that would provide the same instantaneous return as would an option on an Interest Rate Swap. So, the worlds of portfolio theory and options pricing are much closer than one would at first think.

Present Market Conventions for Swaption Pricing

Suppose we decide to follow market convention and use the Black (1976) formula, which assumes the 'correct' underlying asset for European pricing is the forward rate for the Interest Rate Swap. Now all we need to do is to gather the other data required by the formula to proceed. These data include the strike 'rate' of the Swaption, the time until expiration, the government (risk-free) interest rate for the Swaption expiration and the volatility of the forward Interest Rate Swap. All these variables are directly observable, except the volatility (and we will explain how the reader might be able to estimate it). Assuming the trader has all these inputs, he can simply plug the variables into the Black equation to determine a theoretical European Swaption's price.

What about American-style Swaptions? In options theory, if the possibility of an early exercise exists, things can be complicated. If early exercise is not a rational strategy, then the value of an American Swaptions will equal that of European Swaptions. In stock options, the element that makes early exercise rational for calls is generally the payment for dividends (although as it was discussed in Chapter 2, Merton has shown that put options have other aspects that can justify early exercise).

How does this relate to Swaptions? The problem of early exercise (and the American exercise feature) has simply been avoided by most Swaption participants. Those that offer American-style Swaptions, must recognise the element that might cause early exercise in some positive cashflow (i.e. accrued interest) and which would induce the buyer of the Swaption to exercise to obtain it. For standard Swaption transactions this is irrelevant because the term of the Swap begins at the point of exercise and, therefore, cannot involve any cumulative cashflows to that point.

For reversible Swaptions, however, the buyer of the American Receiver Swaption could have an incentive to exercise if floating rates were significantly below the fixed rate (or for the Payer Swaption, if floating rates were significantly higher than the fixed rate). Nevertheless, this 'payment' is not really like a dividend, but is in fact the 'in-the-money amount' for that one segment of the overall Interest Rate Swap Agreement, which would already be embedded in the Swaption price.

Further, if the Swaption is exercised, it may result in a immediate cashflow, but the buyer must consider the rest of the Interest Rate Swap Agreement cashflows that will be deferred into the future. Even so, it is conceivable that a reversible Swaption could potentially be exercised early if the present value of the deferred cashflows is below that of the immediate cashflow. For reversible Swaptions this potential value of early exercise implies that an American Swaption price must be greater than or equal to the

European Swaption price for the same maturity. To value the American Swaption, some valuation model that accounts for early exercise would be more appropriate. The Binomial approach (Cox, Ross, Rubinstein, discussed in Chapter 3) and the Schaefer and Schwartz's formula (presented earlier), which incorporates the term structure of interest rates, are two approaches that market participants are applying to the problem of pricing American Swaptions. However, many market participants approximate the American Swaption price by using a method similar in spirit to Fischer Black's approximation for valuing American call options on dividend paying stock. This approximation is:

American price = MAXIMUM (Intrinsic Value, European price)

Hence, one can avoid the computational complexity associated with using the other approaches. Anyway, as most option dealers will tell you, the choice of models may be important but the determination of the volatility to input into the model is of greater importance.

If Swaption prices are already available, then it is a simple matter to determine the implied volatility by an iterative process. However, if Swaption prices are unavailable, the determination of the projected volatility for the forward Interest Rate Swap requires, in theory, historical analysis. Past Interest Rate Swap data must be collected either for 'spot' Interest Rate Swap rates or for forward Interest Rate Swap rates. Generally it is easier to get 'spot' Interest Rate Swap rates (especially as a spread over treasuries). If the analyst does use 'spot' rates, he must convert these to 'forward' rates using, in theory, the appropriate government-(risk-free) rate. However in practice, what is used to calculate the forward Swap rate is the appropriate deposit rate that the analyst's institution could invest at. With the synthetic or actual forward Interest Rate Swap rate data in hand, the projected volatility is determined by assuming that proportional changes in the interest rates are log normally distributed. With this assumption in hand, the projected volatility is determined using the (historical volatility) methodology in the usual manner.

After all these steps are completed and the data are input in the pricing model, there is one final adjustment to be made to the theoretical prices. This adjustment is required because the 'prices' of Swaptions are expressed in annualised interest rate terms. Quite often the underlying Interest Rate Swap can extend beyond one year and the Swaption price must reflect the fact that the intrinsic value (a positive interest rate spread) increases with the maturity of the Swap. To account for this effect, the intrinsic value of the Swaption must be divided by an (annuity) factor that measures the present value of the positive interest spread extending over the term of the Interest Rate Swap (and then express this at an annual rate).

EXOTIC OPTIONS – AVERAGE RATE AND MIN/MAX OPTIONS

A key feature of OTC options is the ability to customise the transactions to meet individual clients' needs. Examples of how far Investment Banks will go to meet a client's needs are best represented by the Average Rate (Asian-style) Options and the Maximum/Minimum (Look back) Options that have come into prominence in the last few years.

Average Rate Options – the 'Asian'-Style Option[19]

In the field of exotic OTC options, Average Rate Options (also known as Asian options) have a broad appeal for corporate users. An Asian option, when exercised, pays out the difference between the strike rate and the average interest rate for the period of the option.[20]

Asian options tend to be much cheaper than other kinds of options and are particularly well adapted to the needs of borrowers who are uncertain as to the timing and quantity of their exposures. These options tend to have a European exercise feature and are generally cash settled. The term 'Asian' option comes from the fact that Bankers Trust was the first to offer these products out of their Tokyo office. The maturity for these options is typically in the one to two-year range; however, it is not uncommon for these options to have maturities of as long as three years.

Applications of the Average Rate Option

The most obvious interest rate application of Asian options is for firms that have uncertain borrowing needs over the year. If, for example, a firm cannot easily identify exactly when its borrowing needs will be or the quantity, then the Average Rate option will provide a hedge against the overall levels of interest rates that occur for that period.

As was discussed above, the most attractive selling point of the Average Rate option is the fact that the premiums can be substantially lower than the premiums for conventional options. Most Asian options are priced at 60 per cent to 65 per cent of the value of a conventional OTC interest rate option. While the concept is fairly simple in its construction, the pricing of Average Rate options is not.

Pricing of the Average Rate Option

Average Rate options pricing is complicated by the fact that their values depend on how the price of the underlying asset moves over time and not simply on the level of the underlying asset. To date, no (closed form) solution to the problem has been found. Most banks which offer Asian options have come up with an approximation for the price of these securities by either applying a Binomial approach (similar to what I presented in Chapter 3) or by adjusting standard option pricing models for the reduced volatility associated with the average rate of the underlying asset.

When using the standard options pricing models, the adjustments include treating the average interest rate for the period as though it were an ordinary interest rate and reducing the volatility input into a Black and Scholes type model to take into account the reduced volatility. The rule of thumb is that the volatility of the average rate should be $1/\sqrt{3}$ (58 per cent) of the ordinary underlying volatility. According to John Hull of the University of Toronto, this is not too bad an approximation provided that the number of points used in the averaging is sufficiently frequent and the volatility is not too high.[21] However, the big problem with using Black and Scholes (or a modification of this model) is the assumption that the distribution of the underlying asset is lognormal. When one combines a series of assets, each of which is distributed lognormally (as one would do with the estimation of an average), the result is no longer a lognormal distribution (especially if the assets are correlated). So, some theoreticians have applied a variety of technical approaches to the problem with limited success.[22]

Surprisingly, while banks have difficulty in pricing the Average Rate Options, the hedging is less problematic. These Asian options can be delta-hedged in the cash market in a manner similar to standard options (the reader is referred to Chapter 6 for a discussion of delta hedging). The only difference is that it makes much more sense for a bank to have a portfolio of these Asian options on its books since otherwise the transaction costs involved in maintaining a delta neutral hedge can become excessive. Fortunately, the risk to a bank of an Asian option decreases over its life because the uncertainty of what the average rate will be decreases. The maximum risk is at the beginning of the Asian option's life. This means that near the expiration of the Asian option, the bank is fairly certain what the average rate will be and can more accurately calculate the exposure.

MAXIMUM/MINIMUM OPTIONS – THE 'LOOK BACK' OPTION[23]

The concept of the Maximum/Minimum option was built upon the classic customer complaint that they were not able to get the best rate possible over the period. The Maximum/Minimum option (also known as a 'look back' option) gives the holder the right to purchase or sell the underlying asset at the best price attained in the option's lifetime. For a call option, this means the minimum price (or rate) for the period and for a put options this means the maximum price (or rate). For example, consider a Borrower option with this Minimum/Maximum feature. Suppose the holder of the Borrower option held it for a six-month period. At expiration, he could 'look back' over the preceding six-month period and exercise the option at the lowest borrowing rate which occurred in that time. This feature provides the holder with a 'no-regrets' result: the best interest rate is never missed.

Potential Uses for 'Look Back' Options

Obviously, the potential users of 'look back' options are the same clients who would be interested in ordinary options on interest rates. The difference is that the clients who go for 'look back' options want to achieve the very best rate. Examples of potential users include: investors in Floating Rate Note Bonds who would like to assure that the rate they achieve on their floating rate investment is maximised; borrowers who wish to minimise their floating borrowing expense in highly volatile markets; and traders who combine 'look back' options with ordinary options to create a 'zero-cost' hedging strategy. The final example – a 'zero-cost' hedging strategy – will resemble the example I presented in Chapter 8 with the difference that the maximum profit potential would not be bounded as it was with an ordinary option (assuming the hedger bought the 'look back' option and sold an ordinary option).

Pricing of 'Look Back' Options

While this is great for the customer, the institution which must price and hedge this 'look back' option has a much greater problem figuring out the value. To determine the theoretical price of the 'look back', the usual assumptions in option pricing must be made. One must assume that the interest rate underlying the option is distributed lognormally, the volatility for the interest rate is known, and that the market for the interest rate underlying security trades 24 hours and continuously.

   With these assumption in hand, Goldman, Sosin and Gatto[24] were able to create an equivalent portfolio of other securities which would provide exactly the same payoffs as a 'look back' option. Since they could price the components of the equivalent portfolio, they were able both to price the 'look back' and hedge it by dealing in the 'look back' and doing exactly the opposite trades in the equivalent portfolio.

   Let us consider what their equivalent portfolio looks like. Suppose that a financial institution has written the interest rate 'look back' option outlined above. To hedge the risk fully, it would have to purchase immediately a six-month ordinary Borrower option with exactly the same terms as the Borrower option they sold to the client. It will hold that option until a new minimum rate occurs and then, at this point, immediately sell the Borrower option it purchased back into the market and repurchase a new (ordinary) Borrower option with a strike rate equal to the new minimum rate. It will continue this process whenever a new minimum rate is established until the expiration of the option it sold to the client. This strategy is referred to as a 'rollover' strategy and will produce exactly the same payoffs as the 'look back' option at expiration.

   Unfortunately, this 'rollover' strategy will always involve selling the Borrower option with a higher rate when the new minimum rate is established and then buying a new Borrower option which is then at-the-money. This will always require a cash outflow (i.e. a loss) because the premium of the at-the-money option one must now pay will always be greater than the amount of money received for the previously purchased Borrower option which is now out-of-the-money. Then it becomes clear that the 'look back' option has two sources of cost to the writer: one is the cost of buying the ordinary Borrower option, and the other the accumulated losses from having to roll the Borrower option down to assure the minimum rate. This second element is called a 'strike-bonus option'.[25] These two factors imply that the price for an interest rate 'look back' option is equal to the sum of the value of an ordinary interest rate option with a strike price at the minimum level for the period of the options life plus the value of the 'strike-bonus option'.

Pricing the 'Strike-Bonus Option'

The next problem is how to estimate the values of these two components of the 'look back' option. The first element is easy, being simply the value of an ordinary interest rate option, and one could use the forward price for the interest rate, the minimum achieved interest rate as the strike price and the Black (1976) model to estimate the price. The problem is the value of the 'strike-bonus option'. Essentially, to solve the problem, one will apply the same logic that applies to the Black and Scholes formula. This formula is presented in Figure 10.7; as the reader can see, for the first time this model for the 'strike-bonus option' looks somewhat different from the Black and Scholes formula. In reality, the only major difference is that no specific underlying price (F) or exercise price (E) is multiplied by the cumulative normal distribution functions (N). Instead, the ratio of the current price (F) for the interest rate and the minimum interest rate (L) are used as the underlying input. Finally, the τ is what Garman calls the 'speed' factor.[26] So, the value of a 'look back' options is simply the value of an ordinary Borrower options with a strike price equal to the minimum interest rate for the period and the value of this 'strike-bonus option', the formula of which I have just presented.

$$V_{sb}(F, L, t, \sigma, r) = \frac{F}{\tau} e^{-rt} \left[\left(\frac{F}{L} \right)^{-\tau} \right.$$

$$\left. N(y_L + 2 r\sqrt{t}/\sigma) - N(y_L) \right]$$

WHERE:
F = FORWARD INTEREST RATE
L = ACHIEVED MINIMUM ("LOW")
t = TIME REMAINING TO OPTION MATURITY
σ = VOLATILITY OF F
r = INTEREST RATE FOR PERIOD
$\tau = 2 / \sigma^2$ = THE "SPEED" PARAMETER
N(.) = CUMULATIVE NORMAL DENSITY FUNCTION

AND:
$$y_L = \frac{-\ln(F/L) - (\sigma^2/2)t}{\sigma\sqrt{t}}$$

Figure 10.7 'Strike Bonus' Option Pricing Formula for Look Back Options

With these pricing models in place, it is a simple matter to determine the 'look back' options sensitivities to the level of the underlying interest rates. As is the case with any options, the delta and gamma can be estimated to determine the proper hedging ratios for a riskless hedge. The problem with the delta hedging of 'look back' options is that while the deltas are typically smaller, the gammas are generally higher, compared with ordinary options on interest rates. Furthermore, the gamma risk is one-sided (only occurring when a new minimum rate is reached). Nevertheless, research has shown that while these Maximum/ Minimum options must be monitored more closely than regular options, historical data seems to indicate it is possible to hedge them effectively.[27]

One would expect that 'look back' option premiums would have to be more expensive than ordinary interest rate options simply because another option is thrown in. Indeed, this is the case. Sometimes, the 'strike-bonus' option price can be as large as the price of the ordinary interest rate option. Therefore, it is not unreasonable to say, as a rule of thumb, that a 'look back' option price will be twice as expensive as the price of an ordinary interest rate option.

CONCLUSION

The same principles underlying all these exotic options have been applied to other markets such as currencies, commodities and equity products. The driving force for innovation has been the customer's needs and is not dependent on the technological expertise of the market. The recent work in the academic world (just a few examples of these papers were referenced in this chapter) has allowed financial engineers the tools necessary to price almost any kind of contingent claim. So, the reader can expect that this explosion of innovation will most probably continue and spread to other markets. Regardless of the structure of option-like securities yet to be created, it is safe to assume that any of these innovations will most probably be based upon the concepts presented either in this chapter or earlier in the book (Chapters 2 and 3). So, no matter what kind of option the reader must evaluate, remembering the basic principles outlined here should suffice to address the problem.

[1] For a good introduction to how this was done, the reader is referred to 'Strip Mining' in *Risk Magazine* , Vol. 4, No. 2, pp.20-24 (February 1991).

[2] The basis risk is the risk that the relationship between the instrument to be hedged and the instrument used in the hedging strategy diverges overtime. This was discussed extensively in Chapter 7, to which the reader is referred for a discussion of the basis relationship between US Treasury Bonds and the T-Bond futures.

[3] A similar kind of settlement procedure exists for currency options and this is known as a 'Boston' options after the Bank of Boston which was the first institution to offer it.

[4] The construction of synthetic underlying positions using short calls and long puts is discussed extensively in Chapter 11 as the conversion trade.

5 Robert C. Merton, 'On the pricing of corporate debt: The risk structure of interest rates,' *Journal of Finance* , Vol. 29, pp.449-70.

6 At that point, we will introduce the Margrabe model to exchange one asset for another. If one substitutes a Bond for the first asset and a short-term interest security for the second asset, and finally includes the 'average volatility' for the Bond over the life of the option, one will get the Merton model.

7 C.A. Ball and W. Torous, 'Bond price dynamics and options', *Journal of Financial and Quantitative Analysis* , Vol. 18, No. 4, pp.517-30.

8 Steven M. Schaefer and Edwardo S. Schwartz, 'Time Dependent Variance and the Pricing of Bond Options', *Journal of Finance* , Vol. 42, No. 5, pp.1113-28.

9 Duration is a measure of the average life of a Bond and when divided by 1 + yield for the Bond will predict how much a Bond's price will change for a given movement in interest rates.

10 Thomas Ho, and S.Y. and S.B. Lee, 'Term Structure Movements and Pricing Interest Rate Contingent Claims', *Journal of Finance* , Vol. 41, pp.1011-29 (December 1986).

11 Stephen Figlewski, William L. Silber and Marti G. Subrahmanyam, 'Financial Options: From Theory to Practice', *Business One Irwin* , Homewood, Illinois, pp.337-38 (1990).

12 This section is heavily drawn from a paper written by the author and published as 'The A to Z of Caps', in *Risk Magazine* , Vol. 2, No. 3, pp.21-24 (March 1989).

13 The source for this example is Chemical Bank, New York, and is drawn from the article 'Insurance against the Unknown', in *Risk Magazine* , Volume 2, Number 9, pp.20 (October 1989).

14 Robert Geske, 'The Valuation of Compound Options', *Journal of Financial Economics* , Vol. 7, pp.63-81 (1979).

15 Many thanks to Dr. Michael J.P. Selby of the London School of Economics for his advice on how the Geske model applies to Captions. For what may be a more interesting paper on compound options, the reader is referred to Michael J.P. Selby and Stewart D. Hodges, 'On the Evaluation of Compound Options', *Management Science*, Vol. 33, No. 3, pp.347-55 (March 1987).

16 This section is drawn heavily from a paper written by the author which appeared as 'Behind the Mirror', in *Risk Magazine* , Vol. 2, No. 2, pp.17-23 (February 1989).

17 See Clifford W. Smith Jr., Charles W. Smithson, and Lee M. Wakeman, 'The Evolving Market for Swaps', *Midland Corporate Finance Journal* , pp.20-32 (Winter 1986).

18 William Margrabe, 'The Value of an Option to Exchange One Asset for Another', *Journal of Finance* , 33, pp.177-86 (March 1977).

19 This section is drawn heavily from 'Asian Elegance' by Krystyna Kryzak in *Risk Magazine* , Vol. 3 , No. 1, pp.30-34, 49 (December 1989 – January 1990).

20 Asian options are also available on currencies, commodities and stock indices, allowing the holder an average price for the period at risk.

21 Ibid, page 49.

[22] One article which seems to approach a viable solution to the problem of pricing Average Rate options is Andrew Carverhill and Les Clewlow, 'Flexible Convolution', in *Risk Magazine* , Vol. 3, No. 4, pp.25-29 (April 1990).

[23] This section is drawn heavily from 'Recollection in Tranquility', a paper by Mark Garman which appeared in *Risk Magazine* , Vol. 2, No. 3, pp.16-19 (March 1989).

[24] M.B. Goldman, H. Sosin and M. Gatto, 'Path Dependent Options: "Buy at the Low, Sell at the High"', *Journal of Finance* , Vol. 34, No. 5, pp.1111–27.

[25] See the Garman article in *Risk Magazine* previously referenced, page 16.

[26] Ibid, page 17.

[27] Ibid.

11: Structure of Exchange-Traded Options Markets

In this chapter, I will examine how exchange-traded options markets function. Initially, I will explain the role of the clearing house and the mechanics of margining at a typical futures and options exchange. Then, I will examine in detail the structure of four option markets that have different structures: the Philadelphia Stock Exchange, the European Options Exchange, the Option Market (Stockholm) and the Chicago Mercantile Exchange. At that point, I will finish the chapter with a discussion of a new kind of margining system that is based upon the risk analysis techniques presented in Chapter 9.

THE CLEARING HOUSE AND ITS ROLE

A clearing house can be defined as an organisation which guarantees performance and settlement of all exchange traded contracts. In the case of a typical exchange, this task is undertaken by a clearing house which is owned by the exchange (as is the case with the Chicago Mercantile Exchange) or is an independent body (like the London Clearing House which clears all the trades on the London futures and options markets and is a division of the International Commodity Clearing House).

The clearing house plays a crucial role in the operations of every exchange. Once a contract is entered at the futures or options exchange and the confirmation has followed, the clearing house steps in – so to speak – and assumes the opposite side to each transaction. It, therefore, becomes the ultimate buyer for every seller and the ultimate seller for every buyer. Let us assume you place an order with your broker to buy a 350 call option on Gold futures. Your broker passes the order on to his trader on the floor of the exchange (COMEX in this example) and the order is entered into the trading pit. Suppose the order is executed. This means another trader has agreed to sell this 350 Gold call option to your agent (which is the floor broker acting on your behalf). What risks (apart from the price risk of the option) would you potentially have to face? You could potentially face a credit risk and/or default risk if the trader on the opposite side experienced either financial difficulties (credit risk) or failed to fulfil his side of the deal upon your exercise of the option (default risk). Therefore, if you are depending on your counterparty (the individual on the other side of your deal) to perform, you will have to monitor his financial health to make sure that the contract will be honoured upon exercise. To reduce these risks (and the costs you would have to incur to keep an eye on the counterparty), all transactions after they are consummated are reported immediately to the futures or options exchange and then passed on to the clearing house. Then, the clearing house provides a note of confirmation to you and your counterparty. In the confirmation note, the clearing house indicates that the opposite side of the transactions (for both sides) has been taken over by it. In this example, the clearing house would inform you that it is the seller of the 350 call option. Any future obligations or rights you have received from the transaction are now held against the clearing house. The same applies to your counterparty, the seller of the call option, who is now obliged to perform to the clearing house. The overall market risk of this transaction to the clearing house is flat because it is buying the 350 call on Gold from the option seller and selling the 350 call option on Gold to you. The risks that the clearing house assumes are those concerning creditworthiness and potential default.

The net effect of this arrangement is that the clearing house becomes the seller of all contracts bought and at the same time it becomes the buyer of all contracts sold. Its role is to stand in the middle of all transactions and guarantee the fulfilment of each and every contract. How does the clearing house protect itself against the risks outlined above? The answer to this question is through the mechanism of margining, which I will discuss next.

The Mechanism of Margining

To explain the concept of margining, I will once again return to the world of gambling. In the card game of poker, before the participants can play, a deposit has to be placed in the centre of the table by each and every player. This deposit is known as ante and is the 'stake' that each player must put into the 'pot' before receiving cards. As the hand proceeds, more money is put into the 'pot' reflecting each player's view of the final result. When the hands are laid down, one of the players wins and can take all the money in the 'pot'. To begin the next round, each player must once again put the required ante into the pot to continue playing. If he fails to do so, he is not allowed to play that hand. The winner in the previous hand has the choice of either taking all his money from the table and then replacing the ante for the next round, or leaving the ante for the next hand in the 'pot' and taking out the net proceeds he has won.

The concept of margining at a futures or options exchange works in a similar way. Each participant must 'ante' up a deposit with the clearing house (which is acting like the 'pot'). Each day, as the futures or options contracts settle, the hands of all the participants are laid on the table, so to speak. The winners are those who have profited during the trading day from the change in their contract value and the losers are those who have experienced an adverse move in the market. The amount of gains or losses are then taken from the 'pot' and the winners receive the profits and the losers have the amount of the equivalent loss debited from their margin account by the clearing house. To continue trading the next day, both the winners and the losers have to make sure the minimum 'ante' remains in the 'pot' (the clearing house) and generally this implies that the losers have to put more money in.

This is repeated every trading day and every day it is possible that the clearing house may have to shift funds from the accounts of the losers to the winners. Since each participant in the market must deposit this 'ante' with the clearing house, the credit or default risk to it is that on any particular day one of the participants will not be able to pay the loss that occurred during that trading day. To minimise the credit risk, the clearing house requires all market participants to deposit a margin in cash (or post a suitable security such as a stock portfolio) to cover any losses that could potentially occur. The worst possible loss that could occur during a single trading day is determined by the exchange where the futures or options contracts trade, and this amount is called the initial margin. (In our poker analogy, this is comparable to the ante). If, during the next trading day, a participant is unable to maintain the balance in the 'pot' of some minimum amount (known as the maintenance margin), his position will be offset by the clearing house on the floor of the exchange at the best price available, and any remaining funds in the account will be returned to that participant. If the loss exceeds the initial margin, then the participant must pay the difference. If he is unable to do so, then his broker is next in line to pay the loss and if the broker is also unable to do so, then the General Clearing member (whom the broker clears through) is liable. If the General Clearing member has defaulted as well, then the rest of the General Clearing members will get together and make up for the loss. Finally, if all the General Clearing members have gone down, the clearing house will reach into its pocket and cover the loss (by drawing from its capital). This system works remarkably well and the futures industry points with pride to the fact that no individual trader has ever failed to receive his profits in a futures or options contract because of a default.[1]

To discuss the mechanics of margining at a typical futures or options exchange, I will take the reader though a simple example of buying a Bund futures contract at the London International Financial Futures Exchange (LIFFE). Let us imagine that the Bund futures market is currently trading at 87.14 and we want to be exposed to the German government Bond market via the Bund futures. At the same time, someone else has an opposite view and therefore wishes to sell the Bund futures. A contract is agreed upon at 87.14 and consummated. Then both sides of the transaction are assumed by the clearing house. Thus, we are now long one Bund futures contract with the clearing house and the seller is short one Bund futures contract with the clearing house. In order to ensure the performance of both trades and to protect itself against default risk, the clearing house requires a cash guarantee, which is the initial margin (of DM 6,250). This cash can be thought of not as a 'down payment' (which is the case with stock market margin) but rather as a 'Guarantee Bond' to assure the integrity of the positions from one day until the next.

The rationale for margin is the consideration that the Bund futures price could change from one day until the next, and if it does so the clearing house will be at risk from the losing party. Suppose that tomorrow, Bund futures price increases to 87.25. In this case, we are the winners and the clearing house will transfer DM 275 to our margin account (87.25 – 87.14 × DM 25 per point). The DM 275 will come directly from the clearing house, but will ultimately be debited from the account of someone who was short the Bund futures. Since the total number of buyers and sellers must be equal, it is irrelevant which individual account is debited because the clearing house will draw the losses from all short positions in aggregate. The proceeds will be exactly equal to what is required to pay the aggregate long positions. Somehow and from someone, the money will be drawn to provide the DM 275. Then, the clearing house will look at all the accounts of those holding positions with it and determine if they still have enough funds for the next 'hand'. If not, they will require more money (in cash) to be deposited to cover the variation. This payment is referred to as variation margin. The process of daily revaluation of all positions is known as marking to market. Marking to market is similar to our poker game in that after each hand, each gambler knows how much he has. With futures and options markets, the clearing house essentially divides up all daily profits among the winners and pays the profits from the losers. It is as if the contracts were broken each day (settled up) and re-established at the closing price of that day. Over time, the amount in the margin account will reflect the cumulative gains or losses that have occurred since the initiation of the trade.

Let us examine what would happen to the long Bund futures position if the Bund futures price continued to rise on subsequent days to 87.85. Each day, marking to market would occur and we would be credited an additional amount (of course if the futures price fell in any one day, our account would be debited) until at the time the futures price settled at 87.85, we would have an additional DM 1775 in our account above the DM 6250 we must maintain every day to continue 'playing'. Conversely, those who had sold the Bund futures by that date would have had to pay in an additional DM 1775 to remain in the game. The individual we initially traded with may have decided long before to stop 'playing' and would do so by offsetting his short futures position by buying a Bund futures contract. So the reader may wonder who is now on the other side of our long futures position. The person that has assumed the short position is the individual that sold the futures to our previous counterparty that closed out his position. However, we never need to know that this has occurred because the clearing house has stood between ourselves and the counterparty we first traded with and will automatically find a short position that will be opposite to our long position. As far as we are concerned, we do not care who is ultimately on the other side of our trade because the guarantee of the clearing house makes all short (and long) positions fungible.

The Margining of Options at a Typical Options Market

PHLX establishes margin requirements for customer positions on all types of options and stocks traded on the Exchange. Once the appropriate margin requirement has been determined, the requirement can be satisfied by either deposit of cash or securities, or a letter of credit from an approved issuer. For foreign currency options, the margin requirements are as follows. For option buyers and covered writers, no margin is required. For uncovered option writers, 100 per cent of option premium plus 4 per cent of contract spot value less any out-of-the-money amount, down to a minimum of premium plus ¾ per cent of contract spot value. For spreads, where the long position expires *before* the short position, the spread is treated as two separate positions. Where the long position expires at or after the expiration of the short position, the margin required is the *lesser* of the margin required on the short position or the amount by which the exercise price of the long call (or short put) exceeds the exercise price of the short call (or long put). For short uncovered straddles or strangles, the combined margin on either the short call or short put (whichever is *greater*) and any intrinsic value. Both premiums received may be applied toward the total margin due. The initial margin required on a short uncovered position is 100 per cent of option premium plus 4 per cent of the contract spot value less any out-of-the-money amount down to a minimum of the premium received plus ¾ per cent of contract spot value. Uncovered short positions are marked to market daily with the daily contract spot value and the closing price of the short option. The new premium is then used to calculate the margin required, thereby creating a marked-to-market margin position.

The margin must be met in cash or by fully-paid-for securities where the loan value equals or exceeds the margin requirement. When a transaction creates a margin deficiency, additional margin will be required. Alternatively, a letter of credit from an Exchange-approved bank or trust company may be used. When a member firm is a beneficiary under a letter of credit, certain financial information specific to the member firm must be made available to the exchange. Additional margin requirements must be settled promptly to reduce the margin deficit. The broker must collect this margin immediately, or no later than seven business days following the margin call.

STRUCTURE OF DIFFERENT OPTION MARKETS WORLDWIDE

Broadly speaking, three forms of options market exist at the moment: the open outcry market; the open-outcry market with a specialist or market maker; and the electronic or computer-based system. Pure open-outcry systems exist at a number of futures and options exchanges worldwide, examples of which include the Chicago Mercantile Exchange (CME) and the European Options Exchange (EOE) in Amsterdam. The Chicago Board Options Exchange (CBOE) and the Philadelphia Stock Exchange (PHLX) trade options with the open-outcry/specialist system. This requires a market maker to supply representative bids and offers to the market at all times. The Options Market in Stockholm (OM) also employs a market-maker system but most transactions are handled electronically and crossed on a computer without the necessity of an open-outcry auction process.

In this section, I will examine each of these systems to explain how they are structured, the composition of the exchange's membership, any international co-operation that may exist, how the process of trading occurs, the mechanisms of clearing and, finally, how risk is addressed from the point of view of the ultimate guarantor.

The Philadelphia Stock Exchange

Background

The Philadelphia Stock Exchange (PHLX) was officially established in 1790 and trades a variety of cash and derivative instruments. Linkage through the International Trading System enables a broker or market maker on the PHLX floor to display his or her own customers' orders in other market centres. The PHLX also conducts a primary market for more than 100 stocks not listed on other exchanges.

Since 1975, the PHLX has traded stock options and the exchange now lists more than 75 such options. Currently, the PHLX is the only US stock exchange to trade in currency options and offer contracts in British pounds, German marks, Japanese yen, Swiss francs, Canadian dollars, French francs, Australian dollars, and the ECU. All these are against the US dollar.

The exchange operates three subsidiaries:

- Stock Clearing Corporation of Philadelphia, which handles money and stock transfer after trading;
- Philadelphia Depository Trust Company, which physically stores stock and bond certificates for members;
- Financial Automation Corporation of Philadelphia, which implements technological advances in the exchange's various departments.

Membership

The PHLX is regulated in the United States by the Securities and Exchange Commission (SEC). There are two categories of stock exchange members: those who work on the trading floor, and those who execute orders through other members on the floor.

Members on the floor perform one of four functions:

The Specialist. A specialist is registered and thus obliged to perform certain functions related to maintaining an orderly market. These may include trading for his own account. The specialist also maintains an order book acting in the capacity of agent.

The Floor Broker. The floor broker acts as an agent for the customer. It is his responsibility to execute orders at the best price. This can be done through his employing firm or with other firms.

The 'Two Dollar' Broker. The term is a misnomer in today's tiated commission rates. This member, for a fee, executes orders for other members, including floor brokers. Typically, he is used when the floor broker is very busy.

The Market Maker. Like the specialist, he is obliged to assist maintenance of an orderly market. He adds liquidity to the market by buying and selling for his own account.

Regular membership on the PHLX provides access to the equity floor. Access to the options floors are provided by a full-privilege seat. Seats are bought and sold in accordance with supply and demand. However, the exchange's admissions committee imposes basic membership requirements; individuals must exceed 21 years of age and be affiliated either with a partnership or corporation registered as a broker/dealer with the Securities and Exchange Commission.

A special feature of US stock markets is the existence of a member known as a specialist. This member is almost without exception a major brokerage institution or bank. This member is required 'to make a market on the exchange at competitive prices to the best of his ability commensurate with his position and with prevailing market conditions'.[2] These market makers assure that markets exist with real bid and offer prices. In the foreign currency options, large international brokers and banks act as market makers depending on which currencies they specialise in.

Clearing

The Central Clearing House, Stock Clearing Corporation of Philadelphia (SCCP) – a wholly-owned exchange subsidiary – was established in 1870. The SCCP settles each of its member's accounts for the stocks they have traded and cash received or paid. An exchange member need not be a direct member of a clearing corporation but each must make the appropriate arrangements to have its trades settled. Many smaller dealers clear through existing clearing members. Exchange members who join only one clearing corporation specify that all trade settlements be directed to the member's clearing corporation. In reality, the control of the massive trading activity is an extremely complex process. For activity which is settling, members are required to pay or collect the net settlement amount and in this respect the clearing corporation has assumed responsibility for orderly settlement of trading activity.

The clearing services offered by other registered clearing agencies are generally comparable. However, the SCCP does offer margin accounts to members which permit them to purchase stock without paying the full amount of the cost. This financing enables members to gain a greater leverage by maintaining, in cash only, a percentage of the cost of the securities.

Option Settlement

The Options Clearing Corporation (OCC) provides two methods by which OCC Clearing members and/or Clearing member clients can deliver currencies arising from foreign currency option exercises and assignments. These are:

1. 'Regular Way'. The Clearing member must deliver the US dollar payment to OCC's agent bank two days prior to settlement day which is four days after tendering an exercise notice to OCC.

2. Delivery-vs-Payment. The Clearing member instructs its agent bank (for currency options) to pay US dollars and in return receive foreign currency (for call-holder or put-writer) or pay foreign currency to receive US dollars (for call writer and put holder).

Summary
The PHLX trades a variety of option contracts including stock options and foreign exchange options: the trading is conducted physically on the exchange floor. The specialist system assures orderly markets. The roles of the members are determined by their categories of membership. Specialists and market makers are required to maintain orderly markets. Orders are executed through floor brokers who act as agents for customers and are responsible for executing orders at the best price. Customers must ensure that margin accounts are kept with sufficient cash or collateral with margin requirements being calculated on the type of trade and value of the underlying contract. Settlement can be carried out through the exchange's own clearing corporation or that of another exchange.

European Options Exchange

Background
The EOE opened in Amsterdam in 1978 trading American-style options (options that can be exercised at any point during the option's existence). The 10,450,329 contracts traded in 1990 make the EOE the largest option market outside the United States. The options are cleared through four entities: the European Stock Options Clearing Corporation (ESCC), the International Options Clearing Corporation (IOCC), the Associate Clearing House Amsterdam (ACHA), and futures, through the European Futures Clearing Corporation (EFCC). ESCC clears stock, bond and EOE-index options. The ACHA is a clearing member of the Options Clearing Corporation (based in Chicago). It acts as a facility manager in the delivery of transaction data and distribution of reports on Major Market Index (MMI) Stock Index options to EOE clearing members. IOCC clears gold, silver, platinum and currency options traded in a worldwide linkage with the stock exchanges in Montreal, Vancouver and Sydney. Finally, the EFCC clears financial futures.

International Co-operation
The EOE has entered into an agreement with a number of exchanges outside the Netherlands to trade fungible option contracts on precious metals and currencies. The participants in the worldwide backup are:

- The European Options Exchange Amsterdam (EOE);

- The Montreal Exchange (ME);

- The Vancouver Stock Exchange (VSE);

- The Australia Stock Exchange Ltd (ASE).

These four exchanges own the International Option Clearing Corporation B.V. (IOCC), the clearing organisation responsible for the administration and guarantee of options on precious metals and currencies. This co-operation extends the trading hours for contracts to approximately 20 hours per day. Members of participating exchanges have access to each other's floors, and all trades are perfectly fungible. The EOE has also entered into an agreement with the American Stock Exchange (AMEX) in New York to trade the Major Market Index. As discussed before, these options are cleared through the Options Clearing Corporation in Chicago with the Associate Clearing House Amsterdam B.V. operating as a clearing member.

Membership
At the end of 1990 a total of 383 companies and individuals were registered as members of the EOE. The membership categories are as follows:

Public Order Members (POM). POMs are entitled both to accept orders from non-members and to trade for their own account, but all orders must be executed by a Floor Broker on the floor of the EOE.

Public Order Correspondent Members (POCM). POCMs may accept orders from investors for their own account but only for execution through a POM acting as intermediary.

Floor Brokers (FB). FBs execute orders on the floor of the EOE for other members or for members of participating exchanges or for their own account.

Market Makers (MM). MMs trade for their own account and are obliged to make a market in one or more of the option classes to which they are assigned.

Off-Floor Traders (OFT). OFTs may have orders for their own account executed on the floor by a Floor Broker.

Clearing Members (CM). A CM is entitled to settle transactions effected on the floor of the EOE through the intermediary of a clearing organisation, recognised by the EOE, with which he is associated.

Members of the EOE must provide each client (on request) with a statement showing the client's open position in each option series in which the client has conducted a transaction. A client may only exercise an option or effect a closing transaction through the EOE member bank or broker in whose books the open position appears. A client can, however, ask for his position to be transferred to another member of the EOE prepared to accept his account. The EOE is authorised to set limits on the maximum number of options that can be held or written by an investor acting by himself or in concert with others; the EOE can determine that excess positions are liquidated.

Clearing

The ESCC maintains two separate accounts for each Clearing Member: a Public Account (an aggregate of contracts held for POMs in each clearing currency); and a Trader's Account (reflecting options held for the account of each Floor Broker, Market Maker and off-floor trader). Every Clearing Member may enter into clearing contracts with other members but at any one time a member is only permitted to have one clearing contract. Each business day the ESCC issues to each Clearing Member daily reports including: position reports, margin reports, deposit statements, and settlement statements.

On the basis of these statements, the Clearing Member must make provisions on a daily basis to settle the statements.

Margin Requirements

As long as a Clearing Member is obliged to the ESCC as a writer under an options contract, the Clearing Member must maintain the requisite margin. At any time during any business day, the ESCC may recompute the margin and issue a Daily Margin Report to a Clearing Member. Within one hour of the issue of the Margin Report, the Clearing Member must provide the maintenance margin shown to be required. At any time, the ESCC may require a Clearing Member to provide a 'variation margin' beyond the margin otherwise required if it is determined that such variation margin is necessary. Each POM is free to require additional margin requirements from its clients. Margins can be met by a cash deposit or securities with a POM. An increase in the requirement may make an additional deposit necessary.

Margin calculations are based on the actual price of the option plus a percentage of the actual price of the underlying value. The calculation also considers the exercise price of the option and volatility. The margin percentages are set out every month. The following minimum margin requirements apply:

1. Uncovered written calls. The price of the option plus a percentage of subtracting the exercise price from twice the price of the underlying value.

2. Written put options. The price of the option plus a percentage of the result of subtracting the price of the underlying value from twice the exercise price.

For combinations, an opening purchase of options increases a long position. An opening sale increases a short position and a closing transaction reduces a position. Other lower margin calculations apply to certain combinations; for example, to spreads. The margin requirement for call spreads is the long exercise price less the short exercise price, and for put spreads the short exercise price less the long exercise price. The EOE has permitted uncovered options writing, on condition that security is provided worth in principal not less than the current option premium, plus a percentage (of the difference between twice the price of the underlying value and the exercise price for calls and twice the exercise price and the price of the underlying value for puts). The percentage is set at regular intervals by the EOE. Further margin information is provided in a publication from the exchange, *Minimum Margin Requirements.*

Exercise Procedure
A client who wishes to exercise an option must notify his EOE member bank or broker. The latest time at which this can be done is specified in the rules of the option agreement. Under the rules of the EOE, the exchange is authorised to set limits on the number of options that may be exercised by a single holder within a specified period. Put and call classes are separate and are not added together. When options are exercised, an EOE member bank or broker – who acts as an agent for option sellers – is selected at random to deliver the underlying value (where a call is exercised) or buy it (where a put is exercised). The relevant EOE member bank or broker will use its own assignment method to determine which client is to be called on to meet his obligations.

Delivery of, and Payment for, Underlying Value
The underlying value must be delivered to a financial holding institution nominated by the ESCC, IOCC or ACHA. The ESCC, IOCC and ACHA reserve the right to determine that exercised options are settled in cash and not by delivery.

Clearing Fund
Every Clearing Member guarantees to the ESCC the performance of every other Clearing Member, and in accordance with this each Clearing Member pays an initial contribution. Both the initial maintenance and specific maintenance contributions are payable in cash or approved government securities. At the end of each month, the ESCC calculates the daily average open position of every Clearing Member. From this figure, the ESCC determines the monthly maintenance contribution. If a member defaults, the ESCC applies this maintenance contribution deposited by the defaulting Clearing Member. If this is insufficient to meet the deficit then the ESCC can apply every other Clearing Member's maintenance contribution to make up for the deficiency.

Summary
The EOE is a floor-based exchange for options, modelled on the Chicago Board Options Exchange. Various agreements extend the trading day EOE (fungible) products to 20 hours per day. The EOE can restrict the maximum number of options that an investor can hold by himself or when acting in concert with other investors. The ESCC clears transactions on behalf of exchange members and produces four daily reports which include a margin report. A Clearing Member is obliged to the ESCC to maintain the requisite margin and, at any time during the day, maintenance margin can be required. The exact margin requirements are based on the open contract, the 'weightings' placed on such contracts, and the average open position of the member over the previous month. In the event of the default of a Clearing Member, funds of that Clearing Member will be applied to the deficit. If this is insufficient, then any

additional shortfall will be covered by funds placed with the ESCC by every other Clearing Member.

Stockholm Options Market (OM)

Background
Swedish trading in standardised options began on 12 June 1985. The options were standardised call options relating to six stocks traded on the Stockholm Stock Exchange. By the end of 1985, average daily turnover was about 5000 contracts. The turnover continued to rise and by August 1990 amounted to about 34,000 stock options contracts related to 13 underlying stocks. In March 1986, OM introduced standardised call and put options on the Swedish five-year Treasury Note (interest rate options). The average volume at the end of 1990 amounted to 3755 contracts daily.

In December 1986, OM introduced index options, related to the OMX stock market index, and turnover has risen sharply with the product accounting for more than 60 per cent of total volume (an average of 35,000 contracts per day). From 3 August 1987, Swedish non-residents have been able to trade these OMX options.

OM's Function
'OM serves as a neutral marketplace and clearing house for trading in derivative instruments' (SOM Overview 1988, p.3). OM has a trading system based on an electronic marketplace. Within this system, buyers and sellers meet electronically with deals being closed automatically. Additionally, OM provides a parallel system where buyers and sellers meet in telephone-based block order trading. Swedish banks, brokerage firms and independent market makers are linked to the OM. Owing to Swedish laws and regulations, all customer transactions must take place via Swedish banks or brokers.

OM acts as a party to each option contract (i.e. OM acts as seller vis-a-vis the buyer and as buyer vis-a-vis the seller). OM effectively guarantees each option so that a holder of an option is assured of exercising his or her rights. Since the OM is the counterparty to each contract, the buyer and seller have no rights or obligations to anyone other than the OM. OM guarantees through its system of collateral and own capital resources that each option is fulfilled. To ensure this guarantee can be fulfilled, OM allocates pre-tax earnings to a special untaxed reserve to build up a clearing fund (guarantee risk reserve). This reserve now amounts to SEK 317,284,000.

Ownership
According to OM publications, the OM has approximately 1800 shareholders. The owners comprise the following: all Swedish banks and brokerage firms active in the options market in 1990; AB Investor; Forvatnings AB Providentia; Investment AB D. Carnegie and Co; AB Volvo through the subsidiary Fortos AB; the insurance companies, Skandia and Trygg-Hansa.

Organisation of Trading

OM's options trading is based on an electronic marketplace with integrated clearing. Each transaction with OM as a buyer is matched by an identical transaction with OM as seller; thus the OM is neutral. The marketplace and clearing functions are integrated by computer. When an order is transacted it is cleared immediately. Parallel to the electronic trading is telephone trading with the OM's electronic system still used to quote prices, distribute information and clearing. OM officials act as the telephone (block order) brokers.

The Electronic Market System

Parties linked with the electronic terminal-based system place bids and offers via their own terminals. The orders are ranked in accordance with the criteria of price, time and whether the order is from a market maker or end customer. Sixty-five terminals are currently in existence.

The Broker Function

Orders over ten contracts (block orders) are usually executed via OM's block order brokers. Best prices are immediately distributed to market participants via the OM system, which ties into newswire services such as Reuters. Each transaction is recorded on the system after it occurs. Interbank and intrabank trading are also permitted. These transactions, which are not made in the marketplace, are still recorded on the OM's electronic order book. The OM computer system is not equipped to execute special orders; for example, spreads or combinations. The OM broker must display the order onto a wall board display and monitor it continuously. Block order prices are not binding on the OM. Legally, the block order only represents an expression of interest.

Clearing

OM records all transactions in the account of the broker's customer, each of whom has his own account at the OM. Each customer has an account number and therefore remains anonymous. In the morning following a trading day, the broker receives a report containing settlement notes and lists of collateral pertaining to the broker's total account and to the broker's individual customer accounts. Since the OM guarantees the fulfilment of each option it writes, it must ensure all options written to OM will be fulfilled. Collateral arrangements make brokers responsible for their customers. If the customer fails to meet obligations to the OM, the broker must intervene.

Margin Requirements

OM's margin system is designed to protect OM as a clearing house against the risk of non-performance by a customer. The system computes – per product and per customer – the margin requirement for each account at the close of each trading day, expressed as a collateral balance. OM sends a notice of the collateral balance to the broker for the account of the customer. If there is a negative balance, collateral must be provided. The collateral is normally provided to the broker by the customer as an obligation to pay for option transactions. A broker that is not a Swedish bank must in turn provide collateral in the same amount to the OM. Alternatively, at the broker's approval, all or part of the collateral balance may be provided directly by the customer to the OM. The collateral must be provided to the OM or broker by 11.00 am of the first trading day following the day in which the change in collateral balance is attributable.

The cash margin is as follows: the total net value of long positions with positive net value, less the adjusted basic amount for all short positions at the close of each trading day.

Adjusted basic amount is the higher of: 25 per cent of the value of the stock at the close of trading (daily closing value), plus or minus the net value of the option; or a minimum, per short position, of five per cent of the daily closing value of the stock.

The collateral balance equals the positive net value of long positions less the adjusted basic amount for short positions. If the balance is negative, collateral must be provided.

Delivery Capacity
In accordance with a regulation of the Swedish Bank Inspection Board, delivery capacity is required of the writer of a stock call option and the buyer of a stock put option. Delivery may be fulfilled by deposit of underlying stocks or deposit of a long call. If the long call is out-of-the-money, a supplementary cash deposit is required.

Reporting of Deals Closed
OM prepared settlement notes (which show transactions made by the broker for customers) are delivered to the broker the morning following the transaction, together with any collateral/deposit account details. The broker must then in turn prepare settlement notes for his customers. On settlement day, the third day following a transaction, the customer's account is debited or credited in the amount of the premium and fees.

Summary
The OM is an electronic marketplace and links up dealers by a screen-based dealing system. Block orders are conducted by telephone and prices for these orders are treated 'subject'. The OM has its own guarantee risk reserve in the event of default. Clearing is conducted by the exchange's own electronic system with brokers being responsible for their clients' obligations. The margining system computes the margin requirement per product and per customer, cash or collateral must be provided to the broker or in the case of non-Swedish Banks directly to the OM. In the near future the OM plans to update the margin requirements continuously to cater for 'exceptional' markets.

The Chicago Mercantile Exchange (CME)

Background
In 1982, the CME opened its first option contract with options on Deutschmark futures. Rapid growth in the interest of futures and options has led to expansion and development of other option contracts, namely other currencies, interest rate futures commodity futures and Stock Index futures. In 1984, an international trading link was established with the Singapore International Monetary Exchange (SIMEX). The joint 'offset' arrangement on contracts provides a full day and night trading cycle. While the two exchanges maintain separate clearing houses, audits, compliance and surveillance departments, the contracts are completely fungible.

The CME is a non-profit corporation consisting of approximately 2700 members. There are three divisions: the Chicago Mercantile Exchange, where agricultural contracts are traded; the International Monetary Market (IMM) division for the trading of currency and interest rate futures; and the Index Option Market (IOM), trading Stock Index futures and options on futures.

Function of the Exchange
'The exchange provides a physical location where floor traders can trade specific futures and options contracts, and, through the auction process, discover a price.'[3] Buyers and sellers do not deal directly. The actual financial transaction is conducted by a third party, the clearing house of the exchange. The clearing house is charged with the proper conduct of delivery procedures and adequate financing of the whole operation, and deals only with clearing members. Each clearing member must be a member of the exchange (although not all exchange members are clearing members). The clearing house settles all transactions at the end of each day's trading by interposing between the two transactors and guaranteeing the contractual obligations of both parties.

All CME members are approved by the Exchange's Board of Governors. Like the markets they trade, the memberships themselves are traded freely and actively at current 'market prices'. All members are given equal access to the market by the process of open outcry. By a combination of shouting and hand signals, each trader becomes his own auctioneer – openly declaring bids and offers ready to transact. This full open-outcry method of trading fosters the liquidity necessary for an efficient market environment.

Organisation of Trading
The membership of the CME is made up of independent traders as well as representatives of major brokerage firms, banks and institutions. Members can trade futures contracts on physical commodities financial instruments, or options on futures, depending on the type of exchange seat they hold. Delivery of the traded instrument is rare with the contract normally closed out with an offsetting transaction. (Ninety-nine per cent of the time, contracts are offset rather than delivered upon.) The

marketplace is made up of the traders in the pits, floor traders and floor brokers. Floor brokers execute orders for the accounts of the Exchange's member firms.

Trade Execution
Orders are received by firms on the CME floor. These orders are then relayed to the pit by an order clerk. Different contracts are traded in separate pits. No trading may occur outside the designated pit (except for Exchange for physical transactions). In compliance with exchange rules, floor brokers and traders may only announce bids or offers if they are equal to or better than the existing market. When a transaction occurs, participants make a written record and a CME employee enters the price into the computerised reporting system. This price is displayed on electronic boards and stored for later use.

Clearing
The Exchange's clearing house is the repository for all transactions that occur on the trading floor. Ultimately, the capital of the clearing house (from its members) protects all customers. In addition, in 1969 the Exchange created a trust fund for further customer protection. Customer protection is therefore achieved by regulating the relationship between member firms and customers and protecting clearing members of the exchange against non-performance by any other CME member. However, the first line of customer protection lies with the Clearing members themselves.

The *Commodity Exchange Act* requires each clearing member firm to maintain a prescribed level of capital so any insolvency has no direct effect on customer funds. In addition, the Exchange administers financial surveillance which monitors clearing members, and where appropriate can impose higher capital requirements than those of the Commodity Futures Trading Commission (the US government regulator for futures and options on futures).

The CME trust fund is a second level of protection existing to insulate customers against the insolvency of a clearing member. This now has approximately $28 million in capital (see Annual Report). The final level of protection then goes to the clearing house capital and all solvent clearing members. In addition, the Exchange secures payment directly from each of its clearing members, so that the Exchange can insert itself between every transaction it clears. The clearing house by acting as a buyer to each seller and a seller to each buyer can guarantee that any customer's gain will be realised regardless of any possible default from the party with the opposite position.

Margin Requirements
Clearing members are required to collect from customers a minimum initial margin on futures contracts which thereafter must remain at a minimum maintenance level. Margin levels are generally related to prevailing volatilities.

Until recently, the CME required gross margining; i.e. long and short positions cannot be offset to give a margining figure. The 'gross' system assures that necessary margin exists, and that funds have been segregated for the purpose. The initial margin, net capital and position requirements are intended to limit short-term losses so they can be absorbed by a firm, and secondly by the clearing house, without disrupting business.

Should a clearing member fail to meet obligations to the clearing house, the Exchange may apply that member's security deposit and any other available assets to discharge the liabilities of that member. If a shortfall still exists, the security deposits (about $5 million) contributed by CME members may be used to discharge liabilities. Any remaining requirement is found from solvent members (and ultimately the capital of the clearing house).

Daily Settlement
All transactions conducted on the exchange are settled daily. As a result, every account holding futures positions is adjusted daily in a process called marking to market. A loss on a position is treated as a debt to the clearing house which must be paid for before trading begins on the next business day. This loss or gain adjustment is known as variation margin. Variation margin protects the Exchange since its debt exposure is limited to one day's price fluctuation. The exchange only demands this variation margin from the Clearing members. They in turn are required to make margin calls on their customers. If the ultimate customer fails to meet his obligation, the clearing member can close the position of the customer and apply any proceeds remaining in the margin account to settle with the clearing house. If funds are insufficient, the Clearing member must either apply other resources or default. As discussed before, other mechanisms then take place to settle all accounts before the markets can open.

Summary
The CME's financial safeguards regulate and protect member firms and their customers. Firms must maintain capital requirements and segregate customer funds. The CME Trust Fund is available in an emergency situation. 'Margining' of open positions with daily settlement by both clearing members (and their customers) limits the potential for injurious collapse of a clearing member or customer because any risk is confined to daily variations. The clearing house deals only with clearing members and settles all transactions at the end of the day's trading by interposing between the two transacting parties, and thereby guarantees the contractual obligations.

On 6 December 1990, a new era in futures and options margining began at the CME with the introduction of the *Standard Portfolio Analysis of Risk* system (SPAN). Since that time, six futures and options exchanges worldwide have included the SPAN in their clearing system[4] and an additional five exchanges intend to do so sometime in 1992. Before this system, the CME had margined options on futures with a simple system similar to that outlined above for the PHLX. However, as I discussed in Chapter 9, risk management of options is a complicated business. The delta is only one element in a multifaceted risk management measurement problem. The ideal system for margining and risk management would be to apply the methodology underlying the RAP program to assess accurately the true risk of the portfolio of transactions, and then charge a margin based upon the worst case scenario loss. By applying essentially the same methodology as the RAP program, the SPAN system approaches this ideal.

The SPAN System Explained

On 2 April 1991, the London International Financial Futures Exchange (LIFFE) also decided to adopt the SPAN system for margining option positions. As the ultimate counterparty to every trade and guarantor to the markets, the London Clearing House (of the LIFFE) is at risk to the default of a Clearing member. To cover its risk exposure, the LCH requires an initial margin to be placed by each participant who holds open positions in the market. At most options exchanges worldwide, when one buys an option, one must immediately pay a premium for that. The clearing house accepts this payment and as far as it is concerned there is no additional risk from the option buyer because they have already surrendered the amount which is the most they can lose (the premium). For the option writers, most exchanges will require that this premium be held at the clearing house on the behalf of the option writer. In addition, the option writer must post additional margin because his loss potential is unlimited. At the LIFFE, the system is different and the settlement procedure for options on futures is closer to the settlement of futures contracts which was outlined above. LIFFE will margin both buying and selling options positions rather than requiring the immediate payment or receipt of a premium.

An immediate problem with this approach is how much to charge as margin, since the risk of options will not be the same as the risk of the underlying futures contract. The solution to this problem is found in the portfolio risk evaluation I discussed in Chapter 9. Recognising this fact, the London Clearing House has incorporated the concept of portfolio management of options into determining how risky an option position is, and can easily utilise this number to determine the margin required for the portfolio of futures and options as a whole.

The SPAN system simulates how a portfolio of transactions would react to changing market conditions. The margin requirement is equal to the largest possible overnight loss that could occur (exactly as I determined with the RAP system in Chapter 9. Together with the LIFFE, The London Clearing House sets a range of possible futures moves overnight as well as ranges for volatility changes. Then the SPAN system calculates a 'risk array' for each futures and option contract. Each risk array gives the calculated profits or losses for these contracts under 16 different scenarios. These scenarios can be seen in Table 11.1. By valuing positions using these arrays, the SPAN system determines which is the worst scenario for the portfolio of futures and options and assigns the initial margin accordingly. An outstanding feature of the SPAN system is that it will accurately take into account when positions offset the risk of other positions, yielding a net margin. The SPAN system only affects the margin implications of options on Bund futures, the Bund futures themselves will be margined in the way outlined above.

How the Risk Arrays are Constructed
As discussed in Chapter 3, options on futures (or forward) prices are sensitive to changes in the price of the underlying futures, volatility and time to expiration. In the construction of risk arrays, all these elements are taken into account. The futures

```
┌─────────────────────────────────────────────────────────────────────┐
│   1    FUTURES UNCHANGED              VOLATILITY UP                    │
│   2    FUTURES UNCHANGED              VOLATILITY DOWN                  │
│   3    FUTURES UP 1/3 RANGE           VOLATILITY UP                    │
│   4    FUTURES UP 1/3 RANGE           VOLATILITY DOWN                  │
│   5    FUTURES DOWN 1/3 RANGE         VOLATILITY UP                    │
│   6    FUTURES DOWN 1/3 RANGE         VOLATILITY DOWN                  │
│   7    FUTURES UP 2/3 RANGE           VOLATILITY UP                    │
│   8    FUTURES UP 2/3 RANGE           VOLATILITY DOWN                  │
│   9    FUTURES DOWN 2/3 RANGE         VOLATILITY UP                    │
│  10    FUTURES DOWN 2/3 RANGE         VOLATILITY DOWN                  │
│  11    FUTURES UP 3/3 RANGE           VOLATILITY UP                    │
│  12    FUTURES UP 3/3 RANGE           VOLATILITY DOWN                  │
│  13    FUTURES DOWN 3/3 RANGE         VOLATILITY UP                    │
│  14    FUTURES DOWN 3/3 RANGE         VOLATILITY DOWN                  │
│  15    FUTURES UP EXTREME MOVE (COVER 35% OF LOSS)                     │
│  16    FUTURES DOWN EXTREME MOVE (COVER 35% OF LOSS)                   │
└─────────────────────────────────────────────────────────────────────┘
```

Table 11.1 What are the Sixteen Different Scenarios

scanning range is the largest futures price move that the clearing house requires initial margin for. For example, consider the Bund futures and options contracts traded at LIFFE. With the current Bund futures margin at DM 6250, this represents a futures price move of 250 basis points. So if the closing futures price of a Bund futures contract was 86.55, then 'futures up 3/3' (in Table 11.1) would imply a future price of 89.05 and the SPAN system would evaluate the profit and loss at that point. The category of 'futures down 1/3' would imply a futures price of 85.72 (1/3 of 250 basis points) and again the SPAN system would evaluate the profit and loss of the portfolio at that point. In addition to the movement in the underlying Bund futures, the SPAN system also covers the largest volatility move that might reasonably be expected to occur in one day. This is combined with the futures price movements to yield 14 of the possible 16 scenarios. The other two scenarios (at the bottom of Table 11.1) are for extreme moves in the price of the Bund futures. This extreme range is defined as twice the normal futures overnight range and would be equal to 500 basis points up or down. However, all these parameters can change and may be revised by the clearing house after consultation with the LIFFE.

Examples of SPAN Initial Margin Calculations
Suppose that you have the following position: long one (1) March Bund call option at a strike price of 80.50. The SPAN risk array for this trade might look like Table 11.2. In this table, the profit and losses have been determined for each of the 16 scenarios and the margin is determined by looking down the column for the maximum loss, which is the largest positive number. (Note that gains are negative values.) In this case, the maximum loss is on line 14 at DM 4725, therefore the basic initial margin would be DM 4725.

Let us now look at another example of how SPAN works with a more complicated position. Suppose that you had a portfolio containing the following positions: short five (5) March Bund futures, long one (1) 80.50 March Bund call option, and long

80.50 BUND CALL OPTION

1	-125	FUTURES UNCHANGED	VOLATILITY UP
2	150	FUTURES UNCHANGED	VOLATILITY DOWN
3	-2000	FUTURES UP 1/3	VOLATILITY UP
4	-1850	FUTURES UP 1/3	VOLATILITY DOWN
5	1550	FUTURES DOWN 1/3	VOLATILITY UP
6	1975	FUTURES DOWN 1/3	VOLATILITY DOWN
7	-3975	FUTURES UP 2/3	VOLATILITY UP
8	-3900	FUTURES UP 2/3	VOLATILITY DOWN
9	3025	FUTURES DOWN 2/3	VOLATILITY UP
10	3550	FUTURES DOWN 2/3	VOLATILITY DOWN
11	-6000	FUTURES UP 3/3	VOLATILITY UP
12	-5975	FUTURES UP 3/3	VOLATILITY DOWN
13	4175	FUTURES DOWN 3/3	VOLATILITY UP
14	4725	FUTURES DOWN 3/3	VOLATILITY DOWN
15	-4275	FUTURES UP EXTREME MOVE	
16	2100	FUTURES DOWN EXTREME MOVE	

Table 11.2 Example of a Simple Risk Margin Calculation 80.50 Bund Call Option.

five (5) 74.50 March Bund put options. To determine the initial margin required for this portfolio, once again, the 16 scenarios would be evaluated and the worst loss would then be the initial margin. The risk array for this portfolio can be seen in Table 11.3. The profit or loss for each scenario is determined by first multiplying each array value by the appropriate position size (plus for long and minus for short) and then adding across each row to get a total loss for the overall portfolio in that scenario. The reader can see that the greatest loss occurring is associated with scenario number 12 and is equal to DM 25,275. Therefore, this would be the basic SPAN initial margin required by the Clearing House to hold this portfolio overnight.

Each of the scenarios automatically takes into account the passage of time overnight and – like the Risk Analysis Program (RAP) – SPAN also allows for intra-month charges to be added to the basic risk margin calculation. In this case, the intra-month spread credits will be deducted to produce the final initial margin figure.

PORTFOLIO OF BUND FUTURES AND OPTIONS

LINE	FUTURE	PUT 74.50 STRIKE	CALL 80.50 STRIKE	TOTAL LOSS DM
1	-5 x 0	5 x -25	1 x -125	-250
2	-5 x 0	5 x 0	1 x 150	150
3	-5 x -2075	5 x 0	1 x -2000	8375
4	-5 x -2075	5 x 0	1 x -1850	8525
5	-5 x 2075	5 x -25	1 x 1550	-8950
6	-5 x 2075	5 x 0	1 x 1975	-8400
7	-5 x -4175	5 x 0	1 x -3975	16900
8	-5 x -4175	5 x 0	1 x -3900	16975
9	-5 x 4175	5 x -50	1 x 3025	-18100
10	-5 x 4175	5 x 0	1 x 3550	-17325
11	-5 x -6250	5 x 0	1 x -6000	25250
12	-5 x -6250	5 x 0	1 x -5975	25275
13	-5 x 6250	5 x -100	1 x 4175	-27575
14	-5 x 6250	5 x -25	1 x 4725	-26650
15	-5 x -4375	5 x 0	1 x -4275	17800
16	-5 x 4375	5 x -125	1 x 2100	-20400

Table 11.3 Example of a Simple Risk Margin Calculation Portfolio of Bund Futures

The Variation Margin

The variation margin for options, however, is independent of the SCAN system outlined above (because the SCAN system simply determines the initial margin). The amount of variation margin that will be credited or debited from participants' accounts depends only on how much the price of the option has changed from one day until the next. For example, suppose that a particular call option on Bund futures has a price of 50 basis points. The initial margin will be determined by the SCAN system as defined above. Suppose that the next day, the Bund futures price is unchanged and the implied volatility of the market has increased resulting in the option's price increasing to 70 basis points. The variation margin is determined by the difference between the *prices* of the call option from one day until the next. So, the variation margin which would be paid to a call option holder on this day would be DM 500 (and the call option seller would be debited this DM 500 amount). To calculate the variation margin for options on Bund futures, one will simply multiply today's tick change from the previous trading day by the tick size (DM 25 for Bund futures) and the number of contracts.

The reader must be aware that these margin requirements and methods for margin estimates will change from time to time. To keep up to date, you should periodically contact either your broker, the exchange where your futures or options contracts trade, or the clearing house of that exchange.

[1] There was a problem on the London Tin Futures Market once when a consortium of traders cornered the Tin market and then were unable to deliver the tin. However, after closing the exchange for a period, the contracts were eventually settled and the exchange resumed trading.

[2] *Philadelphia Stock Exchange Rule Book*, page 2145.

[3] According to *A World Marketplace*, a Chicago Mercantile Exchange publication, page 6.

[4] The Chicago Board of Trade, The Chicago Mercantile Exchange, The London International Financial Futures Exchange, The Commodity Exchange, The Coffee, Sugar and Cocoa Exchange and the Kansas City Board of Trade.

12: Accounting, Regulation and Taxation Issues for Options

The last chapter of this book addresses the subjects of operational issues, accounting and taxation around the world.[1]

REGULATIONS: A GLOBAL SURVEY

Australia

Accounting: Brokers in futures and options are governed by the *Futures Industry Act.* They are required to produce audited financial statements and to keep detailed accounting records of transactions. However, as no specific Australian accounting standards relate to futures and options accounting, reference is made to the US standards.

Regulation: Regulation of futures and options contracts under the *Futures Industry Act* is overseen partly by the self-regulation of the exchange houses themselves and partly by the National Companies and Securities Commission. Foreign companies which do business in Australia must register under the National Companies and Securities Code. Brokers and other advisors on futures and options must be licensed by the Commission before they may provide such financial services. Client property (such as funds) has to be held in separate designed accounts and dealt with only in accordance with the Act. The Commission is entitled to enquire into all futures and options activities and can demand both written material and affidavits from any connected person.

Tax: Where futures and options are used as part of normal trading activities, whether directly or to hedge underlying trading transactions, the gains are taxable and the losses deductible from income. Those who write or buy options for general business purposes (i.e. banks) may deduct option premiums paid, and will be taxed on those received. In the same way, gains or losses resulting from the exercise or expiry of the option will be taxed or deductible respectively. Apart from where derivatives are used to hedge foreign currency capital exposure (where since February 1986 the gains – after deduction of the premiums – are taxable and the losses deductible), gains and losses resulting from hedging capital transactions are covered by the capital gains tax provisions.

Canada

Accounting: Canada has no specific accounting treatment laid down for derivatives, but generally two methods are used. If derivatives are being used for the designated purpose of hedging activities exposed to price or interest rate risk, and their use reduces the risk, then gains and losses will be deferred. The timing of recognition varies according to the actual asset or liability. For non-hedging transactions, mark-to-market accounting is used. Bought options can be stated at the lower cost and net realisable value, and written options at the higher of sale proceeds and market value. Alternatively, unrealised gains and losses are brought into the current income statement.

Regulation: There is a complex regulatory framework covering Canadian derivative transactions, including a framework recently set up for regulators in Canada and abroad to work together on international activities. Regulatory bodies include Self Regulatory Organisations, the exchanges themselves and provincial securities legislation.

Tax: Gains and losses arising from trading or hedging trading positions with derivatives as part of normal trading activities are taxed or deducted as part of income. However, with the above exception, the reporting method used by the taxpayer, provided it is consistent, will determine the tax treatment applied and so give the taxpayer a choice of treatment. Income methods of reporting give rise to a full deduction for accrued losses and fully taxed accrued gains. By contract, capital reporting means that only three-quarters of the loss may be deducted, but only against other capital gains; and only three-quarters of the gain is included in income (once the contract has been closed down).

Denmark

Accounting: For banks and brokers extensive rules have been set up and these are supervised by the Danish Supervisory Authority of Financial Affairs. The rules are under constant review. However, no specific regulation has been laid down for other traders and general principles are applied. Professional traders must recognise realised and unrealised gains and losses in their income statement at market value, and unrealised gains must be credited to a restricted revaluation reserve in the quality account. Non-professional traders must account for losses in their income statements on a current basis whilst gains are deferred until realised. Hedge accounting is applied where a transaction fulfils the hedging criteria.

Regulation: Trading on the FUTOP market in futures and options takes place at the Copenhagen Stock Exchange (CSE). Trading at the CSE is supervised, cleared and guaranteed by the Guarantee Fund for Danish Options and Futures. Only professional traders who are approved members at the CSE are allowed to trade on the CSE. Both the Guarantee Fund and the CSE clearing and exchange members are under the supervision of the Supervisory Authority of Financial Affairs. Except for margin deposit, no regulatory limitation exists for investors wishing to trade in options and futures through the approved members of the Guarantee Fund for Danish Options and Futures. Foreign participation and transactions involving foreigners are not restricted in any way. The margin rules are as follows: 4 per cent of size for bond futures, 12 per cent of size for Stock Index futures, premium plus 4 per cent for written bond options.

Tax: Legislation is in the process of being developed to cover derivatives specifically, but, in the interim tax rules are based on an interpretation of current practice and basic taxation principles. The gains and losses arising from the activities of professional traders are taxed as normal business income. No stamp duty is charged on futures and options trading. Private investors may not deduct a net realised loss from income, but are taxed on a net realised gain.

France

Accounting: France has brought out new futures and options regulations comparatively recently. These suggest an approach based on the transaction being classified as either hedging or speculation. Speculative gains and losses should be accounted for at mark-to-market on a current basis, whilst those arising from hedging transactions should be accounted for over the period of the hedge.

Regulation: All those entitled under French regulations to trade futures and options in France must be approved by the regulatory organisation, the Clearing House (Chambre de Compensation). Transactions undertaken by French residents may carry on a transaction on interest rate or indices in foreign derivatives without using an intermediary

Tax: The tax treatment of derivatives trading by resident companies is governed mainly by recent legislation as clarified by Administrative Comments dated 20 April 1988. Contracts on non-hedging transactions on all futures, forwards and options that are quoted or traded on a market or by reference to a market must be marked-to-market at year end, and the resulting gain or loss included in current taxable income. On contracts traded outside a market, the unrealised gains can be deferred until after the contract is settled. Where contracts are traded specifically as a hedge against risks from transactions in the subsequent year, and disclosure is made to the tax administration, tax on unrealised gains may be deferred until the contracts are settled. Where contracts are traded specifically as a hedge against exchange risks on future operations, and disclosure is made to the tax administration, tax on unrealised gains may be deferred until the hedge operation is settled. Positions may be offset as follows: where one position has a loss (realised or otherwise) it may only be deducted from the gain on the other position if this has been taxed. If not, subject to the appropriate disclosure, the deduction is held off until the gain is taxed.

Germany

Accounting: According to German accounting principles, each asset and liability has to be evaluated separately. As an exception, micro hedge accounting is applicable if some restrictive requirements are met including that the terms of both the futures or options position and the underlying asset or liability are identical. Macro hedge accounting in general is not accepted. A mark-to-market evaluation does not exist. Non-realised losses have to be accrued for, whereas profits can only be shown in the financial statements if realised, for example through a closing transaction. Purchased options have to be capitalised at original cost, premiums received by the writer can only be shown as income if realised. If the option is not exercised by the holder at expiration date, its book value has to be written off. The purchase or sale of futures is regarded as a pending transaction and therefore an off-balance sheet item. For anticipated losses a respective accrual has to be set up. Variation margins as such do not yet affect the profit and loss account.

Regulation: Recent amendments to German law have made futures trading also binding for private customers. These amendments, which include trading in precious metals (but not trading in commodities), are allied to the opening of the German options and financial futures exchange (DTB – Deutsche Terminbörse) early in 1990. Under these new regulations, private customers are required to sign a risk disclosure statement detailing the risks associated with futures and options contracts, which have to be periodically renewed. In order to become a member of the German options and futures exchange, applicants must have at least a branch office registered and operating in Germany. Since June 1990 a securities lending system has existed which allows writers of options more flexibility. Within certain restrictions, German investment funds (since 1990) and insurance companies (since 1991) have been allowed to trade in options and futures.

Tax: The tax treatment of futures and options for business investors follows the accounting treatment. Profits are taxed as income at standard rates and municipal trade on income. For private investors, premiums received by the writer are taxed as income at standard rates. Losses suffered in the underlying assets or liabilities cannot be offset against the premium. Following recent court decisions, those gains and losses that arise on the disposal of an option are treated as net capital gains. Gains must be short-term (under six months), and worth more than DM 999 per year, before they will be subject to tax. It should be noted that for private investors this treatment is subject to current discussions with the tax authorities. The current position on gains from currency futures is that they are tax-free to private investors because they are gambling profits. This follows a recent Supreme Court ruling and should be applicable to all cash settled futures contracts. Options and futures transactions had been subject to 0.25 per cent stock exchange turnover tax if they resulted in a delivery of securities. However, stock exchange turnover tax has been abolished as of 1 January 1991. Options and futures are not subject to value added tax.

Hong Kong

Accounting: At present, derivatives accounting procedures have not been formally set up. A number of different procedures are currently used and disclosure within financial statement is generally poor. There is a need for standard accounting policies designed to recognise the economic reality of the transaction. It is generally accepted that mark-to-market methods are sufficiently reflective of the economic basis of speculative transactions to be used by active traders. To define a transaction as hedging, the US accounting standard treatment would usually be applied. Hedging transactions would normally be accounted for so as to be in line with the underlying transactions.

Regulation: Trading is regulated by the Commodities Trading Ordinance and the rules of the Futures Exchange. The SFC (Securities and Futures Commission) enforces the rules and regulates brokers. Brokers must comply with regulations concerning levels of capital and liquidity and segregation of client funds. Trading of futures (such as interest rate and community futures) takes place on the Hong Kong Futures Exchange. Banks also trade OTC options amongst themselves.

Tax: Capital gains or profits earned 'offshore' are not liable to Hong Kong tax. Thus gains made on futures exchanges abroad through brokers outside Hong Kong will be exempt from Hong Kong profits tax (although they may be liable to tax in that location abroad). Hong Kong-sourced profits resulting from a trade or business carried on in Hong Kong are liable to tax. This is governed by the location where the activity causing the profit took place – known as 'operations test'. This test is applied to gains and losses on derivatives trading by financial institutions in Hong Kong, and the timing of the taxation will generally follow the accounting treatment. Although capital profits on-shore are non-taxable, it would be difficult for a financial institution to show that profits from futures and options were capital as the hedging transactions relate to underlying assets that make up part of the trading stock of the business. Non-financial institutions and other companies will also have profits measured by the operations test, and the tax treatment of derivatives used for hedging purposes will match that of the underlying assets. This speculative use of derivatives will be treated as giving rise to taxable gains and deductible losses, whilst where the underlying assets or liabilities are capital, no Hong Kong tax will arise.

Ireland

Accounting: There are no accounting standards designed specifically for futures and options. So, accepted accounting standards are applied to provide a method of accounting that reflects the underlying economic effect of the transaction. Where derivatives are used to hedge a position, the underlying asset or liability, and gains and losses may be offset between the two. Financial institutions using derivatives should mark them to market and include the gain or loss within their profit and loss account. As this method is not in line with the rules of valuation in the *Companies (Amendment) Act* (1986), disclosure will be necessary. Other companies speculating in derivatives will usually value positions at the lower of cost or market value.

Regulation: Trading in Ireland takes place on IFOX (Irish Futures and Options Exchange) and is regulated by the *Central Bank Act* (1989), enforced by the Central Bank. IFOX also has a 'guarantee and compliance' officer, who records and controls such things as exposure, position limits and risk management. Four futures contracts are currently traded: on a 20-year Irish gilt; on three-month Dibor; on a short gilt; and on the Irish Stock Exchange Index.

Tax: As no prescriptive tax legislation exists for futures and options and no guidelines are available to date, profits and losses from derivatives are taxed according to general principles, and in practice follow the treatment applied in the UK. Profits and losses from speculative trading, or arising from hedges of trading transactions, are taxed as normal trading income. Where the taxpayer uses derivatives to hedge a capital asset or liability and does not deal in futures and options, then capital gains tax treatment will be afforded to the transaction. Gains will be taxed at various rates (30-50 per cent) depending on the length of ownership. However, the long gilt future contract traded on IFOX is exempt from tax, as are dealing in financial futures and traded options carried out by pension funds.

Italy

No options and financial futures exchange currently exist in Italy, although Parliament has been dealing with this area specifically. The following comments are therefore based on generally applied principles.

Accounting: Contracts used to hedge positions should be accounted for in line with the underlying instruments. Futures transactions carried out for trading purposes are marked to market and options premiums are suspended and valued to market at year end. Provisions must be made for unrealised losses on unmatched positions, and gains on options should be accounted for when realised.

Regulation: No restriction now exists to prevent transaction in foreign currencies. Hence, by operating via a bank authorised to deal in currencies, Italian residents can operate fully on futures and options exchanges.

Tax: All gains and losses arising from futures and options are exempt from tax for individuals, and taxed as normal income on professional traders (whether individuals or companies). All Italian investors are liable to pay the transfer taxes which apply in the foreign markets. Where an option is exercised, the premium paid for the contract is treated as the cost of the underlying instrument. If the option is left to expire, the premium is deducted when the option is abandoned. Premiums are taxed when cashed and losses arising from written options are deducted on realisation. For tax purposes, hedging accounting is not permitted.

Japan

Accounting: Tokyo Stock Exchange (TSE) government bond futures are the only specific area where guidelines exist. The treatment outlined below is also applied to other futures products.

(1) Except where the relevant contract was used to hedge a risk, all material unrealised losses should be disclosed in a note to the accounts at the balance sheet date. (2) Gains and losses arising on futures contracts should be taken into account in the acquisition cost of securities such as government bonds. (3) Profit and losses should be taken into account at the time that the futures contract is settled.

The Japan Securities Dealers Association (JSDA) first developed a preliminary set of accounting rules for options transactions. At the request of the Ministry of Finance, the Federation of Bankers Association of Japan then developed rules for futures accounting following discussions in the Business Accounting. With the exception of currency options held by banks, option premiums paid or received should be capitalised and deferred until exercise, sale or expiry. On sale or expiry, any gain or loss should be immediately recognised. On exercise into a non-cash asset, the premium (together with the strike price) will be capitalised as the cost of the underlying asset. On exercise into cash, any gain or loss will immediately be recognised. Currency options held by banks are not covered by these new rules. Instead, currency option premiums should be carried in the balance sheet and marked to market at the bank's reporting date.

Regulation: Amendments to legislation in May 1988 allowed the creation of cash-settled index futures and options. Such stock index futures were then traded on the TSE and the Osaka Securities exchange along with the already established Japanese government bond futures. Stock index options were first traded on the Osaka, Tokyo and Nagoya exchanges in 1989. Financial futures law covers all financial futures and options except securities (covered by securities and exchange law). The Tokyo International Financial Futures Exchange (Tiffe) started trading new financial futures instruments in 1989. The instruments include: Eurodollar three-month interest rate; Euroyen three-month interest rate; Currency futures (yen and US dollars).

Tax:

DIRECT TAXES: Companies are taxed on all realised income whatever the type of transaction. Gains or losses (except the gains from closing out futures transactions) arising on individuals are taxed under the capital gains tax rule. Instead of being separately taxed, the individual may elect to be taxed at a flat rate of 1 per cent withholding on the gross proceeds from the transfer of securities listed on a security exchange. No inhabitants tax is payable under this election. Gains from closing out futures transactions are taxed according to regular income tax rules, although capital gains tax has been imposed on individuals when selling securities including JGB futures and Kabusaki 50 futures settles by delivery.

TRANSFER TAX AND EXCHANGE MARKET TAX: Many bonds and futures are subject to exchange market tax of between 0.001 per cent and 0.1 per cent. Both government bonds and Kabusaki 50 futures are subject to transfer tax. Exchange market tax will be effective on options premiums as of 1 October 1990. Gains on commodity futures are also subject to direct and exchange market taxes.

OPTIONS PREMIUM: In the absence of specific guidelines, the general rules on tax treatment of options are as follows: (1) gains/losses are recognised when the contract is closed out, and recognition is not on a market basis; (2) where companies buy or sell options the premiums are usually recognised on a current basis as income. The exception is premiums on deep in-the-money options which may not be deductible when paid.

Luxembourg

Accounting: As no specific regulations cover futures and options, generally accepted accounting principles apply. However, the Luxembourg Monetary Institute has issued instructions for banks and other financial institutions which embody these principles. When items are valued in the accounts, the prudence principle must be applied such that only realised profits may be taken into account. Gains and losses resulting from hedging activities can be deferred. Mark-to-market accounting should usually be applied by investment funds under the separate regulations which cover their futures and options transactions.

Regulation: All companies and individuals doing business in Luxembourg are required to be registered under company law. Advisors on derivatives and futures brokers must be licensed and all financial consultants are required to prove they are adequately qualified and financed. Futures contracts, provided they are set up by banks or traded on the Luxembourg Stock Exchange, are traded as commercial rather than gaming contracts under legislation passed in 1984.

Tax: All losses on futures and options transactions are deductible from income (whether realised or otherwise) but only those gains that have been realised will be subject to tax. Unrealised gains are not taxed until such time as the contract is settled. If hedging profits and losses are deferred in the accounts they may both be deferred for tax purposes.

Netherlands

Accounting: There is little Government intervention in Dutch financial markets. Following a change in the Gaming Statute, the EOE index and the US Stock Index have both been permitted by Dutch law to allow index option trading. Professional corporate derivatives traders account for transactions at maker rates. For other non-professional traders, in accordance with general principles, speculative positions are valued at the lower of cost and market value, and gains losses resulting from hedging transaction are deferred over the period of the hedge.

Regulation: Securities legislation governing derivatives was brought in to protect the public from unprincipled dealers. The most recent regulation is thus carried out by the exchanges and implementation of the *Securities Trading Act* and the *Securities Trading Decree*. Brokers may only act in derivatives transactions with professional issuers, dealers and investors, unless the transaction is made by a licensed person. Licenses are given only after the financial situation and the background of the applicant has been accepted by the Dutch Ministry of Finance. Members of certain bodies, such as the US and Swiss stock exchanges, are exempt from these rules.

Tax: The Netherlands does not have a general capital gains tax for individuals. A capital gain can be taxed only in very specific situations, for example when a profit is realised as a consequence of insider trading. Except in these specific situations and for those individuals who are trading, there is no income tax or capital gain tax impact on individuals with gains and losses resulting from transactions in futures and options. However, derivatives are brought into net equity for the calculation of net equity tax. They are taxed on the first of January value at 0.8 per cent. In the case of professional traders, prudent business principles are applied. Until fiscal year 1990 the tax authorities have accepted a system whereby long positions are valued at the lower of cost and market value, while short positions at the higher of cost and market value. In this way, realised gains/losses are treated as normal trading income and expenditure whereas unrealised profit can be deferred and unrealised losses included. In practice, however, this leads to a reduction in the value of the securities to a rather unrealistic level. Hence, recently the tax authorities have put forward a new way of valuing stock, options and futures positions to be used from fiscal year 1990. They propose to categorise securities related to a fund in a separate group. For each group a choice should be made whether all securities are valued at market value or at lower cost price. Both for long and short positions, acceptance of this system would mean that tax payments could no longer be deferred as they were under the old regime. At the moment, this new system is being discussed in depth with the tax authorities. It is anticipated that losses, which economically could not be suffered, will only be permissible to a limited extend.

Singapore

Accounting: 'Recommended Accounting Practices 4' contains guidelines for accounting for financial futures. Foreign currency transactions are regulated by the Statement of Accounting Standard 20. The above accounting standard and practice differentiate between the use of derivatives for speculative purposes and their use for hedging. There is currently no accounting standard for options. In general, reference would be made to the accounting standards and/or practice adopted by the US and UK where the accounting treatment of a transaction is not covered by a Statement of Accounting Standard or Recommended Accounting Practice. Hedging transactions should be treated in the same manner as the underlying asset or security. Where hedging of investments in foreign companies is effected by foreign currency transactions, the related profits and losses should be taken in shareholders' interests. Gains and losses on speculative contracts are usually accounted for on a mark-to-market basis and should be taken to the profit and loss account in the year they arise.

Regulation: The main regulatory body in Singapore, the Monetary Authority of Singapore (MAS) – empowered by the *Futures and Trading Act* (1986) – regulates the futures and options market. In addition, Singapore International Monetary Exchange (Simex) regulates members, firms and individuals in accordance with its rules and regulations. There are minimum requirements on reporting, auditing, capital levels and separation of client funds, and maximum limits on the daily movements in contract process. Brokers, dealers and pool operators in futures must be licensed as futures brokers or futures pool operators. Any person who carries on the business of advising others on futures contracts must be licensed as a futures trading advisor. However, holders of the futures brokers or futures pool operators licence need not apply for the futures trading advisor licence.

Tax: Traders in futures and options (whether companies or individuals) are taxed on trading profits at the following rates: companies and non-resident individuals at 31 per cent; resident individuals at progressive rates of up to 33 per cent.

Non-residents with no presence in Singapore may be exempt from tax. The accounting policy (e.g. mark-to-market) adopted will influence the decision as to whether unrealised profit/losses are subject to tax on an accruals basis. A concessionary rate of 10 per cent will be applied to income from 'relevant transactions' derived by the following persons: members of Simex; and off shore banking units of financial institutions (ACUs).

All the following conditions must be satisfied before a transaction is regarded as a 'relevant transaction' for the 10 per cent tax concession: the transaction must be in gold bullion, gold, financial (other than Singapore dollar) and oil futures; the transaction must be carried out on a specified exchange (i.e. Simex, CME, Comex, Liffe, CBOT, Sydney Futures Exchange or any gold exchange/market); and the transaction must be with an ACU, another Simex member, a non-resident with no permanent establishment in Singapore, or an overseas branch of a Singapore resident company.

Foreign investors making gains on futures and options contracts through funds managed by an approved fund manager of ACU are exempt from tax. Also, non-residents are exempt from paying withholding tax on interest received from Simex members on margin deposits for transactions in gold, gold futures and financial futures. Non-trading (i.e. speculative) profits earned by individuals are not subject to tax.

South Africa

Accounting: In South Africa, any change in the market value of futures contracts should be recognised in the Income Statement in the period in which the change occurs, except in cases where the contract qualifies as a hedge for activities exposed to price or interest rate risk. If the contract qualifies as a hedge, the accounting for the changes in market value should be related to the change in the value of the hedged items.

Regulation: Futures trading in South Africa began in 1987 when a local bank introduced futures contracts on Stock Exchange indices and acted as a clearing house. This market was regulated by informal rules agreed to by market participants. In a move towards greater regulation, the South African Futures Exchange (Safex) commenced operations in 1990. Safex operates under rules approved by the Registrar of Financial Markets, and is controlled by the *Financial Markets Control Act* which came fully into operation on 10 August 1990. Although options are traded informally, a formal market does not yet exist.

Tax: Since there is no specific legislation relating to derivative instruments, each transaction or series of transactions must be examined in accordance with general principles. Gains and losses are usually recognised immediately for taxation purposes. Those arising from trading or the hedging of speculative underlying transactions are taxed as normal trading income. There is no capital gains tax in South Africa and consequently gains and losses arising from the hedging of capital transactions do not attract any tax. Whether or not a specific transaction is of a capital or a revenue nature is determined in accordance with the interpretation of the South African courts.

Spain

Accounting: Only the Bank of Spain circulars sent to financial institutions which apply specifically to banks, savings banks etc. refer to accounting rules for financial futures and options traded in organised markets. Circular 16/89 distinguishes between the treatment of futures used for hedging purposes and other purposes, and gives the criteria necessary to define a hedge. Circular 18/89 states that options must be recorded in the balance sheet at market price, with differences taken to the income statement. Interest rate options used as hedges must be recorded in line with the underlying asset or liability. Non-hedging transactions are accounted for on a current basis, whilst hedges are matched to the income or cost arising from the underlying asset or liability.

Regulation: In Spain, more than 40 finance and credit institutions have recently combined to form a financial futures market corporation, Meff. Meff began trading in March 1990 and is acting as a clearing house. A three-year notional bond with a face value of Pta 10 million and a coupon of 10 per cent per annum will be the first contract to be traded. Initially, margins will be a minimum of 4 per cent with a variation in contract value of +/– 2 per cent. The Madrid Stock Exchange is currently considering introducing a traded equity options market and since November 1989 OM Ibrica has quoted government debt interest rate options.

Tax: As both Meff and OM Ibrica have only recently begun to trade, there has not yet been developed a specific tax regime for futures and options. Current legislation suggests that income from trading in derivatives may be treated as a capital gain, and would not be subject to withholding tax at source as though it were income from capital. Non-residents without tax treaty protection may be liable to Spanish tax.

Sweden

Accounting: Any profits arising from trading futures and options must be accounted for on a realised basis. Unrealised losses must be provided for and may be netted off within a futures and options portfolio. Net unrealised gains may not be recognised. Until income from an option is realised the seller must account for the premium received as deferred income. If, at the balance sheet date, options have not been realised a provision for potential losses on exercise must be set up. Options purchased should be held in the balance sheet at the lower of cost and net realisable value.

Regulation: Most of the exchange control legislation in Sweden has been abolished. Payments made to or received from foreign countries must, however, be made through a currency bank, and non-residents trading in derivatives must also go via either a currency bank or a stockbroker. Debt instruments such as Swedish Bonds must be deposited with a stockbroker or a foreign currency bank.

Tax: Current legislation has been significantly augmented by the rules on options introduced in January 1991. Those for whom dealing in derivatives and other securities is a regular business are taxed according to normal business income rules (30 per cent) with the right to offset losses fully. This would include banks, stockbrokers and insurance companies. For other investing companies the tax rate is also 30 per cent on profit. Companies that do not deal in derivatives and other securities, however, have a limited right for deductions for losses on shares and securities similar to shares. For these companies it is only possible to offset losses from the sale of securities against gains from the sale of securities. Gains on the sale of futures are for natural persons taxed as income from capital at a 30 per cent tax rate. Losses are also treated in the same source of income. Certain limitations on setting off losses apply. For taxpayers, where the provisions regarding income from capital apply, the following is the position on sales and purchases of options. Those selling options are taxed on the premium received at standard income tax rates. The cost of the premium is treated by the buyer as the cost of the underlying asset. From January the rules vary according to the length of the option. For those under one year, the premium (less costs) is taxed on completion of the contract, whilst longer term options are taxed immediately. If the option is offset or expires, the owner is taxed on the cash settlement (less the premium) at the time of settlement. If the options are exercised, call options are taxed when the shares are sold (the premium added to the initial value of the share) and put options are taxed at the same time of exercise (the premium deducted from the capital gain). Following recent legislation, the turnover tax on both buyer and seller on the stock market has been extended to transactions in futures and options. However, not all types of securities are included. The rates of the turnover tax range are between 0.5 and 1 per cent.

Switzerland

Accounting: Accounting guidelines as issued by Soffex (The Swiss Options and Financial Futures Exchange) state that derivatives can be marked to market provided that they are traded on an exchange by banks on a regular basis and the trading is sufficiently executed and regulated. Where trading is of a non-professional nature, losses must be accounted for as soon as they arise. Where futures and options are used for hedging purposes, however, hedge accounting may be used to defer results over the life of the hedge.

Regulation: The basic premise on which Soffex is based is that of self-regulation. The responsibility for setting the rules and regulations lies with the directors and to ensure that non-Soffex members also follow these regulations circular letters have been issued by the Swiss Bankers Association and the Federal Banking Commission which bind all banks and members of the Association. The day-to-day running of the trading and clearing system, the surveillance and compliance is the responsibility of Soffex. As the system is fully automatic it provides a complete audit trail.

Tax: In Switzerland the tax treatment of income is generally determined by the accounting treatment used. Thus, the method of taxation used for futures and options follows the accounting treatment. Gains made by individuals on derivatives trading are exempt from federal taxes. Those gains which can be defined as private capital gains are also exempt from tax in all but one of the 26 Cantons. Net capital gains are, however, taxed in the 26th Canton. Trading in futures and options will not incur duty (except in cases of physical delivery of securities) and options held by individuals are not subject to private wealth tax. No withholding tax is chargeable to Soffex.

United Kingdom

Accounting: No accounting pronouncements relate specifically to futures and options. It is generally accepted that the accounting treatment should be consistent with the underlying economic substance of the transaction. Mark-to-market accounting gives a close approximation of the economic reality in the case of speculative trading, and is becoming generally accepted for active traders. However, futures positions and purchased options may alternatively be stated at the lower of cost and market value and written options at the higher of proceeds and market value. Once a transaction fulfils the necessary criteria to be defined as a hedge, the accounting treatment of the transaction should follow that of the underlying asset or liability. These principles are consistent with those embodied in the recently published *British Bankers Association Exposure Draft* on commitments contingencies.

Regulation: All those involved in futures and options trading, in the United Kingdom and internationally, are governed by the recently enacted *Financial Services Act* (1986). The regulatory structure consists of the Department of Trade and Industry and self-regulation by the markets themselves (as governed by the Securities and Investment Board [SIB]). One of the five self-regulatory bodies (SROs) under the SIB is the AFBD (Association of Futures Brokers and Dealers). This organisation has primary responsibility for authorising and supervising member institutions. On 2 April 1991 the AFBD merged with The Securities Association to form a new SRO – the Securities and Futures Authority (SFA). SROs have the power to investigate members' compliance with the rules set by them on matters such as capital adequacy, segregation of client funds and business conduct; if necessary, they can institute disciplinary proceedings.

Tax: Following the 1988 Statement of Inland Revenue Practice and the 1990 *Finance Act*, the grey area that has traditionally caused difficulty in the taxation of futures and options has partly been cleared up, although many difficulties still remain. The basic tax treatment afforded gains and losses depends on whether they are the result of trading (when they are taxed as income) or of hedging (when they are taxed in accordance with the underlying asset or liability). The definition of hedging was of particular importance to such institutions as unit trusts, investment trusts and pension funds because they are exempt from tax on capital profits and subject to tax on income.

Hence, if they could show the hedged portfolio was capital, no tax would arise. The Statement of Practice attempted to clarify the definition of hedging (and has done to a limited extend) and the 1990 *Finance Act* has granted exemption from tax or derivative transactions for authorised unit trusts and pension funds.

United States of America

Accounting: Futures contracts (with the exception of foreign currency, forward placements and delayed delivery contracts) are dealt with by FASB Statement 80. The exceptions are dealt with partly by FASB Statement 52, although where no specific rules apply FASB 80 will be applied. Accounting treatment differs according to whether the derivatives were used for hedging or speculative purposes. Speculative positions are marked to market and unrealised profits and losses resulting from a change in market value must be recognised on a current basis. In the case of hedged positions, market value changes are recognised as income only when the allied change in the price or interest rate of the underlying asset in recognised.

Regulation: The SEC (Securities & Exchange Commission) regulates equity options. The CFTC (Commodity Futures Trading Commission) governs the commodity, futures and options exchanges. The rules for all futures commission merchants, such as segregation of customers funds, capital adequacy, client relationship and trade reporting, are regulated by the CFTC.

Tax: Whether profits and losses resulting from stock options are treated as capital or ordinary depends on the item underlying the option. If capital treatment applies and the option is held for more than one year, long-term capital gains or losses will be recognised when the option is disposed of. Any premium paid will be treated as a non-deductible capital expenditure. Any premium received is not included in income at the time of receipt. Section 1256 Contract-Regulated Futures Contracts and Foreign Currency Contracts trading on qualifying exchanges and certain non-equity options may be taxed under the year end mark-to-market rules. Unrealised gains and losses mark-to-market at year end are treated as 60 per cent long term and 40 per cent short term. Adjustments to basis are made when the position is subsequently closed. In certain cases Section 1256 Contracts are used for hedging purposes. Mark-to-market and 60/40 rules will not apply where the hedge is entered into in the normal course of the taxpayer's trade or business to reduce the risk of price change, currency fluctuation or interest rate change. Gain or loss on the transaction is ordinary. For corporations, there is currently no difference in tax rates between capital and ordinary income. For tax years beginning in 1991 individual taxpayers may receive a small benefit for net long-term capital gains versus net short-term capital gains and ordinary income.

[1] This entire chapter is a reprint of a special section prepared for *Futures and Options World* by Arthur Andersen & Co. We are using this material with the kind permission of Victor Levy of the London Arthur Andersen & Co. office. All copyrights to the contents of this chapter are retained by Arthur Andersen & Co.

Appendix

WORLDWIDE EXCHANGES TRADING OPTIONS CONTRACTS

Next to the name of each exchange, in brackets, is its abbreviation (when available) followed by the name of the city where the exchange is located (when necessary).

1. Australia

Australia Options Market (AOM), Sydney
- Equity Options (27 [Individual Stocks])
- Gold

Sydney Futures Exchange Ltd (SFE)

- All Ordinaries Share Price Index Futures
- 90-day Bank Accepted Bill Futures
- 10-year Treasury Bond (T-Bond) Futures
- 3-year T-Bond Futures
- 5 & 10-year Semi-Government Bonds Futures
- Australian Dollar Futures

2. Austria

Österreichische Termin und Optionen Börse (ÖTOB), Vienna (Opening Scheduled for October 1991)

- Stock Options
- Stock Index Options (ATX)

3. Brazil

Brazilian Futures Exchange (BM&F), Rio De Janeiro
- US Dollar
- IBV — 12 Stock Index
- IBV Stock Index
- Gold Futures

Rio De Janeiro Stock Exchange

- Individual Stocks

Mercantile and Futures Exchange, Sao Paolo

- Gold Futures
- US Dollar

Sao Paolo Stock Exchange

- Equity Options

4. Canada

Montreal Stock Exchange (MSE)

- 10-year Government of Canada Bond Futures (CGB)
- Canadian T-Bonds
- Equity Options (31)
- Gold

Toronto Futures Exchange (TSE)

- Silver
- Toronto 35 Index
- Long Term Canadian Government Bonds

Vancouver Stock Exchange (VSE)

- Gold
- Silver
- Equity Options (23)

5. Denmark

Guarantee Fund for Danish Options and Futures (FUTOP), Copenhagen

- KFX Futures
- 9 per cent Annuity Mortgage Bond
- FUTOP futures
- Danish T-Bond Futures

6. Finland

Finnish Options Market (FOM), Helsinki

- FOX Index Futures
- Equity Options

7. France

Marché à Terme International de France SA. (MATIF), Paris

- Notional Government Bond Futures
- 3-month Pibor Futures
- 3-month EuroDEM Futures
- White Sugar

Marché des Options Negociables de la Bourse de Paris (MONEP), Paris

- Equity Options (24)
- CAC 40 Stock Index

8. Germany

Deutsche Terminbörse (DTB), Frankfurt

- Equity Options
- DAX Options
- Bund Options

9. Japan

Osaka Securities Exchange

- Nikkei 225 option

Tokyo Stock Exchange (TSE)

- Topix Futures
- Japanese Government Bond Futures

10. Netherlands

European Options Exchange (EOE), Amsterdam

- EOE Stock Index
- Dutch Top 5 Stock Index
- Equity Options (28)
- Dutch Government Bonds
- Dutch Bond Index
- Major Market Index (MMI)
- British Pound
- US Dollar
- Jumbo Dollar
- Gilder Bond Future
- Gold

11. New Zealand

New Zealand Futures and Options Exchange (NZFOE), Auckland

- Option on NZ Dollar Futures (KWO)
- Barclays Stock Index Options (BSO)
- NZ 5-year Government Stock Futures
- 90-day Bank Bill Futures
- NZ 3-year Government Stock Futures

12. Norway

The Oslo Stock Exchange (OSE)

- 5 Equity Options
  Den Norske Bank
  Bergesen B
  Hafslund Nycomed B
  Saga Petroleum
  Norsk Hydro OBK Index
- OBX Stock Index

---

13. Singapore

Singapore International Monetary Exchange (SIMEX)

- 3-month Eurodollar Futures
- 3- month Euroyen Futures
- Japanese Yen
- Japanese Yen Futures
- Deutschmark
- Deutschmark Futures
- British Pound

14. Spain

Om Iberica (OMIb), Madrid

- MIBOR90
- Notional Bond 10 per cent
- Bond 12.50 per cent
- FIEX 35

15. Sweden

Stockholm Options Market (SOM)

- Stock Options
- OMX Stock Index
- OMDM Currency Options
- Interest Rate Options
- Swedish Krona
- Deutschmark
- Equity Options (17)

16. Switzerland

Basle Stock Exchange
- COTO (Cash Order Titel Option)
- Non-Standardised Options on Bonds

Swiss Options and Financial Futures Exchange (SOFFEX), Zurich
- Equity Options

Alusuisse Lonza Holding
BBC Brown Boveri
Ciba-Geigy
Credit Suisse
Hoffmann-La Roche
Nestlé
Sandoz
Swiss Bank Corp.
Swiss Re-Insurance
UBS
Zurich Insurance
Swiss Market Index

17. United Kingdom

International Petroleum Exchange, London

- Gas Oil futures
- Brent Crude Oil Futures

London Options and Futures Exchange (FOX)

- Robusta Coffee
- No 7 Cocoa
- No 6 Raw Sugar
- No 5 White Sugar
- MGMI Metal Index
- Wheat
- Barley
- Potatoes
- Soybean Meal

London International Financial Futures (LIFFE)

- Long Gilt Futures
- US Treasury Bond Futures
- 3-month Eurodollar Futures
- 3-month Sterling Futures
- German Government Bond Futures
- 3-month Euromark Futures

London Metal Exchange (LME)

- Copper Futures
- Zinc Futures
- Lead Futures
- Nickel Futures
- Tin Futures
- LME Futures

London Traded Options Market (LTOM)

- Equity Options (65)
- FT-SE 100 Stock Index (American-Style and European-Style)
- Restricted Life Options

OM London
- Swedish Stock Options
- Norwegian Stock Options
- OMX Stock Index

18. United States of America

American Stock Exchange (AMEX), New York

- Major Market Index (MMI)
- Japan Stock Index
- Institutional Stock Index
- International Market Index
- Computer Stock Index
- Oil Stock Index
- Equity Options (214)

Chicago Board Option Exchange (CBOE)

- Equity Options (222)
- LEAPS (Long Term Equity Anticipation Securities)
- S&P 100 Index (OEX)
- OEX LEAPS
- S&P 500 Index (SPL & SPX)
- SPX LEAPS

- S&P 500 Index NSX
- US 30-year Treasury Bonds
- US 5-year Treasury Notes
- Short-Term (IRX) and Long-Term (LTX) Interest Rate

Chicago Board of Trade (CBOT)

- Corn Futures
- Soybeans Futures
- Soybeans Meal Futures
- Soybean Oil Futures
- Wheat Futures
- Oats Futures
- Silver Futures
- US Treasury Bonds Futures
- 5 and 10-year US Treasury Notes Futures
- Municipal Bond Index Futures
- Mortgage-Backed Securities Futures
- Topix Index

Chicago Mercantile Exchange (CME)

- Pork Bellies Futures
- Live Cattle Futures
- Feeder Cattle Futures
- Live Hogs Futures
- Broiler Chickens Futures
- Lumber
- S&P 500 Index Futures
- Nikkei Dow Stock Index Futures
- Currency Futures
  US Treasury Bill Futures
  Eurodollar Futures
  British Pounds
  Canadian Dollar
  Australian Dollar
  D-Mark Japanese Yen
  Swiss Franc

Coffee Sugar and Cocoa Exchange, New York

- Coffee
- No 11 Sugar
- Cocoa

Commodity Exchange (COMEX), New York

- Gold Futures
- Silver Futures
- Copper Futures

Kansas City Board of Trade (KCBT)

- No 2 Red Wheat

Mid America Commodity Exchange, Chicago

- Soybeans
- Wheat
- Gold

Minneapolis Grain Exchange

- Hard Red Spring Wheat

New York Cotton Exchange (NYCE)

- Cotton Futures
- Frozen Orange Juice Futures

Financial Instruments Exchange, New York

- 5-year Treasury Note Futures
- US Dollar Index Futures

New York Futures Exchange (NYFE)

- NYSE Composite Index Futures
- CRB Index Futures

New York Mercantile Exchange (NYME)

- Crude Oil Futures
- Heating Oil Futures
- Gasoline Futures
- Platinum Futures

New York Stock Exchange (NYSE)

- NYSE Composite Index
- Equity Options (42)

Pacific Stock Exchange, San Francisco
- Financial News Composite Index
- Equity Options (164)
- Extended Term Options

Philadelphia Stock Exchange (PHLX)

- National OTC Stock Index
- Value Line Composite Index
- Gold/silver Stock Index
- Utility Stock Index
- Equity Options (137)
- Currency Options
  Australian Dollar
  British Pound
  Canadian Dollar
  Deutschmark
  French Franc
  Japanese Yen
  Swiss Franc
  ECU

Index

The following titles in the *Finance and Capital Markets* series are also published by The Macmillan Press Ltd:

Off Balance Sheet Finance   ISBN 0-333-56041-8

Written in the light of the Accounting Standards Board, this book discusses the various financing practices which have grown up over recent years and explains how they will be affected by the new accounting standard being developed by the ASB. It will provide an expert analysis of the accounting rules which will govern the treatment of off balance sheet finance when the standard comes into force.

February 1992   £95

Risk Management for Derivatives   ISBN 0-333-55924-X

The full implications of trading these products is examined in depth by leading practitioners in the field, focusing on the use of 3rd generation financial products such as swaps, futures and options, caps and swaptions.

March 1992   £75

Bund Options   ISBN 0-333-56910-5

A comprehensive and practical introduction to these new and active markets, offering an analysis of basics, pricing, trading, hedging and risk management.

December 1991   £75

For fuller information on these and other titles in the Finance and Capital Markets series, or to order copies, please call 0256 29242 or write to Carla Jones, Globe Book Services Ltd, Macmillan, Houndmills, Basingstoke, Hampshire RG21 2XS.